Practical Computer Literacy 2nd Edition

Internet and Computing Core Certification

June Jamrich Parsons • Dan Oja

CONTAINS A BookOnCD FOR A FULLY INTERACTIVE LEARNING EXPERIENCE

COURSE TECHNOLOGY
CENGAGE Learning™

Australia • Brazil • Japan • Korea • Mexico • Singapore • Spain • United Kingdom • United States

COURSE TECHNOLOGY
CENGAGE Learning

Practical Computer Literacy, 2nd Edition
June Jamrich Parsons, Dan Oja

Executive Editor: Marie Lee

Senior Product Manager: Kathy Finnegan

Product Manager: Katherine C. Russillo

Associate Acquisitions Editor: Brandi Shailer

Developmental Editor: Fran Marino

Associate Product Manager: Leigh Robbins

Editorial Assistant: Julia Leroux-Lindsey

Marketing Manager: Ryan DeGrote

Content Project Manager: Heather Furrow

Photo Researcher: Abby Reip

Art Director: Marissa Falco

Cover Designer: Nancy Goulet

BookOnCD Technician: Keefe Crowley

BookOnCD Development: MediaTechnics Corp.

Prepress Production: GEX Publishing Services

For product information and technology assistance, contact us at
Cengage Learning Customer & Sales Support, 1-800-354-9706
For permission to use material from this text or product, submit all requests online at **www.cengage.com/permissions**
Further permissions questions can be emailed to
permissionrequest@cengage.com

ISBN-13: 978-1-4390-3748-5
ISBN-10: 1-4390-3748-5

Cengage Learning
20 Channel Center Street
Boston, MA 02210
USA

Cengage Learning is a leading provider of customized learning solutions with office locations around the globe, including Singapore, the United Kingdom, Australia, Mexico, Brazil, and Japan. Locate your local office at:
international.cengage.com/region

Cengage Learning products are represented in Canada by Nelson Education, Ltd.

Visit our corporate website at **www.cengage.com**

To learn more about Course Technology, visit **www.cengage.com/coursetechnology**

To learn more about Cengage Learning, visit **www.cengage.com**

Purchase any of our products at your local college store or at our preferred online store **www.ichapters.com**

Printed in the United States of America
2 3 4 5 6 7 13 12 11 10 09

Preface

Practical Computer Literacy provides a state-of-the-art introduction to computer concepts and software applications, written in an easy-to-read style.

On the inside front cover you'll find an action-packed, multimedia BookOnCD that mirrors every page of the printed book and contains interactive elements such as guided software tours and end-of-chapter quizzes. The BookOnCD requires no installation, so it's easy to use at home, at school, or at work.

How does it work?

Practical Computer Literacy offers a unique graduated learning environment where you see it, try it, and then apply it.

1. See It

The book provides background information and step-by-step screen illustrations to get you oriented to a task.

2. Try It

Use **the BookOnCD** to work with hands-on, step-by-step task simulations that help you learn the basics even if you don't have access to Windows Vista or Microsoft Office 2007.

3. Apply It

Activities in the **Projects** section challenge you to try your skills on real-word examples using Microsoft Office and other application software.

Use this book because...

- **You want to learn about computers**. *Practical Computer Literacy* helps you understand enough "tech talk" so you can decipher computer ads and hold your own when the conversation turns to computers.

- **You want to learn Windows**. *Practical Computer Literacy* shows you how to use Windows Vista or XP to manage files and customize your on-screen work area.

- **You want to learn Microsoft Office**. *Practical Computer Literacy* teaches you all the key skills for Microsoft Word, Excel, PowerPoint, and Access.

- **You want to learn how to use the Internet**. *Practical Computer Literacy* shows you how to get connected, use a browser, send e-mail, and work with search engines.

- **You want to prepare for the IC3 certification exam**. *Practical Computer Literacy* offers a visual, hands-on way to prepare for CertiPort's IC3 certification. You'll find more details about this globally recognized certification program on page v.

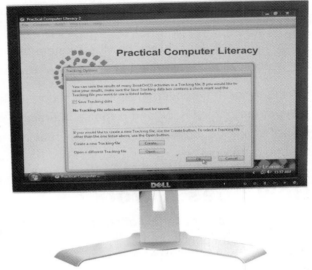

The BookOnCD

Every book includes the innovative BookOnCD, which is loaded with features to enhance and reinforce learning.

On the CD, the Play It! button makes figures come to life as videos and screen animations. You'll see PC hardware in action and interact with some of today's most popular software packages.

The Get It? button, located at the beginning of each section, starts an interactive auto-graded quiz. Take a quiz more than once. Each quiz contains ten randomly selected questions from an extensive test bank. Results can be saved and delivered to an instructor.

Interactive end-of-chapter QuickCheck questions provide instant feedback on what you've learned.

Teaching Tools

ExamView: Our powerful testing software package. With ExamView, instructors can generate printed tests, create LAN-based tests, or test over the Internet.

An **Instructor's Manual** outlines each chapter and provides valuable teaching tips.

WebTrack provides automated delivery of tracking data from any student directly to the instructor with minimal setup or administrative overhead.

Blackboard Learning System and WebCT content are available to simplify the use of *Practical Computer LIteracy 2nd Edition* in distance education settings.

PowerPoint presentations for *Practical Computer LIteracy 2nd Edition are* included with the instructor supplements.

Check with your Course Technology sales representative or go to *www.cengage.com/coursetechnology* to learn more about other valuable Teaching Tools.

INTERNET AND

COMPUTING CORE

CERTIFICATION

SETTING THE STANDARD

Certification

Learning materials provided by the Practical Computer Literacy book and BookOnCD are designed to help you prepare for IC³ certification exams.

IC³...What is it?

IC³ (Internet and Computing Core Certification) is a global training and certification program providing proof to the world that you are:

CERTIFICATION ROADMAP

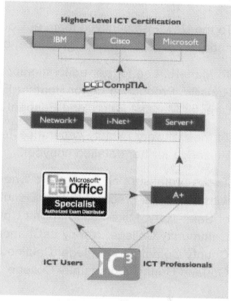

- Equipped with the computer skills necessary to excel in a digital world

- Capable of using a broad range of computer technology—from basic hardware and software, to operating systems, applications, and the Internet

- Ready for the work employers, colleges, and universities want to throw your way

- Positioned to advance your career through additional computer certifications such as CompTIA's A+ and other desktop application exams as shown in the Certification Roadmap

IC³...Why do you need it?

Employers, colleges, and universities now understand that exposure to computers does not equal understanding computers. So now more than ever, basic computer and Internet skills are being considered prerequisites for employment and higher education.

This is where IC³ helps! IC³ provides specific guidelines for the knowledge and skills required to be a functional user of computer hardware, networks, and the Internet. It does this through three exams:

- Computing Fundamentals

- Key Applications

- Living Online

By passing the three IC³ exams, you'll have initiated yourself into today's digital world. You'll have also earned a globally accepted and validated credential that provides the proof employers and higher education institutions need.

Earn your IC³ certification today. Visit **www.certiport.com/ic3** to learn how.

Acknowledgments

The successful launch of this book was possible only because of our extraordinary "ground crews." We would like to extend our profound thanks:

To the students at Northern Michigan University, the University of the Virgin Islands, and countless other universities who have participated in classes and corresponded with us over the 25 (or so) years since we began teaching and producing textbooks.

To our development team: Donna Mulder, Tensi Parsons, Keefe Crowley, and Marilou Potter for content and media development; to Kevin Lappi, Deanna Martinson, Karen Kangas, and Jackie Kangas for testing; and to Chris Robbert for narrations.

To our team members' patient and supportive children, parents, spouses, and significant others.

To the New Perspectives team at Course Technology, who once again provided professional and enthusiastic support, guidance, and advice. Their insights and team spirit were invaluable.

To Marie L. Lee for her editorial support and to our Product Managers Erik Herman and Kate Russillo, Production Editor Heather Furrow, Associate Product Manager Leigh Robbins, Art Director Marissa Falco, and Editorial Assistant Julia Leroux-Lindsey.

To the Software Quality Assurance Team for their valuable QA test comments and to Suzanne Huizenga for her detailed copyedit.

To the professors and reviewers who expressed their ideas and shared their teaching strategies with us for the Practical series: Dennis Anderson, St. Francis College; Mary Dobranski, College of Saint Mary; Mike Feiler, Merritt College; Shmuel Fink, Touro College; Dennette Foy, Edison Community College; Nancy LaChance, DeVry Institute of Technology; Janet Sheppard, Collin County Community College; Pauline Pike, Community College of Morris; and Linda Reis, Garland County Community College.

Contents

Contents

Contents

Contents

Contents

Before You Begin

You are going to enjoy using *Practical Computer Literacy* and the accompanying BookOnCD. It's a snap to start the BookOnCD and use it on your computer. The answers to the FAQs (frequently asked questions) in this section will help you begin.

FAQ Will the BookOnCD work on my computer?

The easiest way to find out if the BookOnCD works on your computer is to try it! Just follow the steps below to start the CD. If it works, you're all set. Otherwise, check with your local technical support person. If you are technically inclined, the system requirements are listed inside the back cover of this book.

FAQ How do I start the BookOnCD?

The BookOnCD is easy to use and requires no installation. Follow these simple steps to get started:

1. Make sure your computer is turned on.

2. Press the button on your computer's CD drive to open the drawer-like "tray," as shown in the photo below.

3. Place the BookOnCD into the tray with the label facing up.

4. Press the button on the CD drive to close the tray, then proceed with Step 5.

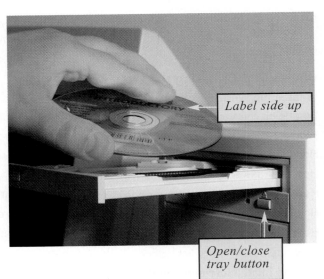

Label side up

Open/close tray button

5. After inserting the CD, wait about 15 seconds. During this time, the light on your CD drive should flicker. If your computer displays an AutoPlay window similar to the one shown below, click the option to Run BookOnCD.exe.

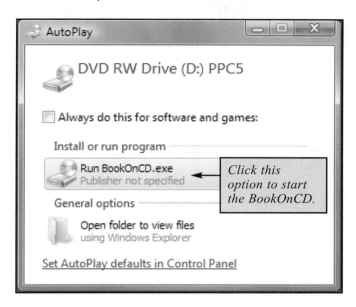

6. If the AutoPlay window does not appear and the Practical Computer Literacy title screen does not appear, you can manually start the BookOnCD by following the steps in the figure below.

Manual Start: *Follow the instructions in this figure only if the Welcome screen did **not** appear automatically in Step 5.*

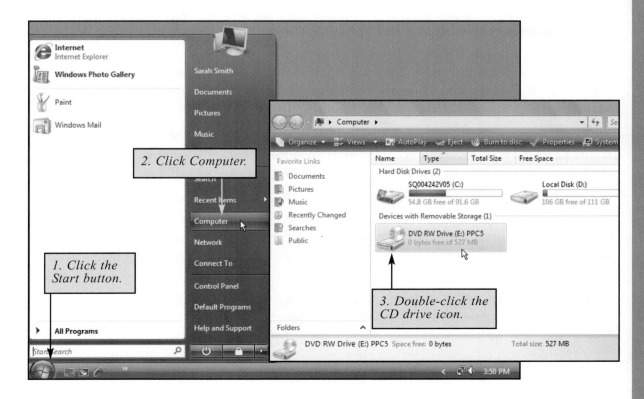

FAQ How should I set my tracking options?

When the BookOnCD starts, it displays the Practical Computer Literacy title screen and a Tracking options window. To proceed, you'll need to select your tracking settings.

A Tracking File records your progress by saving your scores on QuickChecks and chapter quizzes at the end of each chapter. If you don't want to record your scores, simply make sure the *Save Tracking data* box is empty and then click the OK button to proceed straight to the first chapter.

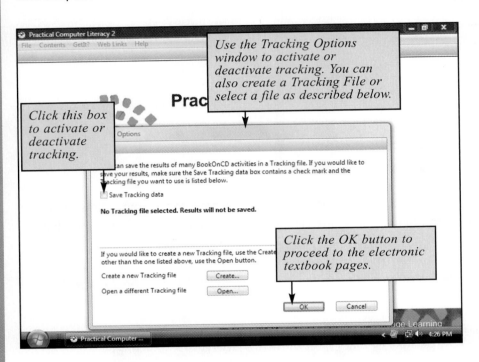

Use the Tracking Options window to activate or deactivate tracking. You can also create a Tracking File or select a file as described below.

Click this box to activate or deactivate tracking.

Click the OK button to proceed to the electronic textbook pages.

If you prefer to track your scores, then you must create a Tracking File. It's easy! Click the Create button and then follow the on-screen prompts to enter your name, student ID, and class section.

When the Save As window appears, you can select the location for your Tracking File. If you are using your own computer, the default location in the Documents folder is a great place to store your Tracking File, so just click the Save button and you're all set!

If you are working on a public computer, such as one in a school lab, be aware that data stored on the hard disk might be erased or changed by other students unless you have a protected personal storage area. When working on a public computer or when you need to transport your data from one computer to another, a floppy disk or USB flash drive would be a better option for storing your Tracking File.

To save your Tracking File in a location other than your computer's Documents folder, click the Computer icon and then double-click a storage location to select it. Click the Save button to finalize your storage selection.

FAQ How do I navigate through the BookOnCD?

Each on-screen page exactly duplicates a page from the paper book. Use the mouse or the vertical scroll bar to scroll up and down the page. Additional navigation controls are explained in the figure below.

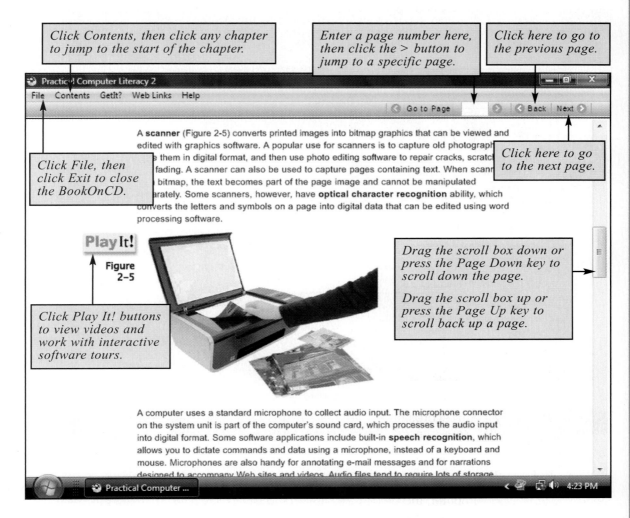

Click Contents, then click any chapter to jump to the start of the chapter.

Enter a page number here, then click the > button to jump to a specific page.

Click here to go to the previous page.

Click here to go to the next page.

Click File, then click Exit to close the BookOnCD.

Click Play It! buttons to view videos and work with interactive software tours.

Drag the scroll box down or press the Page Down key to scroll down the page.

Drag the scroll box up or press the Page Up key to scroll back up a page.

FAQ What should I know about the Projects?

The Project section at the end of each chapter helps you review and apply the concepts presented in the book. Most projects can be completed on computers running Microsoft Windows Vista or XP. Other software and storage media that you'll need are listed at the beginning of each project.

If a project requires you to send an e-mail attachment to your instructor, use your usual e-mail software, such as Thunderbird, Microsoft Outlook, Windows Mail, Eudora, Gmail, or AOL mail. (If you don't have an e-mail account, see Chapter 20 for instructions on how to set one up.) First make sure that you have saved the project file. Next, start your e-mail software. Then, follow your software's procedures for sending an e-mail attachment.

FAQ How does the interactive assessment page work?

Each chapter ends with an assessment page containing interactive activities. You can use these activities to evaluate how well you've mastered the concepts and skills covered in the chapter. If you do well on the QuickChecks, then you're ready to move on to the next chapter. If you don't do well, you might want to review the material before going on to the next chapter.

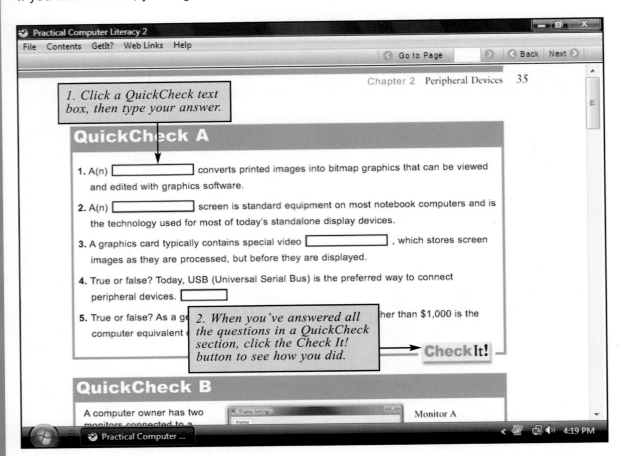

FAQ Are all my scores tracked?

Your scores on QuickChecks and chapter quizzes are tracked if you have activated tracking with a check mark in the *Save Tracking data* box.

FAQ How can I change tracking?

You can access the Tracking Options window at any time by clicking File on the menu bar and selecting Change Tracking Options. When the Tracking Options window appears, you can activate or deactivate tracking, create a new Tracking File, or select a different Tracking File.

FAQ What if the Tracking Options window shows the wrong Tracking File?

When working in a computer lab or using a computer where other students are using the BookOnCD, the Tracking Options window might show the name of a Tracking File that belongs to another person because that person was the last one to use the computer. You can use the Open button on the Tracking Options window to select a different Tracking File.

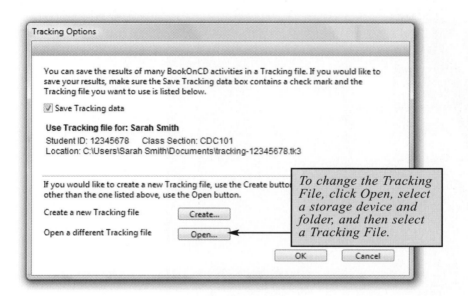

Tracking Options

You can save the results of many BookOnCD activities in a Tracking file. If you would like to save your results, make sure the Save Tracking data box contains a check mark and the Tracking file you want to use is listed below.

☑ Save Tracking data

Use Tracking file for: Sarah Smith
Student ID: 12345678   Class Section: CDC101
Location: C:\Users\Sarah Smith\Documents\tracking-12345678.tk3

If you would like to create a new Tracking file, use the Create butto
other than the one listed above, use the Open button.

Create a new Tracking file   Create...

Open a different Tracking file   Open...

To change the Tracking File, click Open, select a storage device and folder, and then select a Tracking File.

OK   Cancel

FAQ How do I submit my Tracking File?

In an academic setting, your instructor might request your Tracking File data to monitor your progress. Your instructor will tell you if you should submit your Tracking File using the WebTrack system, if you should hand in your entire Tracking File, or if you should send the Tracking File as an e-mail attachment.

FAQ How do I end a session?

Leave the BookOnCD disk in the CD drive while you're using it, or you will encounter an error message. Before you remove the CD from the drive, you must exit the program by clicking File on the BookOnCD menu bar, then clicking Exit. You can also exit by clicking the Close button in the upper-right corner of the window.

FAQ What about sound?

If your computer is equipped for sound, you should hear narrations during videos, screen tours, and interactive simulations. If you don't hear anything, check the volume control on your computer by clicking the speaker icon in the lower-right corner of your screen. If you're working in a lab or office where sound would be disruptive, consider using headphones.

FAQ Which version of Windows do I need?

Your PC's operating system sets the standard for the way all your software looks and works. Most of today's PCs use a version of the Microsoft Windows operating system—"Windows" for short. The BookOnCD is optimized for use with Windows Vista, but will also work on most computers running older versions of Windows, such as Windows XP.

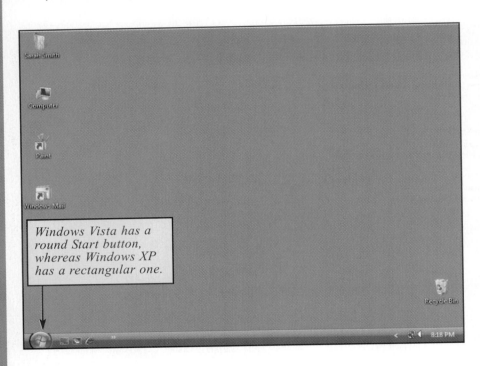

Windows Vista has a round Start button, whereas Windows XP has a rectangular one.

FAQ How do I get the most out of the book and the BookOnCD?

If you have your own computer, you might want to start the CD and do the reading on-screen. You'll then be able to click the Play It! buttons as you come to them and interact immediately with QuickChecks and quizzes.

If you do not have a computer, you should read through the chapter in the book. Later, when it is convenient, take your BookOnCD to a computer at school, home, or work and browse through the chapter, clicking each Play It! activity. After you view the videos, you can complete QuickChecks and quizzes.

You'll get the most out of your book if you experiment with your application software as you read, especially in Section II. For example, while reading the chapters about word processing, use Microsoft Word to experiment with the features described in the figures and bullet points. Feel free to type in a few sentences and then see how the various commands, buttons, and options work. This informal practice will supplement the Play It! activities and give you additional hands-on experience before you tackle projects or certification exams.

Your book is a handy see-it-and-do-it reference, so use it when you work on projects—not only the projects at the end of the book, but for your personal projects as well.

Section I
Computing Fundamentals

When you complete Section I, click the **Get It?** button while using the BookOnCD to take a Practice test.

Computer Hardware

CHAPTER **1**

What's Inside and on the CD?

Chapter 1 provides an overview of computer equipment and terminology. You'll learn how computers are classified and find out how personal computers fit into the gamut of machines ranging from PDAs to supercomputers. You will review the basic components of a typical personal computer system and take a look inside the system unit, which holds the motherboard, processor, and memory. Then, you'll explore the advantages and disadvantages of several computer storage devices. The chapter winds up with some handy information about maintaining your computer and troubleshooting problems.

FAQ What is a computer?

At its core, a **computer** is a multipurpose device that accepts input, processes data, stores data, and produces output, all according to a series of stored instructions.

Computer input is whatever is typed, submitted, or transmitted to a computer system. Input can be supplied by a person, by the environment, or by another computer. Examples of input that a computer can accept include words and symbols in a document, numbers for a calculation, photos from a digital camera, temperatures from a thermostat, audio signals from a microphone, and instructions from a computer program. An input device, such as a keyboard or mouse, gathers data and transforms it into a series of electronic signals for the computer to store and manipulate.

In the context of computing, **data** refers to symbols that represent facts, objects, and ideas. Computers manipulate data in many ways, and this manipulation is called **processing**. In a computer, most processing takes place in a component called the **central processing unit** (**CPU**), which is sometimes described as the computer's "brain." The series of instructions that tell a computer how to carry out a processing task is referred to as a **computer program**, or simply a "program." These programs form the **software** that sets up a computer to do a specific task. An **operating system** is software that helps a computer control itself to operate efficiently and keep track of data. **Application software** helps users "apply" the computer to specific tasks, such as writing documents and editing photos.

A computer stores data so that it is available for processing. Most computers have more than one location for storing data, depending on how the data is being used. **Memory** is an area of a computer that temporarily holds data waiting to be processed, stored, or output. **Storage** is the area where data can be left on a permanent basis when it is not immediately needed for processing.

Computer output is the result produced by a computer. Some examples of computer output include reports, documents, music, graphs, and pictures. An output device displays, prints, or transmits the results of processing. The figure below can help you visualize the input, processing, storage, and output activities of a computer.

Play It!

**Figure
1-1**

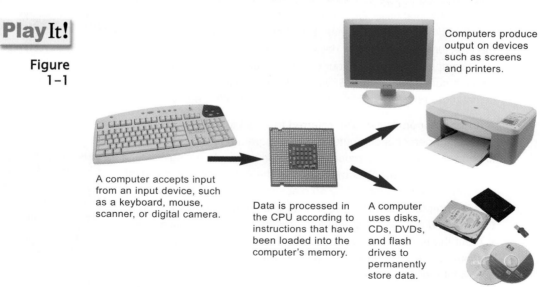

Computers produce output on devices such as screens and printers.

A computer accepts input from an input device, such as a keyboard, mouse, scanner, or digital camera.

Data is processed in the CPU according to instructions that have been loaded into the computer's memory.

A computer uses disks, CDs, DVDs, and flash drives to permanently store data.

FAQ How are computers classified?

Computers are sometimes divided into categories. In order of size and computing power, these categories are: handheld computers, personal computers, servers, mainframe computers, and supercomputers.

Figure 1-2

A **handheld computer**, such the one shown at right, features a small keyboard or touch-sensitive screen and is designed to fit into a pocket, run on batteries, and be used while you are holding it. A handheld **PDA** (personal digital assistant) is typically used as an electronic appointment book, address book, calculator, and notepad. Most of these devices can also send and receive e-mail, collect maps and locations based on the global positioning system, and make voice calls using cellular phone service. Handheld computing devices also include portable e-book readers, smartphones, portable media players, portable game systems, and programmable calculators.

A **personal computer** is designed to meet the computing needs of an individual. These computers are sometimes referred to as "microcomputers." Personal computers typically provide access to a wide variety of computing applications, such as word processing, photo editing, e-mail, and Internet access. Personal computers are available in desktop configurations or in portable configurations such as notebooks, tablets, and minilaptops.

A **desktop computer** fits on a desk and runs on power from an electrical wall outlet. The keyboard is typically a separate component, connected to the main unit by a cable. Although the main unit is sometimes incorporated into the display device or keyboard, more typically the main unit is housed in a vertical case, as shown on the right, or in a horizontal case. Desktop computers are popular for offices, schools, and homes. Because their components can be manufactured economically, desktop computers typically provide the most computing power for your dollar. The price of an entry-level desktop computer starts at $300 or a bit less, but most consumers select more powerful models that cost between $700 and $1,200.

A **notebook computer** (also referred to as a laptop), is a small, lightweight personal computer that incorporates the screen, the keyboard, storage, and processing components into a single portable unit. Notebook computers, like the one shown on the right, can run on power supplied by an electrical outlet or a battery. These computers are ideal for mobile uses because they are easy to carry and can be used outdoors, in airports, and in classrooms without the need for a nearby electrical outlet. Small notebook computers are sometimes called **minilaptops**. Notebook computers cost a bit more than desktop computers with similar computing power and storage capacity. The price of an entry-level notebook computer starts at about $350, but consumers typically spend between $600 and $1,500 to get the performance they desire.

How are computers classified? (continued)

A **tablet computer** is a portable computing device featuring a touch-sensitive screen that can be used as a writing or drawing pad. A slate tablet configuration, shown on the right, lacks a keyboard (although one can be attached) and resembles a high-tech clipboard. A convertible tablet configuration is constructed like a notebook computer, but the screen folds face up over the keyboard to provide a horizontal writing surface. Tablet computers shine for applications that involve handwritten input. When tablet computers were first introduced in 2002, they were priced significantly higher than notebook computers with similar specifications. Currently, however, tablet computers are priced only slightly higher than equivalent notebook computers.

**Figure
1–3**

The purpose of a **server** is to *serve* data to computers connected to a network. Technically, just about any computer can be configured to perform the work of a server. Nonetheless, computer manufacturers such as IBM and Dell offer devices called blade servers and storage servers that are especially suited for storing and distributing data on a network. Despite impressive performance on server-related tasks, these machines do not offer features such as sound cards, DVD players, and other fun accessories, so they are not a suitable alternative to a personal computer.

A **mainframe computer** (or simply a "mainframe") is a large and expensive computer capable of simultaneously processing data for hundreds or thousands of users. Its main processing circuitry is housed in a closet-sized cabinet like the one shown on the right; but after large components are added for storage and output, a mainframe can fill a good-sized room. Originally designed to accept input from devices called terminals, mainframes today are typically accessed by desktop computers.

Mainframes are generally used by businesses and governments to provide centralized storage, processing, and management for large amounts of data. Mainframes remain the computer of choice in situations where reliability, data security, and centralized control are necessary. The price of a mainframe computer typically starts at several hundred thousand dollars and can easily exceed $1 million.

A computer falls into the **supercomputer** category if it is, at the time of construction, one of the fastest computers in the world. Because of their speed, supercomputers, like the one pictured at the right, can tackle complex tasks that just would not be practical for other computers. Typical uses for supercomputers include breaking codes, modeling worldwide weather systems, and simulating nuclear explosions.

Courtesy of Marco Librero, NASA Ames

FAQ Can computers connect to each other?

Computers can connect to each other in a variety of ways. In a very simple computer-to-computer connection, a PDA can connect to a desktop computer using a cable or wireless link to synchronize data between the two devices. More typically, personal computers connect to each other and to larger computers over a wired or wireless **computer network** designed to share hardware, data, and software. A computer network can encompass as few as two or as many as thousands of computers. Today, computer networks are in widespread use at schools, small businesses, and large enterprises. You'll find these networks in homes, college computer labs, university administrative offices, government agencies, retail stores, and multi-location superstores. The **Internet** is the world's largest network, connecting millions of personal computers, servers, mainframes, and supercomputers.

Computers can be connected using a centralized model or a distributed model. A **centralized computing system** depends on a centrally-located computer for processing and storage. A mainframe that services desktop computers is an example of this model. Centralized systems are relatively easy to control, manage, and secure because the main computing hardware is in one place. A **distributed computer network** spreads the processing and storage tasks among many computers. The Internet is an example of a distributed network. Management and security of a distributed computing system are more difficult than for a centralized system because the locations of files, resources, and machines are often geographically disbursed. Figure 1-4 illustrates the different organization of computers in centralized and distributed computing networks.

Figure 1–4

Centralized computer system   Distributed computer network

Large-scale centralized and distributed computer systems are used today for many tasks. Examples of government applications include public records systems, such as tax roles, census records, and vehicle registration. Commercial applications for large retail operations, such as supermarkets and superstores, include inventory, payroll, and point-of-sale. In hospitals and health care organizations, large-scale applications include patient records systems, integrated diagnostic tools, patient billing, and health insurance claims processing. In education, large-scale applications include course registration, student records, budgeting, and payroll.

Networks are monitored by security personnel and supervised by network administrators who set up accounts and passwords for authorized network users. The user ID and password entered during the login process are authenticated against a list of authorized users. Only authorized user IDs and passwords allow access to network data and equipment.

FAQ What are the components of a personal computer system?

The term **personal computer system** usually refers to a desktop or notebook computer and all the input, output, and storage devices connected to it. A typical personal computer system includes the following equipment:

- **System unit.** The system unit is the case that holds the computer's circuit boards, CPU, power supply, memory, and storage devices. Depending on the computer design, the system unit might also include other devices, such as a keyboard and speakers.

- **Display device.** Most desktop computers have a separate display device, whereas the display device for notebook computers is incorporated in the system unit.

- **Keyboard.** Most computers are equipped with a keyboard as the primary input device.

- **Mouse.** A mouse is an input device designed to manipulate on-screen graphical objects and controls.

- **Storage devices.** Most computers include a hard disk drive, and a CD or DVD drive.

- **USB ports.** Sockets called USB ports on the system unit make it easy to plug in various devices, such as external hard disk drives and USB flash drives.

- **Sound card and speakers.** Desktop computers have a rudimentary built-in speaker that is mostly limited to playing beeps. A small circuit board, called a sound card, is required for high-quality music, narration, and sound effects. A desktop computer's sound card sends signals to external speakers. A notebook's sound card sends signals to speakers built into the notebook system unit.

- **Modem.** Some personal computer systems include a built-in modem that can be used to establish an Internet connection using a standard telephone line.

- **Network card.** Many personal computer systems include a network card designed for connecting a computer to a local area network.

- **Printer.** A computer printer is an output device that produces computer-generated text or graphical images on paper.

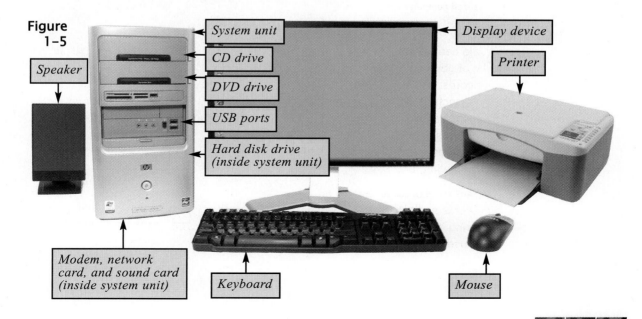

Figure 1–5

Speaker

System unit

CD drive

DVD drive

USB ports

Hard disk drive (inside system unit)

Display device

Printer

Modem, network card, and sound card (inside system unit)

Keyboard

Mouse

FAQ What's inside the system unit?

The system unit contains storage devices, a power supply, and the computer's main circuit board, called a **motherboard**, "system board," or "mainboard." This circuit board houses all essential chips and provides connecting circuitry between them.

The terms "computer chip," "microchip," and "chip" originated as technical jargon for "integrated circuit." An **integrated circuit** is a super-thin slice of semiconducting material packed with microscopic circuit elements, such as wires, transistors, capacitors, logic gates, and resistors. An integrated circuit is usually encapsulated in a small, black plastic case that provides a series of metal connectors. These connectors plug into special chip sockets in the motherboard and other circuit boards.

A **microprocessor** (sometimes simply referred to as a "processor") is an integrated circuit designed to process instructions. Although a microprocessor is sometimes mistakenly referred to as "a computer on a chip," it can be more accurately described as "a CPU on a chip" because it contains—on a single chip—circuitry that performs essentially the same tasks as the CPU of a classic mainframe computer.

The figure below shows the motherboard, chips, and other components housed within a typical desktop computer system unit.

Play It!

Figure 1–6

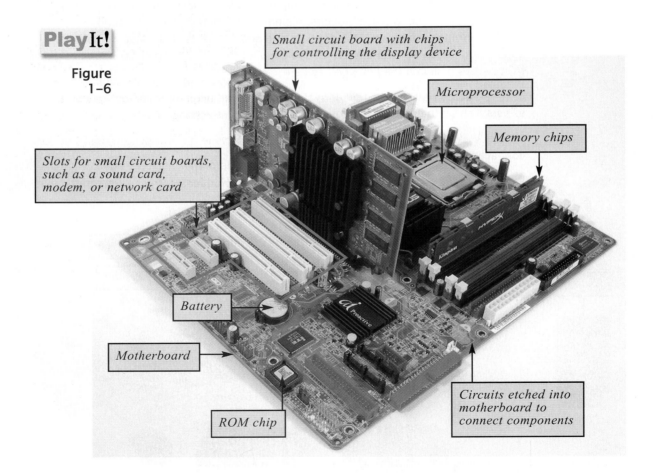

Small circuit board with chips for controlling the display device

Microprocessor

Memory chips

Slots for small circuit boards, such as a sound card, modem, or network card

Battery

Motherboard

ROM chip

Circuits etched into motherboard to connect components

FAQ How do computer circuits manipulate data?

Most computers are electronic, digital devices. A **digital device** works with discrete—distinct and separate—data, such as the digits 1 and 0. In contrast, an **analog device** works with continuous data. For example, a traditional light switch has two discrete states—on and off—so it is a digital device. In contrast, a dimmer switch has a rotating dial that controls a continuous range of brightness. It is, therefore, an analog device.

Most computers use the simplest type of digital technology—their circuits have only two possible states. For convenience, let's say that one of those states is "on" and the other state is "off." When discussing these states, we usually indicate the "on" state with 1 and the "off" state with 0. So the sequence "on" "on" "off" "off" would be written 1100. These 1s and 0s are referred to as binary digits. This term has been shortened to **bit** (*bi*nary digi*t*). Computers use sequences of bits to digitally represent numbers, letters, punctuation marks, music, pictures, and videos.

The binary number system has only two digits: 0 and 1. No numeral like 2 exists in this system, so the number "2" is represented in binary as "10" (pronounced "one zero"). The important point to understand is that the binary number system allows computers to represent virtually any number simply by using 0s and 1s, which conveniently translate into electrical "on" and "off" signals. Using binary arithmetic, a computer can perform calculations.

Computers employ several types of codes to represent character data, including ASCII, EBCDIC, and Unicode. **ASCII** (American Standard Code for Information Interchange, pronounced "ASK ee") requires only seven bits for each character. For example, the ASCII code for an uppercase "A" is 1000001. ASCII provides codes for 128 characters, including uppercase letters, lowercase letters, punctuation symbols, and numerals. As shown in Figure 1-7, a superset of ASCII, called **Extended ASCII**, uses eight bits to represent each character. **EBCDIC** (Extended Binary-Coded Decimal Interchange Code, pronounced "EB seh dick") is another 8-bit code usually used only by older, IBM mainframe computers. **Unicode** (pronounced "YOU ni code") uses 16 bits and provides codes for 65,000 characters—a real bonus for representing the alphabets of multiple languages. For example, Unicode represents an uppercase "A" in the Russian Cyrillic alphabet as 0000010000010000.

Figure 1-7

0	00110000	C	01000011	V	01010110	i	01101001
1	00110001	D	01000100	W	01010111	j	01101010
2	00110010	E	01000101	X	01011000	k	01101011
3	00110011	F	01000110	Y	01011001	l	01101100
4	00110100	G	01000111	Z	01011010	m	01101101
5	00110101	H	01001000	[	01011011	n	01101110
6	00110110	I	01001001	\	01011100	o	01101111
7	00110111	J	01001010	]	01011101	p	01110000
8	00111000	K	01001011	^	01011110	q	01110001
9	00111001	L	01001100	_	01011111	r	01110010
:	00111010	M	01001101	`	01100000	s	01110011
;	00111011	N	01001110	a	01100001	t	01110100
<	00111100	O	01001111	b	01100010	u	01110101
=	00111101	P	01010000	c	01100011	v	01110110
>	00111110	Q	01010001	d	01100100	w	01110111
?	00111111	R	01010010	e	01100101	x	01111000
@	01000000	S	01010011	f	01100110	y	01111001
A	01000001	T	01010100	g	01100111	z	01111010
B	01000010	U	01010101	h	01101000		

FAQ What factors affect computer speed, power, and compatibility?

Computers have three major components: a microprocessor, memory, and storage. In a nutshell, a computer keeps programs and data in storage when they are not immediately needed. When you start a program, it is moved from a storage device into memory. The microprocessor fetches a program instruction from memory, and then begins to execute it. If the instruction requires data, the computer fetches it from storage, loads it into memory, and then transfers it to the microprocessor. Results from processing the data are sent back to memory. From there the results can be stored or output to a printer or screen.

Processing speed and efficiency can be affected by the following factors:

- **Microprocessor type and speed.** Faster processors are able to execute more instructions and manipulate more data than slower processors.

- **Memory capacity.** Transferring data from disk to memory is slower than transferring data from memory to the processor. More memory capacity means your computer can load in lots of program instructions and data while other processing occurs. Once instructions and data are loaded into memory, the microprocessor doesn't have to wait for their arrival from a slow storage device.

- **Hard disk drive speed and organization.** The faster a disk drive transfers data to memory, the faster the data is available for processing. Also, data can be accessed quickly if it is well organized. As explained later in the chapter, running a defragmentation program optimizes disk performance.

- **Display capability and video memory.** When data is output to a display device, your computer has to draw every dot on the screen. As the image changes, the screen image is redrawn. When this process happens quickly, the screen appears crisp and steady. The data used to form the screen image is stored in special video memory. Your screen gives the best performance for videos and fast-action computer games when a large amount of video memory is supplied by the video circuitry that connects your computer and display device.

- **Network and modem connection speed.** When you request data from a network, your computer cannot process the data until it arrives. A slow network connection makes your computer seem to operate slowly when dealing with transmitted data.

Computer ads, like the one in Figure 1-8, include several specifications for computer speed and capacity. A few key concepts can help you understand these specifications and use them to compare computers before making a purchasing decision.

Figure 1-8

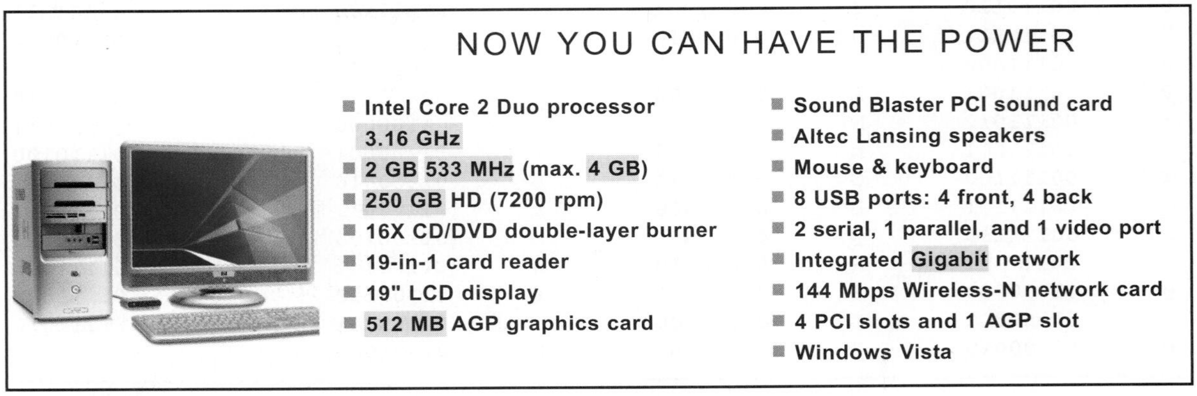

NOW YOU CAN HAVE THE POWER

- Intel Core 2 Duo processor 3.16 GHz
- 2 GB 533 MHz (max. 4 GB)
- 250 GB HD (7200 rpm)
- 16X CD/DVD double-layer burner
- 19-in-1 card reader
- 19" LCD display
- 512 MB AGP graphics card

- Sound Blaster PCI sound card
- Altec Lansing speakers
- Mouse & keyboard
- 8 USB ports: 4 front, 4 back
- 2 serial, 1 parallel, and 1 video port
- Integrated Gigabit network
- 144 Mbps Wireless-N network card
- 4 PCI slots and 1 AGP slot
- Windows Vista

• What factors affect computer speed, power, and compatibility? (continued)

Even though the word "bit" is an abbreviation for "binary digit," it can be further abbreviated, as a lowercase "b." A **byte**, on the other hand, is composed of eight bits and it is abbreviated as an uppercase "B." These abbreviations combine with prefixes such as "kilo" to produce specifications such as KB (kilobyte) and Kb (kilobit).

In common usage, "kilo," abbreviated as "K," means 1,000. In the world of computers, however, "kilo" means 1,024. A kilobit (abbreviated Kb or Kbit) is 1,024 bits. A kilobyte (abbreviated KB or Kbyte) is 1,024 bytes. Kilobytes are often used when referring to the size of small computer files.

The prefix "mega" means a million, or in the context of bits and bytes, precisely 1,048,576. A megabit (Mb or Mbit) is 1,048,576 bits. A megabyte (MB or MByte) is 1,048,576 bytes. Megabits are often used when referring to the speed of data transmission over a computer network connection. Megabytes are often used when referring to the size of medium to large computer files, CD capacity, or video card memory capacity.

The prefix "giga" refers to a billion, or precisely 1,073,741,824. As you might expect, a gigabit (Gb or Gbit) is approximately 1 billion bits. A gigabyte (GB or GByte) is one billion bytes. Gigabytes are typically used to refer to RAM, DVD, and hard disk capacity.

Computers—especially mainframes and supercomputers—sometimes work with huge amounts of data, and so terms such as "tera" (trillion), "peta" (quadrillion), and "exa" (quintillion) are also handy. Figure 1-9 summarizes the terms commonly used to quantify computer data.

Figure 1-9

Bit	1 binary digit	Megabit	1,048,576 bits	Terabyte	1 trillion bytes
Byte	8 bits	Megabyte	1,048,576 bytes	Petabyte	1 quadrillion bytes
Kilobit	1,024 bits	Gigabit	1 billion bits	Exabyte	1 quintillion bytes
Kilobyte	1,024 bytes	Gigabyte	1 billion bytes		

Today, there are three personal computer platforms: PC, Mac, and Linux. The PC platform is based on the design for one of the first personal computer superstars—the IBM PC. The great grandchildren of the IBM PC are on computer store shelves today—a huge selection of personal computer brands and models manufactured by companies such as Lenovo, Hewlett-Packard, Dell, and Acer. The Windows operating system was designed specifically for these personal computers and, therefore, the PC platform is sometimes called the Windows platform.

The Mac platform is based on a proprietary design for a personal computer called the Macintosh (or Mac), manufactured almost exclusively by Apple Computer, Inc. The Mac lineup includes the iMac, MacBook, MacBook Air, MacBook Pro, Mac mini, and Mac Pro computers, all running the Mac OS operating system.

The Linux platform is essentially a standard PC with the Linux operating system installed. Linux is typically the platform selected for servers and other technical applications.

Compatible computers operate in essentially the same way. At one time, PC, Linux, and Mac platforms were not compatible because of hardware and operating system differences. The compatibility situation has changed because most Mac and Linux computers now use the same microprocessors as PCs. For example, if you have a Mac computer with an Intel processor (sometimes called an Intel Mac), you can install Windows on it and run Windows software.

FAQ What's important about microprocessors?

The microprocessor is the most important, and usually the most expensive, component of a computer. Today, microprocessors are used in a variety of devices. Some microprocessors perform general computing tasks in handheld devices, personal computers, servers, mainframes, and supercomputers. Other microprocessors are built into non-computer machinery such as automobiles, appliances, and industrial equipment. These **embedded microprocessors** are designed for specialized tasks, such as monitoring the performance of automobile engines, controlling washing machine spin cycles, or running assembly-line robots.

The miniaturized circuitry in a microprocessor is grouped into important functional areas, such as the ALU and the control unit. The **ALU** (arithmetic logic unit) performs arithmetic operations, such as addition and subtraction. It also performs logical operations, such as comparing two numbers to see if they are the same. The **control unit** directs microprocessor tasks. The ALU uses **registers** to hold data that is being processed.

For a microprocessor analogy, consider the equipment and procedures you use to whip up a batch of brownies. Registers hold data just as a mixing bowl holds ingredients for a batch of brownies. The microprocessor's control unit fetches each instruction, just as you would get each ingredient out of a cupboard or the refrigerator. The computer loads data into the ALU's registers, just as you would add all the ingredients to the mixing bowl. Finally, the control unit gives the ALU the green light to begin processing, just as you would flip the switch on your electric mixer to begin blending the brownie ingredients.

Microprocessor speed is measured in megahertz (MHz) or gigahertz (GHz). One megahertz is one million cycles per second. One gigahertz is one billion cycles per second. Clock speed is analogous to how fast you pedal when you ride a bike. Usually, the faster you pedal, the faster you move. During each clock cycle, the microprocessor executes instructions. The faster the clock speed, the more instructions your microprocessor can carry out in each second. Therefore, a 3.2 GHz microprocessor is faster than a 2.8 GHz processor. The original IBM PC, introduced in 1981, operated at 4.77 MHz. Today's computers with GHz speeds are almost 1,000 times faster.

Microprocessors are also rated by word size. Many of today's computers process a 32-bit word—a chunk of data up to 32 bits long. 64-bit computers are also available and quickly gaining popularity. By handling more data in each clock cycle, these computers are faster than their 32-bit counterparts.

Microprocessors are manufactured by several companies. Intel produces many PC microprocessors, such as the Core, Celeron, Atom, and Xeon. Other microprocessor manufacturers include AMD, Motorola, and IBM.

Figure 1-10

Photos courtesy of Intel Corporation

FAQ What's important about computer memory?

RAM (random access memory) is a temporary holding area for data, application program instructions, and the operating system. In a personal computer, RAM is usually several chips or small circuit boards that plug into the motherboard within the computer's system unit. RAM is the "waiting room" for the computer's processor. It holds program instructions, raw data, and the results of processing. When you start a program, it is loaded from disk into RAM. It remains there until you close the program, which releases the RAM space it used.

RAM also holds data. For example, when you use personal finance software to balance your checkbook, you enter raw data for check amounts. This data is held in RAM. The personal finance software sends the instructions for processing this data to RAM. The processor uses these instructions to calculate your checkbook balance and sends the results back to RAM. From RAM, your checkbook balance can be stored on disk, displayed, or printed. When you close a data file, it releases the space it used in RAM.

Figure 1–11

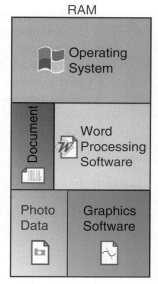

Unlike disk storage, most RAM is **volatile**, which means it requires electrical power to hold data. If the computer is turned off or the power goes out, all data stored in RAM instantly and permanently disappears. You can understand why it is important to frequently save your data in a more permanent storage area, such as the hard disk, as you work. The process of saving data copies it from RAM to a storage device.

In addition to data and application software instructions, RAM also holds operating system instructions that control the basic functions of a computer system. These instructions are loaded into RAM every time you start your computer, and they remain there until you turn off your computer. RAM capacity is measured in megabytes or gigabytes. Today's computers typically feature between 512 MB and 4 GB of RAM. Figure 1-11 illustrates the contents of RAM while your computer is on and running application software.

In addition to RAM, most computers also contain **ROM** (read-only memory)—a type of memory circuitry that holds the computer's startup routine. Whereas RAM is temporary and volatile, ROM is permanent and non-volatile. ROM circuitry holds hardwired instructions that are a permanent part of the circuitry and remain in place even when the computer power is turned off. This is a familiar concept to anyone who has used a handheld calculator that includes various hardwired routines for calculating square roots, cosines, and other functions. The instructions in ROM are permanent, and the only way to change them is to replace the ROM chip.

When you turn on your computer, the microprocessor receives electrical power and is ready to begin executing instructions. As a result of the power being off, however, RAM is empty and doesn't contain any instructions for the microprocessor to execute. Now ROM plays its part. ROM contains a small set of instructions called the **ROM BIOS** (basic input/output system). These instructions tell the computer how to access the hard disk, find the operating system, and load it into RAM. After the operating system is loaded, the computer can understand your input, display output, run software, and access your data.

FAQ Why do computers use multiple storage devices?

The perfect storage device would be inexpensive, high-capacity, portable, and virtually indestructible. Unfortunately, such a device does not exist today. To cover everyone's storage needs, computers typically feature multiple storage devices, such as hard disk drives, CD drives, DVD drives, and USB flash drives. Each one has advantages and disadvantages that make them useful for some tasks, but not appropriate for other tasks.

A **hard disk drive** is the main storage device in most computer systems. It provides economical, high-capacity storage—up to 2 terabytes. It also provides fast access to files. In computer ads, hard disk capacity is specified in gigabytes, and its speed is measured in milliseconds (ms) or revolutions per minute (RPM). Higher GB numbers mean more capacity. Lower ms numbers mean faster speeds. Higher RPMs mean faster speeds.

Figure 1-12

A hard disk drive often contains more than one hard disk platter for data storage.

Read-write heads move in and out from the center of the disk to locate data.

Hard disks are not the most durable type of storage. They use **magnetic storage technology** in which microscopic particles are magnetized to represent 0s and 1s. Hard disk read-write heads, shown in Figure 1-12, hover a microscopic distance above the disk surface. If a read-write head runs into a dust particle or some other contaminant, it can cause a **head crash**, which damages some of the data on the disk. To eliminate contaminants, a hard disk is sealed in its case. A head crash can also be triggered by jarring the hard disk while it is in use. Although hard disks have become considerably more rugged in recent years, you should still handle and transport them with care.

The main hard disk drive for a computer is installed inside the system unit. Additional internal hard drives can be installed if space is provided. Otherwise, external hard drives can be connected to any USB port. Because external drives can be easily removed and stored in a safe place, they work well for holding backups of hard disk data.

Most computers include a **CD drive** or **DVD drive** that uses a small laser light to read data stored on plastic-coated CDs and DVDs. Figure 1-13 illustrates how these drives work.

Figure 1-13

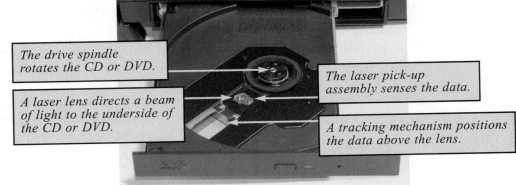

The drive spindle rotates the CD or DVD.

A laser lens directs a beam of light to the underside of the CD or DVD.

The laser pick-up assembly senses the data.

A tracking mechanism positions the data above the lens.

• Why do computers use multiple storage devices? (continued)

A **CD** (compact disc) provides 650–700 MB of storage space for computer data. A **DVD** (digital video disc or digital versatile disc) is a variation of CD technology with a capacity of 4.7 GB. Storage capacity can be doubled if the DVD drive and DVD medium support dual-layer technology.

CDs and DVDs are classified as removable storage technologies because they can be easily removed from the drive and transported to another computer. This characteristic makes them handy for sharing data files and for backing up important work.

CDs and DVDs are durable storage media because their **optical storage technology** essentially etches data onto the disc surface. The process of creating CDs and DVDs is sometimes referred to as "burning" and drives are referred to as CD or DVD "burners." CDs and DVDs have a much higher tolerance for temperature fluctuations than hard disks. They are unaffected by magnetic fields. Dust and dirt can be cleaned off using a soft cloth. Scratches pose the biggest threat to the data stored on CDs and DVDs, so they should be stored in a case or jacket. CDs and DVDs come in several varieties.

- **Read-only** (ROM) versions of CDs and DVDs contain permanent data stored on the disk during the manufacturing process. Data on CD-ROMs and DVD-ROMs cannot be changed or deleted. These discs are typically used to distribute software and movies.

- **Recordable** (R) CDs and DVDs contain a layer of color dye sandwiched beneath the clear plastic disc surfaces. A writable drive can store data on CD-R and DVD-R discs by changing the dye color. The change in the dye is permanent, so data cannot be changed after it has been recorded.

- **Rewritable** (RW) CDs and DVDs contain a crystal structure on the disc surface. The crystal structure of CD-RW, DVD-RW, CD+RW, and DVD+RW discs can be changed many times, making it possible to record and modify data much like on a hard disk. A rewritable CD or DVD drive is a fine addition to a computer system, but is not a good replacement for a hard disk drive because the process of accessing, saving, and modifying data on a rewritable disk is relatively slow compared to the speed of hard disk access.

The original CD drives could access 150 KB of data per second. The next generation of drives doubled the data transfer rate and were consequently dubbed 2X drives. Transfer rates seem to be continually increasing. A 46X CD drive, for example, transfers data at 55.40 Mbps. That rate is relatively slow, however, compared to a hard disk drive's transfer rate of 2,560 Mbps.

The speed of a DVD drive is measured on a different scale than a CD drive. A 1X DVD drive is about the same speed as a 9X CD drive. Today's DVD drives typically have 16X speeds for a data transfer rate of 177.28 Mbps.

Figure 1–14

• **Why do computers use multiple storage devices? (continued)**

**Figure
1-15**

A **USB flash drive** ("flash drive" for short) is a popular removable, portable storage device featuring a built-in connector that plugs directly into a computer's USB port. Nicknamed "jump drives" or "thumb drives," USB flash drives like the one in Figure 1-15 are about the size of a highlighter pen and so durable that you can literally carry them on your key ring.

Flash drives replaced floppy disks, or diskettes, as the most popular portable storage medium for several reasons. Just about every computer has a USB port, so flash drives work virtually everywhere. Data can be written onto a flash drive without a bulky drive or burner; and with capacity that ranges up to 64 GB, flash drives store lots of data.

You can open, edit, delete, and run files stored on a USB flash drive just as though those files were stored on your computer's hard disk. USB flash drives use **solid state storage technology**, which provides fast access to data, and uses very little power. This type of storage is sometimes referred to as "flash memory" or "memory cards," even though it is quite unlike volatile random access memory, which holds data only when the power is on.

In addition to popular storage devices directly connected to your computer, data can also be stored on remote devices, such as network hard disk drives and virtual drives located on the Internet.

Network drives might offer more storage capacity than your PC, but the speed at which you can access data depends on the speed of your network connection. Files stored on network drives are easily accessible to others for collaborative work. Network storage offers a potentially safe place to store data backups in case your computer is damaged or stolen.

Online storage provides space for your files on a server that can be accessed over the Internet, which is handy for files you want to back up, share, or access while you are out and about.

**Figure
1-16**

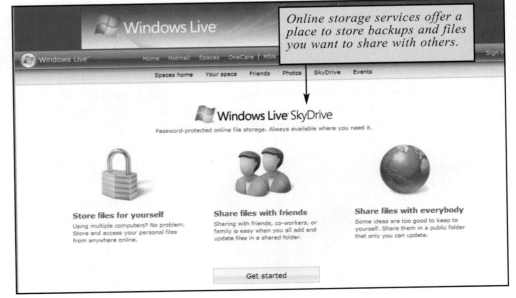

Online storage services offer a place to store backups and files you want to share with others.

FAQ What kind of protection and maintenance does a computer require?

The data stored on your computer can be quite valuable. A damaged or stolen notebook computer can be replaced, but the data it contains might be irreplaceable. Not only could it be difficult to reconstruct assignments, reports, and calculations you might need for school or work, but your computer can contain important personal information, which you don't want to fall into the wrong hands. Therefore, you should take all reasonable steps to protect your computer from theft and damage, and maintain your computer equipment in good working condition.

Large organizations protect computer equipment from theft with high-tech security systems such as building alarms and monitors. To protect your personal computer, you can keep it locked to a desk or within a locked room. When traveling by air, transport your computer in your carry-on bag. Don't leave it unattended in public places, such as a library or coffee shop.

Computers can be easily damaged if dropped. When using your computer, make sure it is resting on a stable surface. When carrying a notebook computer, use a padded carrying case. To transport a desktop computer, use the original box or protect it with foam padding.

Environmental factors can damage computers. Extreme temperatures can damage circuitry. High humidity can corrode contacts and cables. Water leaks can short out circuits. Magnetic fields can erase data. Dust, dirt, and air pollution can cause overheating and clog up mechanical parts.

Routine cleaning of your mouse and keyboard can keep them working smoothly. Follow your printer manufacturer's instructions for periodic cleaning to keep your printer from jamming and the print head from smearing. If a printer jam occurs, follow instructions carefully to clear the jammed paper. Keep floppy disks and hard disks away from strong magnetic fields, which could rearrange the iron oxide particles on the disk surface that stores your data. Refrigerator magnets have no place in your computer area.

Computers are vulnerable to power irregularities and outages. When setting up your computer, make sure the power cable is safely positioned so that it cannot be accidentally disconnected. When transporting a computer to another country that uses a different power system, you should check with the manufacturer to make sure all your equipment can adapt to it. Otherwise, purchase the necessary transformer.

Figure 1-17

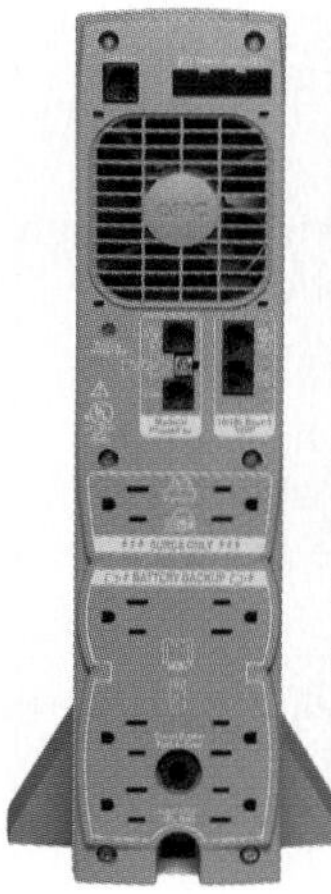

At home, you should use a surge strip to protect your computer from power spikes and surges that could overload circuits and cause permanent damage. A **surge strip** (or "surge suppressor") is typically a row of outlets arranged in a plastic case. The surge strip plugs into a wall outlet, and you can plug your computer equipment into the surge strip's outlets. A surge strip monitors the flow of power and attempts to filter out overloads. For protection against power outages, you can connect your computer to an **uninterruptible power supply** (UPS) that offers battery backup along with surge protection (see Figure 1-17).

Computer owners can safely perform many computer maintenance tasks, such as cleaning the mouse, keyboard, and printer, and replacing printer cartridges and other consumables. Owners should also periodically make backups of data, run a defragmentation utility, and update antivirus software. Backups on CDs, DVDs, USB flash drives, or network storage devices should be made on a file-by-file basis whenever you produce data you don't want to lose. A more comprehensive backup should be scheduled weekly or monthly, depending on how much data you generate.

● **What kind of protection and maintenance does a computer require? (continued)**

A **defragmentation utility** helps your hard disk operate more efficiently. As you store, change, and delete files, the operating system divides each file into manageable chunks and stores them in any available space. Eventually, files become scattered all over the disk and the disk drive has to work hard to round up all the pieces each time you open a file. The defragmentation process consolidates all parts of a file into nearby areas of the disk, so that the disk drive can easily access them. You should defragment your hard disk monthly or bi-annually, depending on the amount of data you work with.

Computer owners should also make sure their computers have up-to-date virus protection. Most antivirus software automatically updates itself by periodically connecting to the Internet. Make sure this feature is activated on your computer.

If you can identify a malfunctioning component, such as the keyboard, mouse, or display device, you might be able to swap it out for a component that works. However, some maintenance and repair work is best left to professionals. If you are not comfortable working with electronic components, ask an experienced professional to replace malfunctioning hardware components and upgrade system unit hardware components, such as microprocessors and RAM.

Most computer owners *can* troubleshoot malfunctioning equipment and at least narrow down the source of a problem. Such problems might include a "crashed" hard drive, newly installed hardware that does not work correctly, or a printer that begins to behave erratically. An organized, step-by-step approach to problem solving can expedite your troubleshooting efforts to get your computer back up and running. Consider the guidelines below when you troubleshoot computer problems.

● Make sure equipment is plugged into a functioning wall outlet and turned on.

● Check all cables between the computer and other devices. A loose cable, for example, can cause intermittent errors.

● Get a clear idea of the problem by trying to isolate the malfunctioning device or replicating the steps that consistently cause the problem.

● Attempt basic solutions, such as restarting the device or rebooting the computer.

● Look for information about the problem in the manual, on the Web, or from the manufacturer's technical support line.

● Write down relevant error messages.

● When communicating with technicians, make sure you explain the problem accurately and be prepared to answer questions about the brand and model of your computer, operating system, and application software.

● Follow the instructions from a manual, Web site, or technician carefully and completely. For example, if the instructions tell you to close all application programs before proceeding, you should do so.

● Before you resume normal computer operations, make sure the problem has been fixed. It is a good idea to turn all your computer equipment off and then reboot. Test out the situation in which you originally encountered the problem to make sure it doesn't reoccur.

● Save a record of the problem and solution in case you need to reference it in the future.

QuickCheck A

1. [＿＿＿＿＿＿＿] is an area of a computer that temporarily holds data waiting to be processed, stored, or output. [＿＿＿＿＿＿＿] is the area where data can be left on a permanent basis when it is not immediately needed for processing.

2. [＿＿＿＿＿＿＿] computer networks spread the processing and storage tasks among many computers.

3. A(n) [＿＿＿＿＿＿＿] circuit is a super-thin slice of semiconducting material packed with microscopic circuit elements, such as wires, transistors, capacitors, logic gates, and resistors.

4. In the world of computers, [＿＿＿＿＿＿＿] is abbreviated MB.

5. Unlike disk storage and solid state storage, most RAM is [＿＿＿＿＿＿＿] , which means it requires electrical power to hold data.

Check It!

QuickCheck B

Examine each specification indicated. If the specification is correct, enter C in the corresponding box below. For incorrect specifications, enter the correct measurement, such as MB, GHz, and so on.

1. [＿＿＿]
2. [＿＿＿]
3. [＿＿＿]
4. [＿＿＿]
5. [＿＿＿]

NOW YOU CAN HAVE THE POWER

1 → ■ Intel Core 2 Duo processor 2.8 GB

2 → ■ 512 Mb RAM (max. 4 GB)

3 → ■ 80 GHz HD (7200 rpm)
■ 16X DVD+RW/+R/CD-RW combo

■ 19" display device

4 → ■ 512 ns AGP graphics card
■ Sound Blaster PCI sound card

■ Altec Lansing speakers

■ U.S. Robotics 56 KB modem

■ Mouse & keyboard

■ 8 USB ports: 2 front, 6 back
■ 2 serial, 1 parallel, and 1 video port

5 → ■ 100 MHz network card

■ 4 PCI slots and 1 AGP slot

■ Windows Vista

Check It!

2

Peripheral Devices

What's Inside and on the CD?

This chapter provides an overview of the most popular peripheral devices for personal computers. It begins with standard input devices—your computer's keyboard and mouse—and then takes a look at some specialized input devices including trackpads, digital cameras, and joysticks. In the FAQs about output devices, you'll learn about computer display devices and printers. Specialized output devices, such as voice synthesizers and plotters, are also explained.

Peripheral devices can be connected to a computer system in a variety of ways. You'll find out which technologies provide the easiest connections.

The chapter winds up with an FAQ about purchasing components for a computer system. Handy tips will help you know what to look for when shopping for a computer, software, and peripheral devices.

FAQ What is a peripheral device?

The term **peripheral device** refers to any input or output component that connects to a computer's system unit. On a personal computer, standard peripheral devices include a keyboard, mouse, display unit, and printer. A wide variety of specialized peripheral devices for playing games, monitoring home security, capturing video images, and all kinds of other activities are also available for your personal computer. You'll learn more about personal computer peripheral devices later in the chapter.

Specialized peripheral devices are a key component of many large-scale computer systems. High-speed printers are instrumental in addressing mass mailing envelopes based on customer lists stored in a database. Mass mailings legitimately assist utility and credit card companies with monthly billing, but unfortunately also generate mountains of junk mail from advertisers and sweepstakes solicitors.

Banks use high-speed optical character readers and other sophisticated imaging peripherals to read and sort millions of paper checks at high speed without halting on creased, torn, or stapled checks. The check amount and account number are read and fed into the bank computer system. Check images generated by any bank can be transported to the Federal Reserve and the issuing bank for verification and archiving.

Some manufacturing firms use computer-controlled robots to carry out tasks such as arc welding, circuit board assembly, and painting. These robots can be reprogrammed as necessary when different models roll onto the assembly line.

Overnight shipping firms, such as UPS and FedEx, use handheld scanning devices to keep track of package deliveries. The shipping label for each package contains a bar code. When a package is delivered, the bar code is scanned and the scanning device automatically adds a date and time stamp. The package recipient's signature can be collected on a pressure sensitive input pad, and stored in memory until the driver returns to base and transfers the scanner's contents to the company's main computer system.

Figure 2-1

Retail stores use UPC scanners at staffed and self-checkout lanes (shown in Figure 2-1). As each item is scanned, its price is pulled from the store's main computer database. At the same time, the inventory count for that item is decreased by one to maintain an up-to-date inventory.

All of these devices—high-speed printers, optical character readers, computer-controlled robots, package scanners, and UPC scanners—can be considered peripheral devices. Although they are not typically part of personal computer systems, these peripherals are important components of large, enterprise computer systems and underscore the key role that digital devices play in business and industry.

FAQ What are the options for standard input devices?

Most personal computer systems include a keyboard and a pointing device for basic data input. These are the tools you use most often when entering data, issuing commands, and manipulating on-screen objects.

The keyboard is the most important input device on desktop and notebook computers, but you can even find tiny keyboards on handheld devices—entering text and numbers is required for just about every computing task. The design of most computer keyboards is based on the typewriter's QWERTY layout. This unusual arrangement of keys was not designed to maximize typing speed, but to keep a typewriter's mechanical keys from jamming. Computers inherited this layout because of its familiarity to millions of typists. In addition to the basic typing keys (Figure 2-2), desktop and notebook computer keyboards include an **editing keypad** to efficiently move the screen-based insertion point. They also include a collection of **function keys** designed for computer-specific tasks. Most desktop computer keyboards also include a calculator-style **numeric keypad**.

Figure 2-2

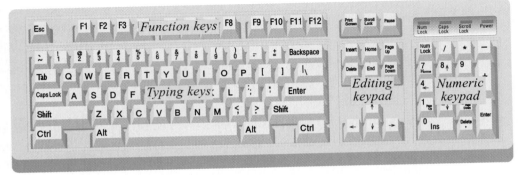

A **pointing device** allows you to manipulate an on-screen pointer and other screen-based graphical controls. The most popular pointing devices for personal computers include mice, trackballs, pointing sticks, trackpads, and joysticks.

A standard desktop computer includes a **mouse** as its primary pointing device. Many computer owners also add a mouse to their notebook computers because it is easier to use than the notebook's standard pointing stick or trackpad.

A **pointing stick**, also called a "TrackPoint," looks like the tip of an eraser embedded in the keyboard of a notebook computer. It is a space-saving device that you can push up, down, or sideways to move the on-screen pointer. A **trackpad** is a touch-sensitive surface on which you can slide your fingers to move the on-screen pointer. A **trackball** looks like a mechanical mouse turned upside down. You use your fingers, thumb, or palm to roll the ball and move the pointer. Pointing sticks, trackpads, and trackballs (Figure 2-3) are typically used with notebook computers as an alternative to a mouse.

Figure 2-3

FAQ What are the options for specialized PC input devices?

Personal computers are used in so many activities that most computer owners have at least one specialized input device for playing computer games, taking digital photos, or scanning printed images. Although the variety of input gadgets seems almost endless, the most popular devices are discussed below.

Figure 2-4

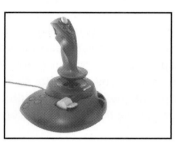

A **joystick** (left) looks like a small version of a car's stick shift. Moving the stick provides input to on-screen objects, such as a pointer or a character in a computer game. Joysticks (also called "game controllers") can include several sticks and buttons for arcade-like control when playing computer games. Joysticks can be also adapted for use by individuals who have difficulty using a keyboard.

A **digital camera** (left) is a peripheral device used to capture still images in a digital format that can be easily transferred into a computer and manipulated using graphics software. Digital cameras eliminate film and processing costs. They produce images that can be stored, manipulated, posted on Web sites, and transmitted as e-mail attachments.

A **digital video camera** (left) captures moving images in a format that can be easily transferred to a computer and manipulated using photo editing software. Digital video eliminates the need for costly editing equipment used to splice film or video tape footage and overlay sound tracks. Using a low-cost digital video camera and entry-level video-editing software, computer owners can produce videos of weddings, vacations, baby's first steps, and other significant events. **Webcams** are a type of inexpensive digital camera that remain tethered to a computer and used for video conferencing, video chatting, and live Web broadcasts.

A **graphics tablet** (left) features a pressure-sensitive surface and pen for free-hand drawing. Pressing hard with the pen creates a thick, dark line; light pressure reduces the line width. The software supplied with a graphics tablet provides a color palette and a variety of brushes, pens, and textures. Serious artists as well as children seem to enjoy the process of using a graphics tablet, as well as the resulting art.

A **digitizing tablet** (left) looks similar to a graphics tablet, but can be much larger in size. It provides a flat surface for a paper-based drawing and a pen or "puck" you can use to click and store endpoints. These endpoints can be used to redraw the image as a vector graphic, which can then be edited using drawing software. Architects and engineers typically use digitizing tablets to create blueprints and technical drawings.

• What are the options for specialized PC input devices? (continued)

A **touch-sensitive screen** can detect the location of a fingertip or stylus within the screen area. Touching the location of a screen-based icon, for example, can activate a menu or similar control. Touch-sensitive screens are used for tablet computers, PDAs, smartphones, and specialized devices such as information kiosks.

A **scanner** (Figure 2-5) converts printed images into bitmap graphics that can be viewed and edited with graphics software. A popular use for scanners is to capture old photographs, store them in digital format, and then use photo editing software to repair cracks, scratches, and fading. A scanner can also be used to capture pages containing text. When scanned as a bitmap, the text becomes part of the page image and cannot be manipulated separately. Some scanners, however, have **optical character recognition** ability, which converts the letters and symbols on a page into digital data that can be edited using word processing software.

Play It!

Figure 2–5

A computer uses a standard microphone to collect audio input. The microphone connector on the system unit is part of the computer's sound card, which processes the audio input into digital format. Some software applications include built-in **speech recognition**, which allows you to dictate commands and data using a microphone, instead of a keyboard and mouse. Microphones are also handy for annotating e-mail messages and for narrations designed to accompany Web sites and videos. Audio files tend to require lots of storage space, however, so you should refrain from recording long audio segments.

Personal computer peripheral devices also include a variety of sensors, such as water, smoke, and motion detectors used in PC-based home security systems. Security devices, such as fingerprint readers, can be connected to a personal computer to prevent unauthorized access to files and network connections.

Remote controls can also be considered peripheral devices when used to control computer applications. For example, when using a personal computer as the base for a home theater system, a remote control can be used to operate the DVD and adjust speaker volume.

A variety of input devices have been designed to assist people with physical challenges. Speech recognition systems are useful when keyboarding is not possible. Adaptive devices such as specialized keyboards and head pointers offer other alternatives to a standard keyboard and mouse.

FAQ What are the most popular display technologies?

Display devices (sometimes referred to as "monitors") are usually classified as output devices because they typically show the results of a processing task. Some displays, however, can be classified as both input and output devices because they include a touch-sensitive screen that accepts input. Today's most popular display devices use LCD, CRT, and plasma technologies.

An **LCD** (liquid crystal display) produces an image by manipulating light within a layer of liquid crystal cells. Modern LCD technology is compact in size, lightweight, and provides an easy-to-read display. LCDs are standard equipment on notebook computers. Standalone LCDs, referred to as "LCD monitors" or "flat panel displays," are also the most popular type of display for desktop computers. The advantages of an LCD monitor include display clarity, low radiation emission, portability, and compactness.

A **CRT** (cathode ray tube) display device uses the same sort of bulky glass tube as an old-style television. Gun-like mechanisms in the tube spray beams of electrons toward the screen and activate individual dots of color that form an image. CRT display devices are inexpensive and dependable, but they are heavy, and consume a fair amount of power.

Plasma screen technology creates an on-screen image by illuminating miniature colored fluorescent lights arrayed in a panel-like screen. The name "plasma" comes from the type of gas that fills fluorescent lights and gives them their luminescence. Plasma screens are compact and lightweight, but more expensive than LCDs and CRTs.

The performance of an LCD display device is a factor of screen size, dot pitch, response time, color depth, brightness, and resolution. When selecting a display device, it is important to keep these factors in mind.

- **Screen size** is the measurement in inches from one corner of the screen diagonally across to the opposite corner. Typical screen sizes range from 13" to 22".

- **Dot pitch** (or pixel pitch) is a measure of image clarity. Technically, dot pitch is the distance in millimeters between like-colored pixels—the small dots of light that form an image. A dot pitch between .28 mm and .22 mm is typical for today's display devices; a smaller dot pitch produces a crisper image.

- **Response time** is the length of time required for a pixel to change color to keep pace with the image being displayed on screen. For example, when playing an action game, the screen image is constantly changing. A display device with good response time will maintain a crisp image without the appearance of smearing or ghosting. Response time is measured in milliseconds, with lower numbers indicating better response times. Typical response times vary from 6 ms to 2 ms.

- The number of colors a monitor can display is referred to as **color depth** or "bit depth." Most PC display devices have the capability to display millions of colors. When set at 24-bit color depth (sometimes called "True Color"), your PC can display more than 16 million colors and produce what are considered photographic-quality images.

• What are the most popular display technologies? (continued)

• Screen brightness can be measured as luminance or as a contrast ratio. **Luminance** is usually expressed in candela per square meter (cd/m2), with higher numbers indicating a brighter display. **Contrast ratio** is the difference between the luminance of white and black pixels. You can adjust a display's brightness level, but if you plan to use your computer outdoors, make sure the screen has a good brightness rating and contrast ratio.

• The number of horizontal and vertical pixels that a device displays on a screen is referred to as **screen resolution**. The resolution for many early PC displays was referred to as VGA (Video Graphics Array). Higher resolutions were later provided by SVGA (Super VGA), XGA (eXtended Graphics Array), SXGA (Super XGA), and UXGA (Ultra XGA). These resolutions were supplemented by wide-screen versions such as WUXGA, indicated by prefixing the acronym with "W."

Resolution is adjustable up to the maximum capacity of the display device. At higher resolutions, text and other objects appear smaller, but the computer can display a larger work area, such as an entire page of a document. In Figure 2-6 the screen on the left is set at 1162 X 864 resolution. The desktop appears larger, but text and controls are reduced in size to allow all of the screen elements to fit. The screen on the right is set at 800 X 600 resolution. The desktop appears smaller—the application windows fit only with significant overlap. At this resolution, however, the larger text and controls are easier to see and use.

Figure 2-6

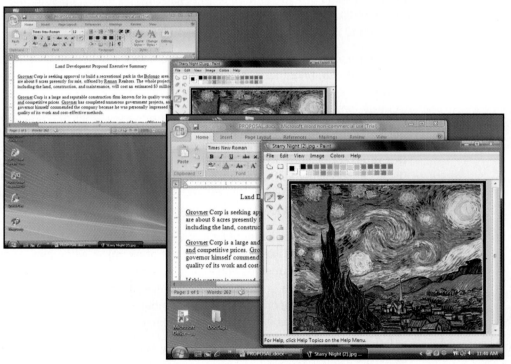

In addition to a display device, such as a monitor, a computer display system also requires graphics circuitry that generates the signals for displaying an image on the screen. Graphics circuitry can be built into a computer's motherboard or supplied as a small circuit board that plugs into the motherboard. This circuit board is called a **graphics card** (also called a "graphics board" or a "video card"). A graphics card typically contains special **video memory**, which stores screen images as they are processed, but before they are displayed. Lots of video memory is the key to lightning-fast screen updating for fast action games, 3D modeling, and graphics-intensive desktop publishing.

FAQ What are the most popular printer technologies?

Printers are one of the most popular output devices available for personal computers. Today's best-selling printers typically use ink jet or laser technology.

An **ink jet printer** has a nozzle-like print head that sprays ink onto paper to form characters and graphics. The print head in a color ink jet printer consists of a series of nozzles, each with its own ink cartridge. Most ink jet printers use CMYK color, which requires only cyan (blue), magenta (pink), yellow, and black inks to create a printout that appears to have thousands of colors. Alternatively, some printers use six ink colors to print midtone shades that create slightly more realistic photographic images.

**Figure
2–7**

Ink jet printers, such as the one in Figure 2-7, outsell all other types of printers because they are inexpensive and produce both color and black-and-white printouts. They work well for most home and small business applications. Small, portable ink jet printers meet the needs of many mobile computer owners. Ink jet technology also powers many photo printers, which are optimized to print high-quality images produced by digital cameras and scanners.

A **laser printer**, such as the one in Figure 2-8, uses the same technology as a photocopier to paint dots of light on a light-sensitive drum. Electrostatically charged ink is applied to the drum and then transferred to paper. Laser technology is more complex than ink jet technology, which accounts for the higher price of laser printers.

A basic laser printer produces only black-and-white printouts. Color laser printers are available, but are somewhat more costly than basic black-and-white models. Laser printers are often the choice for business printers, particularly for applications that produce a high volume of printed material.

**Figure
2–8**

• **What are the most popular printer technologies? (continued)**

When selecting a printer for your personal computer system, you should consider if its resolution, speed, duty cycle, and operating costs meet your printing needs.

- **Print resolution.** The quality or sharpness of printed images and text depends on the printer's resolution—the density of dots that create an image. Printer resolution is measured by the number of dots per linear inch, abbreviated as dpi. At normal reading distance, a resolution of about 900 dpi appears solid to the human eye, but a close examination reveals a dot pattern. If you want magazine-quality printouts, 900 dpi is sufficient resolution. If you are aiming for resolution similar to expensive coffee-table books, look for printer resolution of 2,400 dpi or higher.

- **Print speed.** Printer speeds are measured either by pages per minute (ppm) or characters per second (cps). Color printouts typically take longer than black-and-white printouts. Pages that contain mostly text tend to print more rapidly than pages that contain graphics. Typical speeds for personal computer printers range from 6 to 30 pages of text per minute. A full-page 8.5 X 11 photo can take about a minute to print.

- **Duty cycle.** In addition to printer speed, a printer's **duty cycle** determines how many pages a printer is able to churn out. Printer duty cycle is usually measured in pages per month. For example, a personal laser printer has a duty cycle of about 3,000 pages per month—that means roughly 100 pages per day. You wouldn't want to use it to produce 5,000 campaign brochures for next Monday, but you would find it quite suitable for printing 10 copies of a five-page outline for a meeting tomorrow.

- **Operating costs.** The initial cost of a printer is only one of the expenses associated with printed output. Ink jet printers require frequent replacements of relatively expensive print heads. Laser printers require toner cartridge refills or replacements. When shopping for a printer, you can check online resources to determine how often you can expect to replace printer supplies and how much they are likely to cost.

- **Memory.** A computer sends data for a printout to the printer along with a set of instructions on how to print that data. **Printer Command Language** (PCL) is the most widely used language for communication between computers and printers, but **PostScript** is an alternative printer language preferred by many publishing professionals. The data that arrives at a printer along with its printer language instructions require memory. A large memory capacity is required to print color images and graphics-intensive documents. Some printers accept additional memory, so you might be able to upgrade if your printer requires more memory for the types of documents you typically print.

- **Duplex printing.** Some printers are capable of printing on both sides of the paper, a feature referred to as **duplex printing**. The main advantage of duplex printing is cost—you use half the paper required for single-sided printing. Saving paper is also good for the environment; so next time you shop for a printer, consider one that offers the option of duplex printing.

- **Networkability.** Virtually every business has a computer network, and many households have them, too. Networks allow multiple computers to share a single printer. Any standard printer can be accessed over a network as long as it is connected to a computer on a network that is turned on and allows printer sharing. Some printers, however, contain circuitry that connects directly to a network rather than to a computer. Network circuitry adds to the cost of a printer, but is worth considering if you don't want to leave one of the computers on your network running all the time.

FAQ What are the options for specialized output devices?

Personal computer owners tend to collect fewer specialized output devices than input devices. Nevertheless, specialized output devices are available.

Many computer owners decide to upgrade their computers' speaker systems to get better sound quality when listening to digital music and watching digital videos. High-end computer audio systems include surround sound speakers and a subwoofer to blast out mellow bass tones. If you live in an environment where a sound system is not appreciated by your neighbors, you might opt for a set of high-quality earphones, instead.

A **plotter** is a special type of printer designed to produce line drawings, such as blueprints. Many plotters are designed to produce large-format printouts—some up to six feet wide. Plotters are typically purchased for computer systems owned by architects, engineers, and interior designers.

Figure 2-9

A **voice synthesizer** converts digital text into audio output. Many people are familiar with the synthesized voice that narrates weather reports on National Weather Service radio stations. Voice synthesizers are also an integral part of telephone directory assistance and other automated calling systems.

Voice synthesizers are used as adaptive devices on personal computers. They can read the text displayed in a word processor or on a Web page, making these computer services available to people with visual handicaps. For these applications, voice synthesis has a great advantage over recorded audio files because they are generated "on-the-fly" and can adapt to changes that appear on the screen. Windows Vista includes an application called Narrator (Figure 2-9) that reads the contents of the screen and names screen-based objects as the mouse pointer encounters them.

Computer projection devices are popular with busines people, teachers, and students who make lots of presentations. A **computer projection device** (Figure 2-10) uses digital light processing technology to display a computer-generated image on a large-size screen. It is the ideal device for delivering PowerPoint presentations to large groups. As an added bonus, these projection devices can be connected to the DVD player in a home theater system.

Figure 2-10

FAQ How do I connect peripheral devices to my computer?

When you install a peripheral device, you are basically creating a pathway for data to flow between the device and the computer. The channel that transmits data between these devices could be wired or wireless.

Establishing a wired connection between your computer and a peripheral device might be as simple as connecting a cable, or it could require you to install an expansion card inside the computer system unit.

Figure 2-11

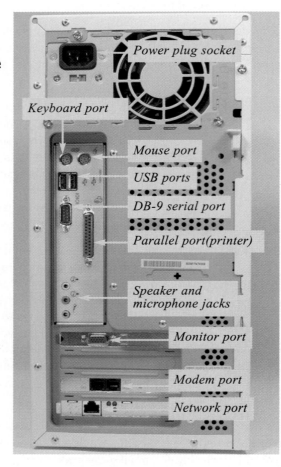

Power plug socket

Keyboard port

Mouse port

USB ports

DB-9 serial port

Parallel port(printer)

Speaker and microphone jacks

Monitor port

Modem port

Network port

Today, **USB** (Universal Serial Bus) is the preferred way to connect peripheral devices. On most new computer models, USB ports are conveniently located on the front and sides of the system unit, so that peripherals can be easily connected and disconnected.

Many kinds of peripheral devices, including mice, scanners, and joysticks, are available with USB connections. Several types of storage devices, such as USB flash drives and external hard drives, also use USB connections. Windows automatically recognizes most USB devices, which makes installation simple.

Most personal computers also include a variety of other built-in ports for connecting peripheral devices. These ports are pictured in Figure 2-11. When purchasing a peripheral device, read its specifications to determine what type of port it requires. Make sure that you use the right cable and insert it correctly into the port.

Establishing a wireless connection between your computer and a peripheral device typically requires some type of transceiver on both devices. A **transceiver** transmits and receives signals. Those signals could be generated as **infrared** light, like those used on a television remote control. Signals could also be generated as radio waves by popular wireless technologies, such as Bluetooth and Wi-Fi, that you'll learn about in the Networks chapter.

Wireless peripheral devices typically have a built-in transceiver for a specific wireless technology. Your computer might have a matching built-in wireless transceiver. If not, you can usually connect a transceiver to one of your computer's USB ports.

• How do I connect peripheral devices to my computer? (continued)

If a peripheral device requires a port that is not available on your computer, you might have to install an **expansion card** (also called an "expansion board," a "controller card," or an "adapter"). Today, installing an expansion card is typically necessary only for some network cards, graphics cards, and sound cards. Figure 2-12 shows how to plug an expansion card into an expansion slot inside the system unit.

**Figure
2-12**

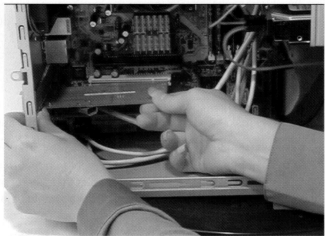

In addition to a physical or wireless connection, some peripheral devices also require software, called a **device driver**, to establish communication with a computer. If needed, directions for installing the device driver are supplied along with the device. Typically, you use the device driver CD one time to get everything set up, and then you can put the CD away in a safe place.

Many long-time computer techies remember the days when installing a peripheral device meant messing around with little electronic components called dip switches and a host of complex software settings called IRQs. Fortunately, today's PCs include a feature called **Plug and Play** that automatically takes care of these technical details. Although it took several years to refine Plug and Play technology, it works quite well for just about every popular peripheral device. If Plug and Play doesn't work, your computer simply won't recognize the device and won't be able to transmit data to it or receive data from it. If you've got a stubborn peripheral device, check the manufacturer's Web site for a device driver update, or call the manufacturer's technical support department.

FAQ How do I select components for my computer system?

Computer technology changes with great frequency. Sorting through computer and peripheral device choices can challenge even the most savvy shopper. The following guidelines should help you navigate through computer, software, and peripheral device purchases.

Consider the tasks for which you'll use the computer. Begin by making a list of activities you'll expect to do with your computer system. For example, do you want to use your PC for gaming, word processing, Internet access, graphics, music, or something entirely different? Will you use your computer system for a combination of tasks, or will it be dedicated to one particular task, such as small business accounting? Do you want to use your computer for applications, such as home security monitoring, that might require specialized hardware or software? Does anyone who will use the computer have special needs that might require adaptive devices, such as a voice synthesizer or one-handed keyboard? If you are planning to use specialized peripheral devices or software, check their system requirements to make sure you purchase a computer that supports them.

Determine your budget. Ask yourself how much money you can afford to spend on your new computer. Set a price range and shop for the best computer in that range. As a general rule of thumb, a computer priced higher than U.S.$2,000 is the computer equivalent of a luxury automobile. A computer in this price range contains a fast processor, a generous amount of RAM, and copious amounts of disk space. These computers contain state-of-the-art components and should not have to be replaced as quickly as less expensive computers.

Computers that retail for between U.S.$500 and $2,000 might be considered the four-door sedans of the computer marketplace because a majority of buyers select computers in this price range. These popular computers lack the flashy specifications of their state-of-the-art cousins, but provide ample computing power for average users.

In the computer industry, the equivalent of a compact car is a sub-$500 computer. The technology in these computers is usually older by a year or two and you can expect reduced processor speed, memory capacity, and drive capacity. Nevertheless, budget computers feature many of the same components that owners coveted in their state-of-the-art computers a few years back. You might, however, have to replace a budget computer sooner than a more expensive computer.

Select a computer platform. Before you start shopping, you should determine whether you want a Mac or a PC. To make this decision, consider the platform used by the majority of your friends and coworkers. If PCs are the standard platform at work, you should probably purchase a PC for yourself. PCs are the choice of most businesses, except those focused on artistic endeavors, such as advertising agencies. Many elementary schools have standardized on the Mac platform, so if you are a teacher or have children who use Macs at school, that should be your platform of choice.

Choose a desktop, notebook, or tablet configuration. If you want portability, or if you don't have much desk space, consider a notebook or tablet computer. Otherwise, a desktop computer might fulfill your needs. The features of today's notebook computers essentially match those of desktop models, but at a somewhat higher price. If you are on a tight budget and don't require portability, then go for a desktop model. Another reason for selecting a desktop model is the amount of expandability it can provide. If you plan to install lots of peripherals, and you want an ergonomically designed keyboard, and you prefer a large screen display device, you might not be happy with a notebook computer.

● How do I select components for my computer system? (continued)

Select processor type and speed. Even after you've identified a brand and model, you might have a choice of microprocessors. Processor speed directly affects computer performance. A fast processor is essential for some applications such as desktop publishing, video editing, and serious computer gaming. The fastest processors are expensive, however, and unnecessary for most routine computing tasks.

Select an operating system. Macintosh computers are shipped with the current version of Mac OS, but you can add Windows to an Intel Mac computer using software such as Boot Camp or Parallels. PCs can be shipped with Windows or Linux, but that choice is typically easy to make. Linux would be the operating system of choice if you plan to operate a network or Web server. For the typical personal computer system, Linux limits your choice of software applications and might not provide device drivers for some of the peripheral devices you want to install. PC buyers typically choose the Windows operating system because of its flexibility and because it is the PC standard.

When you purchase a PC, you might have a choice of Windows versions. Microsoft typically offers Windows in a Home version and a Professional version. The Professional version provides some enhanced security and networking options not available on the Home version. Unless you plan to operate a small business network, the Home version should be sufficient for your needs. Don't be intimidated, however, if the PC you purchase comes with the Professional version of Windows—it operates in basically the same way and has essentially the same graphical user interface as the Home version.

Regardless of the operating system you select, make sure it is the most recent version. Older operating systems might not support the newest software applications or some new peripheral devices.

Consider your storage needs. A hard disk serves as the main storage device for your computer. Most of today's computers offer at least 80 GB of hard disk space. That amount should be sufficient for most personal computer owners. Music, video, and graphics files are large; so if you plan to store many of these files, you might want to upgrade to a larger hard disk.

Your computer should include at least one rewritable CD or DVD drive for making backups and installing software from distribution disks. Many computer buyers want two CD or DVD drives, with at least one of them providing rewritable capabilities. With this configuration, it is possible to copy CDs.

Consider RAM and video memory capacity. Today's computers include between 512 MB and 4 GB of RAM. Lots of RAM capacity is better for memory-intensive applications such as desktop publishing and video editing. Additional RAM raises the price of a computer. If you are on a tight budget, remember that you can add RAM later if your applications demand it.

If the computer you're purchasing has a graphics card, it contains some amount of video memory. You'll want the maximum amount of video memory if you intend to use your computer for 3D action games, video editing, or desktop publishing. On some computers, the graphics card circuitry is built into the motherboard and a section of RAM is dedicated to handling graphics-related tasks. This technology, usually referred to as **shared memory** (or "integrated graphics"), does not match the performance of a dedicated graphics card and video memory.

• How do I select components for my computer system? (continued)

Evaluate the computer's upgradeability. Some computers are easier than others to expand and upgrade. As a rule of thumb, desktop models are easier to upgrade than notebooks, which often contain specialized components designed to fit in the small system unit. If you want expandability, look for open drive bays that can hold additional hard disk, CD, and DVD drives. Ask about the number of expansion slots provided for network, video, and audio expansion cards. Also, look at the position and number of ports for connecting peripheral devices. Multiple USB ports are handy—especially if they are easily accessible.

Select software. Most computers are shipped with the operating system preinstalled. Remember that Windows includes several utilities and applications, such as rudimentary graphics, compression, backup, defragmentation, Web browsing, and e-mail software. Many computer vendors also install a "bundle" of application software packages. A typical software bundle includes word processing, spreadsheet, presentation, and antivirus software. This software is handy for just about everyone, and computer buyers can typically save money by purchasing a bundle along with a new PC. Some of the software bundled with a PC is typically trial software that you can use without charge for a short period of time, but have to pay to use after the trial period ends. Make sure you understand if an application is trialware. If you don't pay when the trial period ends, you could lose access to data files that you created when using it.

Select peripheral devices and accessories. Always find out what is included in the price of a computer system, and think carefully whether each device will be useful for your computing projects. Many companies advertise low-cost computer systems that don't include display devices. After factoring in the price of a display device, these systems might not be such a good deal. In contrast, some vendors offer special hardware bundles that include an LCD display, printer, PDA, and digital camera. When purchasing a notebook computer, you should consider buying an extra battery, carrying case, A/C adapter for using an electrical wall outlet, and D/C adapter for in-car use. Because many of these accessories are designed specifically for a particular notebook model, they might not be available in a year or two.

Evaluate manufacturer and vendor support and warranty. When you encounter hardware and software problems, you want them fixed as quickly as possible. Technical support and repair service is usually available from the company that manufactured the equipment or published the software. Support and service might also be available from the merchant or vendor. Before you make a final decision on computer equipment or software, ask the following questions: Does the price of the equipment or software include technical support? How long does the support last? How can you contact technical support? Is it free? Is the support staff knowledgeable? What is the duration of the equipment warranty? Does it cover the cost of parts and labor? Where do repairs take place and is there a shipping cost? How long do repairs typically take?

Shopping for computer equipment and software can be a challenge; but if you take a careful, organized approach, you can usually buy with confidence. Remember to use all available resources, such as vendor Web sites, magazine reviews, and recommendations from friends and experts.

QuickCheck A

1. A(n) [＿＿＿＿＿＿] converts printed images into bitmap graphics that can be viewed and edited with graphics software.

2. A(n) [＿＿＿＿＿＿] screen is standard equipment on most notebook computers and is the technology used for most of today's standalone display devices.

3. A graphics card typically contains special video [＿＿＿＿＿＿] , which stores screen images as they are processed, but before they are displayed.

4. True or false? Today, USB (Universal Serial Bus) is the preferred way to connect peripheral devices. [＿＿＿＿]

5. True or false? As a general rule of thumb, a computer priced higher than $1,000 is the computer equivalent of a luxury automobile. [＿＿＿＿]

CheckIt!

QuickCheck B

A computer owner has two monitors connected to a computer. Fill in each answer box with 1 or 2, depending on the monitor description:

1. Which monitor is the default? [＿＿＿]

2. Which monitor is set for the highest resolution? [＿＿＿]

3. Which monitor will display the largest desktop? [＿＿＿]

4. Which monitor will display the largest icons and text? [＿＿＿]

5. Which monitor has the highest bit depth? [＿＿＿]

Monitor A

Display Settings

Monitor

Drag the icons to match your monitors.   Identify Monitors

1   **2**

1. Generic PnP Monitor on NVIDIA GeForce Go 6150

☑ This is my main monitor
☑ Extend the desktop onto this monitor

Resolution: Colors:
Low ———————————○ High   Highest (32 bit)

1440 by 900 pixels

How do I g

Monitor B

Display Settings

Monitor

Drag the icons to match your monitors.   Identify Monitors

1   **2**

2. Generic PnP Monitor on NVIDIA GeForce Go 6150

☐ This is my main monitor
☑ Extend the desktop onto this monitor

Resolution: Colors:
Low ○——————————— High   Medium (16 bit)

800 by 600 pixels

How do I get the best display?   Advanced Settings...

OK   Cancel   Apply

CheckIt!

CHAPTER

3

System and Application Software

What's Inside and on the CD?

Choosing the right software to complete a task is sometimes tricky. Different types of software can help you accomplish similar tasks. For example, word processing software, spreadsheet software, and database software are all capable of creating tables of text and numbers. How do you decide which to use? Should you use a spreadsheet, a database, or a financial software package to balance your checkbook? Is it better to use word processing or desktop publishing software to write a report?

Choosing the wrong software can cause problems as you try to complete a task. For example, although word processing software might allow you to create a nicely formatted table of numbers, it might not provide much flexibility for manipulating those numbers to produce totals and other calculations. For balancing your checkbook, spreadsheet or personal accounting software would be more appropriate. In this chapter you'll learn about many kinds of software and the types of tasks they can carry out.

● FAQs:

FAQ What is software?

The instructions that tell a computer how to carry out a task are referred to as a computer program. These programs form the software that prepares a computer to do a specific task, such as document production, video editing, graphic design, or Web browsing.

Software applies rules, also called algorithms, to process data. An **algorithm** is basically the steps necessary to complete a task. For example, suppose you want to listen to a playlist on your iPod. Your iPod's software follows an algorithm to start at the beginning of your list to play the first song, and then it steps down the list to play the next song. Although the algorithms for creating a document or looking at Web pages might not seem as clear-cut as the iPod example, they are programmed into all the software you use.

Software is categorized as system software or application software. The primary purpose of **system software**—your computer's operating system, device drivers, and utilities—is to help the computer carry out its basic operating functions. System software helps computers manage files, interact with peripheral devices, send data over networks, and filter out viruses.

In contrast to system software, the primary purpose of application software is to help people use a computer to carry out tasks, such as creating documents, tracking finances, and editing photos. Figure 3-1 illustrates the division between system software and application software, and lists some specific types of software included in each category.

Figure 3–1

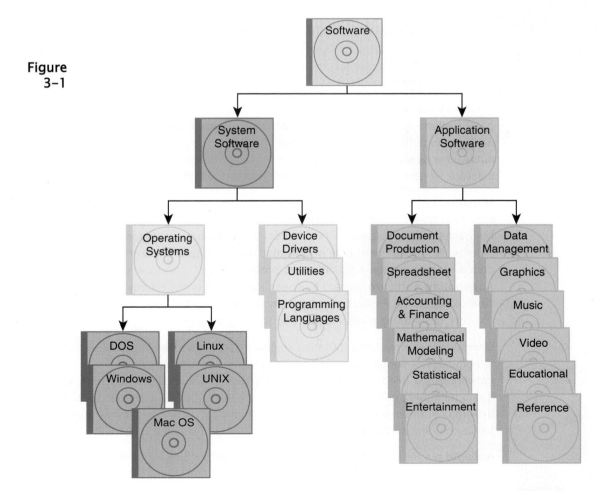

• What is software? (continued)

System and application software work together in a way that is similar to the chain of command in an army. You issue a command using application software. Application software tells the operating system what to do. The operating system tells the device drivers, device drivers tell the hardware, and the hardware actually does the work. Figure 3-2 illustrates this chain of command for printing a document or photo.

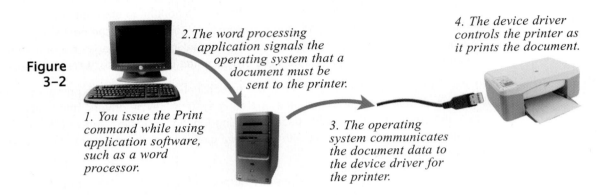

Figure 3–2

2. The word processing application signals the operating system that a document must be sent to the printer.

4. The device driver controls the printer as it prints the document.

1. You issue the Print command while using application software, such as a word processor.

3. The operating system communicates the document data to the device driver for the printer.

Application software is subcategorized in a variety of ways. **Productivity software** refers to word processing, spreadsheet, presentation, and database applications, all of which are designed to increase individual productivity at home, school, and work.

Related software packages are often bundled together in a **software suite**. For example, you can purchase Microsoft Word, Excel, and PowerPoint together as the Microsoft Office Suite. Or, you can purchase photo-editing, drawing, and animation software in the CorelDRAW Graphics Suite.

Business software is a broad umbrella for applications designed to help businesses and organizations accomplish routine or specialized tasks. **Vertical market software** is designed to automate specialized tasks in a specific market or business. Examples include patient management and billing software specially designed for hospitals, job estimating software for construction businesses, and student record management software for schools.

Horizontal market software is generic software that just about any kind of business can use. Payroll, accounting, and project management software are good examples of horizontal market software. Almost every business has employees and maintains payroll records. No matter what type of business uses it, payroll software must collect similar data and make similar calculations to produce payroll checks and W-2 forms. **Accounting software** helps a business keep track of the money flowing in to and out of various accounts. **Project management software** is an important tool for planning large projects, scheduling project tasks, and tracking project costs.

Groupware is a type of application software frequently used in businesses. It is designed to help several people collaborate on projects using connections provided by a local network or the Internet. Groupware usually provides capabilities to maintain schedules for group members, automatically select meeting times for the group, facilitate communication by e-mail or other channels, distribute documents according to a prearranged schedule or sequence, and allow multiple people to contribute to a single document.

A **media player** is software that plays media files, such as music and videos. Examples include Windows Media Player and Quicktime Player. Players that add functionality to other programs, such as browsers, are referred to as **plug-ins**.

FAQ What is an operating system?

An operating system (OS) is essentially the master controller for all the activities that take place within a computer. Operating systems are classified as system software, not application software, because their primary purpose is to help the computer system monitor itself in order to function efficiently. Operating systems keep track of files, manage the memory allocated for programs and data, regulate the flow of data to the processor, and provide a basic level of system security through passwords and encryption. For example, an operating system might require a valid user ID and password before allowing access to a computer, its files, and network connections.

Unlike application software, an operating system does not directly help people perform application-specific tasks, such as word processing. People do, however, interact with the operating system for certain operational and storage tasks, such as starting programs and locating data files. As you perform everyday tasks, you're likely to interact with multiple operating systems running on personal computers, networks, Web servers, and mobile phones. Even some embedded microcontrollers have operating systems.

Historically, Microsoft DOS was one of the first operating systems for personal computers. Installed on the original IBM PCs, DOS used a **command-line interface** that simply displayed a "prompt" such as C:\ on the screen and waited for users to type commands. Figure 3-3 shows the DOS interface and C:\ prompt.

Figure 3-3

```
C:\MYDATA>PAINT
Bad command or file name

C:\MYDATA>CD\

C:\_
```

Many people found it difficult to remember DOS commands, and computers did not gain widespread popularity until graphical user interfaces became available. Today's popular operating systems, such as Windows, Mac OS, and Linux, feature easy-to-use graphical user interfaces. A **graphical user interface**, abbreviated as GUI and pronounced as "gooey" or "gee you eye," displays controls and commands as pictures that users can manipulate with a mouse or other pointing device.

GUIs establish standardized controls for all applications that run on their platforms. This standardization simplifies the process of learning to use new software. For example, most GUIs offer a standard dialog box that's used for saving files regardless of the software being used. A standard Save dialog box means you don't have to discover the procedure for saving files when learning to use a new application.

● **What is an operating system? (continued)**

Microsoft Windows is an operating system that has evolved through several generations. Windows Vista, released in 2007, and Windows XP, released in 2001, are in widespread use. Their GUIs operate in a similar way, but the shape and placement of controls differ slightly. Figure 3-4 shows the graphical controls provided by Microsoft Windows Vista (top) and Microsoft Windows XP (bottom).

Figure 3-4

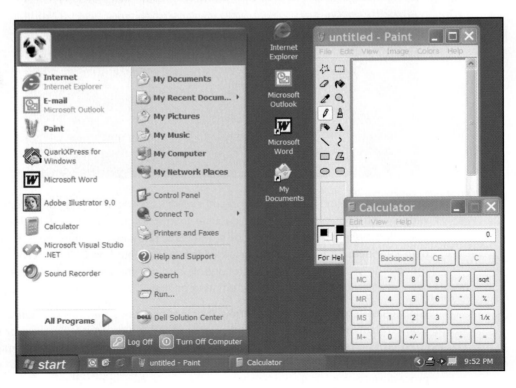

• What is an operating system? (continued)

Operating systems such as Mac OS X, Linux, and UNIX also feature graphical user interfaces. Even when installed on large scale computer systems, Linux and UNIX sport graphical user interfaces that allow system administrators to monitor multiple users, set up network security, maintain regular backups, and optimize performance. Figure 3-5 illustrates the GUIs for Linux (top) and Mac OS X (bottom) installed on personal computers.

PlayIt!

Figure 3-5

PlayIt!

Operating systems, such as Windows Mobile OS, Symbian, and Palm OS, designed for handheld devices also feature GUIs. These GUIs perform basic file functions, run a limited set of programs, control touch-sensitive screens, and establish communication links.

Operating systems equip computers with a wide range of capabilities, including the ability to run multiple programs and provide access to multiple users. However, operating systems also establish limits. For example, DOS limits program names to eight characters, making it difficult to identify the contents of files by their names. Operating systems also limit the amount of memory that can be installed, and can limit the size of disk storage.

Operating system problems can be frustrating and difficult to diagnose. Corrupted operating system files on disk or in memory can result in an unstable computer, requiring frequent reboots into a "safe mode" designed for troubleshooting. Incompatibilities between the operating system and application software, files, or devices can cause a computer to become nonresponsive to input from the keyboard or mouse. If you encounter operating system problems, you might have to work with technical support resources to fix them. Check the help desk at your business or school, access the operating system publisher online, or call the computer manufacturer for assistance.

FAQ What is document processing software?

Whether you are writing a 10-page paper, preparing software documentation, designing a brochure for your new startup company, or laying out the school newspaper, you probably use some form of document production software. This software assists you with composing, editing, designing, printing, and electronically publishing documents. The three most popular types of document production software are word processing, desktop publishing, and Web authoring.

Word processing software, such as Microsoft Word and OpenOffice Writer, replaced typewriters for producing documents such as reports, letters, memos, papers, and manuscripts. Word processing software gives you the ability to create, spell-check, edit, and format a document on the screen before you commit it to paper.

Desktop publishing software (abbreviated DTP) takes word processing software one step further by helping you use graphic design techniques to enhance the format and appearance of a document. Although today's word processing software offers many page layout and design features, DTP software products, such as QuarkXPress and Adobe InDesign, provide even more sophisticated features to help you produce professional-quality output for newspapers, newsletters, brochures, magazines, and books.

Web authoring software helps you design and develop customized Web pages that you can publish electronically on the Internet. Only a few years ago, creating Web pages was a fairly technical task that required authors to insert special formatting HTML tags, such as <a href="contents.htm">. Now Web authoring software products, such as Adobe Dreamweaver and KompoZer, help nontechnical Web authors by providing easy-to-use tools for composing the text for a Web page, assembling graphical elements, and automatically generating HTML tags.

Figure 3-6

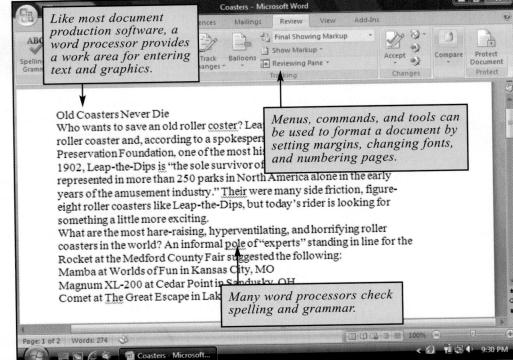

FAQ What is spreadsheet software?

A **spreadsheet** uses rows and columns of numbers to create a model or representation of a real situation. For example, your checkbook register is a type of spreadsheet because it is a numerical representation of the cash flowing in to and out of your bank account.

Today, **spreadsheet software**, such as Microsoft Excel and OpenOffice Calc, provides tools to create electronic spreadsheets, called worksheets. A worksheet is similar to a "smart" piece of paper that automatically adds up the columns of numbers you write on it. You can also use it to make other calculations based on simple formulas that you enter, or more complex built-in functions. Worksheets can be grouped together into a workbook to share data.

As an added bonus, spreadsheet software helps you turn your data into a variety of colorful graphs. It also includes special data-handling features that allow you to sort data, search for data that meets specific criteria, and print reports.

Spreadsheet software was initially popular with accountants and financial managers who dealt with paper-based spreadsheets, but found the electronic version far easier to use and less prone to errors than manual calculations. Other people soon discovered the benefits of spreadsheets for projects that require repetitive calculations—budgeting, maintaining a grade book, balancing a checkbook, tracking investments, calculating loan payments, and estimating project costs.

Because it is so easy to experiment with different numbers, spreadsheet software is particularly useful for what-if analysis. You can use what-if analysis to answer questions such as "What if I get an A on my next two economics exams? But what if I get only Bs?" or "What if I invest $100 a month in my retirement plan? But what if I invest $200 a month?" Figure 3-7 illustrates the components of a basic worksheet.

Figure 3-7

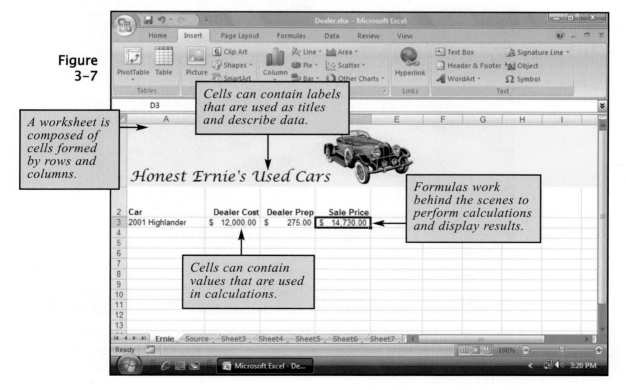

A worksheet is composed of cells formed by rows and columns.

Cells can contain labels that are used as titles and describe data.

Formulas work behind the scenes to perform calculations and display results.

Cells can contain values that are used in calculations.

FAQ What is presentation software?

Presentation software supplies the tools you need for combining text, photos, clip art, graphs, animations, and sound clips into a series of electronic slides. You can display electronic slides on a color monitor for a one-on-one presentation or use a computer projection device for group presentations. You can also output a presentation as overhead transparencies, paper copies, or 35 mm slides. You can even post presentations on the Internet. Microsoft PowerPoint and OpenOffice Impress are two of today's most popular presentation software applications.

Presentation software is used by instructors and students to create slides for use in classroom lectures and oral presentations. Instructors can use presentation technologies to create virtual classrooms for distance education courses. Businesspeople use presentation software to present and illustrate ideas at company meetings, conferences, and sales events.

Presentation software typically includes tools for creating speaker notes that help the presenter remember important information to supplement the slide display. Presentation software also includes basic tools for creating line drawings, arrows, and other simple shapes. Complex diagrams, digital photographs, animations, or videos can be incorporated into slides created with presentation software, but the presentation software itself does not include the necessary tools to create these types of content. Presentation software includes templates, master slides, and themes that can be used to ensure that all presentations created by an organization, person, or department have a uniform style.

Figure 3-8

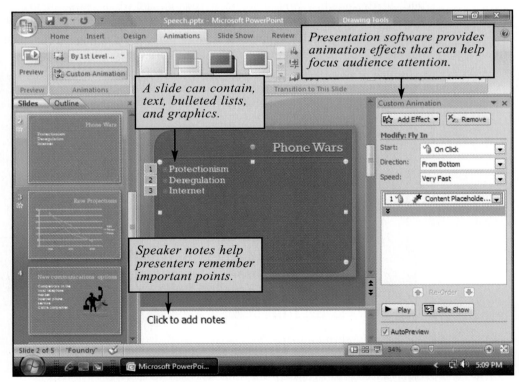

Presentation software provides animation effects that can help focus audience attention.

A slide can contain, text, bulleted lists, and graphics.

Speaker notes help presenters remember important points.

PowerPoint's ability to work with text, charts, images, and tables illustrates how applications can interact and share data. You can create speaker notes using Word and pull them up with PowerPoint. You can even paste data and charts from Excel worksheets onto PowerPoint slides.

FAQ What is database software?

The term "database" has evolved from a specialized technical term into a part of our everyday vocabulary. In the context of modern usage, a **database** is simply a collection of data that is stored on one or more computers. A database can contain any sort of data, such as university student records, a library card catalog, or customer e-mail addresses. Databases can be stored on personal computers, servers, mainframes, supercomputers, and even handheld computers. Working behind the scenes, databases play an important role in maintaining data for e-commerce sites and other data-driven applications.

Database software, sometimes referred to as a "database management system" or "DBMS," helps you enter, find, organize, update, and report information stored in a database. Microsoft Access is a well-known database software product for personal computers. It can be used for mailing lists and household inventories, but is more typically used in small business applications. SQLite, Oracle, and MySQL are popular server database software packages. These high-powered applications can manage large amounts of complex data for airline reservation systems and corporate accounting systems.

Database software stores data as a series of records, which are composed of fields that hold data. A **record** holds data for a single entity—a person, place, thing, or event. A **field** holds one item of data relevant to a record. Key fields contain unique identifiers, such as Social Security numbers, and are used to sort and quickly search for data. Most database software for personal computers and servers supports the **relational database** model in which records are grouped into tables and related to each other by common characteristics.

Most database software includes tools to create queries, electronic forms, and reports. A query is used to formulate search criteria. Electronic forms are used to enter information into the database. Reports gather, format, and present information in the database, and can typically be printed, published on the Web, or e-mailed to other people.

Figure 3–9

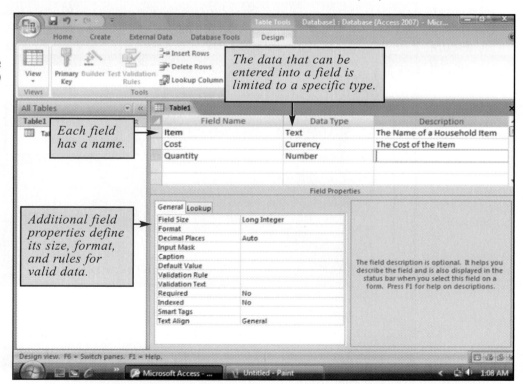

FAQ What about graphics software?

In computer lingo, the term **graphics** refers to pictures, drawings, sketches, photographs, images, or icons that appear on your computer screen. **Graphics software** is designed to help you create, manipulate, and print graphics. Some graphics software products specialize in a particular type of graphic, while others allow you to work with multiple graphics formats. Graphics software not only provides professional artists with the tools of their trade, but promotes creativity for children and adults by encouraging the use of photos and art in documents, posters, and flyers.

Paint software (sometimes called "image editing software") provides a set of electronic pens, brushes, and paints for painting images on the screen. A simple program called Microsoft Paint is included with Windows. Many graphic artists, Web page designers, and illustrators use paint software as their primary computer-based graphics tool to work with bitmap graphics file typs such as JPEG, GIF, TIFF, PNG, and BMP.

Photo editing software, such as Adobe Photoshop, includes features specially designed to fix poor-quality photos by modifying contrast and brightness, cropping out unwanted objects, and removing "red eye." Photos can also be edited using paint software, but photo editing software typically offers tools and wizards that simplify common photo editing tasks.

Drawing software and **CAD** (computer aided design) software provide tools for assembling lines, shapes, and colors into diagrams, corporate logos, architectural blueprints, and schematics. The drawings created with tools such as Adobe Illustrator, Corel DESIGNER, and OpenOffice Draw tend to have a "flat" cartoon-like quality, but they are very easy to modify, and look good at just about any size. Drawing software is designed to work with vector graphics file types such as EPS, WMF, and AI.

Figure 3-10

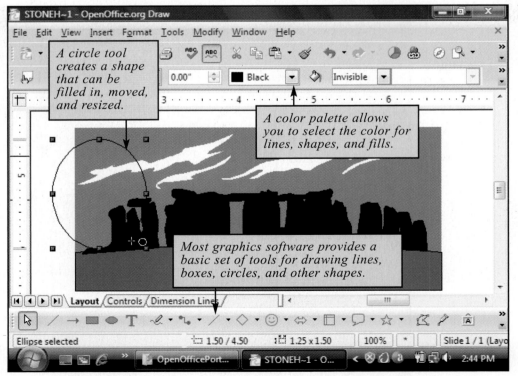

A circle tool creates a shape that can be filled in, moved, and resized.

A color palette allows you to select the color for lines, shapes, and fills.

Most graphics software provides a basic set of tools for drawing lines, boxes, circles, and other shapes.

FAQ Can I create animations and videos on my computer?

An **animation** is a series of still images, each slightly different, that creates the illusion of movement when displayed. Animations are used to create dynamic Web page elements, computer games, and movie special effects. Animations can be based on 2D bitmaps or vector graphics, or they can be based on 3D vector graphics. Flash and animated GIFs are popular file types for animations.

Flash is a popular file type for static graphics or animations. Flash players are shipped with most browsers and can be easily downloaded from the Web, so most computers have the software to display SWF files containing Flash animations, though additional software is required to create them. Animated GIFs are essentially a series of bitmap images displayed in sequence to achieve animation effects. GIF files are fairly large, however, and require longer download times than Flash animations.

Digital video is based on footage of real objects filmed and then stored as bits. It is used for consumer-level YouTube-style videos as well as professionally produced full-length films. Digital videos can be uploaded and downloaded over networks, such as the Internet, though files are large and require a fairly speedy connection.

Computers can work with several types of video files, including QuickTime (MOV), Windows Media Video (WMV), Flash video (FLV), Audio Video Interleave (AVI), and Moving Pictures Experts Group (MPEG). The growing popularity of computer-based video editing can be attributed to video editing software, such as Windows Movie Maker and Apple iMovie, now included with just about any new computer.

Video editing software provides a set of tools for transferring video footage from a camcorder to a computer, clipping out unwanted footage, assembling video segments in any sequence, adding special visual effects, and adding a sound track. Despite an impressive array of features, video editing software is relatively easy to use.

Figure 3–11

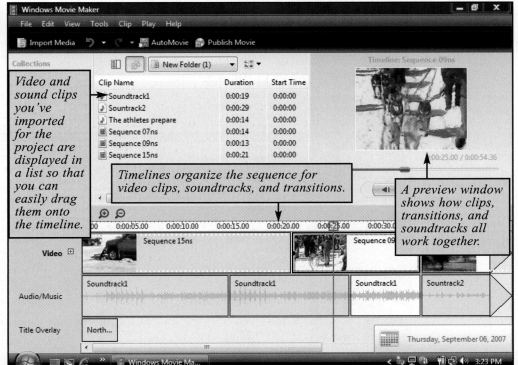

Video and sound clips you've imported for the project are displayed in a list so that you can easily drag them onto the timeline.

Timelines organize the sequence for video clips, soundtracks, and transitions.

A preview window shows how clips, transitions, and soundtracks all work together.

FAQ What software do I need for music and other audio applications?

You don't have to be a musician or composer to have a use for music software. Many types of music software are available. You can use it to make your own digital voice and music recordings, download popular music and play it on your iPod or other portable audio player, set up your computer to act under voice command, and configure your operating system to read the screen aloud.

Digital audio is music, speech, and other sounds represented in binary format for use in digital devices. Sounds can be digitized by a process called **sampling**, which converts a sound wave into digital bits and stores those bits in a computer file. Digital audio files can hold music tracks, narrations, and sound effects. They can be played on a personal computer, portable music player, or computer-based home entertainment center, and they can be incorporated into Web pages and digital videos. Digital audio is stored in a variety of file types, including WAV, MP3, M4P, and MIDI.

Waveform audio (WAV) is a popular audio format for PCs. Software that works with WAV files is supplied along with the Windows operating system. Sound Recorder can be used for recording from your PC's microphone. Windows Media Player, which plays digital video, can also play audio files.

MP3 software is popular for converting music from CDs into a digital format called **MP3** that can be stored on a computer hard disk. Once in MP3 format, music can be arranged into customized playlists and output to portable music players. A proprietary version of MP3, designated as M4P, is used for iTunes music and shown in Figure 3-12.

Computers also work with **MIDI** (Musical Instrument Digital Interface), which allows computers to communicate with music synthesizers. Thousands of MIDI files are available for downloading and can be played back through a computer speaker, electronic keyboard, or other MIDI instrument. MIDI sequencing software and software synthesizers are an important part of the studio musician's toolbox.

Figure 3-12

FAQ What about educational and entertainment software?

Educational software helps you learn and practice new skills. For the youngest students, educational software offerings, such as MindTwister Math and Carmen Sandiego Word Detective, teach basic arithmetic and reading skills. Instruction is presented in game format, and the levels of play are adapted to the player's age and ability.

For older students and adults, software is available for such diverse educational endeavors as learning languages, training yourself to use new software, learning how to play the piano or guitar, improving keyboarding skills, and even learning managerial skills for a diverse workplace. Exam preparation software is available for standardized tests such as the SAT.

Computer-based training (CBT), sometimes referred to as **e-Learning**, can refer to a variety ways of using computers for teaching and learning. Some CBT software creates a learning environment by presenting a series of tutorials, typically beginning with a pretest to see whether students have the prerequisite skills and ending with a post-test to determine whether students can move on to the next tutorial segment. Today, CBT is a popular approach to learning how to use computer software.

Other approaches to e-Learning include teleconferencing, Web-based tutorials, and virtual classrooms. Social networking sites, such as MySpace, and other Internet-based technologies, such as blogs, wikis, and podcasts, are also employed as teaching and learning tools.

Computer games are the most popular type of entertainment software, appealing to players of all ages. Computer games are generally classified into subcategories, such as roleplaying, action, adventure, puzzles, simulations, sports, and strategy/war games.

Multiplayer games provide an environment in which two or more players can participate in the same game. Even some of the earliest computer games, like Pong, supplied joysticks for two players. Today's multiplayer games are a far cry from those simplistic games. Now numerous players can use Internet technology to band together or battle one another in sophisticated virtual environments.

Figure 3–13

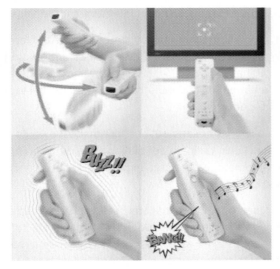

Computer games are moving closer and closer to **virtual reality**, which allows players to interact with computer-simulated environments. Although most virtual environments are primarily visual and auditory experiences, new technologies are adding other sensory elements. For example, the wildly popular Nintendo Wii game console uses gyroscopically-equipped handheld force-feedback controllers (shown at left) to simulate sword fights, golfing, bowling, and other activities. The gyroscope tracks the handheld controller's position in space, while the force-feedback technology provides tactile information by vibrating, clicking, and buzzing.

FAQ What is utility software?

Figure 3-14

Utility software is a category of system software that includes programs designed to optimize your computer's performance, protect data, and facilitate communication. Some of the most popular types of utility software include the following:

* Desktop widgets (also called gadgets) are specialized utility programs that appear on a computer's screen-based desktop, look like a control, and display a snippet of information. Some examples of desktop widgets include clocks, calendars, calculators, news aggregators, sticky notes, and weather stations (Figure 3-14).

* Antivirus software protects your computer from viruses by looking for telltale virus signatures in files that arrive in your computer as e-mail attachments and downloads. Most antivirus software runs continuously whenever your computer is on, so you do not have to manually activate it each time a file arrives. It is important, however, to make sure your antivirus software subscription is current so that you receive regular updates.

* Antispyware utilities notify you when software attempts to spy on your activities. Spyware is usually generated at Web sites and is designed to report your online activities to marketing companies that use the information to send you advertisements. People who would rather not allow marketers to gather this information have found anti-spyware to be a fairly effective deterrent.

* Compression utilities (sometimes referred to as "zip software") shrink the size of a file by applying a mathematical algorithm that allows the file to be later reconstituted to its original form. **File Compression** shrinks the size of a file so it requires less storage space. Compression can also be used to shrink graphics and other files that you attach to e-mail messages and send over the Internet. Compressed files contain fewer bits than the originals and therefore can be transmitted faster.

* A defragmentation utility rearranges segments of files that have become scattered on the hard disk as files are created, edited, and deleted. Usually included with the operating system, a defragmentation utility should be used periodically to reestablish peak hard drive performance.

* Backup software provides options that make it easy to schedule periodic backups, define a set of files that you want to regularly back up, and automate the restoration process in case files become damaged or lost.

* Various types of communications software that handle data transport over networks are also considered utilities. E-mail software is sometimes classified as utility software because it manages the flow of data to and from your electronic post office box. Web browsers and the software that handles chat and instant messaging can also be classified as utility software.

QuickCheck A

1. [_____] software helps you perform a particular task; for example, writing a document or calculating a row of numbers.

2. A computer's [_____] system is the master controller for all the activities that take place within a computer.

3. [_____] software is a good choice for projects that require repetitive calculations or what-if analysis.

4. True or false? Word processing software is a good choice if you want to keep track of a collection of data. [_____]

5. MOV, WMV, and FLV files typically store digital [_____] .

QuickCheck B

Answer each question with T or F, based on the information shown on the screen below.

1. The software would be classified as utility software. [____]

2. The software would be classified as paint software. [____]

3. The image is a vector graphic. [____]

4. This software would be a good choice for editing photos. [____]

5. This software is designed to create gadgets, sometimes referred to as widgets. [____]

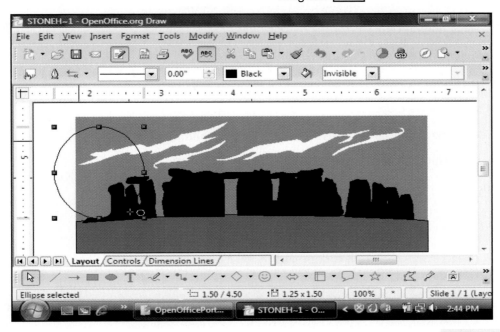

4 Installing Software

What's Inside and on the CD?

It's surprising how quickly your collection of software can grow as you discover new ways to use your computer for school, work, and play. New software is distributed on CDs or DVDs, or it can be downloaded from the Web. Before you can use most new software, it has to be installed on your computer, and that is the focus of this chapter.

Installing new software involves some degree of risk. Viruses and other harmful software can be hiding on distribution disks and in downloaded files, so make sure your computer is protected by antivirus software. Sometimes newly installed software disrupts the normal functioning of your computer system, causing printer malfunctions or glitches in other software. It is prudent, therefore, to make sure you have a backup of your hard disk before you attempt to install new software.

If you're using a computer at work or at school, check with a supervisor to make sure that you're allowed to download and install software. Some organizations strictly control who is allowed to install software to avoid problems with unlicensed or destructive software.

To ensure that the installation process proceeds smoothly, check that your computer meets the software's system requirements and read all pertinent installation instructions on the software's packaging or Web site.

FAQ How do I install software from CDs, DVDs, and downloads?

You might be surprised to learn that a software application is not a single huge computer program, but rather a collection of program modules that work together to accomplish a task. When you **install** software, these program modules are copied from a distribution CD to your computer's hard disk, or they are unzipped from a compressed distribution file that you've downloaded. Making a copy of the distribution CD or copying the distribution download file to a CD gives you a backup in case you lose the original and later need to reinstall the software.

The installation process also adds the software's name to the All Programs menu and provides Windows with the technical information it needs to efficiently run the new software on your PC. This information is stored on the hard disk in a special file called the **Windows Registry**, which keeps track of software that's added or removed, hardware that's connected or disconnected, and settings that customize your work environment.

Software installation is automated by a **setup program** that's included on the distribution CD or download. The installation process is a one-time procedure. Once a software package has been installed, you don't have to install it again unless its files inadvertently get deleted or your computer's hard disk develops problems.

When installing software from a CD or DVD, the setup program usually starts automatically when you insert the disc. If the setup program does not start after a few seconds, use Windows to look for a program called Setup.exe and double-click it.

Once the setup program is running, simply follow the on-screen prompts to accept the terms of the license agreement and select a destination folder for the new program. On Windows computers, most software is installed in a subfolder of the Program Files folder. For example, Adobe Reader software might be stored in a folder called Adobe that is a subfolder of the Program Files folder. The setup program usually suggests a folder name for the new software, and most computer owners use the suggested folder rather than make up an alternative folder name.

Figure
4-1

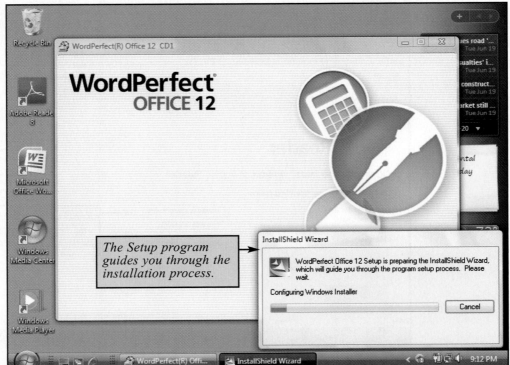

The Setup program guides you through the installation process.

• **How do I install software from CDs, DVDs, and downloads? (continued)**

Software activation is a means of protecting software from illegal copying by requiring users to enter a product key or activation code before the software can be used. Usually an on-screen message instructs you to enter a serial number or validation code supplied on the distribution medium, packaging material, or download site. Keep a record of activation codes because you might need them if it becomes necessary to reinstall a software application.

Installing software you've downloaded follows a procedure similar to installing software from a CD or DVD, but you might have to take a few preliminary steps to unzip the program files and get the setup program started.

Downloaded programs are often zipped to reduce download times, and they have to be unzipped before the installation can proceed. If the setup program doesn't start when the download is complete, look for the downloaded file on your computer's hard disk. You'll find it in a subfolder of your user folder called "Downloads," unless you provided a different name for the file when you started the download process. The file should have .zip at the end of the file name. Double-click this ZIP file to unzip it. If you are asked for a destination, you can accept the default location in the Downloads folder.

Among the unzipped files you should find a program called Setup.exe or Install.exe. Double-click this file to start the program and then follow its prompts to accept the license agreement and specify a folder to hold the installed software.

Be careful not to lose track of files and their locations. You could potentially be dealing with three sets of files: the downloaded ZIP file in the Downloads folder, the unzipped set of files also in the Downloads folder, and the final set of program files in the Program Files folder.

Figure
4-2

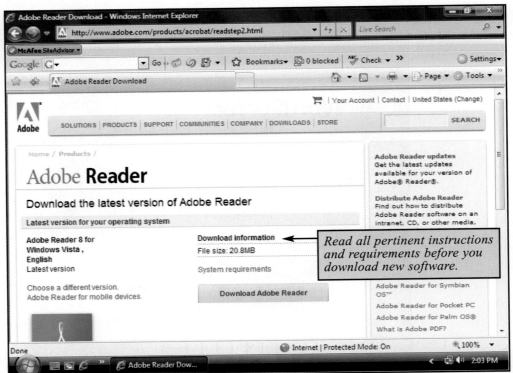

Read all pertinent instructions and requirements before you download new software.

FAQ What about portable software?

Portable software (sometimes referred to as "portable apps") is designed to run from removable storage, such as a CD or USB flash drive. Program files do not exist on the hard disk, no configuration data is stored on the hard disk, and no entries need to be made in the Windows Registry. When the media containing portable software is removed from the computer, no trace of it is left there.

The beauty of portable apps is that you can carry your software and your data on removable storage, such as a USB flash drive, and plug it into any computer. You won't have to worry if the computer contains software to open your data files because the software you need is also on the USB drive.

Your BookOnCD is an example of portable software. To use it, you simply insert the CD containing the program files. Other examples of portable applications include OpenOffice.org Portable, Thunderbird (e-mail), Firefox (browser), and FileZilla (upload and download), which are designed to run from USB flash drives.

Portable software is so simple to install that it is sometimes referred to as install-free software. Installation is simply a matter of getting program files to the media on which they are supposed to run. For example, suppose that you want to run OpenOffice.org Portable from a USB flash drive. You can download the OpenOffice.org Portable ZIP file and then simply unzip it so that the files end up on the USB flash drive.

Much of the information in this book focuses on Microsoft Office, a commercial application that requires installation. OpenOffice.org Portable is a free, open source application that offers features similar to Microsoft Office, but requires no installation. For a quick tour of OpenOffice.org Portable, click the PlayIt! button for Figure 4-3.

Figure 4-3

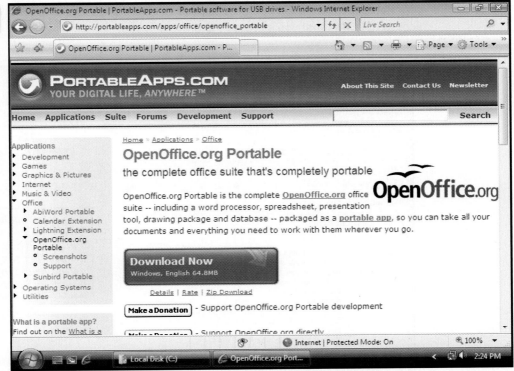

FAQ How do I get started with Web apps?

A **Web application** (or Web app) is software that is accessed with a Web browser. Instead of running locally, much of the program code for the software runs on a remote computer connected to the Internet or other computer network.

Web apps are available for many of the same applications that run locally, such as e-mail, photo sharing, project management, maps, and games. In addition, Google, Microsoft, and other software vendors offer popular spreadsheet and word processing Web apps that allow participants in multiple locations to collaborate on projects.

Many Web apps, such as Gmail and Yahoo! Mail, require no installation at all on your local computer. These applications are said to "run in your browser." Other Web-based applications, require a client-side program to be installed on your local computer.

Some Web apps are free, whereas others require a one-time registration fee or ongoing monthly usage fees. Companies supplying software that runs from the Internet are referred to as **application service providers** (ASPs). The process of deploying software over the Internet is termed **Software as a Service** (SaaS). One advantage of Web-deployed software is that consumers don't have to worry about installing updates because the Web app site always carries the most current version. Web apps are available from any computer with a Web connection, and that is another advantage. However, Web apps and corresponding data files might not be accessible if the ASP service goes down, if you attempt to access the apps with an unsupported browser, or if security software blocks access to the Web app site.

Even free Web apps usually require users to register by supplying a bit of personal information, choosing a user ID, and selecting a password. Before registering, however, read the terms of use and privacy policy. Find out if you'll be subjected to advertising, if your personal information can be disclosed to third parties, and if anyone else can access data files that you store on the provider's site.

Figure 4-4

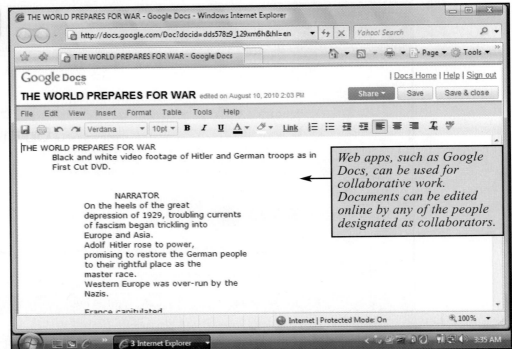

Web apps, such as Google Docs, can be used for collaborative work. Documents can be edited online by any of the people designated as collaborators.

FAQ How do I deal with software installation and access problems?

Usually the installation process proceeds smoothly, but occasionally you'll encounter problems that require a bit of troubleshooting.

- **Defective distribution media.** You insert the distribution CD and your computer's CD drive spins the disk, but can't seem to load it. You might have a defective distribution disk. Before you return or exchange the CD, try it on another computer just to make sure that your computer's CD drive hasn't developed problems.

- **Installation program will not start.** If you insert a distribution CD into the drive and the setup program does not automatically start, Windows security might be configured not to autorun programs from the CD. You can either change the security setting or use Windows Explorer to list the files on the CD. Look for a file called Setup.exe or Install.exe. Double-click it to get it started.

- **Installation stops before completion.** When the setup program is unable to complete an installation, it usually displays an error message specifying a problem, such as running out of hard disk space or missing a file. If the error message does not suggest steps for resolving the problem, try an online search using the error message wording to discover what you can do to bypass this installation hurdle.

- **Installed program does not appear on the computer.** Installed programs should be accessible by clicking the Start button and accessing the All Programs menu. If not, look for the program's executable file in the destination folder you selected during the installation process. You can set up a shortcut to the program by right-clicking it.

- **Installed program fails to work.** If an installed program does not open, consider uninstalling it and then try the installation again. Seek technical support if the program still doesn't start.

- **Other programs fail to work after a new product is installed.** If a newly installed program disrupts other software, check the publisher's Web site to see if an update or setting can return normal functionality. Otherwise, you might have to uninstall the new software.

- **Files cannot be read by the new application.** New versions of software generally read files from previous versions, but sometimes a conversion process is necessary. The conversion process is usually automated so that as you open a file it is converted into the right format for the new software. If you save the file in its new format, however, be aware that the old software might not be able to open it.

- **Access to online application denied.** When you're denied access to online applications, the first step is to make sure you are using a valid user ID and password. Also, make sure your account has not expired or been cancelled for non-payment.

- **Online application not available.** Technical problems sometimes make online applications unavailable. Make sure your Internet connection is working and that the application site is not being blocked by your computer's security software. If an online application is not working, make sure you are using a compatible browser and it is not out of date. Also make sure that your computer has all required auxiliary files, such as media players or plug-ins.

FAQ What about software updates?

Periodically, software publishers produce new versions of software designed to replace older versions. Each version carries a designated version or revision number, such as version 1.1 or version 2.0. Upgrading to a new version usually involves a fee, but it is typically less costly than purchasing the new version off the shelf.

If you've registered your current software, you're likely to receive e-mail notification when new versions are available. Otherwise, you can keep informed of upgrades by periodically visiting the publisher's Web site. Before you decide to upgrade, make sure that you understand its features, purpose, and installation procedures. While an upgrade usually fixes some bugs, it might introduce new bugs. Upgrades can also introduce hardware or software compatibility problems, so make sure you have a recent backup before proceeding.

Instead of migrating to a new version as soon as it is available, many savvy computer owners wait for a few weeks or months to find out how other users like the new version. If Internet chatter indicates some major flaws, it can be prudent to stick with an older version of the software until the publisher is able to make improvements.

A new software version usually installs in a similar way as the original version; by activating a setup program, displaying a license agreement, and adding updated entries to your computer's Start menu. To combat piracy, many software publishers require users to enter a validation code to complete an update.

In between major new software versions, publishers often release software updates, referred to as patches and service packs, designed to fix bugs and update security. A **software patch** is a small section of program code that replaces part of the software you currently have installed. The term **service pack**, which usually applies to operating system updates, is a set of patches that correct problems and address security vulnerabilities. Software patches and service packs are usually free.

Patches and service packs are typically distributed over the Internet and can automatically install themselves. This **automatic update** option periodically checks the software publisher's Web site for updates, downloads updates automatically, and installs them without user intervention. The advantage of automatic updating is convenience. The disadvantage is that changes can be made to your computer without your knowledge.

It is always a good idea to install patches and service packs when they become available. The revised code they contain often addresses security vulnerabilities; and the sooner you patch those holes, the better. Updates to the Windows operating system are common, and it is recommended that you turn on automatic updating to make sure your computer system receives the latest security patches (Figure 4-5).

Figure 4-5

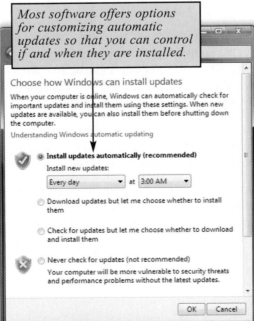

Most software offers options for customizing automatic updates so that you can control if and when they are installed.

Choose how Windows can install updates

When your computer is online, Windows can automatically check for important updates and install them using these settings. When new updates are available, you can also install them before shutting down the computer.

Understanding Windows automatic updating

○ **Install updates automatically (recommended)**
    Install new updates:
    [Every day ▼] at [3:00 AM ▼]

○ Download updates but let me choose whether to install them

○ Check for updates but let me choose whether to download and install them

○ Never check for updates (not recommended)
    Your computer will be more vulnerable to security threats and performance problems without the latest updates.

[OK] [Cancel]

FAQ How do I remove software?

At some point, you might choose to remove software from your computer. You might want to make room on the hard disk for other programs, documents, or graphics. You might no longer need one of your programs, You might want to replace a program with one that has a better collection of features. The process to **uninstall software** removes specific program files from the hard disk, removes the program name from the All Programs menu, and updates the Windows Registry.

In the days when computer software contained only one or two modules, you could uninstall software simply by locating the program modules and deleting them. Today, however, program modules can be housed in various folders and some can be shared by multiple programs. For example, both your word processing software and your graphics software might use the same program module containing a collection of clip art pictures. If you uninstall the graphics software, should your computer delete the clip art module from the disk and remove its entry from the Registry? No, because then the clip art would not be available when you use your word processing software. Generally, your computer should not delete shared program modules when you uninstall software. When in doubt, don't delete!

In addition to the problem of shared program modules, removing software is complicated by the necessity of keeping the Windows Registry up to date. Remember that the Registry keeps track of all hardware and software in a computer system. When software is removed, the Registry files have to be modified accordingly.

To correctly uninstall software, it is essential to use an uninstall procedure. Some software includes its own uninstall module, usually listed along with the program in the All Programs menu. Windows also offers an uninstall utility that can be used to remove any software from your computer. To access this uninstall utility, select Control Panel from the Start menu, and then select Uninstall a Program.

Figure 4–6

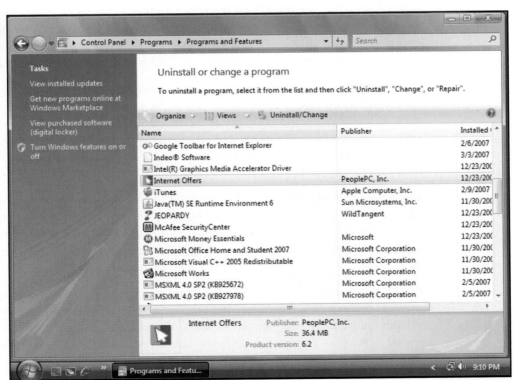

FAQ What's the significance of software licenses and copyrights?

After you purchase software, you might assume that you can install it and use it in any way you like. In fact, your "purchase" entitles you to use the software only in certain prescribed ways. In most countries, computer software, like a book or movie, is protected by copyright. A **copyright** is a form of legal protection that grants the author of an original "work" an exclusive right to copy, distribute, sell, and modify that work, except under special circumstances described by copyright laws.

In addition to copyright protection, computer software is often protected by the terms of a software license. A **software license**, or "end user license agreement (EULA)," is a legal contract that defines the ways in which you may use a computer program. For personal computer software, you will find the license on the outside of the package, on a separate card inside the package, on the CD packaging, or in one of the program files. Make sure to read the license agreement to discover how you can legally use the software.

Commercial software is typically sold in computer stores or at Web sites. Although you "buy" this software, you actually purchase only the right to use it under the terms of the software license. A **single-user license** for commercial software typically adheres closely to the limitations provided by copyright law. It permits the software to be used by one person. Sometimes a single-user license permits you to install the software on a computer at work and on a computer at home, provided that you use only one of them at a time. Special **multi-user licenses** and **network licenses** permit multiple users, but are more costly than single-user licenses.

Demoware and shareware licenses allow you to "try before you buy." **Demoware** (or "trialware") is a version of commercial software that is free, but limited in some way. Commonly, demoware use is free for a limited period of time. At the end of the trial period, the software stops working if you don't pay for it. **Shareware** is another type of software licensed for free use during a trial period, after which users are supposed to pay a registration fee. Payment is on the honor system, however, so shareware authors collect only a fraction of the money they deserve for their programming efforts. Shareware users are encouraged to make copies of the software and distribute them to others. These shared copies provide a low-cost marketing and distribution channel.

Freeware is copyrighted software that—as you might expect—is available for free. Because the software is protected by copyright, you cannot do anything with it that is not expressly allowed by copyright law or by the author. Typically, the license for freeware permits you to use the software, copy it, and give it away, but does not permit you to alter it or sell it. Many utility programs and device drivers as well as some games are available as freeware.

Open source software makes uncompiled program instructions—the source code—available to programmers who want to modify and improve the software. Open source software may be sold or distributed free of charge in compiled form, but it must, in every case, also include the source code. Linux is an example of open source software, as is FreeBSD—a version of UNIX designed for personal computers.

Public domain software is not protected by copyright because the copyright has expired, or the author has placed the program in the public domain, making it available without restriction. Public domain software may be freely copied, distributed, and even resold. The primary restriction on public domain software is that you are not allowed to apply for a copyright on it.

QuickCheck A

1. The Windows [_____] is a file that keeps track of all installed hardware and software within a computer system.

2. The process of software installation is automated by a [_____] program that's included on a distribution CD or in downloaded files for new software.

3. Portable software products, also referred to as Web apps, are supplied by companies called application service providers (ASPs). True or false? [_____]

4. Software [_____] and service packs are software updates designed to fix bugs and update security of existing software programs.

5. Two types of software allow you to "try before you buy:" demoware and [_____] .

CheckIt!

QuickCheck B

Answer each question with Y or N, based on the information provided in the software license agreement on the right:

1. Can I install the software and then decide if I agree to the license? [____]

2. Can I rent the software to my friends? [____]

3. Can I sell the software at my Web site? [____]

4. Can I install the software on three of my computers? [____]

5. If I sell my computer, can the buyer legally use the software if I no longer use it? [____]

Software License Agreement

Important - READ CAREFULLY: This License Agreement ("Agreement") is a legal agreement between you and eCourse Corporation for the software product, eCourse GraphWare ("The SOFTWARE"). By installing, copying, or otherwise using the SOFTWARE, you agree to be bound by the terms of this Agreement. The SOFTWARE is protected by copyright laws and international copyright treaties. The SOFTWARE is licensed, not sold.

GRANT OF LICENSE. This Agreement gives you the right to install and use one copy of the SOFTWARE on a single computer. The primary user of the computer on which the SOFTWARE is installed may make a second copy for his or her exclusive use on a portable computer.

OTHER RIGHTS AND LIMITATIONS. You may not reverse engineer, decompile, or disassemble the SOFTWARE except and only to the extent that such activity is expressly permitted by applicable law.

The SOFTWARE is licensed as a single product; its components may not be separated for use on more than one computer. You may not rent, lease, or lend the SOFTWARE.

You may permanently transfer all of your rights under this Agreement, provided you retain no copies, you transfer all of the SOFTWARE, and the recipient agrees to the terms of this Agreement. If the software product is an upgrade, any transfer must include all prior versions of the SOFTWARE. You may receive the SOFTWARE in more than one medium. Regardless of the type of medium you receive, you may use only one medium that is appropriate for your single computer. You may not use or install the other medium on another computer.

CheckIt!

5

Getting Started with Windows XP

What's Inside and on the CD?

Microsoft Windows is one of today's most popular computer operating systems. First introduced in 1985, Windows has evolved through several generations, Currently, Windows Vista and Windows XP are in widespread use. Chapter 5 focuses on Windows XP, which was released in 2001; Chapter 6 focuses on Windows Vista, released in 2007. You can work through both chapters if you want to compare and contrast the two operating systems. Alternatively, you can concentrate on the chapter that covers the operating system you normally use.

In this chapter, you'll learn how to start and shut down Windows XP. You'll learn how to launch programs and work with the Windows taskbar. In addition, you'll learn how to customize your screen-based desktop and designate printers using the Control Panel. To assist you with troubleshooting, the chapter provides information about the Windows Help and Support Center. You'll also learn where to find information about your computer's Windows version and service packs.

FAQ How do I turn on my computer and start Windows XP?

To start Windows XP, simply turn your computer on. As your computer powers up and completes its boot process, Windows starts automatically. During the boot process, you might be prompted to enter a username and password. Your **Windows password** allows you to view, change, and delete files in your document folders. It is associated with user rights that monitor who is allowed to access various programs and data files. If your computer is connected to a network, entering your **network password** allows you to access network resources, such as shared files and printers. When the Windows XP desktop appears on the screen, your computer is ready to use.

Play It!

Figure 5-1

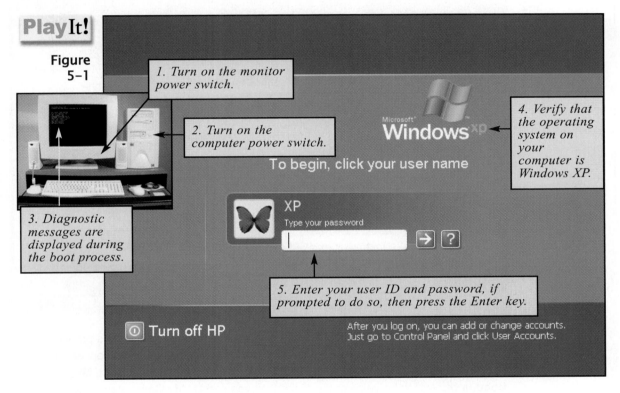

1. Turn on the monitor power switch.

2. Turn on the computer power switch.

3. Diagnostic messages are displayed during the boot process.

4. Verify that the operating system on your computer is Windows XP.

To begin, click your user name

XP
Type your password

5. Enter your user ID and password, if prompted to do so, then press the Enter key.

Turn off HP

After you log on, you can add or change accounts. Just go to Control Panel and click User Accounts.

- A computer might look like it is off, but simply be in a **power-saving mode** that turns off the monitor and other devices when your computer has been idle for a period of time. Your computer is in sleep mode if the power light is on, but the screen is blank. Press any key on the keyboard or move the mouse to "wake up" your computer.

- If your computer displays a "non-system disk" message during the boot process, it probably means that a floppy disk has been left in the disk drive. Remove the disk and press any key to continue the boot process.

- When prompted, type your password in the password box, and then press the Enter key to continue. You must use the correct uppercase and lowercase characters when typing your password. When you type each character of your password, you will see an asterisk (*) or circle (•). These symbols are a security feature that hides your password from an onlooker.

FAQ What's on the Windows XP desktop?

The **Windows XP desktop** is the gateway to all the tasks you perform with your PC. It is the screen you see when the boot process is complete, and it remains in the background as you use other software. You can use controls on the Windows desktop to start a program, to switch from one program to another, and to access information about your computer hardware.

Figure 5-2

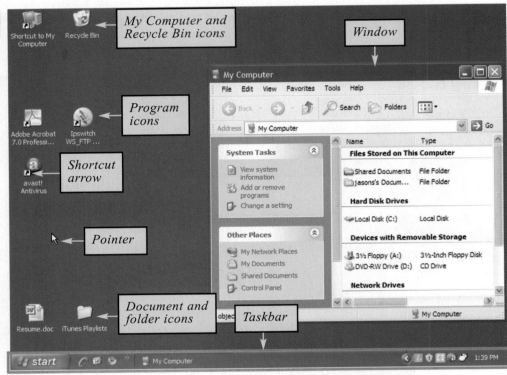

- The desktop contains small graphics called icons. Each **icon** represents a program, hardware device, folder, or document. Double-clicking an icon gives you access to the computer component it represents. Frequently used desktop icons include **My Documents**, which contains many of the files you create; **My Computer**, which provides access to hardware, networks, and software; and the **Recycle Bin**, which holds files scheduled for deletion.

- A **shortcut icon**, indicated by a small arrow, provides alternative access to programs and documents. Deleting a shortcut does not delete the item it represents.

- The desktop provides a work area where programs and files appear in "windows" (with a lowercase w.) A **window** is a rectangular area on the screen. Some windows hold applications and files, whereas another type of window, called a **dialog box**, contains controls for specifying and customizing commands.

- The **pointer** is used to select and manipulate on-screen objects. It is usually shaped like an arrow, but it can change shape when positioned over different objects on the screen or while an action is in progress. For example, the pointer sometimes changes to an hourglass shape to indicate that the computer is busy and you must wait until Windows is ready to accept further commands.

- The **taskbar**, located at the base of the desktop, contains several important controls that help you launch programs, switch between windows, and access system settings.

FAQ How do I use the taskbar?

The taskbar is typically divided into several areas. The **Start button** provides access to programs, documents, system settings, and Help. The **Quick Launch toolbar** gives you one-click access to frequently used programs, and lets you quickly return to the desktop while using other programs. Program buttons show you what's open on the desktop. Each **program button** represents a window. The **Notification area** displays the time and also contains shortcuts to programs and utilities, such as Volume Control, Power Options, and antivirus software.

Figure 5-3

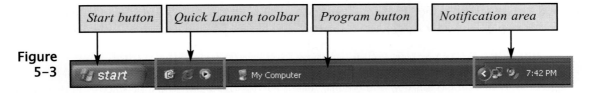

* To find out what each taskbar icon does, point to it and wait. In a second or two, a ScreenTip appears with the icon's title. A **ScreenTip** is a message that pops up to identify unlabeled buttons.

* On some computers, the taskbar is set to disappear when it is not in use. To reveal it, pass the mouse pointer off the bottom edge of the screen. You can also change the size of the taskbar to display more or fewer program buttons.

* A computer keeps track of the current date and time using a battery-operated internal clock, sometimes called a "real-time clock." Your computer uses the clock when recording the date and time when files are created or modified. The time is always displayed in the taskbar notification area. To see the date, point to the time and wait for a second or two. The clock automatically keeps track of daylight savings time, but you might have to adjust the date and time on a new computer or when you take your computer to other time zones. Right-click the time and click Adjust Date/Time to change the clock. Make sure you maintain the correct date and time so that your file date stamps are accurate.

* The taskbar's [image] Volume icon lets you quickly adjust the sound level emitted by your computer's speakers. Click the Volume icon to display the adjustment control.

* Program buttons on the taskbar represent open, or "running," programs. It is possible to have multiple programs open at the same time, but only one program can be active. To activate a program, click its button on the taskbar.

* You can add toolbars and icons to the taskbar by right-clicking any empty area of the taskbar. In addition to the Quick Launch toolbar, the following toolbars are available:

Address toolbar	Quickly go to a specific Web page.
Links toolbar	Link to product information on the Web and add Web links by dragging them to the toolbar.
Desktop toolbar	Access desktop icons, such as the Recycle Bin and My Documents, from the taskbar.
New toolbar	Access a specific folder from the taskbar.

FAQ How do I arrange icons and windows on the desktop?

You can control the placement of icons and windows that appear on your desktop. It is simple to rearrange icons so that those you use most often are easy to find. You can also create new folder and file icons for quick access to documents you frequently use.

- To create a new icon on the Windows desktop, right-click any empty area of the desktop and select New. Select an icon type from the list, then assign it a name.

- To delete an icon from the desktop, right-click it and then click Delete.

- To arrange icons on the desktop, right-click anywhere on the desktop and select *Arrange Icons By*. You can arrange icons in a variety of ways including by name, size, or date of last modification.

- You can also arrange icons by dragging them to a new location. First, right-click anywhere on the desktop and choose *Arrange Icons By*. Make sure that Auto Arrange and Align to Grid are not checked. You can then drag icons to any desktop location.

- To move a file into a folder or storage device, simply drag it to the folder or storage icon device in which you wish to place it.

- To rename an icon, right-click the icon and select Rename.

- To display the properties of an icon, right-click the icon and select Properties.

When several windows are open on the desktop, you can manipulate them in a variety of ways to arrange your desktop for maximum efficiency. You can maximize a window so that it fills the screen and provides the largest amount of working space. When working back and forth between two windows, you might want to size them to fit side by side. Windows automatically tiles all open windows to fit on the screen when you right-click the taskbar and select one of the Tile or Cascade options.

Figure 5–4

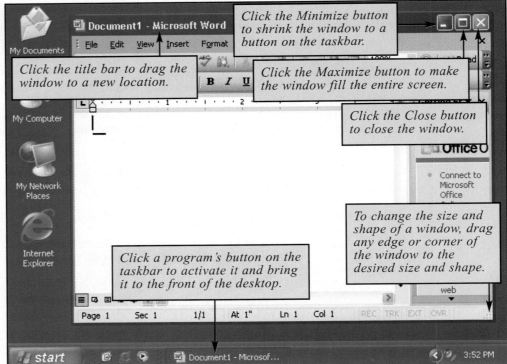

FAQ How do I use the Start menu?

The **Start menu** appears when you click the Start button. The top of the Start menu displays the user ID of the person who is logged on.

The left side of the Start menu features the **All Programs option**, which produces a list of software installed on your computer. You'll refer to this list often to start programs. The upper-left area of the Start menu is the **Pinned Items list**. You can customize this list to show your favorite programs. The lower-left area of the Start menu contains the programs you've used most recently. These programs are automatically added by Windows as it monitors your program usage.

The right side of the Start menu provides options for viewing stored files, opening recently used documents, adjusting system settings, accessing the Internet, controlling printers, getting help, and shutting down your computer.

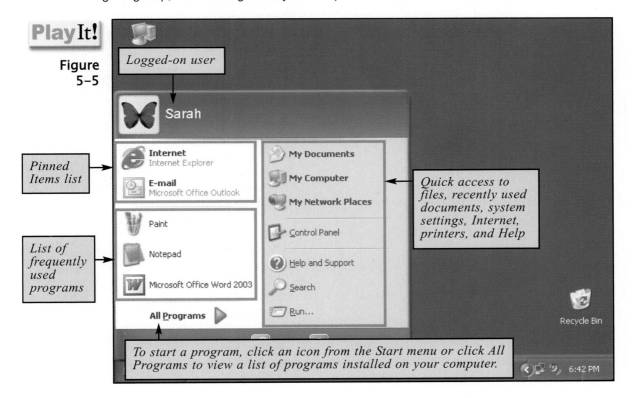

Play It!

Figure 5–5

Logged-on user

Sarah

Pinned Items list

List of frequently used programs

Internet
Internet Explorer

E-mail
Microsoft Office Outlook

Paint

Notepad

Microsoft Office Word 2003

All Programs

My Documents

My Computer

My Network Places

Control Panel

Help and Support

Search

Run...

Quick access to files, recently used documents, system settings, Internet, printers, and Help

Recycle Bin

To start a program, click an icon from the Start menu or click All Programs to view a list of programs installed on your computer.

6:42 PM

- Windows gives you the choice of two Start menu styles. The default style is shown above. The other style, referred to as the **Classic Start menu**, appears in single-column format and has fewer options. To change the Start menu style, right-click the taskbar, click Properties, and select the Start Menu tab.

- To add a program to the Pinned Items list, you can right-click any program shown in the All Programs list, then click Pin to Start Menu. You can also drag any program or document icon to the Pinned Items list area of the Start menu.

FAQ What is the Control Panel?

The **Control Panel** is a collection of tools for customizing Windows system settings so that you can work more efficiently. To open the Control Panel, click the Start button and then select the Control Panel option. From the Control Panel window, select one of the tools by double-clicking. The most commonly used Control Panel tools are the following:

	Accessibility Options	Adjust computer settings to make the computer easier to use for people with vision, hearing, and mobility difficulties.
	Add Hardware	Install and troubleshoot hardware devices.
	Display	Change the desktop, select a screen saver, and adjust screen resolution.
	Fonts	Install new fonts.
	Keyboard	Customize keyboard sensitivity and cursor blink rate.
	Mouse	Adjust mouse sensitivity, customize the mouse pointer, and configure the mouse for left-handed use.
	Speech	Adjust settings for speech recognition and speech synthesis.
	System	Access version information and specifications for hardware components, and change hardware settings.
	Security Center	Manage security settings to block intruders and viruses.

- Some Control Panel tools can be accessed directly from the Start menu. Others can be accessed by right-clicking the taskbar or desktop. If you can't remember these shortcuts, simply open the Control Panel where you can access all of the tools.

- Be careful when you use the Control Panel to change system settings. Changes to network settings can disable your Internet and e-mail connections. Incorrect hardware settings can make a peripheral device unusable. Before you change system settings using the Control Panel, make sure you understand the effect of those changes on the computer. It is always a good idea to jot down the original settings so that you can undo changes that cause problems.

- In businesses and in school computer labs, users are sometimes prevented from making changes to some or all system settings. If you work in such an environment and the Control Panel tools don't seem to work, check with your system administrator.

- Some system settings take effect only for the person who is logged onto the computer. For example, if you can't seem to modify an e-mail account, check the top of the Start menu to make sure you are the user who is logged on.

FAQ How do I change display settings?

The Control Panel's Display tool provides all kinds of options for customizing the look of your Windows XP desktop. You can use it to select a predefined **desktop theme** that includes a background, sounds, and icons for your on-screen desktop. You can select a **screen saver** that appears after your computer is idle for a specified period of time. You can even choose screen resolution and color quality for your computer's display device.

Figure 5-6

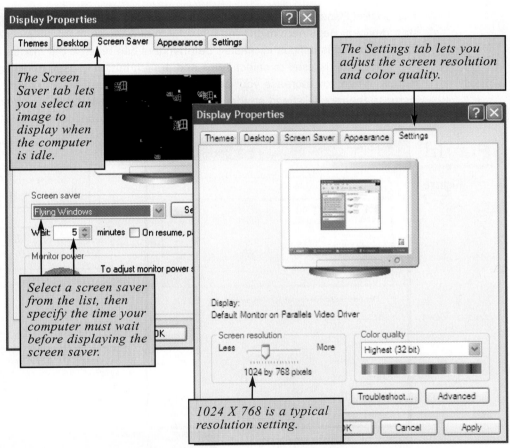

The Screen Saver tab lets you select an image to display when the computer is idle.

Select a screen saver from the list, then specify the time your computer must wait before displaying the screen saver.

The Settings tab lets you adjust the screen resolution and color quality.

1024 X 768 is a typical resolution setting.

- To open the Display Properties dialog box, double-click the Display tool in the Control Panel window. You can also right-click any empty area of the desktop.

- Most computer owners set their displays to 1024 X 768 resolution, but most displays are capable of higher resolutions that display a larger workspace. Fonts and icons, however, appear smaller than at lower resolutions. You can experiment with resolution settings to determine what's best for your work style.

- Screen savers were originally designed so that the same image would not be displayed for hours while the computer was not in use. On older CRT monitors, a sustained image could get "burned" into the screen and show a ghost of the image even when other windows were displayed. LCD display devices don't have this problem, but screen savers are still popular because they are fun and they can hide work in progress while you are away from your desk. When a screen saver is running, however, the display is consuming power. For energy efficiency and to prolong the life of a display device, it is more effective to turn it off when not in use.

FAQ How do I adjust keyboard and mouse settings?

The Control Panel includes a Keyboard tool for adjusting the sensitivity of your keyboard. You can increase or decrease the repeat delay, which is the time that elapses after you press a key until your computer starts displaying repeat characters. You can adjust the repeat rate, or speed at which the repeated characters appear. You can also change the rate at which the cursor (or insertion point) blinks. If your keyboard seems too sensitive, use the Keyboard tool to adjust it.

The Control Panel also includes a Mouse tool for customizing mouse, trackpad, or pointing stick devices. Beginners might find it helpful to slow down the double-click speed if double-clicking is difficult to master. Left-handers can reverse the mouse buttons so that the right button is used to select items and the left button is used to display shortcut menus. When you increase your computer's screen resolution, you might want to increase the mouse speed so that it travels quickly across the large workspace. You can also have some fun by selecting a different collection of mouse pointer shapes.

Play It!

Figure 5-7

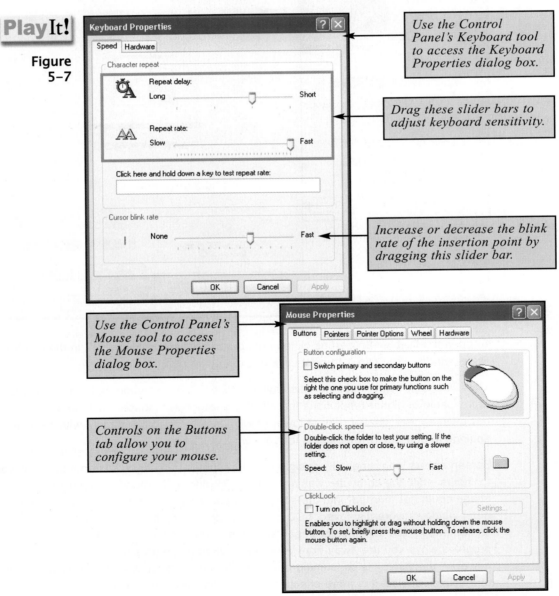

Use the Control Panel's Keyboard tool to access the Keyboard Properties dialog box.

Drag these slider bars to adjust keyboard sensitivity.

Increase or decrease the blink rate of the insertion point by dragging this slider bar.

Use the Control Panel's Mouse tool to access the Mouse Properties dialog box.

Controls on the Buttons tab allow you to configure your mouse.

FAQ How does the Control Panel help me work with printers?

Your computer might have multiple printers attached, or you might have access to several printers on a network. The Control Panel includes a Printers and Faxes tool that helps you work with printers and fax machines. It displays a list of all the printers and fax machines your computer can access. You can use the Printers and Faxes tool to add new printers, add new fax machines, and create connections to network printers.

The printer you want to use automatically, unless you specify otherwise, is called the **default printer**. You can use the Printers and Faxes tool to designate your default printer. You should change your default printer if you replace your old printer or if your network provides access to a new printer. When you no longer plan to use a printer, you should delete it from the Printers and Faxes list.

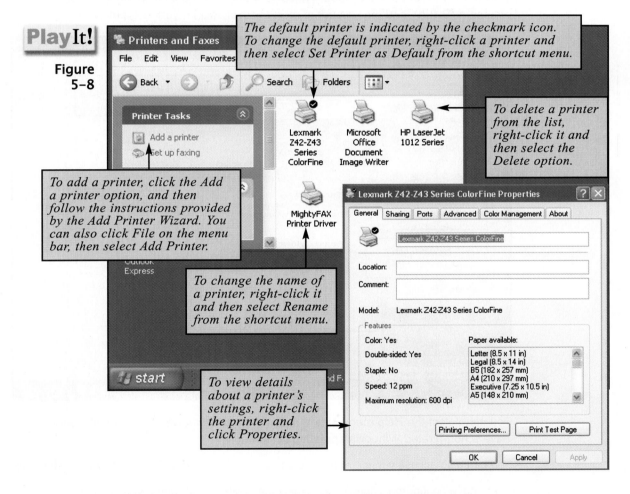

Figure 5-8

The default printer is indicated by the checkmark icon. To change the default printer, right-click a printer and then select Set Printer as Default from the shortcut menu.

To delete a printer from the list, right-click it and then select the Delete option.

To add a printer, click the Add a printer option, and then follow the instructions provided by the Add Printer Wizard. You can also click File on the menu bar, then select Add Printer.

To change the name of a printer, right-click it and then select Rename from the shortcut menu.

To view details about a printer's settings, right-click the printer and click Properties.

- You can open the Printers and Faxes window from the Control Panel or directly from the Start menu.

- When your computer has access to several printers, it is useful to name them by function. For example, you might name one printer "Photo Printer" and name another printer "Black and White Laser Printer." It is also useful to include the word "Network" with the names of printers you can only access when connected to a network. Although the icons for network and local printers are slightly different, the icons can be small and hard to distinguish.

FAQ Which version of Windows XP do I have?

Windows XP was released in several editions, including a Home Edition and a Professional Edition. These editions have been updated numerous times with patches and service packs. If you ever need to troubleshoot Windows or contact a support technician, you should know which edition, version, and service pack are installed on your computer.

The Help menus provided by Windows Explorer and My Computer offer a variety of useful information. To access the Help menu, click the Start button and then select My Computer. When the My Computer window opens, select Help from the menu bar.

The Help menu offers several options. You can use the About Windows menu option to find the version number of your Windows operating system and any service packs you've installed. Also included in the About Windows dialog box are links to the End-User License Agreement (EULA), and the amount of memory available on your computer.

Figure 5-9

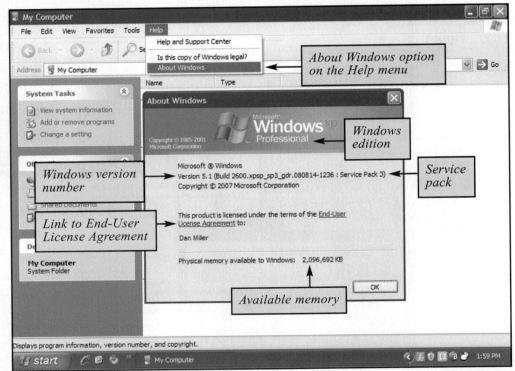

• You can select the Help menu option *Is this copy of Windows legal?* to make sure you have a non-pirated Windows operating system.

• You can also access version and system information using the Control Panel's System tool.

• If you have configured Windows to display the Classic Start menu, your Windows version is displayed on the left side of it. To find information about service packs, memory, and the license agreement, however, you must use the Help About dialog box.

FAQ How do I access Windows XP Help?

To access information about Windows features, look for the Help and Support option on the Start menu. You can also access the Help and Support Center from the Help option on the Windows Explorer or My Computer menu bars.

The Windows Help and Support Center is your gateway to Windows manuals, FAQs, and troubleshooting wizards. Computer manufacturers sometimes customize the Help and Support Center to include specific information about a particular brand of computer. This information can include troubleshooting tips, links to Internet-based help systems, and even links to brand-specific message boards and forums.

Figure 5-10

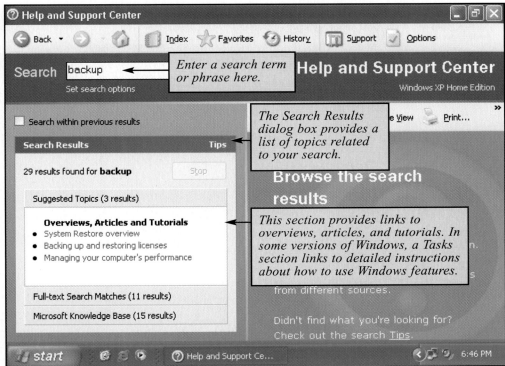

- If the Help and Support Center does not link you to the information you need, you can use a search engine, such as Google, to hunt for user groups, online forums, or articles containing relevant information.

- You might also consider asking local experts. For example, you might have a friend who has extensive Windows experience; your school might provide a student help desk; or your workplace might employ a staff of IT technicians.

- Help is a two-way street. As you gain expertise, consider sharing your knowledge in return for the help you received from others.

FAQ How do I shut down Windows XP?

The Start menu provides several useful options when you have completed a computing session. You can use the Log Off option in any situation where multiple users access the computer. The Log Off option leaves the computer on, but closes your files so that the next person who logs on cannot access them.

The Start menu also provides a Turn Off Computer option. You should use this option before you turn off your computer's power switch. This option ensures that your work during a computing session is saved, and it cleans out any temporary "scratchpad" data that the operating system created but doesn't need to save. As the shutdown proceeds, Windows closes and your computer powers itself off or prompts you to do so.

Figure 5–11

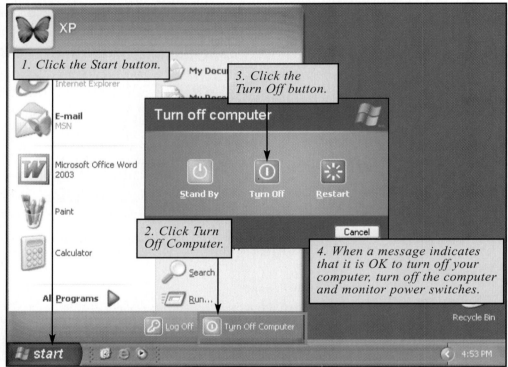

- The *Turn off computer* dialog box offers three options. Use the Turn Off option when you want to power down the computer. The Stand By option puts your computer in a state that requires only enough power to maintain the contents of memory. Use Stand By mode when you're planning not to use your computer for a short time and want it to reactivate quickly. The Restart option powers your computer down and then reboots it. Use this option when you are troubleshooting and want to clear memory then restart Windows.

- If your computer was turned off without being shut down, Windows might run a short disk test the next time you start your computer. Just follow the instructions on the screen to continue the boot process.

- Software programs have "bugs" or errors that sometimes cause your computer to "freeze up" or "hang" so that it doesn't respond to your mouse clicks or keyboard commands. If this situation occurs, you won't be able to issue the regular Turn Off commands. Don't panic and hit the "off" button. Hold down the Ctrl, Alt, and Delete keys at the same time. Then follow the directions in the dialog box that appears. If only one program has frozen, you'll be able to end it without closing other programs you are still using.

QuickCheck A

1. The Windows XP [_____] includes a taskbar with a Start button, Quick Launch toolbar, and Notification area.

2. The [_____] to Start Menu option allows you to add your favorite programs to the Start menu.

3. 1024 X 768 is a popular setting for display [_____] .

4. The [_____] Panel is a collection of tools for customizing Windows system settings so that you can work more efficiently.

5. True or false? You should use the Turn Off Computer option when you are not planning to use your computer for a short period of time. [_____]

Check It!

QuickCheck B

Indicate the letter of the desktop element that best matches the following:

1. Quick Launch toolbar [___]

2. Maximize button [___]

3. Minimize button [___]

4. Start button [___]

5. Pointer [___]

Check It!

6

Getting Started with Windows Vista

What's Inside and on the CD?

Microsoft released Windows Vista in 2007, touting it as more stable and more secure than previous versions of Windows. Notable differences between Windows Vista and Windows XP include an updated user interface, the Start menu's Search box, desktop gadgets, enhanced file management, a more prominent role for user accounts, a revamped system for sharing files, speech recognition, and tightened security.

In this chapter, you'll learn how to start and shut down Windows Vista. You'll learn how to launch programs, navigate the Windows taskbar, and work with user accounts. In addition, you'll learn how to customize your screen-based desktop and designate printers using the Control Panel. To assist you with troubleshooting, the chapter provides information about the Windows Help and Support Center. You'll also learn where to find information about your computer's Windows version and service packs.

FAQ How do I turn on my computer and start Windows Vista?

To start Windows Vista, simply turn your computer on. As your computer powers up and completes its boot process, Windows starts automatically. During the boot process, you might be prompted to enter a username and password. Your **Windows password** allows you to view, change, and delete files in your document folders. It is associated with user rights that monitor who is allowed to access various programs and data files. When the Windows Vista desktop appears on the screen, your computer is ready to use.

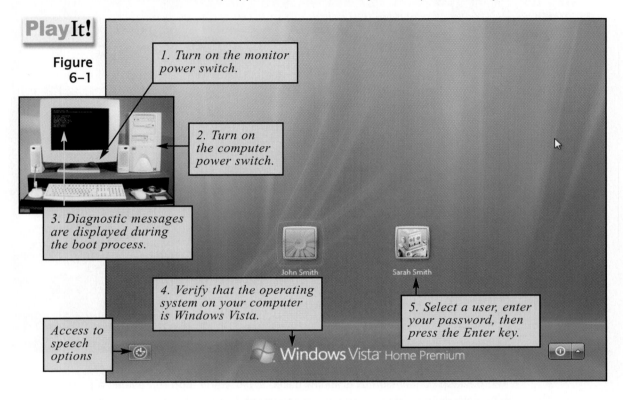

PlayIt!

Figure 6–1

1. *Turn on the monitor power switch.*

2. *Turn on the computer power switch.*

3. *Diagnostic messages are displayed during the boot process.*

4. *Verify that the operating system on your computer is Windows Vista.*

Access to speech options

John Smith

Sarah Smith

5. *Select a user, enter your password, then press the Enter key.*

Windows Vista Home Premium

- A computer might look like it is off, but simply be in a **power-saving mode** that turns off the monitor and other devices when your computer has been idle for a period of time. Your computer is in a power-saving mode if the power light is on, but the screen is blank. Press any key on the keyboard or move the mouse to "wake up" your computer.

- When typing your password, you must use the correct uppercase and lowercase characters. As you type each character of your password, you will see an asterisk (*) or circle (•). These symbols are a security feature that hides your password from an onlooker.

- The Windows Vista login screen displays an icon in the lower-left corner that provides access to speech options. If you'd like Windows to read screens aloud, click this option before you log in.

FAQ What's on the Windows Vista desktop?

The **Windows Vista desktop** is the gateway to all of the tasks you perform with your PC. It is the screen you see when the boot process is complete, and it remains in the background as you use other software. You use controls on the Windows desktop for tasks such as starting programs and accessing information about your computer hardware.

Play It!

Figure 6-2

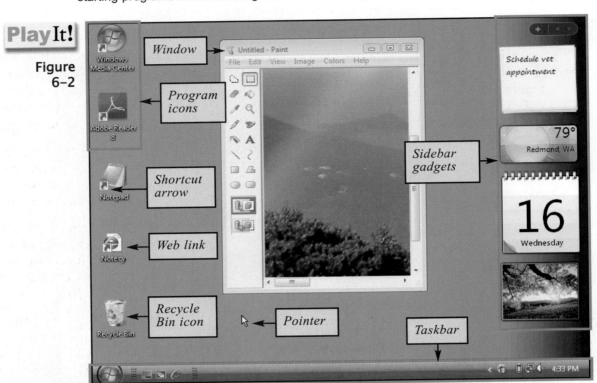

- The desktop contains small graphics called icons. Each **icon** represents a program, hardware device, folder, Web link, or document. Double-clicking an icon gives you access to the computer component it represents. Frequently used desktop icons include the **Recycle Bin**, which holds files scheduled for deletion.

- A **shortcut icon**, indicated by a small arrow, provides alternative access to programs and documents. Deleting a shortcut does not delete the item it represents.

- The desktop provides a work area where programs and files appear in "windows" (with a lowercase w.) A **window** is a rectangular area on the screen. Some windows hold applications and files, whereas another type of window, called a **dialog box**, contains controls for specifying and customizing commands.

- The **pointer** is used to select and manipulate on-screen objects. It is usually shaped like an arrow, but it can change shape when positioned over different objects on the screen or while an action is in progress. For example, an hourglass pointer indicates that the computer is busy and you must wait.

- The **taskbar**, located at the base of the desktop, contains several important controls that help you launch programs, switch between windows, and access system settings.

- The **Sidebar** contains customizable gadgets that perform various tasks, such as reporting the weather, tracking "sticky notes," and displaying current stock market data.

FAQ How do I use the taskbar?

The taskbar is typically divided into several areas. The **Start button** provides access to programs, documents, system settings, and Help. The **Quick Launch toolbar** gives you one-click access to frequently used programs, and lets you quickly return to the desktop while using other programs. Program buttons show you what's open on the desktop. Each **program button** represents a window. The **Notification area** displays the time and also contains shortcuts to programs and utilities, such as Volume Control, Power Options, and antivirus software.

Figure 6–3

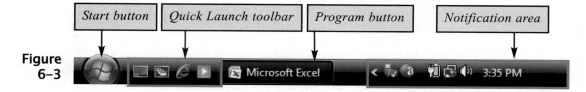

* The Windows Vista Start button is round, whereas the Windows XP Start button is rectangular. This difference offers a quick visual clue to the version of Windows installed on any computer you happen to use.

* To find out what each taskbar icon does, point to it and wait. In a second or two, a ScreenTip appears with the icon's title. A **ScreenTip** is a message that pops up to identify unlabeled buttons.

* Program buttons on the taskbar represent open, or "running," programs. It is possible to have multiple programs open at the same time, but only one program can be active. To activate a program, click its button on the taskbar.

* The Notification area might contain more icons than can fit in the allocated space. The ◄ button displays additional Notification area icons.

* A computer keeps track of the current date and time using a battery-operated internal clock, sometimes called a "real-time clock." Your computer uses the clock when recording the date and time when files are created or modified. The time is always displayed in the taskbar notification area. To see the date, point to the time and the date will appear after a second or two. The clock automatically keeps track of daylight savings time, but you might have to adjust the date and time on a new computer or when you take your computer to other time zones. To change the time, right-click the displayed time and select Adjust Date/Time. Make sure you maintain the correct date and time so that your file date stamps are accurate.

* The taskbar's 🔊 Volume icon lets you quickly adjust the sound level emitted by your computer's speakers. Click the Volume icon to display the adjustment control.

* On some computers, the taskbar is set to disappear when it is not in use. To reveal it, pass the mouse pointer off the bottom edge of the screen. You can also change the size of the task bar to display more or fewer program buttons.

* To customize the taskbar, right-click it and then select Properties from the shortcut menu.

FAQ How do I arrange icons and windows on the desktop?

You can control the placement of icons and windows that appear on your desktop. It is simple to rearrange icons so that those you use most often are easy to find. You can also create new folder and file icons for quick access to documents you frequently use.

- To create a new icon on the Windows desktop, right-click any empty area of the desktop and select New. Select an icon type from the list, then assign it a name.

- To delete an icon from the desktop, right-click it and then click Delete.

- To arrange icons on the desktop, right-click anywhere on the desktop and select Sort By. You can arrange icons by name, size, type, or date of last modification.

- You can also arrange icons by dragging them to a new location. First, right-click anywhere on the desktop and choose View. Make sure that Auto Arrange and Align to Grid are not checked. You can then drag icons to any desktop location.

- To move a file into a folder or storage device, simply drag it to the folder or storage icon device in which you wish to place it.

- To rename an icon, right-click the icon and select Rename.

- To display the properties of an icon, right-click the icon and select Properties.

- When several windows are open on the desktop, you can manipulate them in a variety of ways to arrange your desktop for maximum efficiency. You can maximize a window so that it fills the screen and provides the largest amount of working space. When working back and forth between two windows, you might want to size them to fit side by side. Windows automatically tiles all open windows to fit on the screen when you right-click the taskbar and select the option to Show Windows Side by Side.

 Play It!

Figure 6–4

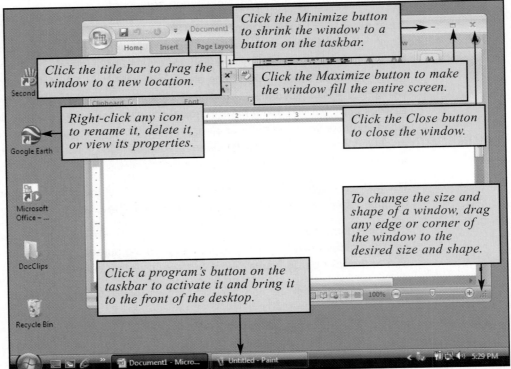

Click the Minimize button to shrink the window to a button on the taskbar.

Click the title bar to drag the window to a new location.

Click the Maximize button to make the window fill the entire screen.

Right-click any icon to rename it, delete it, or view its properties.

Click the Close button to close the window.

To change the size and shape of a window, drag any edge or corner of the window to the desired size and shape.

Click a program's button on the taskbar to activate it and bring it to the front of the desktop.

FAQ How do I use the Start menu and Search box?

The **Start menu** that appears when you click the Start button contains a handy collection of controls for starting programs, searching for files, getting help, adjusting system settings, and shutting down your computer.

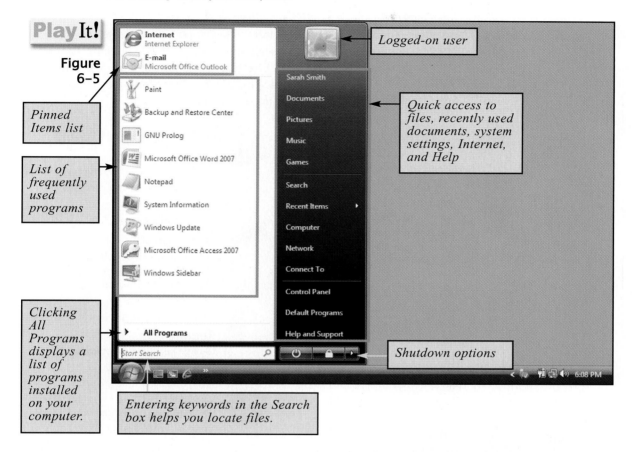

Figure 6-5

Pinned Items list

List of frequently used programs

Clicking All Programs displays a list of programs installed on your computer.

Logged-on user

Quick access to files, recently used documents, system settings, Internet, and Help

Shutdown options

Entering keywords in the Search box helps you locate files.

- The **Search box** is a feature unique to Windows Vista that helps you quickly find files and programs. Just above the Search box, the **All Programs option** produces a list of software installed on your computer. You'll refer to this list often to start programs.

- You can customize the **Pinned Items list** to show your favorite programs. To add a program to the Pinned Items list, you can right-click any program shown in the All Programs list, then click Pin to Start Menu. You can also drag any program or document icon to the Pinned Items list area of the Start Menu.

- Below the Pinned Items list, Windows displays the programs you've used most recently. These programs are automatically added by Windows as it monitors your program usage.

- The right side of the Start menu provides options for viewing files in your personal folders, opening recently used documents, adjusting system settings, connecting to networks, getting help, and shutting down your computer.

- Windows gives you the choice of two Start menu styles. The default style is shown above. The other style, referred to as the **Classic Start menu**, appears in single-column format and has fewer options. To change the Start menu style, right-click the taskbar, click Properties, and select the Start menu tab.

FAQ What is the Control Panel?

The **Control Panel** is a collection of tools for customizing Windows system settings so that you can work more efficiently. To open the Control Panel, click the Start button and then select the Control Panel option. From the Control Panel window, click any graphic or text link.

Windows Vista offers a choice of Control Panel views: Control Panel Home View organizes controls into groups that are accessible by clicking underlined links. Classic View displays icons instead of links to dialog boxes for adjusting settings. The one you use is simply a matter of personal preference. The Control Panel examples in this book show the Control Panel's Home View, which looks like Figure 6-6.

Figure 6-6

 System and Maintenance
Get started with Windows
Back up your computer

 User Accounts and Family Safety
Set up parental controls for any user
Add or remove user accounts

 Security
Check for updates
Check this computer's security status
Allow a program through Windows Firewall

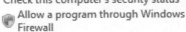 Appearance and Personalization
Change desktop background
Change the color scheme
Adjust screen resolution

 Network and Internet
View network status and tasks
Set up file sharing

 Clock, Language, and Region
Change keyboards or other input methods

 Hardware and Sound
Play CDs or other media automatically
Printer
Mouse

 Ease of Access
Let Windows suggest settings
Optimize visual display

 Programs
Uninstall a program
Change startup programs

 Additional Options

 Mobile PC
Change battery settings
Adjust commonly used mobility settings

- Be careful when you use the Control Panel to change system settings. Changes to network settings can disable your Internet and e-mail connections. Incorrect hardware settings can make a peripheral device unusable. Before you change system settings using the Control Panel, make sure you understand the effect of those changes on the computer. It is always a good idea to jot down the original settings so that you can undo changes that cause problems.

- In businesses and in school computer labs, users are sometimes prevented from making changes to some or all system settings. If you work in such an environment and the Control Panel tools don't seem to work, check with your system administrator.

- Some system settings require administrator rights. You'll learn more about this topic in the FAQ: *How do I work with user accounts?*.

FAQ How do I change display settings?

Windows provides all kinds of options for customizing the look of your on-screen desktop. Access these settings from the Control Panel's Appearance and Personalization link, or right-click any empty area of the desktop and select Personalize from the shortcut menu.

Play It!

Figure 6–7

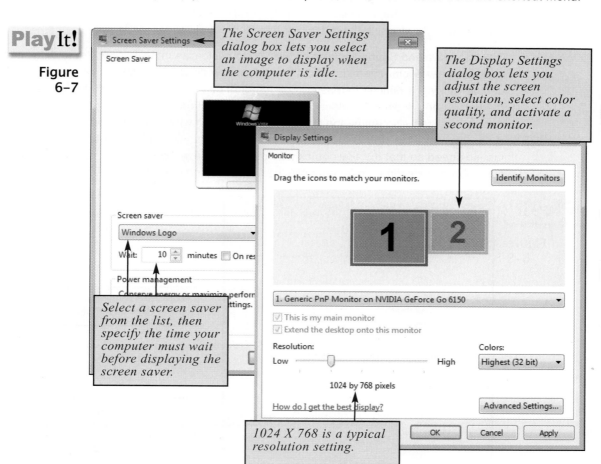

The Screen Saver Settings dialog box lets you select an image to display when the computer is idle.

The Display Settings dialog box lets you adjust the screen resolution, select color quality, and activate a second monitor.

Select a screen saver from the list, then specify the time your computer must wait before displaying the screen saver.

1024 X 768 is a typical resolution setting.

- You can adjust the screen resolution and color quality for up to two monitors. Many computer owners set their displays to 1024 X 768 resolution. Most displays, however, are capable of higher resolutions. You can experiment with resolution settings to determine what's best for your work style.

- You can personalize the look of your Windows desktop by working with color schemes, backgrounds, and themes. A **desktop theme** is a predefined set of colors, sounds, and backgrounds that can transform your desktop from boring to brilliant.

- You can select a **screen saver** that appears after your computer is idle for a specified period of time. Screen savers were originally designed so that a static image would not get "burned" into the screen and show a ghost of the image even when other windows were displayed. LCD display devices don't have this problem, but screen savers are still popular because they are fun and they can hide work in progress while you are away from your desk. When a screen saver is running, however, the display is consuming power. For energy efficiency and to prolong the life of a display device, it is more effective to turn it off when not in use.

FAQ How do I adjust keyboard and mouse settings?

The Control Panel's Hardware and Sound link allows you to adjust the sensitivity of your keyboard. You can increase or decrease the repeat delay, which is the time that elapses after you press a key until your computer starts displaying repeat characters. You can adjust the repeat rate, or speed at which the repeated characters appear. You can also change the rate at which the cursor (or insertion point) blinks.

The Hardware and Sound link also allows you to customize mouse, trackpad, and pointing stick devices. Beginners might find it helpful to slow down the double-click speed if double-clicking is difficult to master. Left-handers can reverse the mouse buttons so that the right button is used to select items and the left button is used to display shortcut menus. You can also adjust the sensitivity of the scroll wheel and the mouse speed. When you increase your computer's screen resolution, you might want to increase the mouse speed so that it travels quickly across the large workspace. You can also have some fun by selecting a different collection of mouse pointer shapes.

Play It!

Figure 6–8

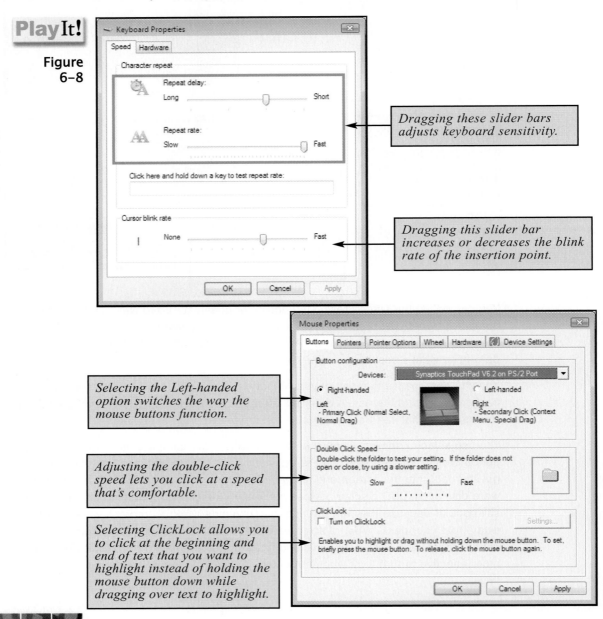

Dragging these slider bars adjusts keyboard sensitivity.

Dragging this slider bar increases or decreases the blink rate of the insertion point.

Selecting the Left-handed option switches the way the mouse buttons function.

Adjusting the double-click speed lets you click at a speed that's comfortable.

Selecting ClickLock allows you to click at the beginning and end of text that you want to highlight instead of holding the mouse button down while dragging over text to highlight.

FAQ How does the Control Panel help me work with printers?

Your computer might have multiple printers attached, or you might have access to several printers on a network. Control Panel's Hardware and Sound link includes a Printer option that displays a list of all the printers your computer can access. It allows you to add new printers, create connections to network printers, and select a default printer.

The printer you want to use automatically, unless you specify otherwise, is called the **default printer**. You can change your default printer if you replace your old printer or if your network provides access to a new printer. When you no longer plan to use a printer, you should delete it from the list of printers.

Play It!

Figure 6-9

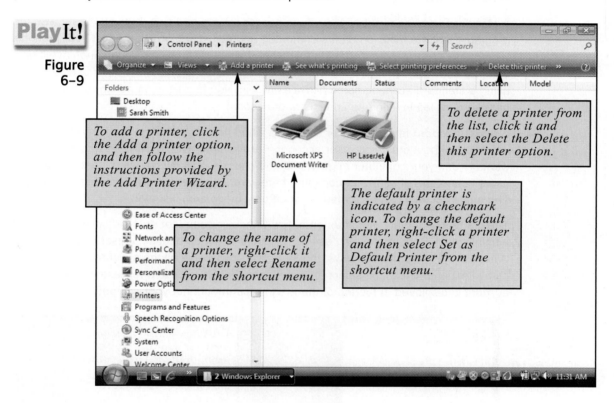

- When your computer has access to several printers, it is useful to name them by function. For example, you might name one printer "Photo Printer" and name another printer "Black and White Laser Printer." It is also useful to include the word "Network" with the names of printers you can only access when connected to a network. Although the icons for network and local printers are slightly different, in some views the icons can be small and hard to distinguish.

FAQ How do I work with user accounts?

User accounts are one of Windows Vista's weapons in the battle against unauthorized access and other surreptitious computer activity. A **user account** includes a user ID and password, plus specifications about which files can be accessed and what settings can be adjusted. Vista offers three types of user accounts: administrator, standard, and guest.

An **administrator account** lets you change any settings, access and change any other users' accounts, install software, connect hardware, and access all the files on a computer. Anyone with an administrator account is considered an "administrator" in Windows lingo.

A **standard user account** allows you to access folders and files that you create, use most programs that are installed on the computer, and adjust settings that affect your personal view of the Windows desktop. With this type of account, however, you cannot install or uninstall software, configure hardware, or change settings that affect other users. While using a standard account, some activities require you to supply an administrator password, or log in using an administrator account.

A **guest account** is designed for situations when you want to allow someone to use your computer without creating a user account. For example, you might have a visitor who wants to use your computer to go online and check e-mail messages. Guest account users cannot install software, configure hardware, change settings, or create accounts. The guest account can be turned on or off only by an administrator.

The first account that you set up on a new Windows computer automatically becomes an administrator account. You can use this account to set up additional user accounts. Whenever you log into Windows, the login screen displays all the accounts so that you can select one. Once you select an account and log in, a picture representing your account is displayed at the top of the Start menu throughout your computing session.

Figure 6-10

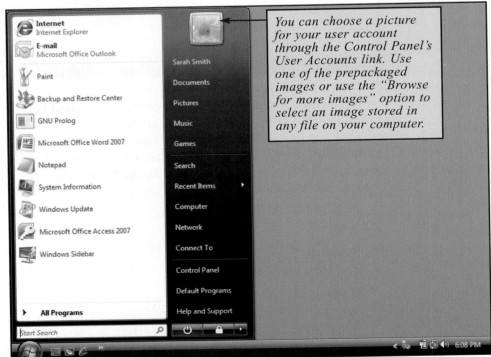

You can choose a picture for your user account through the Control Panel's User Accounts link. Use one of the prepackaged images or use the "Browse for more images" option to select an image stored in any file on your computer.

• **How do I work with user accounts? (continued)**

Although your user account prevents other users from accessing your files, you can allow access to all or some of your files through a process called **file sharing**. Windows Vista offers two ways to share files: by storing them in a public folder or by setting sharing permissions to files that exist in your personal folders.

Windows Vista is preconfigured with a Public folder and subfolders such as Public Documents, Public Music, and Public Pictures. You can access these folders by typing "Public" in the Start menu's Search box. As long as an administrator has activated file sharing for the Public folder, files that you store in public folders are available to anyone with a user account on your computer or with access to your computer through a network.

A second method of file sharing is to right-click one of your folders or files and then click Share. A dialog box prompts you to enter the user ID for one or more people who will be allowed access. With this file sharing method, you can designate access to specific people. You can also designate **permissions** that specify whether users can change files and delete them. Reader permission allows a user to only view a file; changing or deleting it is prohibited. Contributor permission allows a user to view a file, but to change or delete it only if they created it. Co-owner permission allows a user to view, change, or delete a file regardless of who created it.

Figure 6–11

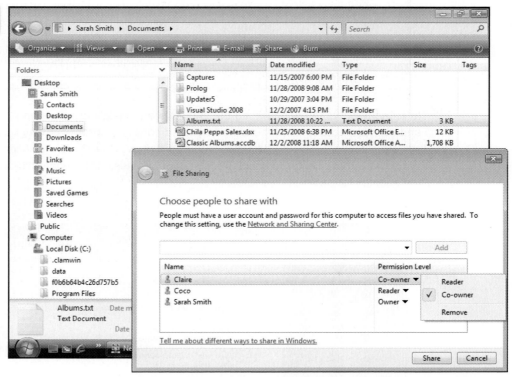

• Although Windows Vista offers very flexible file sharing options, to maintain your computer's security you should try to minimize the number of files you share and the number of people allowed to access them.

FAQ Which version of Windows Vista do I have?

Windows Vista was released in several editions. Windows Vista Home Basic and Home Premium editions include multimedia applications and target the consumer market. Windows Vista Business and Enterprise editions are designed for businesses. These editions have been updated numerous times with patches and service packs.

If you ever need to troubleshoot Windows or contact a support technician, you should know which edition, version, and service pack are installed on your computer. This information is displayed in the System Information window accessible by typing "system" in the Start menu's Search box.

Figure 6-12

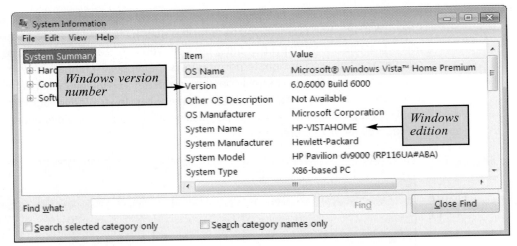

In an earlier chapter, you learned the importance of installing operating system updates and service packs to patch security holes and correct program bugs that might cause system glitches. By typing "Update" in the Start menu Search box, you can access the Windows Update center to check the status of updates, view update history, and change the settings for automatic updates.

Figure 6-13

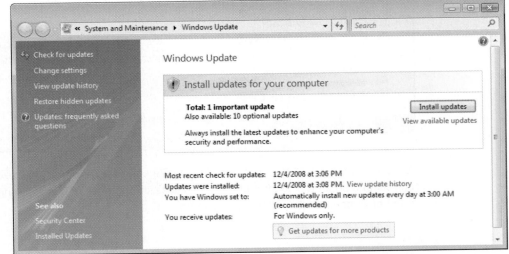

FAQ How do I access Windows Vista Help?

To access information about Windows features, look for the Help and Support option on the Start menu. The Windows Help and Support Center is your gateway to Windows manuals, FAQs, and troubleshooting wizards. Basic help information is stored on your computer as part of Windows; additional help is supplied by Microsoft's online support center.

Computer manufacturers sometimes customize the Help and Support Center to include specific information about a particular brand of computer. This information can include troubleshooting tips, links to Internet-based help systems, and even links to brand-specific message boards and forums.

**Figure
6–14**

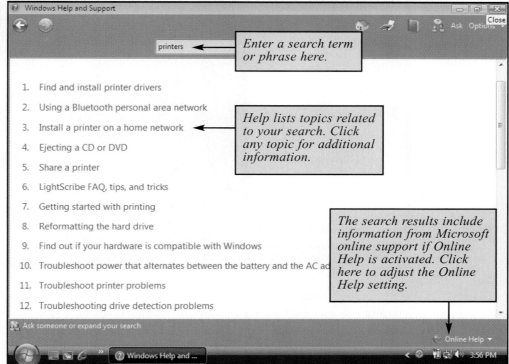

- If the Help and Support Center does not link you to the information you need, you can use a search engine, such as Google, to hunt for user groups, online forums, or articles containing relevant information.

- You might also consider asking local experts. For example, you might have a friend who has extensive Windows experience; your school might provide a student help desk; or your workplace might employ a staff of IT technicians.

- Help is a two-way street. As you gain expertise, consider sharing your knowledge in return for the help you received from others.

FAQ How do I shut down Windows Vista?

Although it might seem counterintuitive, you use the Start menu when you're ready to complete a computing session. The Start menu provides access to a shortcut menu with several useful options for shutting down, logging off, switching users, and restarting.

Figure 6-15

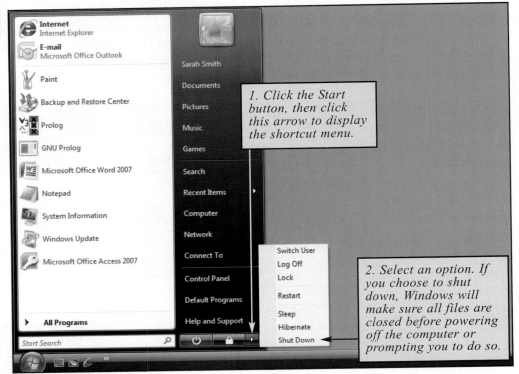

1. Click the Start button, then click this arrow to display the shortcut menu.

2. Select an option. If you choose to shut down, Windows will make sure all files are closed before powering off the computer or prompting you to do so.

- Use the **Shut Down option** before you turn off your computer's power switch. This option ensures that your work during a computing session is saved, and temporary "scratchpad" data created by the operating system is deleted. As the shutdown proceeds, Windows closes and your computer powers itself off or prompts you to do so.

- You can use the **Log Off option** or **Switch User option** in situations where multiple users access the computer. The Log Off option leaves the computer on, but closes your files so that the next person who logs on cannot access them. Switch User is applicable if you want to stay logged in while another person uses the computer.

- Use the **Sleep option** when you're planning not to use your computer for a short time and want it to reactivate quickly. Sleep mode keeps open programs and data files in memory, but puts the computer into a low-power state.

- The **Hibernate option** saves a record of the programs and files that you have open, but closes them before turning off the computer. When you next turn on the computer, your session is restored.

- The **Restart option** powers your computer down and then reboots it. Use this option when you are troubleshooting and want to clear memory then restart Windows.

- Software programs have "bugs" that sometimes cause your computer to "freeze up" or "hang" so that it doesn't respond to your mouse clicks or keyboard commands. If this situation occurs, don't panic and hit the "off" button. Hold down the Ctrl, Alt, and Delete keys at the same time. Then follow the directions that appear. If only one program has frozen, you'll be able to end it without closing other programs you are still using.

QuickCheck A

1. The Windows Vista [   ] includes a taskbar with a Start button, Quick Launch toolbar, and Notification area.

2. The [   ] to Start Menu option allows you to add your favorite programs to the Start menu.

3. 1024 X 768 is a popular setting for the [   ] of a display device.

4. The [   ] Panel is a collection of tools for customizing Windows system settings so that you can work more efficiently.

5. True or false? You should use the Shut Down option when you are not planning to use your computer for a short period of time. [   ]

CheckIt!

QuickCheck B

Indicate the letter of the desktop element that best matches the following:

1. Quick Launch toolbar [   ]

2. Sidebar gadget [   ]

3. Shortcut icon [   ]

4. Start button [   ]

5. Notification area [   ]

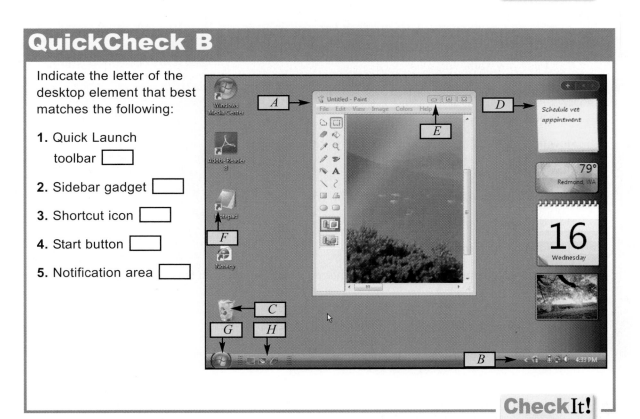

CheckIt!

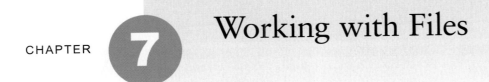

CHAPTER **7**

Working with Files

What's Inside and on the CD?

All the documents, pictures, and music you create with your computer are stored as files. This chapter helps you understand how to best name your files, where to store them, and how to access them. It also emphasizes how to maintain an orderly set of files on your disks.

Although the general concepts are similar, the details of file management are somewhat different for Windows XP than for Windows Vista. These differences are explained in this chapter. If you use a computer with the Windows XP operating system, take note of XP-specific procedures and keep them in mind as you continue on to subsequent chapters where examples are typically presented in the context of Windows Vista.

FAQ What's a file?

A **file** is a collection of data that has a name and is stored on a computer disk, tape, CD, DVD, or USB flash drive. Virtually all the information you can access from your computer is stored as files. For example, each document, graph, or picture you create with application software is stored as a file. The Web pages you view from the Internet are also stored as files, as are the program modules shipped on the distribution CD of a software package.

Files can be divided into two categories: executable files and data files. An **executable file** is a program module containing instructions that tell your computer how to perform specific tasks. Your computer "executes" these instructions to complete tasks such as sorting lists, searching for information, printing, or making calculations. For example, the word processing program that tells your computer how to display and print text is an executable file. Your computer's All Programs menu displays a list of software; when you select one of these programs, the computer runs its executable file.

A **data file** contains words, numbers, and pictures you can manipulate. For example, a document created using word processing software is a data file. You have several ways to access a data file, including the Open option on your application software's File menu, the Start menu's Documents option (Windows Vista) or My Documents option (Windows XP), and the Windows Explorer file management utility.

Every data file or executable file has **file properties** that describe its name, type, location, and size. A file's properties also include the dates when the file was created, modified, and last accessed. Some files are designated as read-only or hidden. A **read-only file** cannot be modified or deleted. A **hidden file** does not appear in file lists and cannot be used unless you know its name and location. Some files are marked for archiving to identify them for backup programs. Other files can be protected by passwords to prevent unauthorized access.

File properties are assigned by the operating system. Files created in Windows Vista can also have descriptive **tags** assigned by users. For example, a photographer might assign tags such as "Nikon" and "Neutral density filter" to the file that holds a digital photo.

Figure 7-1

A file's properties are displayed in a dialog box when you right-click the file name and select Properties from the shortcut menu.

File tags and ratings are assigned by users.

FAQ Can I use any name for a file?

As you create documents, graphs, and pictures, your computer holds the data in memory. When you're ready to save a file by transferring it to more permanent disk or USB flash drive storage, you must give it a unique name.

PC operating systems originally limited the length of a file name to eight characters or less. Also, a file name could not contain any spaces. These limitations made it difficult to create descriptive file names. For example, *Orgch510* might be the name of a file containing an organizational chart updated in May 2010.

With current versions of Windows, you can use more descriptive file names such as *Organizational Chart Updated May 2010*. This capability, which came to be known as "long file names," makes it much easier to find a specific file based on its name.

Long file names also allow you to control capitalization. Most people tend to use the same capitalization for file names as they would use for a title, using uppercase for the first letter of every word except articles and prepositions. Windows is not case sensitive, however. Even though you can use uppercase and lowercase, the file name *Report* is the same as *report* or *REPORT*.

Even in long file names, some symbols and file names are not allowed. When naming files, keep the following file naming conventions in mind.

Figure 7-2

Characters not allowed	File names not allowed	Maximum length
/ < > " \ :	* ?	Aux, Com1, Com2, Com3, Com4, Con, Lpt1, Lpt2, Prn, Nul	255 characters, including spaces

A **file extension** is a set of characters added to a file name to indicate the file's type or origin. For example, in the file name *Letter to the Editor.docx*, the file extension .docx indicates the file type is a Microsoft Word Document. A file extension is separated from the main file name with a period, but no spaces. File extensions are typically three characters in length.

Hundreds of file extensions exist, and the situation would be pretty grim if you had to remember the extension for each program you use. Happily, you don't generally have to memorize file extensions—instead, your software automatically adds the correct one when you save a file. However, knowing the file types that correspond to common file extensions such as those in the table below can be handy when looking at file lists.

Figure 7-3

File Contents	File Extensions
Documents	.doc or .docx (Microsoft Word) .odt (OpenOffice Writer) .txt .rtf .wpd .wps
Databases	.mdb or .accdb (Microsoft Access) .dbf .odb (OpenOffice Base)
Spreadsheets	.xls or .xlsx (Microsoft Excel) .ods (OpenOffice Calc)
Graphics	.bmp .tif .gif .jpg .png
Sound	.wav .mid .aif .mp3 .m4p
Video	.wmv .mpg .mov .avi .flv
Web pages	.htm .html
Programs	.exe .com .sys .dll .drv .ocx

FAQ Can I change the name of a file?

It is easy to change the name of a file. This process is called "renaming." You might want to rename a file so its name better describes its contents. You might also want to standardize the names of similar files—Playoff 2008, Playoff 2009, Playoff 2010—so that they appear in sequence.

Renaming files is fairly straightforward, except for a little twist involving file extensions. Windows allows you to hide file extensions. When this option is in effect, file extensions are not displayed, but they still exist. Windows has simply hidden them from your view. If you would like to change this setting, select Folder Options from the Windows Explorer Tools menu (Windows XP) or use the Organize button to access folder and Search Options (Windows Vista).

Before you rename a file, look at the file name to see if it includes an extension. If you see .docx or another extension, then Windows is set to display file extensions. When file extensions are displayed and you rename a file, you must make sure the new name includes the correct file extension. As a rule, you should use the same file extension as the original. If a file extension is omitted in the new name, Windows displays a reminder. When Windows is hiding file extensions, it is not necessary to type them—Windows automatically retains the old file extension and appends it to the new file name.

Figure 7-4

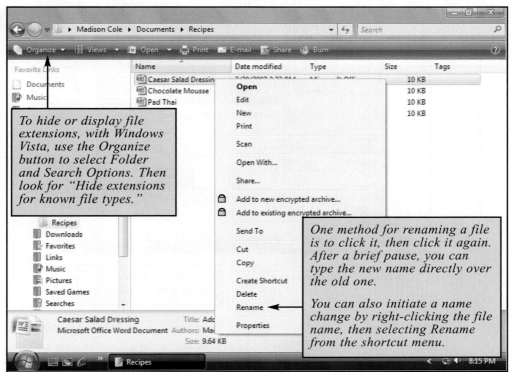

To hide or display file extensions, with Windows Vista, use the Organize button to select Folder and Search Options. Then look for "Hide extensions for known file types."

One method for renaming a file is to click it, then click it again. After a brief pause, you can type the new name directly over the old one.

You can also initiate a name change by right-clicking the file name, then selecting Rename from the shortcut menu.

• You should be careful when renaming files. Changing the file name extension can make the file unaccessible for editing. For example, if you change a .docx extension to .mp3, you will not be able to open and edit the file using Microsoft Word.

FAQ How do I get a list of my files?

You can use a folder window to view a list of files and organize them. Folder windows displayed by Windows Vista are somewhat different than those displayed by Windows XP. You'll look at a Windows Vista example on this page and a Windows XP example on the next page.

When using Windows Vista, the quickest way to view a list of files is to click your user name on the Start menu to display a folder window. The parts of a folder window are illustrated in Figure 7-5. You should become familiar with them so that you can manage your files efficiently.

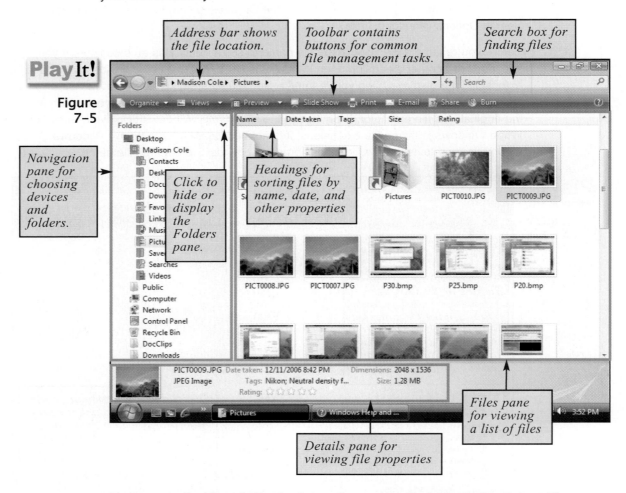

Figure 7-5

Address bar shows the file location.

Toolbar contains buttons for common file management tasks.

Search box for finding files

Navigation pane for choosing devices and folders.

Click to hide or display the Folders pane.

Headings for sorting files by name, date, and other properties

Files pane for viewing a list of files

Details pane for viewing file properties

- You can use the Views button to change the way the file list is displayed. **Icon Views** display a picture to represent each file along with its name. The example above shows the Large Icons view. **List View** displays the name of each file along with a small icon that indicates its type. **Details View** displays the file name, size, type, and date modified. **Tiles View** displays a large icon for each file, plus the file's name, type, and size.

- A folder window can be customized by clicking the Organize button and selecting Layout or Folder and Search Options.

- If you want to manipulate a listed file—delete it or copy it, for example—you can first click it to select it. If you want to open a file, double-click it.

• How do I get a list of my files? (continued)

When using Windows XP, the preferred way to display folder windows is by starting Windows Explorer. To start Windows Explorer, right-click the Start button and then click Explore. The Explorer window is divided into two panes. The Folders pane (or Navigation pane) lists devices and folders. The Files pane lists files. An icon helps you identify each file type. For example, the ▣ icon represents a Microsoft Word document. The ▭ icon represents the file for an executable program.

Figure 7–6

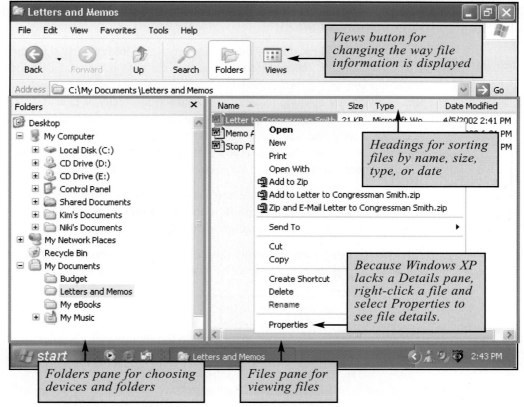

Views button for changing the way file information is displayed

Headings for sorting files by name, size, type, or date

Because Windows XP lacks a Details pane, right-click a file and select Properties to see file details.

Folders pane for choosing devices and folders

Files pane for viewing files

• Use the gray heading bars at the top of each column to rearrange the list. You can adjust the order of files to display them in alphabetical order by title, in order by size, by type, or by date modified.

• You can use the Views button or the View menu to change the way the file list is displayed. **Thumbnails View** shows tiny versions of graphics files—handy when you are selecting photos. **Tiles View** displays a large icon for each file, plus the file's name, type, and size. **Icons View** displays a medium-sized icon for each file along with its name. **List View** displays the name of each file along with a small icon that indicates its type. **Details View** (shown in the figure above) displays the file name, size, type, and date modified. This view is preferred by experienced Windows XP users because it provides the most information about the file.

• If you want to manipulate a listed file—delete it or copy it, for example—you can first click it to select it. If you want to open a file, double-click it.

FAQ How do I navigate to various folders and storage devices?

Most files are stored on your computer's hard disk. To transport a file, however, you might store it on a USB flash drive or CD. To share a file with others, you might store it on a network drive. As you work with files, it is important to keep track of the device where a particular file is stored.

Each storage device on a Windows-based computer is identified by a unique **device letter**. The device letter for the hard disk drive is usually C. Windows displays a unique icon for each type of storage device, though the icons look slightly different in Windows Vista than in Windows XP.

Most of the files on a storage device are organized into folders. A **folder** (sometimes called a "directory") allows you to group files for easy retrieval. Folders can hold other folders called **subfolders**, creating a hierarchical structure. Windows allows you to view this hierarchy by opening folders to expand the hierarchy or closing folders to collapse the hierarchy. Your files are typically stored in a set of predefined personal folders associated with your username. In Windows Vista, those folders include Contacts, Documents, Downloads, Music, and Pictures. In Windows XP, the main personal folder is My Documents and it contains subfolders such as My Music and My Pictures.

A device letter, folder, file name, and extension specify a file's location. This specification is sometimes referred to as a **path**. In the figure below, the path to the highlighted file is C:\Users\Madison Cole\Pictures\Vacations\Kyle's Deck.jpg.

Controls for navigating to various devices and folders when using Windows Vista are illustrated in Figure 7-7. Windows XP controls are shown on the next page.

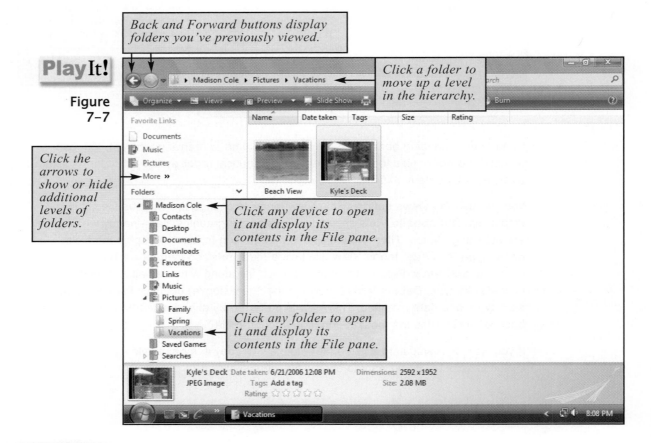

PlayIt!

Figure 7-7

Back and Forward buttons display folders you've previously viewed.

Click a folder to move up a level in the hierarchy.

Click the arrows to show or hide additional levels of folders.

Click any device to open it and display its contents in the File pane.

Click any folder to open it and display its contents in the File pane.

• How do I navigate to various folders and storage devices? (continued)

When using Windows XP, the controls for navigating through your computer's devices and folders are slightly different from those provided by Windows Vista. Most notable is XP's use of ⊞ plus and ⊟ minus icons instead of ▷ arrows to show or hide additional levels of folders. In addition, elements of the Windows XP Address bar cannot be clicked to navigate up through the folder hierarchy. Instead, you can use the Up button for this purpose.

Figure 7-8

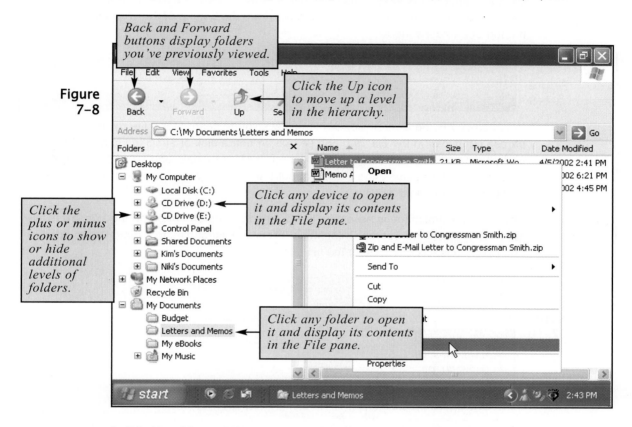

Back and Forward buttons display folders you've previously viewed.

Click the Up icon to move up a level in the hierarchy.

Click the plus or minus icons to show or hide additional levels of folders.

Click any device to open it and display its contents in the File pane.

Click any folder to open it and display its contents in the File pane.

• In Windows Vista, click a ▷ icon to expand the directory hierarchy and show subfolders. Click a ◢ icon to collapse the directory and hide subfolders.

• In Windows XP, click a ⊞ plus-sign icon to expand the directory hierarchy and show subfolders. Click a ⊟ minus-sign icon to collapse the directory and hide subfolders.

• In either version of Windows, click a device or folder to open it and display a list of files it contains.

• Each storage device on your computer has an associated icon. The icon identifies the device as a hard disk, CD, DVD, or USB flash drive. It also indicates whether the storage is a local device attached directly to your computer or a remote device accessed over a network. Remote storage devices, such as the FTP Site shown at right have a green (Vista) or yellow (XP) connector at the bottom of the icon.

FAQ How do I find a specific file?

When you know the folder in which a file is stored, you can easily use a folder window or Windows Explorer to open the folder and scroll through the list of files it contains. If, however, you don't know where to find a file, you can use Windows Vista's Search box or Windows XP's Search Companion.

Vista's Search box is easy to use. Simply enter all or part of a file name. Matches appear as you type. You can access the Search box from the bottom of the Start menu or from the top of a folder window.

Figure 7-9

In Windows XP, the Search Companion allows you to search for a file by name, or by a phrase contained in the file. You can search an entire disk or specified folders. The Search Companion also allows you to search for files by date and size. Searching by date is useful if you don't know much about the file, but can remember a time period in which you last worked with it.

The Search Companion is accessed by clicking the Search button on the Windows Explorer toolbar. The Search Companion displays a list of files that match your criteria. You can double-click any file in the list to open it.

Figure 7-10

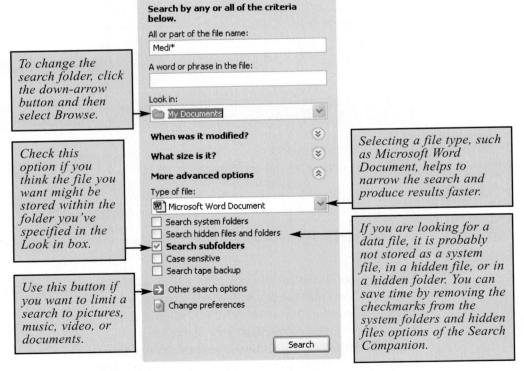

To change the search folder, click the down-arrow button and then select Browse.

Check this option if you think the file you want might be stored within the folder you've specified in the Look in box.

Use this button if you want to limit a search to pictures, music, video, or documents.

Selecting a file type, such as Microsoft Word Document, helps to narrow the search and produce results faster.

If you are looking for a data file, it is probably not stored as a system file, in a hidden file, or in a hidden folder. You can save time by removing the checkmarks from the system folders and hidden files options of the Search Companion.

- A **search wildcard** helps you create search specifications when you don't know the exact title of a file. The * wildcard stands for a series of unknown characters. For example, a search for Medi* would locate files such as Medicine, Medical Treatment, and Mediterranean Cruise. The ? wildcard stands for a single unknown character. For example, a search for Budget 201? would locate files such as Budget 2010 and Budget 2011.

FAQ What's the best organization for my files?

The key to organizing your files is to create a clearly structured set of folders. Here are a few hints to help you improve the organization of your files:

- Use descriptive names for files and folders.

- Always store your data files in a folder. The first level under a device should contain only folders, not files.

- Whenever possible, store your files in your personal folders: Documents, Music, and so on.

- Create subfolders of your personal folders as necessary to group files logically by project or by type.

- Try not to store your data files in the folders that contain program modules for your application software.

- Delete unneeded files and folders.

If the number of files in a folder becomes difficult to manage, don't hesitate to create additional folders and move files into them. To create a new folder, first click the device or folder in which you want the new folder located. When using Windows Vista, the next step is to click the Organize button and then select New Folder. In Windows XP, click the File menu, then select New. You can move new or existing folders within the folder hierarchy to create a logical structure of folders and subfolders.

In order to maintain logical groupings of files in your folders, you can move or copy files from one folder to another. The process is similar in Windows XP and Windows Vista. Files can be moved and copied one at a time or in groups. To select a single file, simply click it. To select multiple files, use either the Control (Ctrl) key or the Shift key while you click, as shown in Figure 7-11.

Figure 7-11

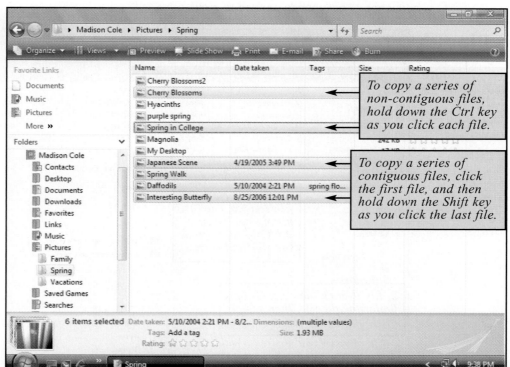

To copy a series of non-contiguous files, hold down the Ctrl key as you click each file.

To copy a series of contiguous files, click the first file, and then hold down the Shift key as you click the last file.

• **What's the best organization for my files? (continued)**

Typically, you copy a file when you want to create a duplicate. You can copy a file into another folder before modifying it. You might copy a group of important files to a CD, which you could store in a secure location. You can also copy files to a USB flash drive if you want to access them on a computer other than your own. You can even copy files to a Web site to access them from a public computer while you're traveling.

When you copy a file, Windows places a duplicate of the file on the **Windows Clipboard**—a temporary holding area in your computer's memory. The original file remains in its original location. After you select a location for the copy, Windows pastes the file from the Clipboard to the new location. Think of copying files as "copy and paste" to remember this sequence of commands. Copying multiple files follows a similar process, except you use the Ctrl or Shift keys to select the files before copying them to the Clipboard. You can copy folders using the same procedure as for copying files.

In the context of file management, you'll find yourself more frequently moving files than copying them. Consider moving files as necessary to group similar files into folders where you can easily find them.

You can move a file simply by dragging it from the Files pane to a folder listed in the Folders pane. This procedure sometimes misfires, however. If you don't carefully position the file on the destination folder, the file can drop into an unintended folder where it could be difficult to find. To avoid this problem, use the cut and paste method.

When you use the cut and paste method to move a file, Windows removes or "cuts" the file from its current location and places it on the Clipboard. After you select a new location for the file, Windows "pastes" it from the Clipboard to the new location. Associating the process of moving files with "cut and paste" can help you remember the sequence of commands needed to move a file.

Figure 7-12

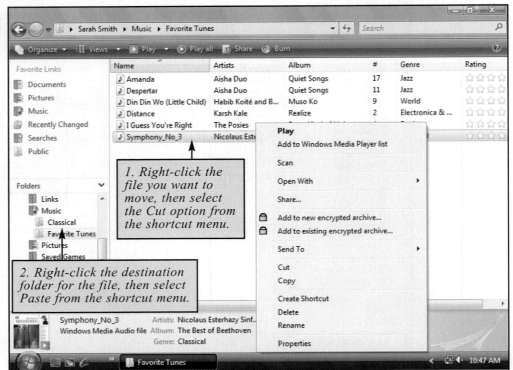

FAQ How do I delete files and folders?

When you no longer need files or folders, you should delete them so that your computer's hard disk drive works more efficiently. Deleting unneeded files also pares down directory listings to avoid clutter. Deleting old versions of files helps you avoid revising an outdated version of a file when you meant to revise the current version.

To delete a file, simply right-click it and select Delete from the shortcut menu. You can delete a folder using the same procedure, but be aware that when you delete a folder, you delete all the files it contains. You can use the Ctrl key, Shift key, or Select All options to delete more than one file or folder at a time.

If you run out of disk space, Windows displays a "Disk Full" message. This message usually means it's time for some PC housecleaning. If your hard disk is full, you might eventually have to delete old files and unneeded software. When removing software, remember to use an uninstall procedure, rather than manually deleting program files.

Before you delete files and software, however, you can usually clear lots of hard disk space by emptying your computer's Recycle Bin. The Recycle Bin is a holding area for the files you've deleted from your PC's hard disk. When you delete a file from the hard disk, its name is removed from the Windows Explorer file list, but the file itself remains on the disk and continues to occupy disk space. This space is not released until you empty the Recycle Bin.

It is nice to know that a deleted file is not gone forever until you empty the Recycle Bin. You can retrieve files from the Recycle Bin and restore them to their previous folders. This feature is an excellent safety net if you mistakenly delete a file. Remember, however, that the Recycle Bin holds only hard disk files. It doesn't retain files you've deleted from USB flash drives and other storage devices.

**Figure
7–13**

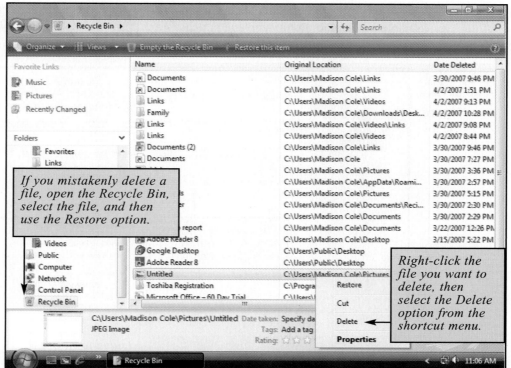

If you mistakenly delete a file, open the Recycle Bin, select the file, and then use the Restore option.

Right-click the file you want to delete, then select the Delete option from the shortcut menu.

FAQ How do I back up important files?

Have you ever mistakenly copied an old version of a document over a new version? Has your computer's hard disk drive gone on the fritz? Did a virus wipe out your files? Has lightning "fried" your computer system? These kinds of data disasters are not rare; they happen to everyone. You can't always prevent them, so you need a backup plan to recover data that's been wiped out by operator error, viruses, or hardware failures.

A **backup** is a copy of one or more files that is made in case the original files become damaged. A backup is usually stored on a different storage medium than the original files. For example, you could back up files from your hard disk to a different hard disk, a writable CD or DVD, USB flash drive, or Web site. The exact steps you follow to make a backup depend on your backup equipment, the software you use to make backups, and your personal backup plan.

One way to back up your important data files is to periodically copy them to a CD, DVD, or USB flash drive. This method depends on you remembering to copy files, however, and it is easy to procrastinate.

If you'd prefer to automate the process, you can use file synchronization software to automatically make copies of files in specified folders. **File synchronization** (sometimes referred to as "mirroring") ensures that files in two or more locations contain the same data. Synchronization software designed for file backup monitors the files on your hard disk, watches for changes, and automatically makes the same changes to files on your designated backup device—preferably an external hard drive.

Both Windows Vista and Windows XP offer a utility that creates restore points. A **restore point** is a snapshot of your computer settings, essentially a backup of the Windows Registry. If a hard disk problem causes system instability, you might be able to roll back to a restore point when your computer was operational.

Restore points are set automatically when you install new software. You can manually set restore points, too. For example, you might want to set a restore point before setting up a network or installing new hardware.

Figure
7–14

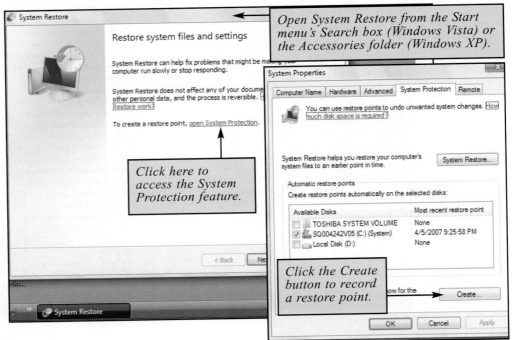

• How do I back up important files? (continued)

Most computer manufacturers provide a way to create a **recovery disk** you can use if your computer's hard disk fails. The contents and capabilities of recovery disks vary. Some are designed to restore your computer to its "like new" state, but wipe out all your data. Others attempt to restore user settings, programs, and data. Before you depend on a recovery disk, make sure you know what it contains and how to use it in case of a system failure. The process of creating a recovery disk depends on your computer manufacturer. Use the Help and Support Center to look for information and instructions.

File backups, restore points, and recovery disks typically do not restore all programs and data to their state just before a hard disk failure or massive virus infection. For a full-system backup, you need backup software. **Backup software** is a set of utility programs designed to back up and restore some or all of the files on a computer's primary storage device. Backup software usually includes options that make it easy to schedule periodic backups, define a set of files that you want to regularly back up, and automate the restoration process.

Backup software differs from most copy and synchronization routines because it typically compresses all the files for a backup and places them in one large file. Under the direction of backup software, this file can spread across multiple disks, CDs, or DVDs if necessary. The backup file is indexed so that individual files can be located, uncompressed, and restored. Backup software is supplied with most operating systems and from third-party vendors.

To use backup software, you typically begin by specifying which files you want to back up, selecting the location of the backup device, and selecting the days and times for automatic backups to proceed. Because the backup process uses system resources, most people schedule backups for times when their computer is on, but when they are not typically using it.

Figure 7–15

FAQ How do I solve common problems encountered when working with files?

File management usually proceeds smoothly, especially if your files are well organized and you are keeping your computer equipment well maintained. Occasionally, file problems do occur and you should be prepared to handle them. The most common file problems are listed below. If you encounter less common problems, you can usually turn to online user forums and the support center at the software publisher's Web site.

File can't be found. If you don't see a file in its expected location, the file might be designated as hidden or it might have been moved. To display hidden files when working with Windows Vista, click the Organize button in a folder window and then select Folder and Search Options. Use the View tab to activate the option *Show hidden files and folders*.

Cannot modify a file. When a file is designated as read-only, it cannot be modified. Right-click the file name to display its properties. You can remove the read-only designation only if you have user rights or permission to do so as the file's creator, as a system administrator, or as a co-owner of a shared file.

Access denied. When trying to open a file or folder, you might see an "Access Denied" or "Folder is not accessible" message. These messages can come from the file or from a network. You can be denied access to a file if its owner has not activated sharing, if you do not have permission to access a shared file, if Windows detects a change in your security ID, or if you have limited access rights on your network.

Cannot open a shared file. If you did not create a file, you might not have permission to open it. Check with the file's owner to find out if you can be given permission.

Cannot open a locked or encrypted file. Files can be locked or encrypted in various ways. If you have locked or encrypted a file that you created, then it is essential that you remember the password needed to access the file. If the file was created by someone else, access might be restricted for a reason. Check with the file's owner to find out how to proceed.

Cannot open a corrupted file. A corrupted file is one that has been inadvertently altered in such a way that data becomes scrambled. Files can become corrupted as a result of defective hardware, storage media, or software. Error messages such as "Corrupted file" or "Unexpected end of file" indicate a file might have become corrupted. Corrupted files can rarely be repaired. Instead, they must be replaced from a copy or backup.

• How do I solve common problems encountered when working with files? (continued)

Bad sectors. Files can become corrupted when parts of a storage medium become damaged. Before a hard disk, CD, or DVD can be used to store data, it is formatted in a process that divides the disk surface into circular **tracks**, divides the tracks into wedge-shaped **sectors**, and then numbers them. The formatting process also looks for defective areas of the disk, called "bad sectors," and cordons them off so data cannot be stored there. Sometimes, the formatting process misses a few bad sectors and data is eventually stored where it cannot be retrieved.

Hard disk failure. The operating system uses a special file to keep track of numbered sectors and the data they contain. If this file becomes damaged, you can lose access to all the files on the disk. In this situation, you might need to install a different hard disk and retrieve your files from backups.

"Can't read file" error message. An error message that your computer cannot read a file could mean that the file is corrupted, but it might also mean that the file's content cannot be read by the program you're using to open it. This problem can occur if the file extension is inadvertently changed. It can also occur if Windows does not have the correct file association. A **file association** links file types with the programs that can open them. For example, suppose the association for Microsoft Paint inadvertently gets switched from .bmp to .docx. You look through your list of files and double-click Report.docx to open it. Windows associates .docx with Paint, so it opens Paint and tries unsuccessfully to use it to open Report.docx. An error message results. If you suspect this problem, right-click the file, select Properties, and then click the Change button next to the *Opens with* specification. You can change the application that opens that particular file or all files with the same file extension.

Figure 7-16

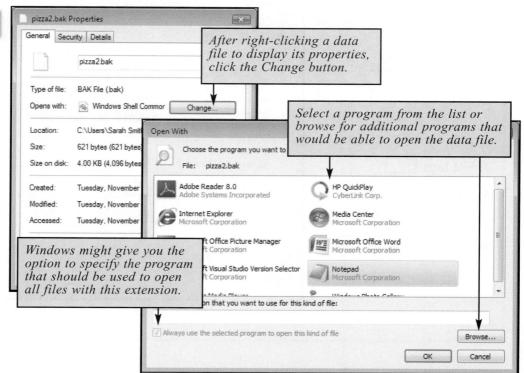

After right-clicking a data file to display its properties, click the Change button.

Select a program from the list or browse for additional programs that would be able to open the data file.

Windows might give you the option to specify the program that should be used to open all files with this extension.

QuickCheck A

1. A(n) [＿＿＿＿＿] file is a program module containing instructions that tell your computer how to perform a specific task, whereas a(n) [＿＿＿＿＿] file contains words, numbers, and pictures you can manipulate.

2. To select several files listed consecutively, click the first file, then hold down the [＿＿＿＿＿] key and click the last file.

3. When used as a search wildcard, the [＿＿＿＿＿] symbol stands for a series of unknown characters.

4. C:\JobSearch\Resume.doc would be referred to as a file [＿＿＿＿＿] .

5. A(n) [＿＿＿＿＿] point is a snapshot of your computer settings that can be used to roll your computer back to a previous state.

Check It!

QuickCheck B

For each description below, enter the letter of the corresponding folder window object:

1. The storage device that contains listed files [＿＿]

2. The folder that contains the listed files [＿＿]

3. File tags [＿＿]

4. The button that would create a new folder [＿＿]

5. The Search box [＿＿]

Check It!

Section II
Key Applications

When you complete Section II, click the **Get It?** button while using the BookOnCD to take a Practice test.

CHAPTER **8**

Getting Started with Application Software

What's Inside and on the CD?

Application software helps you use your computer to accomplish many useful tasks. Some of today's most popular software is included in the Microsoft Office suite. The suite's flagship software is Microsoft Word—a word processing application that has become a worldwide standard. Microsoft Excel is the spreadsheet software of choice for many computer owners. Microsoft PowerPoint is top-rated presentation software. Microsoft Access is among the most frequently used PC database software packages.

A software program designed for the Windows operating system is often referred to as a **Windows application**. Understanding the features common to most Windows applications makes it easy to learn new software. In this chapter, you'll take a look at features common to many Windows applications. You can use what you learn in this chapter as a foundation for working with Word, Excel, PowerPoint, and Access in later chapters. This material also applies to working with a browser and e-mail.

FAQ How do I start and exit Windows applications?

Windows applications are sometimes referred to simply as "applications" or "programs." This book uses the term "program" because it is consistent with Windows terminology. Before you can start a program, such as Microsoft Word, your computer should be on; and the Start button, supplied by the Windows operating system, should be displayed at the bottom of your screen. Windows provides several ways to start a program, but you'll typically use the Start button.

Windows allows you to run several programs at the same time, but it's best to close, or exit, a program when you're finished using it. Closing unused programs frees up memory and helps your computer run more efficiently. Also, remember to close all programs before you initiate the shut down procedure to turn off your computer.

Figure 8-1

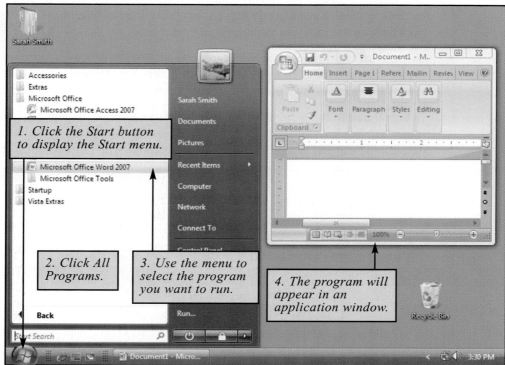

1. Click the Start button to display the Start menu.

2. Click All Programs.

3. Use the menu to select the program you want to run.

4. The program will appear in an application window.

- When you install a new program on your computer, it is typically added to the All Programs menu. To start the program, click its name on the All Programs menu.

- Some menu options, indicated by a ▣ symbol, represent multiple programs. When you click one of these options, a list of program names is displayed. Click the program you want to start from the list.

- In addition to appearing in the All Programs menu, some programs, such as Internet Explorer, are represented by an icon on the Windows desktop. To use one of these icons to start a program, just double-click it.

- To close a program, click the X Close button.

FAQ   What are the components of an application window?

An open program is displayed in a rectangular **application window** on the Windows desktop. Application windows contain many similar elements, even when they hold very different kinds of programs.

An application window's title bar displays the name of the program, the name of the open file, and a set of sizing buttons for minimizing, maximizing, and closing the window.

Many application windows include a **menu bar** that provides access to commands for controlling the program. Below the menu bar, you might see one or more **toolbars** containing small pictures. Each picture is a **toolbar button** that provides a shortcut for accomplishing a task.

Microsoft Office 2007 modules include a **ribbon** instead of a menu bar that provides access to commands and options. For example, the ribbon's Insert tab displays options for inserting headers and footers into a document.

A status bar runs across the bottom of most application windows. A **status bar** contains information about the current condition of the program. Depending on the program, the status bar might display the current page number, the zoom level, or a Web page address.

A **scroll bar** on the side of the window helps you move a document or graphic up and down within the window. A horizontal scroll bar might also appear at the bottom of an application window to help you scroll wide documents and graphics from left to right.

Figure 8–2

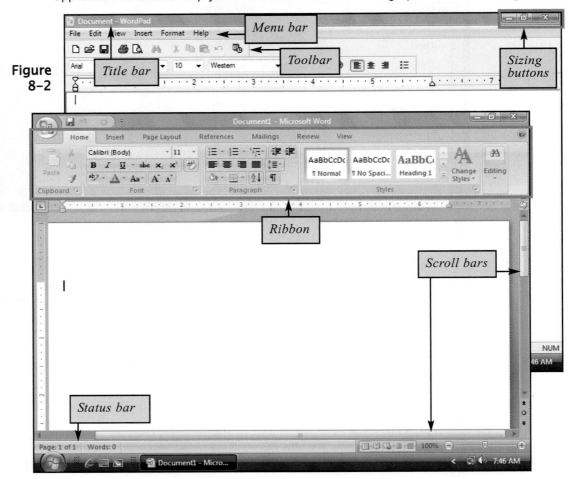

FAQ   How do I switch between application windows?

You can have more than one application window open, or "running," on the desktop. This Windows feature is handy if you want to work on two projects at the same time or if you want to copy a photo from your photo editing software to a document. Open application windows are represented by buttons on the taskbar. Clicking one of these buttons brings the window to the front of the desktop. Although multiple programs can be open at the same time, only one program can be active. The active program is indicated by a distinctly colored taskbar button.

Some programs also allow several data files to be open at the same time. For example, when using Microsoft Word, you could have your to-do list open at the same time you are working on a term paper. When your desktop contains only a few windows, each data file has its own taskbar button. As you open more windows, the data files are combined into a single button that opens to display a list of files.

Figure 8-3

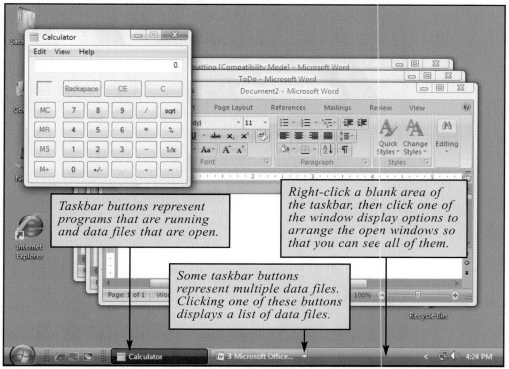

- If a program window is open but hidden underneath another program window, clicking the program's button on the taskbar brings that window to the front, overlapping other windows on the desktop. You can also click any visible part of the hidden window to make it active.

- If a program window is minimized, clicking the program's button on the taskbar restores the window to its previous size and location.

- When multiple data files are open in a single program, such as Microsoft Word, you can click the Switch Windows command from the Windows group on the View tab to see a list of files and switch from one to another.

FAQ How do menus and toolbars work?

Most application windows include a menu bar. Clicking an option from the menu bar displays a menu with a list of choices. For example, clicking Edit on the menu bar displays the Edit menu. You can use this menu to accomplish several tasks. For example, the Copy option allows you to copy a selected item onto the Clipboard.

Typically, a menu bar provides access to all the features of a program. If you don't remember how to access a program feature, you can browse through the menu options to find it.

Most application windows display one or more toolbars, typically located below the menu bar near the top of the window. Toolbars contain several buttons, sometimes called "tools," that provide a single-click shortcut for the most commonly used menu options.

Figure 8-4

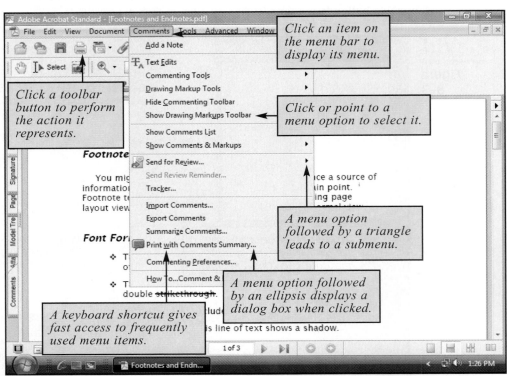

- If you open a menu and then decide you don't want to select an option after all, click the menu title again or press the Esc key to close the menu.

- You can use a **keyboard shortcut** for fast access to frequently used menu items. Hold down the Alt key and press the underlined letter to display a menu. Press the underlined letter to select an option from an open menu. As an example, for the menu item *Hide Commenting Toolbar*, the keyboard shortcut is Alt+C because "C" is the underlined letter.

- Some programs have a Goto command that allows you to specify a page and jump to it. Look for this command on the menu bar or ribbon.

FAQ How does the ribbon work?

In Microsoft Office 2007, the ribbon replaces the menu bar and toolbars at the top of the application window. The ribbon has been divided into a hierarchy consisting of **tabs**, **groups**, and **commands**. The tabs are divided into groups. The groups contain the commands to perform an action. For example, the Home tab contains a Styles group with options for fonts to use for various levels of headings in a document.

Figure 8-5

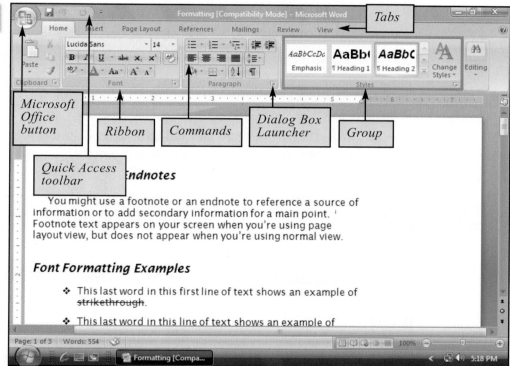

- The **Microsoft Office button** leads to many of the commands that existed on the File menu in previous versions of Office. You can use the Microsoft Office button to create new documents, open existing documents, save documents, print documents, and customize your preferences for Word options such as display elements, document locations, and dictionaries.

- The **Quick Access toolbar** contains commands that you use regularly. Elements of the Quick Access toolbar are completely customizable. Commands can be added by right-clicking a command and then selecting Add to Quick Access toolbar from the shortcut menu.

- **Contextual tabs**, which contain formatting options for an object, appear when the object is selected. For example, in Word after a table is inserted, the Table Tools tab appears. From this tab, you can change borders, insert or delete columns, and change cell properties.

- Dialog boxes can be opened from the **Dialog Box Launcher** in the lower-right corner of a group. For example, in Word the Paragraph dialog box can be launched from the Paragraph group on the Home tab.

FAQ How do I open a file?

Data can be stored in files on your computer's hard disk and on CDs, DVDs, USB flash drives, and other storage media. Files can be referred to in different ways in different programs. For example, a file created with Microsoft Word is usually called a "document," while a Microsoft PowerPoint file is usually called a "presentation."

Before you can work with a file, you must open it. There are several ways to open a file. You can:

● Use the Recent Items option on the Start menu to view a list of recently saved files.

● Double-click a file shortcut icon if one exists on the Windows desktop.

● Double-click a file name from within Windows Explorer.

● Use the Open dialog box provided by an application.

When you use the Open dialog box from within an application window, you'll see a list of files and folders. The dialog box uses file extensions to filter the list of files so that it displays only those files that can be opened with the program.

Figure 8-6

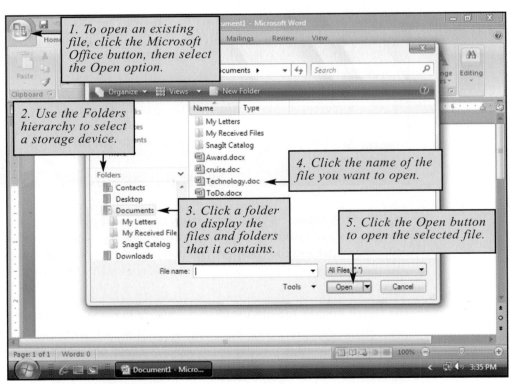

1. To open an existing file, click the Microsoft Office button, then select the Open option.

2. Use the Folders hierarchy to select a storage device.

3. Click a folder to display the files and folders that it contains.

4. Click the name of the file you want to open.

5. Click the Open button to open the selected file.

● Many Windows applications, including Microsoft Office, store files in the Documents folder if no other drive or folder is specified. If you save a file but forget where it went, look in the Documents folder.

FAQ   What if a file doesn't open?

The process of saving and opening files usually goes smoothly, but occasionally you'll encounter file problems. Here's a summary of common problems and their solutions:

- **Storage device not available.** Files can be accessed only if the device on which they are stored is connected to your computer. Before you attempt to open files from a USB flash drive, a LAN server, or Web-based online storage, make sure your computer can access the storage device. As necessary, plug in your USB drive, make sure your LAN connection is active, or make sure you have an Internet connection.

- **File not saved.** If you forgot to save a file before exiting, there's not much hope of retrieving it unless your software provides an autosave feature. **Autosave** periodically saves a file as you're working on it. Check your software's settings to find out if autosave is activated. If so, check Help to find out how to retrieve an autosaved file.

- **File stored in the wrong folder.** If you can't find a file, it might have been inadvertently saved in an unexpected location. Use your operating system's search feature to find the file by name, date, or file type.

- **File moved.** If you moved a file from one folder to another, you won't be able to access it from your software or operating system's recently used files list because those lists point to the original file location. Use your software's Open dialog box to locate and open the file.

- **File is corrupted.** The file might have been damaged—a techie would call it "corrupted"—by a transmission or disk error. You might be able to use file recovery software to repair the damage, but it is usually easier to obtain an undamaged copy of the file from its original source.

- **Incompatible file type.** Most software applications work with a limited number of file types (also referred to as "file formats"), identified by the file's three-character extension. For example, Microsoft Paint opens file types such as Windows Bitmap (.bmp), GIF (.gif), and JPEG (.jpg). If you attempt to use Paint to open a Word document (.docx) file, however, your computer will display an error message: "Paint cannot read this file." To avoid this error, make sure to use the correct application software when you open a file.

- **Wrong association.** Windows Explorer maintains a list of file associations. Each **file association** specifies the software application you'd prefer to use to open files of that type. For example, if Bitmap files are associated with Paint, every time you double-click a file with a .bmp extension, Windows will try to open it in Paint. If the association is wrong, the file might not open. Check Help if you want to alter file associations.

- **File has the wrong extension.** File extensions are sometimes inadvertently changed when a file is renamed. The most prevalent case is when a renamed file ends up with no extension and your computer does not know what software can open it. You can try to guess the file extension and add it. For example, if a file contains a graphic, chances are that it should have an extension such as .bmp, .gif, .jpg, .tif, or .png. If you can't guess the file type, you'll have to locate the original file with its extension intact.

- **Product or version incompatibility.** Some file formats exist in several variations, and your software might not have the capability to open a particular variation of the format. You might be able to open the file if you use different application software. For example, Photoshop might not be able to open a particular file with a .tif file extension, but Corel Paint Shop Pro might open it.

FAQ How do I save a file?

When you create a file on your computer, you must save it if you want to be able to use it again in the future. Make sure you save files before you close their application windows; otherwise, you could lose the work in progress.

Figure 8-7

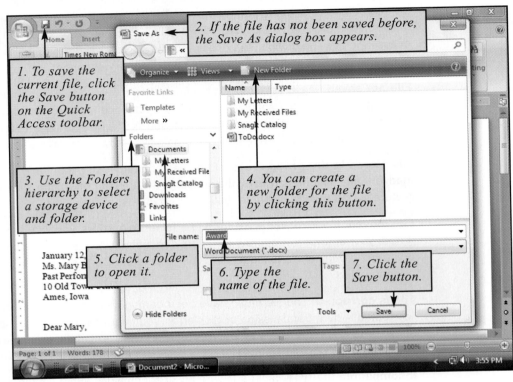

- When you first save a file, you must name it. File names can consist of letters, spaces, numbers, and certain punctuation symbols. File names cannot include the symbols / ? : = < > | and must not be longer than 255 characters. Each folder can contain only one file with a particular file name. However, different documents with the same name can be stored in different folders.

- A file extension is a set of up to four characters that indicates the file type. A file extension is separated from the file name by a period. Windows programs add the appropriate file extension automatically, so you don't have to type it when saving a file. In Office 2007, Word documents are usually saved in with .docx extensions, Excel files with .xlsx extensions, PowerPoint presentations with .pptx extensions, and Access databases with .accdb extensions.

- The Save button works differently, depending on whether the file was previously saved. Clicking the Save button automatically stores a file using the original name, drive, and folder where it was previously stored. If the file hasn't been saved before, clicking the Save button opens the Save As dialog box so that you can select the drive and folder where you want to save the file, enter a file name, then click the Save button.

- If you've modified an existing file and want to save the new version under a different name, click the Microsoft Office button, then click Save As to display the Save As dialog box. Enter a new name and select the drive and folder in which to store the file. The modified version of the file is saved under the new name, leaving the original version of the file unchanged under the original name.

• How do I save a file? (continued)

Many Windows programs are configured to automatically save files in the Documents folder. Other programs are configured to save files in the same directory used for the last save operation. Regardless of the configuration, you have full control over the destination of your files. You can save to the desktop, or to any storage device connected to your computer, including the hard disk drive, floppy disk drive, CD drive, or USB flash drive. You can also save to a network or Internet server if you have access rights and permission to save files.

Each file name extension is associated with a particular file format. For example, the .docx file extension is associated with data files created by Microsoft Word. You can, however, change the format in which a file is saved by using the *Save as type* list provided by the Save As dialog box. For example, you might want to save a document as a template (.dotx) to be used in generating a series of similar documents. You might save a document in Rich Text format (.rtf) or plain text (.txt) format so it can be opened by other word processing software.

You can also use the *Save as type* list to save documents in a format that can be opened by earlier versions of Microsoft Word in case a friend or colleague has not updated to a version of Word that stores files in a format compatible with yours.

Figure 8-8

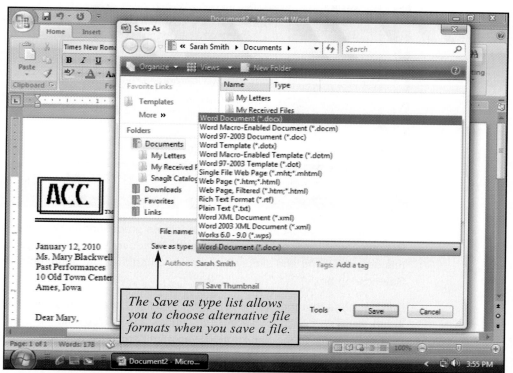

The Save as type list allows you to choose alternative file formats when you save a file.

After you save a file, you can close it or exit the application. Simply closing the file leaves the application open so that you can work on a different file. Closing the application, sometimes referred to as "exiting," closes the file and the application.

- To close a file, but leave the application open, use the Office button or File menu to select the Close option.

- To close the application, click the Close button in the upper-right corner of the application window. Or, you can use the Office button or File menu to select the Exit option.

FAQ How do I change the settings for an application?

Most application software is preconfigured with a set of **application defaults** (sometimes called "preferences" or "default settings") that specify settings, such as where files are stored, which fonts are used to display text, how often files are autosaved, and which printer is used for output. Most software allows you to modify application defaults. Look for Options or Preferences on the File menu or on the Tools menu. Some application defaults, such as settings for autosaving, printing, and file locations, are similar across applications. Other defaults are application specific. Carefully review your application defaults and change those that will streamline your work flow.

Figure 8-9

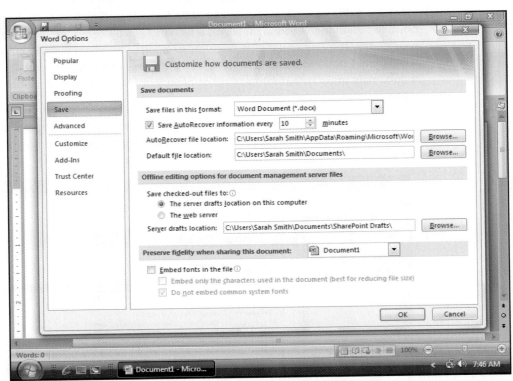

- Microsoft Office applications default to folders predefined in Windows as My Documents (Windows XP) or Documents (Windows Vista). It is a good practice to keep this default setting and simply navigate to an appropriate subdirectory when using the Save dialog box.

- Don't assume that the autosave feature is activated as your application default. Check it and make sure. Although autosave causes a slight reduction in system performance as it saves a file in the background, you'll be happy it is saving copies of your work in case of a power outage or software glitch.

- Be conservative when you change application defaults. Some applications offer hundreds of settings, but the preset defaults usually work for most tasks. When reviewing application defaults, just change a few at a time so that you can easily back track and reestablish the original defaults.

FAQ How do I access help for an application?

While using application software, you can access help from a variety of sources, including on-screen help, printed user manuals, Readme files on a CD, and third-party reference books. The source you turn to first depends on the type of help you need. Typically, general questions about how to use software features can be best answered by on-screen help that explains features and provides step-by-step instructions for their use.

On-screen help is probably the most frequently used help resource. Different programs offer different ways to access on-screen help. For example, Microsoft Office modules offer help through a comprehensive electronic user manual that also connects to Office Online. The help manual provides tools to scan through its Table of Contents, type a question, or look for keywords in the Help window.

Play It!

Figure 8–10

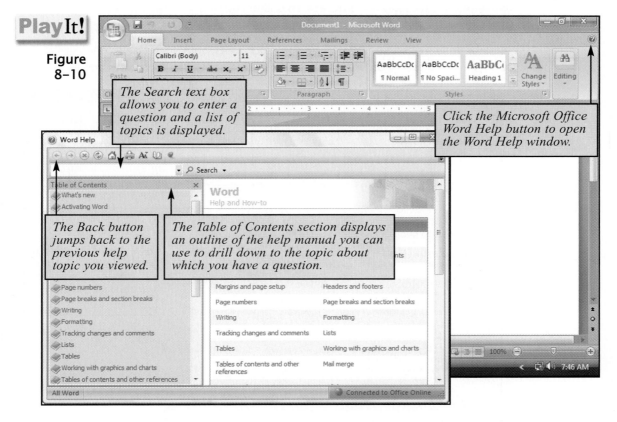

The Search text box allows you to enter a question and a list of topics is displayed.

Click the Microsoft Office Word Help button to open the Word Help window.

The Back button jumps back to the previous help topic you viewed.

The Table of Contents section displays an outline of the help manual you can use to drill down to the topic about which you have a question.

- You can access the electronic user manual for Microsoft Office modules by clicking the Help button in the top-right corner of the application window. You can also access the manual by pressing the F1 function key at the top of your keyboard.

- The Office Help window remains open on the desktop until you click its Close button. If the Help window drops back behind other windows, you can use its taskbar button to bring it to the top of the desktop.

- Microsoft Office applications automatically include online help if your computer is connected to the Internet. The Help window toolbar lets you know if you're not connected and gives you the option of going online.

● How do I access help for an application? (continued)

When on-screen help does not provide answers, you can turn to other sources of information. If you have questions about work-related procedures, your first source of information should be your organization's help desk. Sometimes, coworkers and friends are willing to answer your questions.

If a feature doesn't seem to work as explained in documentation and user manuals, consider checking online user groups or the publisher's Web site for up-to-date information. Some software publishers offer phone support to customers, but you might experience a long wait before a technician is available. You can often find answers more quickly by searching through the publisher's knowledge base or list of FAQs. These sources of information are particularly useful for troubleshooting problems and making sense of error messages. To access an online knowledge base, connect to the publisher's Web site and look for a Support link.

Another option is to use a search engine, such as Google, to get help. For example, you can type in the text of an error message to find the cause of a problem and its solution.

Figure 8–11

When you use a search engine such as Google to get help, you'll get targeted results if you include the full title and version of the software you're using, along with keywords specifically related to your question.

QuickCheck A

1. Before you close an application window, you should [   ] any work in progress.

2. Although multiple programs can be open at the same time, only one program can be [   ].

3. True or false? When you open a file, you have to know which file name extensions the program can work with. [   ]

4. Most applications save files in the [   ] folder.

5. True or false? The first time you save a file, you will use the Save As dialog box to assign the file a name and specify its location. [   ]

Check It!

QuickCheck B

Indicate the letter of the application window element that best matches the following:

1. The Save button [   ]

2. The application window's taskbar button [   ]

3. The Close button [   ]

4. The horizontal scroll bar [   ]

5. The Home tab [   ]

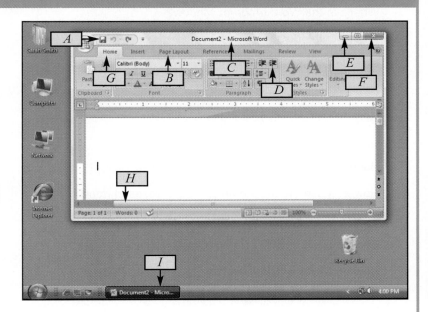

Check It!

CHAPTER **9**

Creating a Document

What's Inside and on the CD?

Microsoft Word is the component of Microsoft Office best suited for creating documents such as letters and reports. As word processing software, Microsoft Word provides a set of tools for entering and revising text, adding graphical elements such as color and tables, and then formatting and printing completed documents.

Most people use Microsoft Word more frequently than any other component of Microsoft Office. Microsoft Word is an excellent tool for creating documents of all sorts—from personal letters to business proposals.

In this chapter, you'll learn how to create documents using Microsoft Word. Then you'll learn how to select and edit text, check spelling, use the electronic thesaurus, and specify print options. You'll also learn how to use document templates to quickly generate common types of documents.

FAQ What's in the Word program window?

The Word program window appears when you start Microsoft Word. To start Word, click Start, point to All Programs, click Microsoft Office, then click Microsoft Office Word 2007. Components of the Word program window include the title bar, ribbon, status bar, views, and document workspace. You'll use these elements of the Word program window to create, edit, save, print, and format your documents.

Figure 9–1

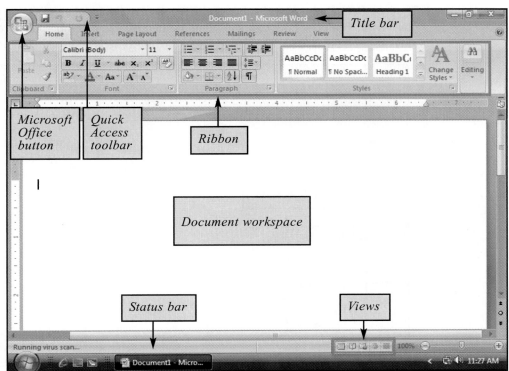

- The **document workspace** represents a blank piece of paper. Characters that you type on the keyboard appear in the document workspace. The title bar indicates the name of the current document. If the current document has never been saved, the title bar displays the generic title Document1. Word's ribbon contains commands and tools that you can use to create and edit your document.

- There are different ways to view your document. The **Draft view** allows quick text editing and formatting; headers and footers are not visible. The **Web Layout view** shows how your document would look in a Web browser. The **Print Layout view** shows how the content will look on the printed page, complete with margins, headers, and footers. The **Full Screen Reading view** displays your document with minimized toolbars at the top of the window. You can also work in **Outline view** to look at the structure of a document.

- The status bar provides information about the document displayed in the window and displays a Zoom control. The information can include page numbers and word count. If you right-click the status bar, you can customize the information displayed.

- You can increase or decrease the zoom level to view the document at various sizes by adjusting the Zoom level on the status bar.

FAQ What's in the document workspace?

The blank document workspace is bordered by scroll bars and a ruler. The scroll bars help you quickly navigate through a document. The rulers help you gauge how the spacing of your on-screen document translates to the space on a printed page. For example, if you've specified one-inch margins, the text that you enter into the workspace will be positioned to the right of the 1" mark on the ruler.

The insertion point is a vertical bar, which indicates the location of the next character you'll type. The I-bar pointer is different than the insertion point. You move the I-bar by moving the mouse. Use the I-bar to select text and reposition the insertion point.

Figure 9–2

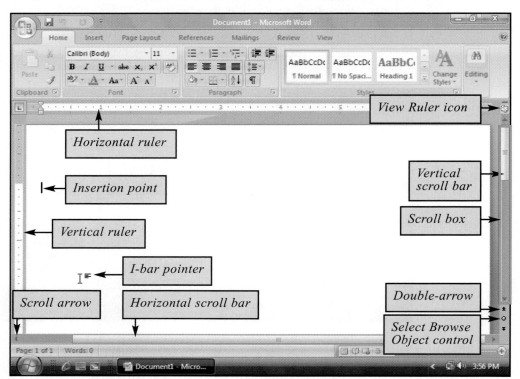

- You can set Word to display a horizontal ruler, a vertical ruler, both, or none. Use the View Ruler icon or the View menu to display or hide rulers.

- The scroll bars offer several ways to navigate a document. Drag the scroll box to smoothly scroll to any part of the document. Click the scroll arrows to move up or down one line at a time.

- When working with lengthy documents, the Select Browse Object control lets you jump to various objects, such as charts, comments, footnotes, tables, or headings.

- Double-arrows on the vertical scroll bar work in conjunction with the Select Browse Object control. If that control is set to *Page*, then the double-arrows take you to the previous or next page. If you have the Browse control set to *Charts*, the double-arrows take you to the previous or next chart.

FAQ How do I create a document?

To create a new document, just click the blank document workspace and start typing. When typing a document, don't worry too much about spelling, formatting, or arranging the document. It is very easy to edit and format a document after you've entered the text.

Figure 9–3

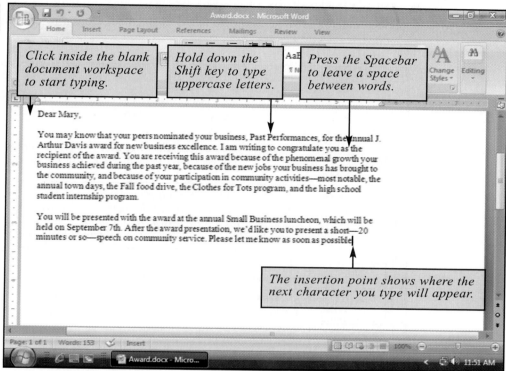

- The **insertion point** indicates your current location in the document. As you type, the insertion point moves to show where the next character will appear. Click anywhere in the document workspace to move the insertion point to that location. The insertion point is sometimes referred to as the cursor.

- Through a feature known as **word wrap**, the insertion point automatically jumps down to the beginning of the next line when you reach the right margin of the current line. If the last word you type is too long for the line, it is moved down to the beginning of the next line. Press the Enter key only when you complete a paragraph. Press the Enter key a second time to create a blank line between paragraphs.

- Press the Backspace key to delete the character to the *left* of the insertion point. You can also press the Delete key to delete the character to the *right* of the insertion point. These keys also work to erase spaces and blank lines.

- To add text in the middle of a line or word, use the mouse or arrow keys to move the insertion point to the desired location, then type the text you want to add. To make room for new text, everything to the right of the insertion point is pushed to the right and down as you type.

- Use the Insert key to toggle between Overtype and Insert mode. Overtype mode causes new characters to be typed over existing characters. Insert mode causes new characters to be inserted at the current location in the document.

- Insert special characters, such as the trademark symbol, by clicking the Insert tab, clicking the Symbol command, then clicking More Symbols. Select the symbol you want to insert, click Insert, then click Close to close the Symbols dialog box.

FAQ How do I select text for editing?

Many word processing features require you to select a section of text before you edit, change, or format it. When you **select text**, you are marking characters, words, phrases, sentences, or paragraphs to modify in some way. Selecting text doesn't do anything useful by itself, but combined with other commands, it enables you to use many of the other important features of Word. Selected text is highlighted. Word provides several ways to select text.

Figure 9–4

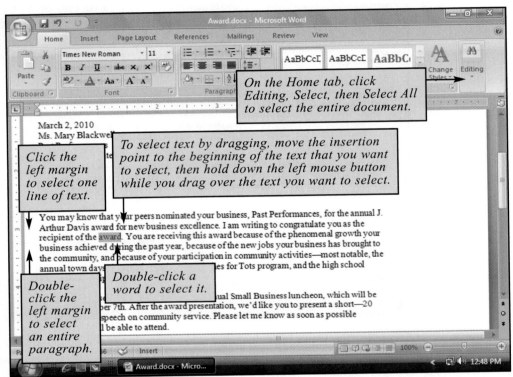

On the Home tab, click Editing, Select, then Select All to select the entire document.

To select text by dragging, move the insertion point to the beginning of the text that you want to select, then hold down the left mouse button while you drag over the text you want to select.

Click the left margin to select one line of text.

Double-click a word to select it.

Double-click the left margin to select an entire paragraph.

- Use the drag method to select short sections of text, such as a few characters or several words. Use one of the other selection methods when you need to select a single word, a line, a paragraph, or the entire document.

- When you point to a word, you can double-click to select only that word. You can triple-click to select the current paragraph.

- When you point to the left margin, the pointer changes to a white arrow. You can click once to select a line of text or double-click to select a paragraph.

- If you have trouble using the mouse, you can also use the keyboard to select text. Use the mouse or arrow keys to move the insertion point to the beginning of the text that you want to select. Hold the Shift key down while you use the arrow keys to select text.

- To deselect text, you should click away from the text that is currently selected. You can also press one of the arrow keys to deselect text.

- To select a section of text, such as several paragraphs, click at the beginning of the selection, then Shift-click at the end. You can also select non-contiguous text by selecting the first word or section, then using Ctrl-click to select subsequent sections.

FAQ How do I move, copy, and delete text?

As you create a document, you might want to move or copy sections of text—words, paragraphs, or even entire pages—from one part of the document to another. To copy or move text, you use the **Clipboard**, a special memory location that temporarily holds sections of your document.

Play It!

Figure 9–5

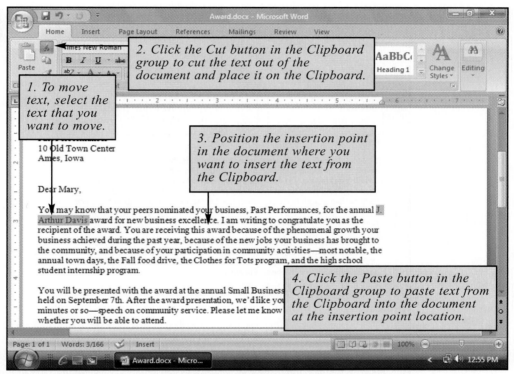

- To move a section of text from one part of your document to another, first select the text, then click the ✂ Cut button. The selected text is cut out of the document and placed on the Clipboard. To paste that text back into the document, move the insertion point to the place where you want to position the text, then click the 📋 Paste button. The text is copied from the Clipboard and placed into the document. This operation is known as **cut and paste**.

- You can also cut and paste using the drag-and-drop method. Select the text you wish to cut, and use the mouse to drag it to the new location.

- **Copy and paste** works much the same way as cut and paste, except that the text is not removed from its original location. Select the text you want to copy, then click the 📋 Copy button. The selected text is copied to the Clipboard, but the original text is not removed from the document. Move the insertion point to the place where you want to place the copy, then click the Paste button.

- After you cut or copy, the copied text remains on the Clipboard. You can use this feature when you need to put several copies of the same text into your document. Just move the insertion point to the location where you want to place the next copy and click the Paste button. You can paste as many copies of the text as you like.

- You can cut and paste text, hypertext links, graphics, tables, and other objects between different applications, such as pasting Excel worksheet data into a Word document.

FAQ Can I undo a command?

If you perform an action and then change your mind, you may be able to use the Undo button to undo the action. The Undo button has a counterpart—the Redo button—that allows you to repeat an action that you mistakenly undid. The Repeat button is used to repeat your last action.

Play It!

Figure 9-6

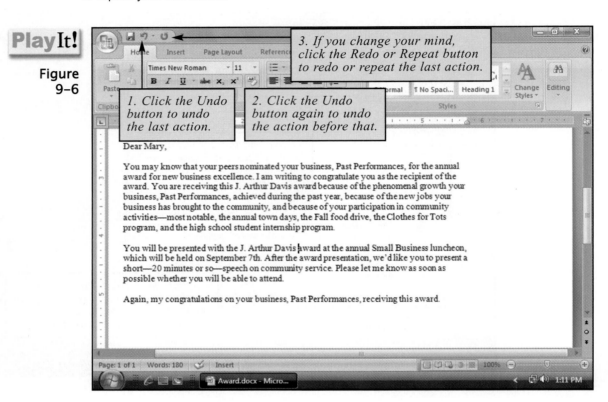

3. If you change your mind, click the Redo or Repeat button to redo or repeat the last action.

1. Click the Undo button to undo the last action.

2. Click the Undo button again to undo the action before that.

- If there are no actions that can be undone or redone, the Undo and Redo buttons are disabled—they appear grayed out and nothing happens if you click them.

- The Undo button works best when undoing an editing or formatting command. Actions such as saving and printing files cannot be undone.

- If you need to undo a series of actions, click the down-arrow button on the right side of the Undo button to display a list of actions that can be undone. Drag down the list to highlight the actions you want to undo. You can also click a specific action to select it, but all the actions prior to that one will also be performed.

- To repeat an action, click the Repeat button.

FAQ How do I check spelling, grammar, and readability?

Microsoft Word provides tools to help you check spelling and grammar in your documents. You should use these tools for all documents before printing them—it only takes a few minutes and can help you catch embarrassing mistakes. However, you should also proofread your documents carefully. You can't depend on the spelling and grammar checker to identify all mistakes or to make sure your document says what you really mean it to say.

In addition to spelling and grammar, you can check the readability of a document by displaying **readability statistics** based on your document's average number of syllables per word and words per sentence. Readability statistics are summarized as a score between 1 and 100 (aim for a score of 60–70) or a grade level (aim for 7th or 8th grade).

Figure 9–7

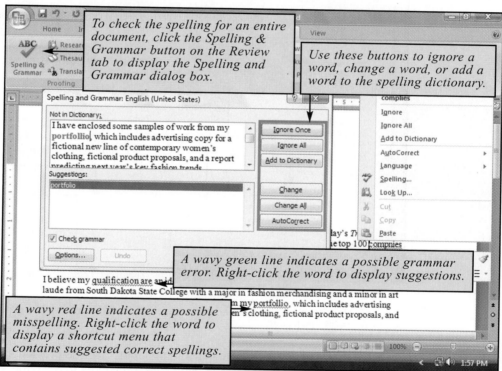

To check the spelling for an entire document, click the Spelling & Grammar button on the Review tab to display the Spelling and Grammar dialog box.

Use these buttons to ignore a word, change a word, or add a word to the spelling dictionary.

A wavy green line indicates a possible grammar error. Right-click the word to display suggestions.

A wavy red line indicates a possible misspelling. Right-click the word to display a shortcut menu that contains suggested correct spellings.

- If you don't see any wavy lines, spelling and grammar checking might be turned off. Click the Microsoft Office button, then click the Word Options button. On the Proofing tab, select *Check spelling as you type*.

- You can also check the spelling and grammar of a complete document by clicking the Spelling & Grammar button on the Review tab. Words that might be misspelled are shown in red. Possible grammar mistakes are shown in green. You can click the appropriate buttons to ignore or replace each word or phrase.

- Readability statistics are shown at the end of a spelling and grammar check if the statistics feature is turned on. To turn on this feature, click the Microsoft Office button, then click the Word Options button. On the Proofing tab, select *Show readability statistics*.

FAQ How do I use the thesaurus and other research tools?

A thesaurus contains synonyms for words and some common phrases. When you are composing a document and can't think of just the right word, you can type the closest word that comes to mind, and then use Word's thesaurus to search for words with a similar meaning.

Figure 9–8

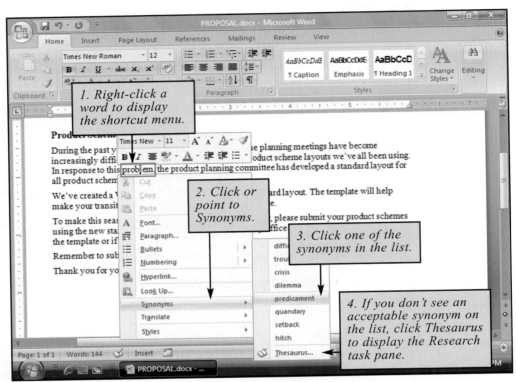

- You can also access Word's thesaurus through the Review tab. Click the Review tab, then click Thesaurus.

- To find a synonym for a phrase, select the phrase, then right-click it to display the shortcut menu. Point to Synonyms, then click Thesaurus to open the Research task pane. A list of phrases appears. Sometimes you'll find an acceptable alternate phrase, but beware—some of the phrases listed might not be appropriate substitutes.

- Microsoft Word's Proofing group offers additional wordsmithing tools that are especially handy when working with multiple-language documents and when English is your second language. The Translate tool translates a word or sentence into another language. The Research tool lets you search for a word or phrase in a variety of local and online sources, such as encyclopedias, atlases, and multi-language thesauri.

FAQ Can I search for text and make global changes?

Suppose you've written a short story and just as you're about to wind up the plot, you decide to change the name of the main character. Or imagine that you discover you've misspelled the name of a pharmaceutical product that's the topic of a lengthy report. Will you have to carefully read through your document to locate every instance that needs to be changed? No, you can use Word's search and replace function.

Figure
9-9

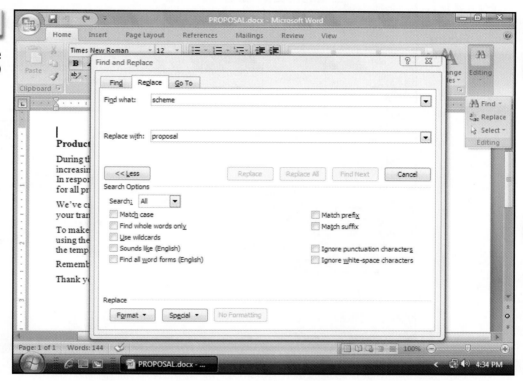

- When you enter replacement text, use capitalization only if you want all instances of the replacement text to be capitalized, as would be the case with proper names.

- If you enter the replacement text in all lowercase, Word will change the case to match the original text. For example, if you want to replace "tornado" with "windstorm," enter "windstorm" in lowercase. If Word finds "tornado" it will replace it with "windstorm," but "Tornado" will be replaced with "Windstorm."

- Word looks for your search string in any part of a word, so searching for "process" will produce matches for "microprocessor" and "processing." If you are simply looking for the word "process," use the *Find whole words only* option in the Find and Replace dialog box.

- The *Sounds like* option lets you find words even if you are not sure how to spell them.

- You can use wildcards, such as ? and *. For example, searching for b?n finds ban and bin. Searching for b*k finds beak, book, back, and so on. Refer to Word Help for more details about wildcards.

FAQ How do I use a document template?

You can create a document from scratch by entering text in the blank, new document workspace. As an alternative, you can use a **document template**, which is a pre-formatted document that can be used as the foundation for creating a new document. Word includes templates for many basic document types, such as letters, faxes, and resumes.

Play It!

Figure
9–10

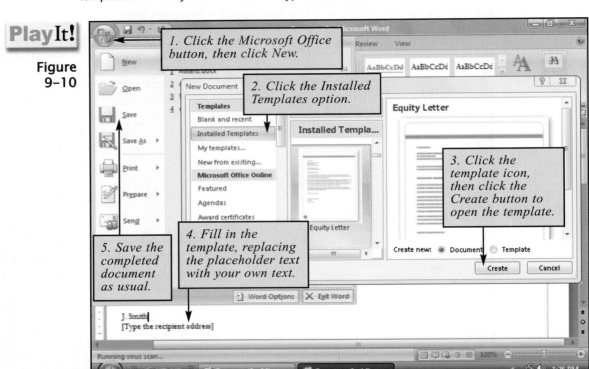

1. Click the Microsoft Office button, then click New.

2. Click the Installed Templates option.

3. Click the template icon, then click the Create button to open the template.

4. Fill in the template, replacing the placeholder text with your own text.

5. Save the completed document as usual.

- A **placeholder** is an element in a document template into which you enter text that personalizes your document. Common placeholders provide entry areas for today's date, your name, or your fax number. To use a placeholder, click inside it and type your own text. The placeholder disappears and your text is displayed.

- Word allows you to create your own document templates. After you're more familiar with Word, you might want to explore this feature to create templates for documents that you create on a regular basis. You can find more information about creating templates in Word Help and in the program documentation.

- If you work in a large business or organization, you might be required to use templates created by managers, supervisors, or designers. Some examples of document templates used in businesses are letterheads, fax cover sheets, memos, and reports. Requiring these official templates helps businesses maintain professional standards.

FAQ How do I save a document?

After you have created a document from scratch or personalized a document template, it's important to save the document properly so that you can find and use it again. The first time you save your document, be sure to store it in the correct location with the appropriate file type.

Play It!

Figure 9–11

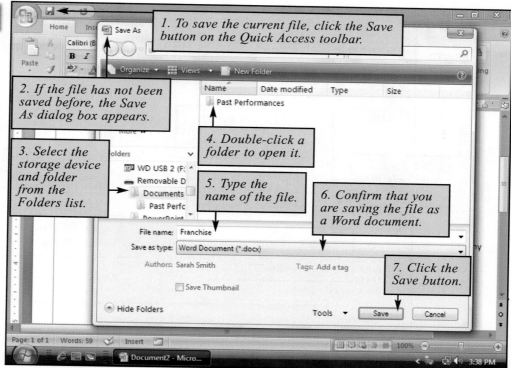

1. To save the current file, click the Save button on the Quick Access toolbar.

2. If the file has not been saved before, the Save As dialog box appears.

3. Select the storage device and folder from the Folders list.

4. Double-click a folder to open it.

5. Type the name of the file.

6. Confirm that you are saving the file as a Word document.

7. Click the Save button.

- The first time you save your document, the Save As dialog box appears. By default, Word saves your file in the Documents folder as a Word document with a .docx extension. You can save the document in another location by selecting a different drive and folder.

- You can save your document as a different file type if you click the down-arrow button to the right of the *Save as type* text box. For instance, you might want to save the document in DOC format so it can be opened on a computer with an earlier version of Microsoft Office, such as Office 2003. You can also save a document in formats such as PDF, TXT, and RTF.

- After you save the document the first time, you can save it more quickly by using the Save button. This action automatically saves the document using the original file name and storage location. It's a good idea to save frequently as you work on a document to minimize the chance of losing data as a result of a power outage, software bug, or other unforeseen event.

FAQ How do I print a document?

You can print a document using the Print option available through the Microsoft Office button. Options to print multiple copies of a document, print selected pages, or select an alternate printer are displayed in the Print dialog box. To access the Print dialog box, click the Microsoft Office button and then click Print.

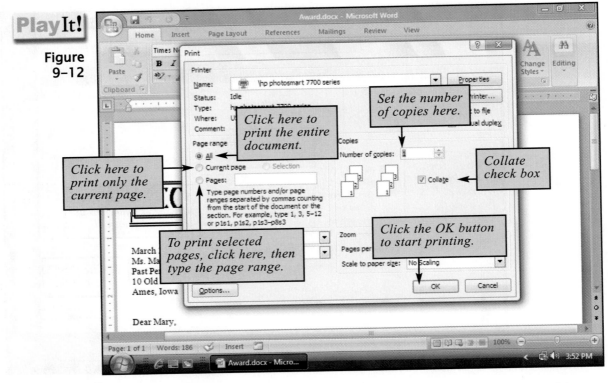

Play It!

Figure 9-12

- You can select a printer by clicking the down-arrow button at the right side of the Printer list, then clicking the printer you want to use.

- To print a range of pages, enter the first page, a hyphen, then the last page in the range. For example, to print pages 13 through 28, you would enter 13–28. To print specific pages that are not in a sequence, click the Pages option button, then enter the page numbers, such as 3, 7, 12, in the Pages text box, separated by commas.

- To print more than one copy of a document, use the *Number of copies* spin box.

- When the Collate option is checked, each copy of a document prints in sequential page number so you don't have to collate it manually.

- Duplex printers can automatically print on both sides of the paper. You can simulate duplex printing using the Manual duplex option and turning the paper when prompted to do so.

- Before you print a document, you can use Print Preview to see how it will look when printed. The preview appears when you click the Microsoft Office button, click the arrow next to Print, then click Print Preview. The Print Preview toolbar provides options for adjusting the magnification and number of pages displayed. If the preview is acceptable, click the Print button provided on the preview screen to print the document. To exit Print Preview without printing, click the Close Print Preview button.

FAQ How can I troubleshoot printing problems?

Suppose you print a document but nothing happens! Printing problems can be caused by the printer, by the software that controls the printer, or by installation glitches. Luckily, most printing problems are easily fixed. Your first step is to check the power light to make sure the printer is turned on. Also, verify that the printer is ready to print by pressing the appropriate buttons on the printer's control panel. You should also make sure the printer is loaded with the correct size and type of paper, and the ribbon, print cartridge, or toner cartridge is properly installed.

If the printer checks out, your next step is to check the print queue. A **print queue** manages multiple documents waiting to be printed. When one document is printed, the next document in the print queue is sent to the printer. Each printer connected to your computer has a separate print queue. You can use a print queue to display information about each print job; to pause, restart, or cancel print jobs; and to move documents higher or lower in the queue. If your computer is connected to more than one printer, use the print queue to make sure you sent the document to the correct printer.

Figure 9–13

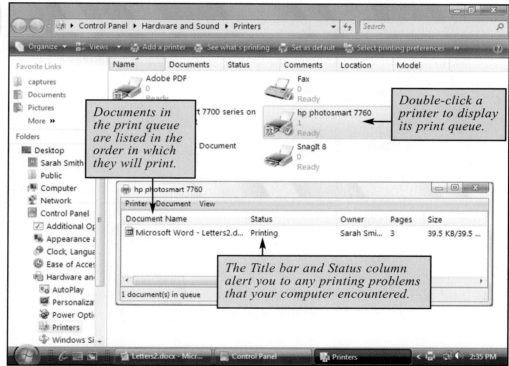

Documents in the print queue are listed in the order in which they will print.

Double-click a printer to display its print queue.

The Title bar and Status column alert you to any printing problems that your computer encountered.

- You can view the print queue at any time by clicking the Start button, clicking Control Panel, and then clicking Printers under the Hardware and Sound section. Double-click the printer that corresponds to the print queue you want to view.

- To pause, restart, or cancel a print job, right-click the name of the print job and choose the desired option from the shortcut menu.

- If the printer is shared, other people might have documents in the print queue ahead of yours. Check the print queue to see if your document is waiting to be printed.

• How can I troubleshoot printing problems? (continued)

If your computer's Printers window contains icons for several printers, only one of those printers can be designated as the default printer. All documents are sent to the default printer unless you specify otherwise. A common printing problem occurs when you connect a different printer to your computer but forget to change the default printer. When a printing problem occurs, make sure the default printer setting is correct.

To change the default printer, click the Start button, click Control Panel, and then click Printers under the Hardware and Sound section. Right-click the printer you want to set as the default printer, and choose Set as Default Printer.

The Printer Properties dialog box is another useful tool for troubleshooting printing problems. From the Printers window, right-click a printer and select Properties. You can use this dialog box to change print settings, activate printer sharing, check the port used to connect your printer and computer, and even print out a test page. Printing a test page can help you determine if the printer is connected correctly.

Figure 9–14

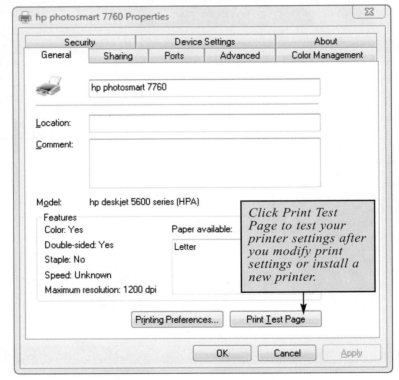

A document might not print if the page settings are not specified correctly on the Page Setup dialog box. Some printers cannot print outside of certain page boundaries, or are limited to certain page sizes. Check your printer documentation for details, and verify that the margins and page size are correct by clicking the Page Layout tab, then clicking the Page Setup Dialog Box Launcher.

Another potential cause of printing problems is the printer driver software used by your computer to control the printer. If you can't find any other solution, check with your printer's manufacturer to see if an updated printer driver is available. Updated printer drivers are typically posted online and can be easily downloaded and installed.

QuickCheck A

1. True or false? In the document workspace, the insertion point is shaped like an I-bar.

   [＿＿＿＿＿]

2. Press the [＿＿＿＿＿＿＿＿＿＿] key to delete the character to the right of the insertion point.

3. When you copy text, the selected text is copied from the original location and placed on the [＿＿＿＿＿＿＿＿] .

4. True or false? If you accidentally delete the wrong text, you can click the Redo button to cancel the deletion and display the original text. [＿＿＿＿＿]

5. A document [＿＿＿＿＿] allows you to create a new document from a pre-formatted document.

Check It!

QuickCheck B

Indicate the letter of the desktop element that best matches the following:

1. Selected text [＿＿＿]

2. The Copy button [＿＿＿]

3. The Paste button [＿＿＿]

4. The Cut button [＿＿＿]

5. The end of a line of text where the Enter key was pressed [＿＿＿]

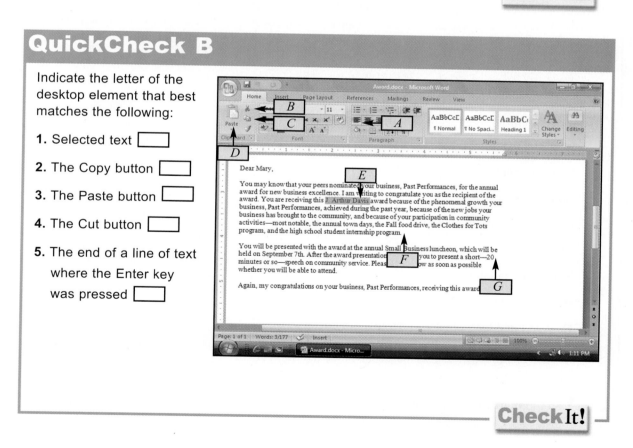

Check It!

Formatting a Document

What's Inside and on the CD?

In this chapter, you'll learn how to format your documents using features such as bold and italic text, different fonts and font sizes, line spacing, and paragraph alignment. You'll also learn how to use tables, bullets, and numbered lists to organize and present information.

Experienced word processing software users find that it's useful to apply formatting after writing the document. The idea is to focus initially on the content of the document, while adding, deleting, and moving text as needed. After you're satisfied with the content and order of the document, you can go back and format the document as needed.

Appropriate formatting can greatly increase the attractiveness and readability of your documents. However, it's important not to get carried away with formatting. Use different fonts, font sizes, and colors only where they add to the appearance or readability of the document. After all, you wouldn't want your documents to look like a ransom note pasted together with letters from a variety of newspaper stories!

FAQ How do I select different fonts, font sizes, and text colors?

You can use the commands on the Home tab to select different text attributes for letters, words, sentences, or paragraphs. The term **font** refers to the design or typeface of each character. Don't use too many fonts—documents look more professional when limited to one or two basic fonts.

Figure 10-1

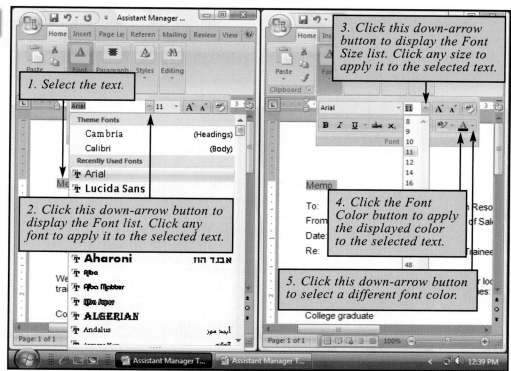

- **Text attributes** include font, font size, bold, italic, underline, and text color. Font size is normally 9–12 points, but you can select any font size up to 72 points, which is equal to one inch. You can make text even larger by typing in a number larger than 72 up to 1638. This feature is useful for making signs and posters.

- Once you've selected text, you can change the font, font size, and color without reselecting the text. As long as the text remains selected, you can apply additional formatting options to it. After you've formatted the text, click anywhere outside of the highlighted area to deselect it.

- **Font effects** include superscript, subscript, shadow, outline, and emboss. To apply font effects, select the text, then click the Font Dialog Box Launcher in the Font group. Choose the effects you want to apply, and click OK.

- If you want to change the font or font size for an entire document, click Editing, Select, then Select All on the Home tab to select the entire document. Using Select All, you can apply any text attributes to all the text in a document, even to multiple pages.

FAQ How do I apply bold, italic, and underlining attributes?

You can use the commands in the Font group to apply text attributes such as bold, italic, and underlining to text within your document.

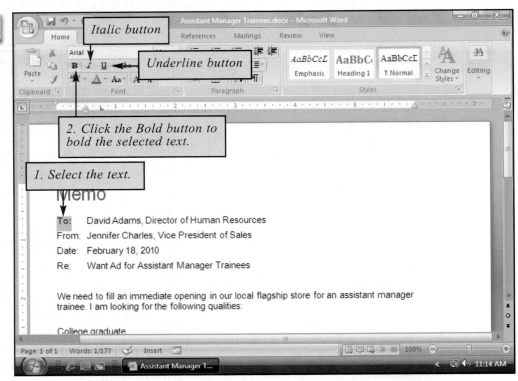

Play It!

Figure 10–2

- Typically, you'll apply text attributes to text you've already typed. Just select the text, then use the desired command button in the Font group to apply the text attribute.

- You can apply the bold text attribute before typing new text. Click the Bold button, then type the text. Click the Bold button again to discontinue bold and continue typing normal text. The Italic button and the Underline button work the same way as the Bold button, but they apply different text attributes.

- Toolbar buttons both apply and remove text attributes. For instance, suppose that you apply the bold attribute, but then change your mind and want to display the text as normal. Select the text, and then click the Bold button again to remove the bold attribute.

- If you select a section of text that includes both normal and bold text, the first time you click the Bold button, all the selected text is displayed as bold. Click the Bold button again to display all of the selected text as normal text.

- Word automatically formats hyperlinks to Web pages such as www.facebook.com and displays them in underlined, blue text. This is a special type of underlining; it is not controlled by the Underline command button. To change the format of a hyperlink, right-click it and select an option from the shortcut menu that appears.

- WordArt offers fancy font effects that you can use for the text on posters and elsewhere. To add WordArt effects to selected text, click WordArt on the Insert tab, select a style, specify a font size, and then apply any additional formatting using the WordArt styles group.

FAQ How do I use the Font dialog box?

As you've already learned, you can apply some text attributes—such as bold, italic, and underlining—using the Font group on the Home tab. But other text attribute options, such as character-spacing options, are only available from the Font dialog box.

You can also use the Font dialog box if you want to apply multiple formatting options to selected text. It's faster to use the Font dialog box to apply all the attributes in one operation than to apply the attributes one at a time using the command buttons.

Figure 10-3

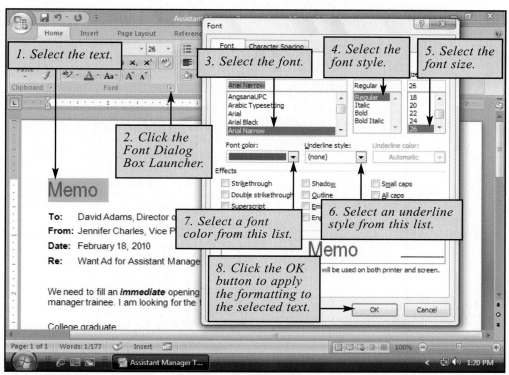

- Use the Character Spacing tab in the Font dialog box if you need to change the scale, spacing, vertical position, or kerning of selected text. Changing the **kerning**—the space between each letter—can be particularly useful when you need to make text fit into a limited space.

- The Preview area of the Font dialog box shows how your formatting affects the selected text. You'll see the selected font, font styles, colors, and effects before you click the OK button to accept your changes. If you don't like what you see in the Preview area, you can adjust the format settings or click the Cancel button to close the Font dialog box without applying the formatting options.

FAQ How do I center and align text?

The Paragraph group on the Home tab provides options for centering, right-aligning, left-aligning, and justifying text.

Left-aligned text is positioned straight against the left margin, but appears uneven, or "ragged," on the right margin. **Centered text** is positioned between the margins and is typically used for titles. **Justified text** has both left and right margins aligned. You might want to use justified text in the body of a formal document to give it a more professional look. **Right-aligned text** is rarely used, but can be useful for headings in a paper, for example, or for the return address in a letter.

Figure 10-4

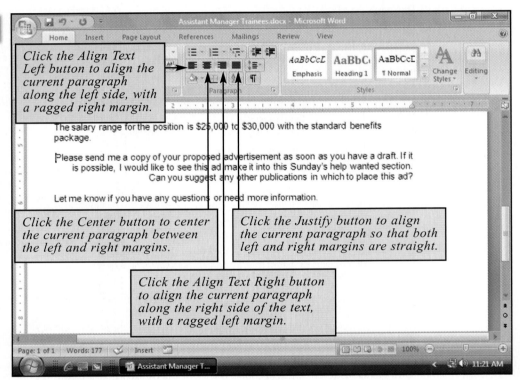

- Unlike bold, italic, and underlining, alignment options apply to an entire paragraph. You don't have to select the text to align it—just click in the paragraph you want to align, then click the appropriate alignment button.

- To center a title, press the Enter key at the end of the title so it becomes a separate paragraph. Click anywhere in the title, then click the Center button. Single lines, such as titles, are centered between the left and right margins. If the paragraph consists of multiple lines, every line in the paragraph is centered.

- To return a centered paragraph to left alignment, click in the paragraph, then click the Align Text Left button.

FAQ How do I use styles?

When formatting a document, select font and paragraph styles that fit the purpose of your document and the needs of the reader. A **style** consists of predefined formatting that you can apply to selected text. Word comes with several predefined styles. Using them will help you avoid design errors such as tight line spacing and ragged margins. Styles also allow you to be consistent in formatting text throughout a document.

In addition to predefined styles, you can create your own. If you find yourself regularly applying multiple format settings to sections of text, you can save time by defining your own style, then applying it as needed.

Figure 10–5

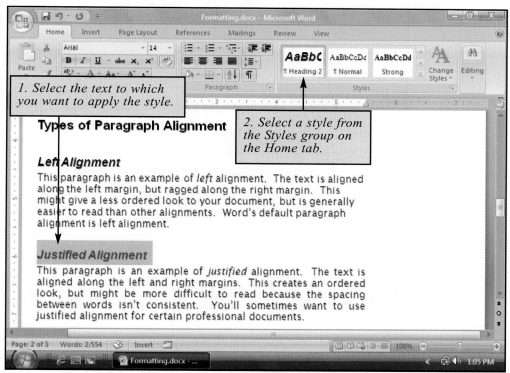

1. Select the text to which you want to apply the style.

2. Select a style from the Styles group on the Home tab.

- To create a style, format a section of text using the desired font, font size, and font styles. Click the Styles Dialog Box Launcher to display the Styles dialog box. Click the New Style button to display the Create New Style from Formatting dialog box. Click the Name text box, then type the name for your new style. Click the OK button to close the Create New Style from Formatting dialog box. Click the Close button to close the Styles dialog box. Your new style is added to the Styles list. To apply the style to other text, select the text, then select your style from the Styles list.

- To remove a style from a section of text, select the text, then select the Normal style from the Styles list.

- To delete a style so that it no longer appears in the Styles list, click the Styles Dialog Box Launcher to display the Styles dialog box. Right-click the style you want to delete, then select Delete. Click Yes, then click the Close button to close the Styles dialog box.

FAQ How do I add numbering and bullets to a list?

Word's Paragraph group on the Home tab contains buttons to format a list with bullets or numbers. A **bullet** is a symbol placed before each item in a list. You can use bullets when you want to set off the items in a list but don't want to imply a specific order. A numbered list is a list with a number in front of each item on the list, which implies the items are listed in order.

Play It!

Figure 10-6

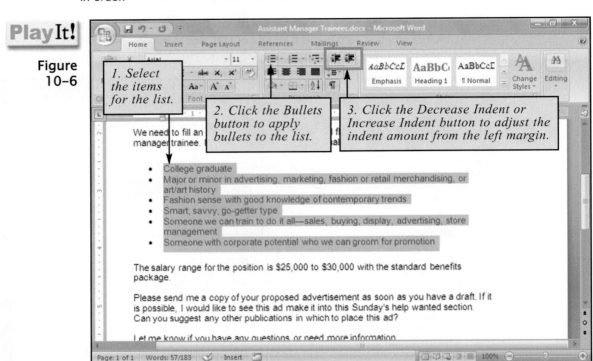

1. Select the items for the list.

2. Click the Bullets button to apply bullets to the list.

3. Click the Decrease Indent or Increase Indent button to adjust the indent amount from the left margin.

- Numbered lists work the same as bulleted lists. Select the items on the list, then click the ⊞ Numbering button to add numbers to the list.

- If you haven't typed the list yet, click the Numbering or Bullets button, then type the items on the list. Each time you press the Enter key, a new number or bullet is inserted before the next list item. At the end of the list, press the Enter key and click the Numbering or Bullets button to discontinue the numbering for the next line of text.

- To remove numbering or bullets from a list, select the list, then click the Numbering or Bullets button.

- If you add, delete, or move the items on a numbered list, Word renumbers the list for you. If the numbering is incorrect, select the list, then click the Numbering button twice. This procedure removes and then reapplies the numbering, which usually corrects any problem with the numbers on the list.

- To change the numbered or bulleted list style, select the list, then right-click the list to display the shortcut menu. Point to Bullets or Numbering, then select a format.

● **How do I add numbering and bullets to a list? (continued)**

A multilevel list displays list items in levels and sublevels. Common uses for multilevel lists include topic outlines and legal documents. Multilevel lists can be numbered, lettered, or bulleted using a variety of predefined or customized styles.

Although you can apply bullets or numbering to a multilevel list after entering the list, the more typical procedure is to activate the Multilevel List button before you enter the list items.

Figure 10–7

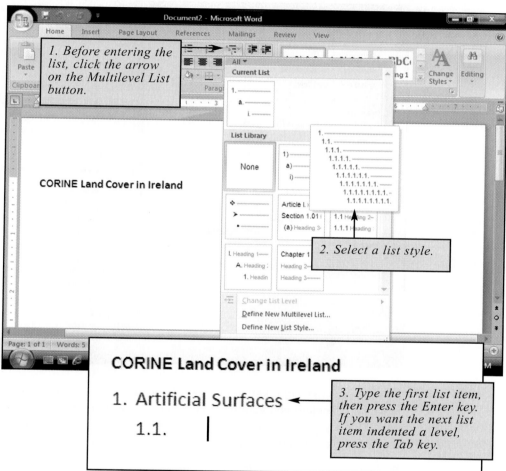

● Pressing the Enter key as you type a list automatically displays the next list number, letter, or bullet.

● Press the Tab key to change a list item to the next level down. Use Shift+Tab to move a list item up a level.

● You can define custom styles for the text, numbers, and bullets in a list by clicking the arrow next to the Multilevel List button, then selecting Define New Paragraph. This option is especially handy for creating a list format that you want to reuse for multiple documents.

● When entering a list, you can change a number manually by right-clicking the number and selecting Set Numbering Value from the shortcut menu. The shortcut menu contains options for starting a new list and continuing the numbering from a previous list.

FAQ How do I adjust line spacing?

Your Word document is single-spaced unless you specify another spacing option, such as double- or triple-spacing. You can apply line-spacing options to a single paragraph, to a group of paragraphs, or to the entire document. You can also adjust the space between paragraphs. Single-spacing is appropriate for letters and memos, whereas double-spacing is often used for first drafts of manuscripts and reports.

Figure 10-8

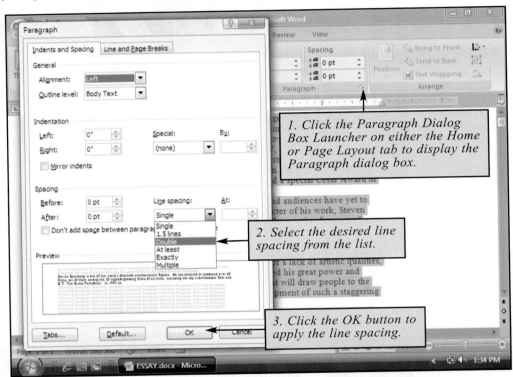

1. Click the Paragraph Dialog Box Launcher on either the Home or Page Layout tab to display the Paragraph dialog box.

2. Select the desired line spacing from the list.

3. Click the OK button to apply the line spacing.

- Do not press the Enter key at the end of each line to create double-spaced text. This makes it difficult to edit your document because words won't wrap from one line to the next. The preferred way to double-space a document is to type the document as regular single-spaced text, then set the line spacing to double.

- To adjust the line spacing for one paragraph of text, position the insertion point in the paragraph, then click the Paragraph Dialog Box Launcher on the Home or Page Layout tab to display the Paragraph dialog box. Select the desired spacing from the Line spacing drop-down list on the Indents and Spacing tab. Single- and double-spacing are the most commonly used spacing settings.

- To adjust the line spacing for more than one paragraph, select the paragraphs, then adjust the line spacing as described above.

- To adjust the space between paragraphs, click the Paragraph Dialog Box Launcher on the Home or Page Layout tab to display the Paragraph dialog box. Select the desired paragraph spacing from the Before and After boxes on the Indents and Spacing tab.

- You can set the line spacing for the entire document before you begin typing. Click Editing, Select, then Select All on the Home tab. Click the Paragraph Dialog Box Launcher on the Home or Page Layout tab. Select the desired line spacing, then click the OK button. As you type, the text appears on the screen with the selected line spacing.

FAQ How do I use tabs?

Setting a **tab** provides an easy way to align text in columns. Word provides default tab stops at 1/2" intervals, but you can change the default tab settings and add your own tab stops. The position of a tab stop is measured from the left margin.

Figure
10-9

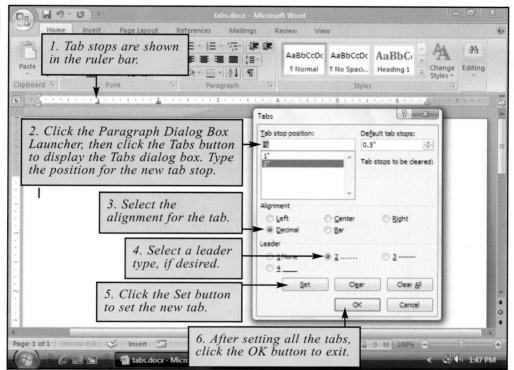

- There are many types of tab stops. A left tab stop means that text will be aligned on the left side of the tab. A right tab stop means that text will be aligned on the right side of the tab. A center tab stop centers text at that location, while a decimal tab stop aligns numbers with the decimal at the tab location. A bar tab stop places a vertical bar at the tab location.

- A **leader** is a line of punctuation characters, such as periods, that fills the area between text and a tab stop. Leaders are typically used in a table of contents to associate a page number with a chapter title or heading. To add a leader to a tab stop, click the option button to select the leader type. When you tab to that tab stop, the leader character—usually a series of periods—fills the area to the tab stop.

- To clear one tab stop, click that tab stop in the Tab stop position box, then click the Clear button. To clear all tab stops, click the Clear All button in the Tabs dialog box.

- On the Word ruler bar, tab stops are represented by these small icons:

∟	Left tab	⊥	Center tab	ı	Bar tab
⌐	Right tab	⊥	Decimal tab		

- To set tabs using the ruler, select the type of tab stop by clicking the icon at the left end of the ruler. Click a location on the ruler to set the tab stop. You can move a tab stop by selecting it, then sliding it right or left on the ruler bar.

- If the ruler bar is not displayed, click the View tab and then select the Ruler option in the Show/Hide group.

FAQ How do I indent text?

You can indent text from the left margin, from the right margin, or from both margins. You can also indent the first line of text differently from the rest of a paragraph. Normally, the first line is indented farther to the right than the rest of the paragraph, but you can use a **hanging indent** to move the first line of text more to the left than the rest of the paragraph. Word's Paragraph dialog box provides several options for indenting text.

Figure 10–10

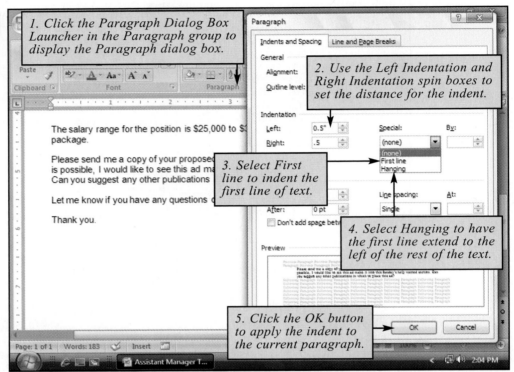

1. Click the Paragraph Dialog Box Launcher in the Paragraph group to display the Paragraph dialog box.

2. Use the Left Indentation and Right Indentation spin boxes to set the distance for the indent.

3. Select First line to indent the first line of text.

4. Select Hanging to have the first line extend to the left of the rest of the text.

5. Click the OK button to apply the indent to the current paragraph.

- To indent an entire paragraph from the left, click the spin box buttons in the Left Indentation box to increase or decrease the indent distance. Use the same process with the Right Indentation box to increase or decrease the right indentation.

- The Preview section shows how the paragraph will look after it is indented. As you change your selections, the Preview is updated.

- To indent the first line of text, select First line from the Special pull-down list. Select the amount of indentation for the first line of the paragraph from the By spin box.

- To create a hanging indent in which the first line of text extends more to the left than the rest of the text, select Hanging from the Special pull-down list. Select the amount of negative indent for the first line of the paragraph from the By spin box.

- Indent settings apply to the paragraph that contains the insertion point. To apply an indent to more than one paragraph, select the paragraphs, then use the Paragraph dialog box to set the indent.

FAQ How do I add footnotes or endnotes to a document?

Footnotes and endnotes are typically used to add comments to blocks of text or cite references to other documents. An asterisk or superscript number appearing in the main text of a document indicates a footnote or endnote. A **footnote** appears at the bottom of the page that contains the corresponding superscript number. An **endnote** appears at the end of a section or chapter.

**Figure
10–11**

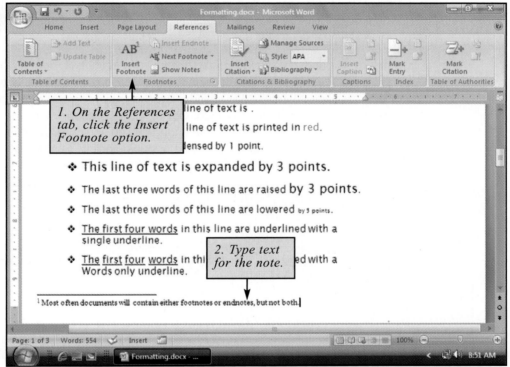

1. On the References tab, click the Insert Footnote option.

2. Type text for the note.

- To insert a footnote or endnote, click the References tab. Click the Insert Footnote or Insert Endnote button. A text area appears on the bottom of your screen that allows you to type the note text.

- To modify the format of a footnote or endnote, open the Footnote and Endnote dialog box by clicking the arrow box next to "Footnotes."

- To delete a footnote or endnote, select the number that corresponds to the note in the text, and press the Delete key.

- The Reference tab contains several tools for adding citations to a document. You can select a citation style, such as APA or MLA, and Word will automatically add the required formatting and punctuation to book titles and other materials you cite. Word can even produce a bibliography based on all the citations in a document.

FAQ How do I work with outlines and other document views?

Word provides several ways to view a document. You can display **format marks** to reveal hidden symbols that indicate paragraph breaks ¶ , spaces · , and tab stops → . To display hidden formatting marks, click the ¶ Show/Hide button in the Paragraph group on the Home tab.

You can also change the document view to see how it will look when printed (Print Layout view), as a Web page (Web Layout view), or as an outline (Outline view). To change the document view, click one of the view buttons in the status bar. You can also change the view by clicking the View tab, then clicking one of the views listed.

Outline view is handy for organizing the content of a document. You can assign outline levels to each title, heading, and paragraph, and view any level of the outline to get an overview or include all details. In Outline view, it is easy to rearrange sections of a document to streamline its organization. Outline view is best used to work on the structure of a document, but it is not meant to be used when you want to create a document that displays paragraph numbers or outline levels. For tools to create multilevel outlines, refer to the FAQ about bulleted and numbered lists.

Play It!

Figure 10-12

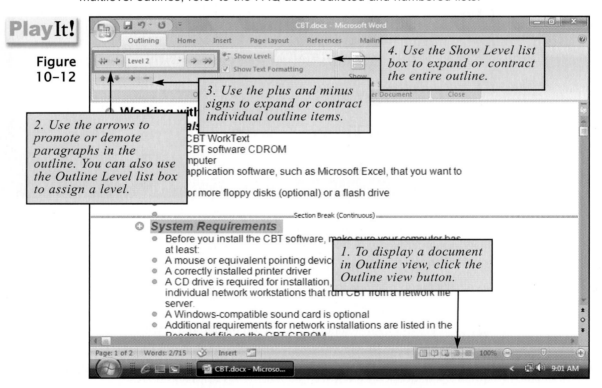

4. Use the Show Level list box to expand or contract the entire outline.

3. Use the plus and minus signs to expand or contract individual outline items.

2. Use the arrows to promote or demote paragraphs in the outline. You can also use the Outline Level list box to assign a level.

1. To display a document in Outline view, click the Outline view button.

- Microsoft Word uses the following conventions to indicate outline levels:

  A plus sign ⊕ indicates a heading with subtext.

  A small solid circle ● indicates body text at the lowest level of the outline.

  A gray line under a heading indicates subordinate text that is not displayed.

  A dash ⊖ indicates a heading without subordinate text.

FAQ How do I create a table?

A **table** is a grid consisting of rows and columns. The intersection of each row and column is called a **cell**. Each cell can hold text, numbers, or a graphic. You can format an entire table or individual cells.

Figure 10–13

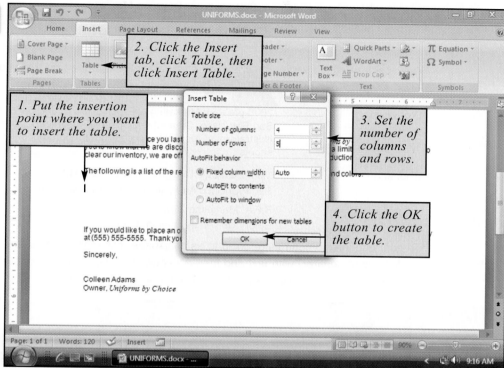

- To add text to a table, click any cell, then type text in that cell. The word wrap feature moves text down while you type and expands the size of the cell to make room for all of your text. To move to another cell, press the arrow keys, press the Tab key, or click the desired cell.

- To quickly format a table, make sure the insertion point is in the table, then click the Design tab under the Table Tools contextual tab. Select a table style from the Table Styles group. You can then modify the format to change the font or other table attributes.

- To insert a new row or column, place the insertion point in the cell closest to where you want the new row or column to appear. Click the Layout tab under the Table Tools contextual tab, then choose from among the options to specify the placement of the new row or column from the Rows & Columns group.

- To delete unused rows or columns, position the insertion point in the column or row you want to delete. Click the Layout tab under the Table Tools contextual tab, then click the Delete command in the Rows & Columns group. Select from among the options to specify what you want to delete.

- To adjust the width of a column, position the pointer over the dividing line between the columns. When the pointer changes to a ◄║► shape, press the left mouse button and drag the column to the correct width.

- You can convert table text into normal text or vice versa using the Table button on the Insert tab. When converting text into a table, use commas to separate the text for columns and paragraph marks (Enter key) to separate the text that will become each row.

FAQ Can I format a document into columns?

There are three ways to format text into columns: tabs, tables, and columns. Tabs are most effectively used when you want to enter a single line of parallel text in each column. Tabs work for well for short, multi-column lists:

Address	List Price	Days on Market
12 Main St.	$349,000	38
322 North Rd.	$149,500	36

Tables are effective when you want to enter parallel text, but some text requires multiple lines. A typical use of table-style columns is the text layout of a resume:

Work History	2008-present: Marketing & Graphics Assistant, Smith & Co., San Francisco: Created designs for consumer packaging using Adobe Illustrator and four-color processing; prepared designs for photo shoots
Education	M.F.A. Graphic Design & Marketing, 2010 San Francisco Art Institute, San Francisco, CA
	B.F.A. Marketing 2006 Emory University, Atlanta, GA

The third option, sometimes referred to as newspaper columns or newsletter columns, fills the left column entirely with text and then continues into the right column as shown below. Use newspaper-style columns when you want to format full paragraphs of text into columns.

Figure 10-14

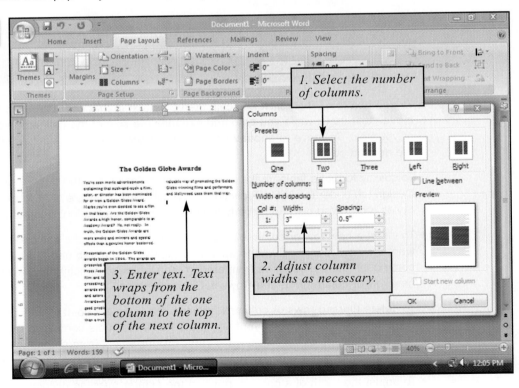

1. Select the number of columns.

2. Adjust column widths as necessary.

3. Enter text. Text wraps from the bottom of the one column to the top of the next column.

• If you want to jump to the next column before reaching the end, Ctrl+Shift+Enter inserts a column break into the text.

QuickCheck A

1. True or false? To create an active hyperlink in a document, select one or more words, click the Underline button, and then change the font color to blue. ⬚

2. Centering and alignment formats apply to an entire ⬚ of text.

3. You should use the ⬚ dialog box to apply multiple formatting options in a single operation.

4. A(n) ⬚ is a symbol, such as a square or circle, placed before an item in a list.

5. True or false? To double-space a document, you should press the Enter key two times at the end of every line of text. ⬚

Check It!

QuickCheck B

Indicate the letter of the desktop element that best matches the following:

1. Underline a single word ⬚

2. Change the font size ⬚

3. Center a title ⬚

4. Create a bulleted list ⬚

5. Select a style ⬚

Check It!

CHAPTER **11**

Finalizing a Document

What's Inside and on the CD?

Writing a document is only half the battle. Once the first draft is done, you'll typically want to check spelling and grammar, apply some formatting, and maybe even change a few words here and there. In this chapter, you'll learn how to add the finishing touches to prepare your document for printing or posting as a Web page.

Important features covered in this chapter include adding headers and footers, setting margins, and incorporating graphics. You'll learn how to save your document in HTML format so it can be posted as a Web page. Also, you'll find out how adding comments and tracking changes make it easy for multiple people to collaborate on a single document.

FAQ How do I create headers and footers?

A **header** is text that appears at the top of every page of a document. A **footer** is text that appears at the bottom of every page. Headers and footers typically contain information such as the title of the document, the date, the name of the author, and the current page number. Headers and footers are useful for keeping documents intact, for example, when a document is dropped or a part of it is misfiled.

Play It!

Figure
11-1

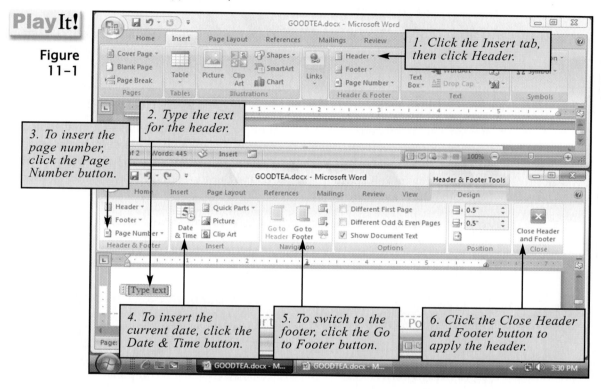

1. Click the Insert tab, then click Header.

2. Type the text for the header.

3. To insert the page number, click the Page Number button.

4. To insert the current date, click the Date & Time button.

5. To switch to the footer, click the Go to Footer button.

6. Click the Close Header and Footer button to apply the header.

- Headers and footers are displayed only in Print Layout view, in Full Screen Reading view, in a print preview, and on printed pages.

- The header and footer have preset tabs—a center tab in the middle of the page, and a right tab near the right margin. Press the Tab key to move the insertion point to the next tab to enter text at that location.

- If you want to include text such as "Page 6" in your header or footer, click the Page Number button in the Header & Footer group, then select the desired format. Page numbers are automatically updated when page content changes during editing.

- To insert the current date and time, click the Date & Time button in the Insert group, select the desired format from the Date and Time dialog box, then click OK. The date and time are automatically updated each time you open the document.

- Click the Go to Header or Go to Footer button to switch between the header and footer. You can edit the header or the footer, but not both at the same time.

- You can change the font and style of page numbers just as you would change any text by using the formatting options on the Home tab.

FAQ How do I insert page breaks and section breaks?

A **page break** occurs within a document where one page ends and the next page begins. When a page is filled with text or graphics, Word automatically inserts a page break. In Draft view, a horizontal dotted line indicates an automatic page break. You can also insert a manual, or "forced," page break at any point in the document. In Print Layout view, both automatic and manual page breaks are displayed as the end of a sheet, or page, within the document.

A **section break**, displayed as a double dotted line in Draft view, divides a document into sections. You can apply different formatting to each section of a document. For example, you might define the title page of a term paper as a section, and format it as a single column with no headers. You could then define the body of the document as a separate section formatted with two columns and headers that contain page numbers.

- Use sections when parts of a document require different page-based format settings for margins, borders, vertical alignment, columns, headers and footers, footnotes and endnotes, page numbering, and line numbers. Paragraph and text-based formatting options—such as line spacing, font, size, and bullets—are typically applied to selected text, rather than to sections.

- To insert a break, click the Page Layout tab, then click Breaks to open the Break dialog box. Select the type of break you want, then click OK. You can also insert a page break with the Page Break button in the Pages group on the Insert tab or by using the keyboard shortcut Ctrl+Enter.

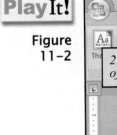

Figure 11-2

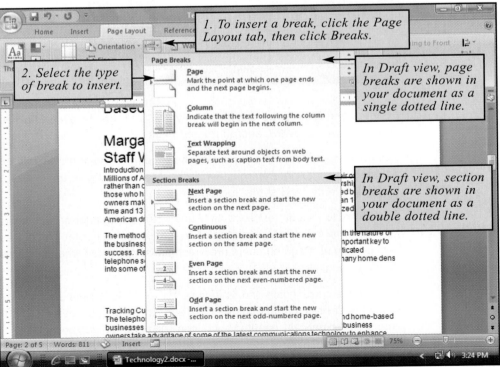

FAQ Can I insert photos into a document?

You can use two types of graphics to enhance documents created with Microsoft Word: vector graphics and bitmap graphics. Both types of graphics can be used to add pizzazz to a page, draw interest to certain text selections, or illustrate important points. Don't overuse pictures, however. Too many can cause a page to look cluttered and confusing.

A **bitmap graphic**, referred to in Word as a "picture," is composed of a grid of colored dots. Digital photos and scanned images are typically stored as bitmap graphics with extensions such as .bmp, .png, .jpg, .tif, or .gif. Word does not provide a feature to create bitmap graphics, but you can insert photos and other bitmaps stored in files on your computer. Word provides a Picture Tools contextual tab to help you adjust the color, contrast, and brightness of inserted bitmap graphics. You can also use this tab to crop or rotate a picture.

- To insert a bitmap graphic into a document, click the Insert tab, then click Picture from the Illustrations group. Use the Open dialog box to navigate to the folder that contains the picture you want to insert, and then click Insert.

- To crop a picture, select the picture, click the Crop button from the Size group, then drag the edges of the picture to frame the part of the image you want to display.

- Adjust the brightness, contrast, and color of a picture by selecting the graphic and then clicking the Brightness, Contrast, or Recolor buttons in the Adjust group.

- You can control the way text flows around a picture in a document. To wrap text around a picture, select the picture. From the Arrange group, click the Text Wrapping button, and then select a text flow option from the list.

- To delete a picture, click it, and then press the Delete key.

**Figure
11–3**

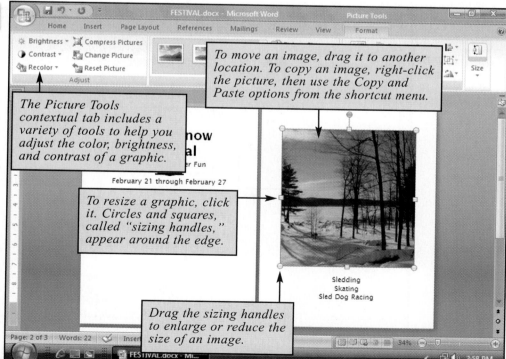

The Picture Tools contextual tab includes a variety of tools to help you adjust the color, brightness, and contrast of a graphic.

To move an image, drag it to another location. To copy an image, right-click the picture, then use the Copy and Paste options from the shortcut menu.

To resize a graphic, click it. Circles and squares, called "sizing handles," appear around the edge.

Drag the sizing handles to enlarge or reduce the size of an image.

FAQ Can I insert line art into a document?

A **vector graphic**, sometimes called a "drawing," is created with basic shapes, such as lines, curves, and rectangles. Clip art, logos, and organizational charts are often created using vector graphics, and have extensions such as .wmf and .ai. Microsoft Office includes a clip art collection you can access by clicking the Insert tab, then clicking Clip Art in the Illustrations group.

You can use Word's Shapes to create your own simple vector graphics within a document. You can also use it to enhance vector graphics you've obtained from other sources and inserted into a document.

• You can create vector drawings by combining several shapes within a rectangular area called a "canvas." To open a blank canvas, click the Insert tab, click the Shapes button in the Illustrations group, then click New Drawing Canvas. When the canvas is selected, you can use the Insert Shapes group on the Drawing Tools contextual tab to add shapes to the canvas.

• Multiple shapes can be grouped together so that they can be moved and resized as a single unit. To group objects, hold down the Ctrl key and select the shapes you want to group. Right-click the shapes, point to Grouping, and then click Group. Shapes can be ungrouped using a similar procedure, but clicking Ungroup instead of Group.

• You can use layers to make shapes appear to be stacked on top of one another or to appear in front of or behind text. To move a shape from one layer to another, right-click the shape, and then click Order. Choose an order from the list.

• To control the way text flows around a vector graphic, click Text Wrapping from the Arrange group, and then select an option from the list.

 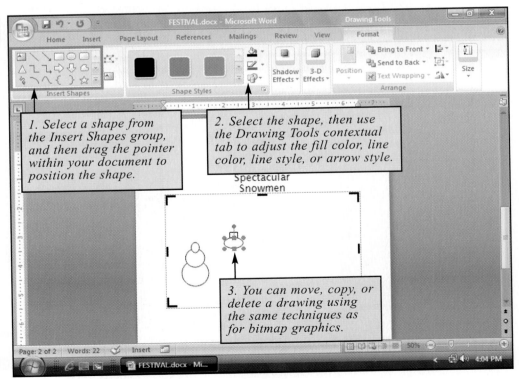

Figure 11-4

1. Select a shape from the Insert Shapes group, and then drag the pointer within your document to position the shape.

2. Select the shape, then use the Drawing Tools contextual tab to adjust the fill color, line color, line style, or arrow style.

3. You can move, copy, or delete a drawing using the same techniques as for bitmap graphics.

FAQ How do I set margins?

Margin settings typically apply to an entire document and are changed using the Page Setup group on the Page Layout tab.

In a Word document, the default margins are 1". Margin settings affect the amount of text that fits on a page. Small margins leave more room on a page for text than large margins.

Figure 11–5

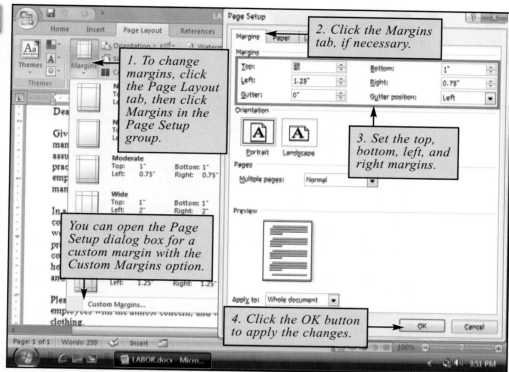

- Don't set the top and bottom margins too small if you're using headers and footers. Headers and footers do not print correctly if there isn't enough room in the top and bottom margins.

- Select Portrait orientation to print the page vertically. If you have a wide document, select Landscape orientation to print the page sideways.

- You can use the Paper tab in the Page Setup dialog box to set the paper size and control how paper feeds into your default printer. Select the appropriate paper size from the Paper size list. You can find more information about printing options in the printer documentation.

- The Layout tab in the Page Setup dialog box is useful for creating different headers and footers on odd and even pages. Other layout options allow you to center text vertically on the page, insert line numbers, and add graphical elements, such as borders, to the document.

- Margin settings and other page formatting options can apply to the whole document, to selected sections of the document, or to the rest of the document that follows the current location of the insertion point. You can find more information about page setup options in Word Help.

FAQ How do I perform a mail merge?

A **mail merge** allows you to create multiple documents from a starting document and a data source. The starting document can be a letter, a label template, or an envelope template. The starting document usually contains formatted information that you want to be the same for all of the document recipients. The data source, or list, contains the information that will be merged into the starting document. After the information is merged, the final documents can be printed or saved for future use.

Figure 11-6

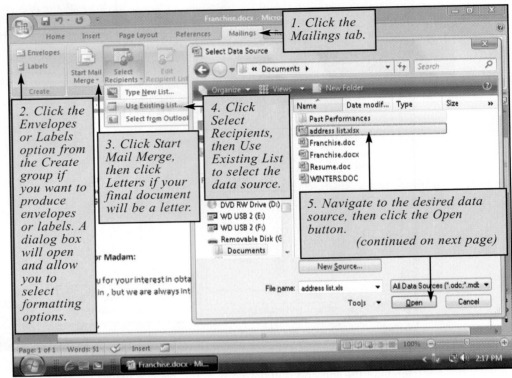

1. Click the Mailings tab.

2. Click the Envelopes or Labels option from the Create group if you want to produce envelopes or labels. A dialog box will open and allow you to select formatting options.

3. Click Start Mail Merge, then click Letters if your final document will be a letter.

4. Click Select Recipients, then Use Existing List to select the data source.

5. Navigate to the desired data source, then click the Open button.

(continued on next page)

- You can compose your starting document from scratch or from a document template.

- The data source can come from a database file, Outlook, an Excel spreadsheet, or a Word document.

• How do I perform a mail merge? (continued)

Merge lists contain data such as names or addresses. Each item in a merge list is considered a field. The data from a field can be inserted into a document during a merge. The location where data is to be inserted is specified by a merge field or merge block. A merge field, such as <<FirstName>>, contains one item of data. A merge block such as <<AddressBlock>> can contain multiple lines of data.

Merge fields are enclosed in angle brackets to show that they will not be printed in the final document. Instead, the data represented by the merge field, such as person's first name, is inserted and printed during the merge.

Figure 11–7

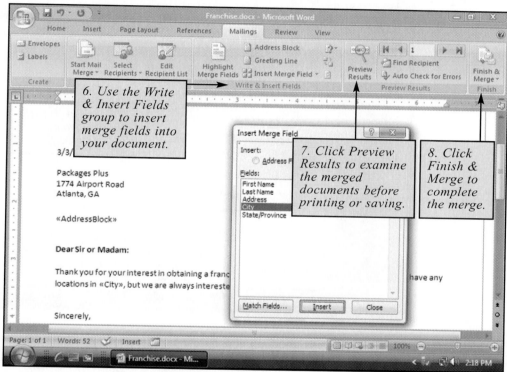

- You can insert pre-formatted merge field blocks or individual merge fields from the Write & Insert Fields group. Use the Match Fields button if there are any discrepancies with field names.

- Preview your final documents to make sure they are exactly what you want before saving or printing them.

FAQ How do I save a document as a Web page?

Instead of printing a document, you might want to post it on the Internet as a Web page. As with other Web pages, your document must be in HTML (Hypertext Markup Language) format to be accessible to Web browsers, such as Internet Explorer or Mozilla Firefox. You can use the Save As option accessed from the Microsoft Office button to save a document in HTML format.

Figure 11-8

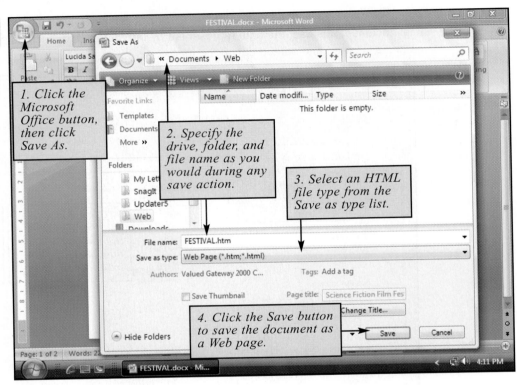

1. Click the Microsoft Office button, then click Save As.

2. Specify the drive, folder, and file name as you would during any save action.

3. Select an HTML file type from the Save as type list.

4. Click the Save button to save the document as a Web page.

- Word does a fairly good job of converting a document to HTML, but several formatting options available in Word cannot be duplicated in HTML documents. If a document contains formatting that cannot be duplicated in HTML, Word displays a message during the conversion process that describes the problem areas. You then have the option of canceling or continuing with the save.

- To see how the document will look when viewed in a Web browser, locate the file with Windows Explorer, then double-click the file to open it in a Web browser.

- Documents saved as Web pages are displayed as a single long page—sort of like a papyrus scroll—even though the original Word document consisted of multiple pages. When viewing a long document in a Web browser, you can use the vertical scroll bar to move through the document.

- Contact your Internet service provider (ISP) or technical support person if you need instructions for posting your Web pages on the Internet.

FAQ How do I convert a document into a PDF?

PDF (Portable Document Format) was created by Adobe Systems and has become a universal standard for exchanging documents, spreadsheets, and other types of data files. Converting a file into a PDF ensures that when the file is viewed or printed, it retains the original layout. PDF is sometimes referred to as a fixed-layout format because once a document has been converted to a PDF, it cannot be edited.

Software for viewing PDFs is free and therefore most computers have the ability to display PDF files. You can convert Word documents into PDF files if you want to distribute them but you're not sure if the recipients have Microsoft Word.

To convert a document into a PDF file, make sure you save it first as a normal Word document. Then use the Save As command and select PDF from the *Save As type* list.

Figure 11-9

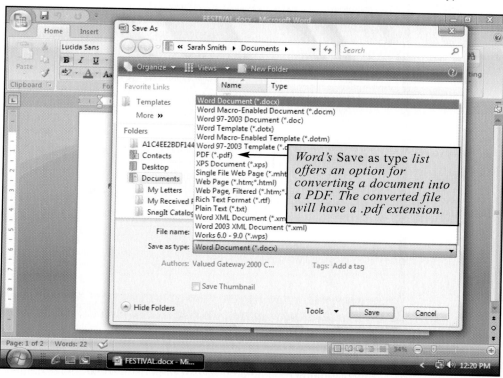

Word's Save as type *list offers an option for converting a document into a PDF. The converted file will have a .pdf extension.*

- Before you can convert a Word document into a PDF, you might have to install the *Publish as PDF or XPS Add-in* for Microsoft Office 2007. Once installed, you'll have a PDF option in the *Save as type* list.

- Software for creating PDFs can be obtained in a number of ways. It is included with the Mac OS X operating system, OpenOffice, and Microsoft Office. You can download the free Adobe Reader from the Adobe Web site. Free PDF software usually allows you to create, read, and print PDF files.

- Some PDF software offers additional features. For the fullest feature set, Adobe offers Adobe Acrobat Professional. In addition to creating, viewing, and printing, Acrobat Professional allows you to annotate a PDF by inserting text, making line-out deletions, highlighting passages, and adding comments.

- **XPS** (XML Paper Specification) is a file format, similar to PDF, but created by Microsoft. XPS does not have the widespread popularity of PDFs.

FAQ How do I work with electronic documents?

Whereas word processors were once used primarily to prepare documents for printing, today many documents remain in electronic formats that are transmitted by e-mail, sent directly to a fax machine, shared on an FTP site, or posted as Web pages and blogs.

Word has several built-in features that help you work with electronic documents. For example, the Office button's Send option can be used to attach a document to an e-mail message or send it over an Internet fax service. The Publish option is useful for creating blogs. Word even includes fax templates so you can easily create a fax cover sheet.

Figure 11–10

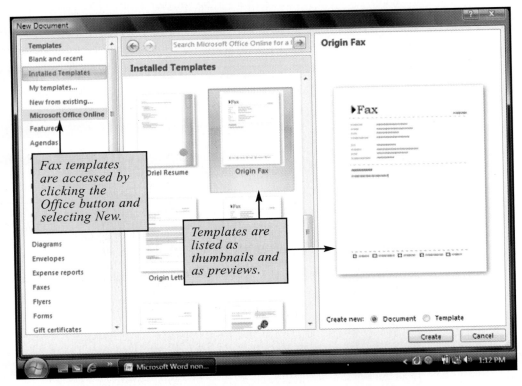

Fax templates are accessed by clicking the Office button and selecting New.

Templates are listed as thumbnails and as previews.

The way you plan to use a document affects the way you handle it. For most applications, you'll typically first save your document normally as a Word DOCX file. The table below contains recommendations for handling electronic documents.

E-mail attachment	Send DOCX files if you are certain the recipient has Word 2007; otherwise convert to DOC or PDF files. Large files might need to be zipped.
Web page	Save in HTM or HTML format. If your Web page includes graphics or links to other pages, make sure they are posted along with the document containing the primary content.
Blog	Save as a DOCX file if you are using Word's blog publishing feature.
Fax	Send any type of file that is accepted by the fax service.
FTP	Post DOCX files if you are certain the recipient has Word 2007; otherwise convert to PDF. Large files will transmit faster if they are zipped.

How do I work with electronic documents? (continued)

When working with electronic documents, remain alert to avoid the following problems:

- **Loss of information or formatting.** When files are converted from one file type to another, some aspects of the original document might be lost. In an earlier FAQ, you learned that a Word document converted into HTML loses its pagination when all the text is incorporated into a single long Web page. Other formatting that might be lost or garbled during conversion includes columns, tabs, highlighting, comments, and graphic placement. After converting a document into a different file type, compare the two versions for significant differences.

- **Necessary software not installed.** Before e-mailing or posting a file, consider the software that's needed to view it. Not everyone has Office 2007, so DOCX is not a universal format. PDF is more universal and might be a better choice, especially if you're not certain of the software installed on your recipient's computer.

- **Missing linked data.** Word documents and e-mail messages can contain hyperlinks to Web sites, spreadsheets can be linked to document files, and Web pages can include links to graphics and other Web pages. When e-mailing or posting documents that incorporate links, make sure to also post all the data files referred to by the links.

- **Blocked file types.** Most computers are protected against viruses and other exploits, but the protective software and hardware can inadvertently block innocent files, too. E-mail attachments with extensions such as .scr .bat, .hlp and .exe are especially vulnerable to being blocked, but .doc and .docx files are sometimes blocked, too. To make sure your files haven't been blocked, ask for confirmation of their arrival. Compressed files with .zip extensions tend not to get blocked, so you might consider zipping documents and other files before you send them.

- **Large files.** File size and connection speed affect upload and download times when transferring electronic documents over the Internet. You can shrink the size of a file using a process called **compression** or zipping.

Figure 11–11

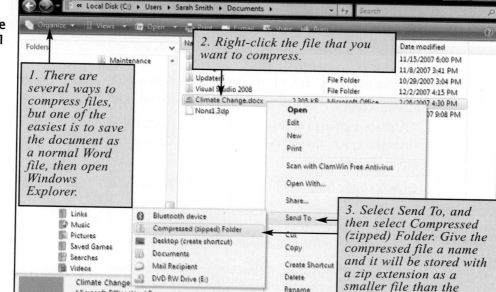

1. There are several ways to compress files, but one of the easiest is to save the document as a normal Word file, then open Windows Explorer.

2. Right-click the file that you want to compress.

3. Select Send To, and then select Compressed (zipped) Folder. Give the compressed file a name and it will be stored with a zip extension as a smaller file than the original DOCX file.

FAQ Can I track changes and insert comments in a document?

As a document is revised, you might want to maintain a record of the original wording. This capability is especially important in the development of legal documents and when multiple people collaborate on a single document. Microsoft Word provides several features for such situations.

The Track Changes feature maintains all deleted, changed, and inserted text for a document and displays it in a contrasting font color. You can hide or display these changes and integrate them in the document by accepting them. Word's comment feature allows you to insert the electronic version of "sticky notes" in your document. Comments are displayed as balloons in the margins and can be displayed or hidden as needed.

Figure 11–12

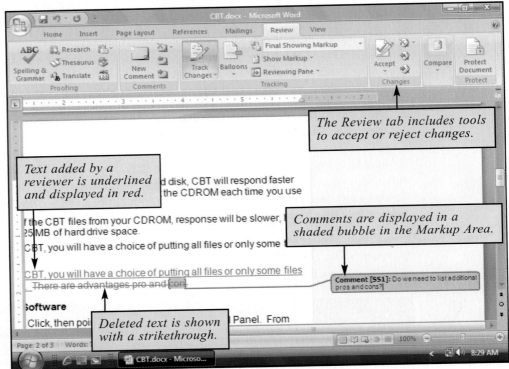

The Review tab includes tools to accept or reject changes.

Text added by a reviewer is underlined and displayed in red.

Comments are displayed in a shaded bubble in the Markup Area.

Deleted text is shown with a strikethrough.

- To track changes, click the Review tab, then click Track Changes in the Tracking group. As you edit the document, changes are indicated in a contrasting font color.

- To accept a change in an edited document, click the changed text, click Accept in the Changes group, then click Accept Change. To reject a change, use the Reject options in the Changes group.

- To accept all changes in a document, click Accept in the Changes group, then click *Accept All Changes in Document*.

- To reject all changes in a document, click Reject in the Changes group, then click *Reject All Changes in Document*.

- To insert a comment, click New Comment on the Review tab. Type your comment in the comment bubble displayed in the Markup Area.

FAQ Is there a way to protect documents from unauthorized access?

You can protect your documents from unauthorized access in several ways. One option is to encrypt the document so that it can be opened only when a valid password is entered.

Figure 11-13

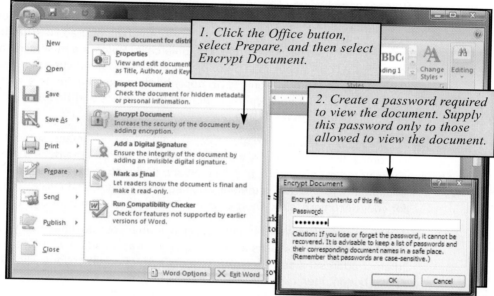

1. Click the Office button, select Prepare, and then select Encrypt Document.

2. Create a password required to view the document. Supply this password only to those allowed to view the document.

Another way to protect your documents is to allow anyone to open a document, but restrict the types of edits that can be made. You can set up these restrictions using Word's Protect Document group.

Play It!

Figure 11-14

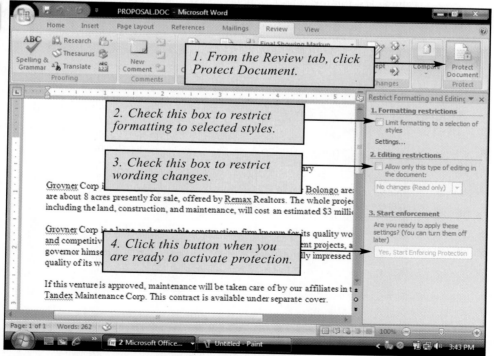

1. From the Review tab, click Protect Document.

2. Check this box to restrict formatting to selected styles.

3. Check this box to restrict wording changes.

4. Click this button when you are ready to activate protection.

• If you would like to deactivate document protection, use the Protect Document button to access the Restrict Formatting and Editing task pane. Scroll to the bottom of the task pane and click the Stop Protection button.

FAQ What other features can I use to finalize my documents?

Use the following tips and tricks to create more professional-looking documents, automate document formatting, or simply spruce up your existing documents:

- Borders and shading allow you to emphasize certain sections of text or parts of a table. A **border** is a line or graphic drawn around a page or section of text. Borders can be customized by width, color, number of lines, and type of graphic. **Shading** is grayscale or color background applied to text or table cells. Borders and shading are often used together to highlight sections of text, differentiate cells and titles in a table, or create an eye-catching page or document. To apply borders and shading to a section of a document, click the down-arrow button on the Borders and Shading button in the Paragraph group on the Home tab.

- Themes make it easy to create professional-looking documents without having to customize the style of every element in the document. A **theme** is a predefined set of coordinated styles, colors, and text options designed to be applied to an existing document. Word includes themes such as Apex, Metro, and Office. To choose a theme for your document, click Themes in the Themes group on the Page Layout tab.

- **AutoFormat** allows Word to automatically format your document as you type. AutoFormat performs tasks such as replacing fractions (1/4 with ¼) and formatting Internet addresses as hyperlinks. To modify AutoFormat options, click the Microsoft Office button, then click the Word Options button. Click the Proofing tab, then click the AutoCorrect Options button to open the AutoCorrect dialog box.

- The Format Painter feature makes it easy to replicate formats from one text selection to another. Click any text that has the format you would like to replicate, click the Format Painter button in the Clipboard group on the Home tab to capture the format, then click the text where you would like the format applied. If you double-click the Format Painter button, you can copy the format to several locations. When you are finished copying the format to the desired locations, simply click the Format Painter button to stop the paste process.

Play It!

Figure 11–15

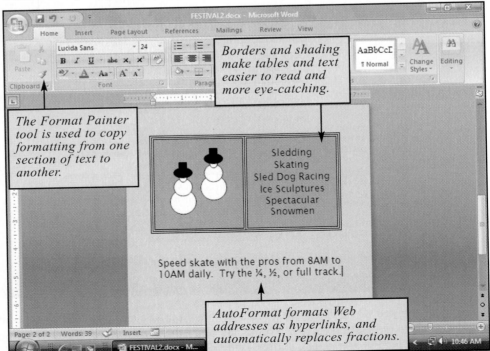

Borders and shading make tables and text easier to read and more eye-catching.

The Format Painter tool is used to copy formatting from one section of text to another.

AutoFormat formats Web addresses as hyperlinks, and automatically replaces fractions.

QuickCheck A

1. If you'd like a title page formatted separately from other pages in a document, add a [_____] break.

2. You can use Word's Shapes to create simple [_____] graphics, such as line drawings, arrows, and stars.

3. A(n) [_____] is text placed at the bottom of every page of a Word document.

4. When you save a Word document as a Web page, it is converted to [_____] markup language format.

5. You can convert a Word document into a(n) [_____] file if you are going to send it to someone who might not have Word, but is likely to have Adobe Reader.

CheckIt!

QuickCheck B

Indicate the letter of the desktop element that best matches the following:

1. Turn commenting off or on [____]

2. Text added by a reviewer [____]

3. Comment added by reviewer [____]

4. Text deleted by reviewer [____]

5. Button for rejecting a suggested change [____]

CheckIt!

CHAPTER 12

Creating a Worksheet

What's Inside and on the CD?

In this chapter, you'll learn the essentials of creating a worksheet with Microsoft Excel. **Microsoft Excel** is the component of the Microsoft Office suite best suited for working with numbers and formulas. As spreadsheet software, Microsoft Excel provides a set of tools for simple or complex calculations, such as creating a budget, estimating expenses, and creating an income and expense projection.

An electronic spreadsheet, often referred to as a worksheet, functions much like a visual calculator. You place each number needed for a calculation into a cell of the grid. You then enter formulas to add, subtract, or otherwise manipulate these numbers. The spreadsheet software automatically performs the calculations and displays the results.

FAQ What's in the Excel window?

To start Excel, click Start, point to All Programs, click Microsoft Office, then click Microsoft Excel 2007. You should notice that Excel's ribbon contains tabs, groups, and commands similar to those you learned to use in Microsoft Word. In this chapter, you will learn some of the important features of Excel that are different from the features of Word.

Play It!

Figure
12–1

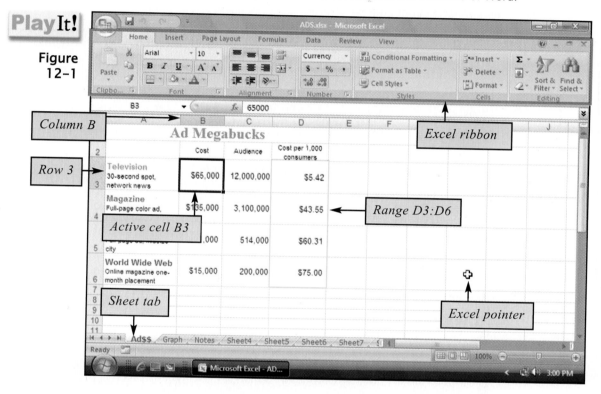

* A **worksheet** consists of a grid of columns and rows. The columns are typically labeled with letters, starting with A as the column farthest to the left. The rows are typically labeled with numbers, starting with 1 as the top row.

* Excel worksheets are saved in a three-dimensional **workbook**. A workbook contains one or more worksheets, each represented by a tab at the bottom of the Excel window. When you save or open a workbook, all worksheets in that workbook are automatically saved or opened. To switch to a different worksheet in the current workbook, click its sheet tab. Right-click a sheet tab to rename, insert, or delete a worksheet.

* A **worksheet cell** (or "cell" for short) is the rectangle formed by the intersection of a column and row. Each cell has a unique name consisting of the column letter and row number. For example, cell B3 is located in the second column of the third row.

* The **active cell** is the cell you can currently edit or modify, and it is marked with a black outline. You can change the active cell by clicking any other cell. You can also change the active cell by pressing the arrow keys to move the black outline up, down, left, or right.

* A **range** is a series of cells. For example, D3:D6 is a range that contains all cells from D3 through D6, inclusive. When specifying a range, use a colon to separate the first and last cells. To select a range of cells, click the cell in the top-left corner of the range, then drag the mouse to the bottom-right cell in the range.

FAQ How do I enter labels?

A **label** is any text entered into a cell of the worksheet. You can use labels for a worksheet title, to describe the numbers you've entered in other cells, and for text data, such as the names of people or cities. Any numerical data you do not intend to use in a calculation should be entered as a label. This data might be a telephone number, a Social Security number, or a street address.

Play It!

Figure 12-2

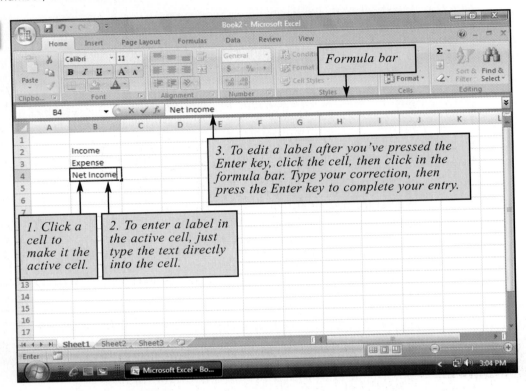

Formula bar

3. To edit a label after you've pressed the Enter key, click the cell, then click in the formula bar. Type your correction, then press the Enter key to complete your entry.

1. Click a cell to make it the active cell.

2. To enter a label in the active cell, just type the text directly into the cell.

- If a label is too long to fit in the current cell, it extends into the cells to the right if they are empty. If the cells on the right are not empty, part of the label will be truncated, which means it will be hidden behind the adjacent cell's content.

- It's possible to make a long label wrap so that it is displayed in two or more lines of text inside the same cell. Select the cell or cells. From the Home tab, click the Wrap Text button in the Alignment group.

- To edit a label after you've pressed the Enter key, click the cell, then click in the **formula bar**. Use the left and right arrow keys to move the insertion point in the formula bar, and use the Backspace and Delete keys to delete characters. Press the Enter key when you finish editing the label. You can also press the ☑ Enter button on the formula bar to complete your entry. Press the ☒ Cancel button to exit the formula bar without keeping any changes.

- It's possible to edit a label inside a cell. Double-click the cell to activate it, then edit the contents using the arrow, Backspace, and Delete keys. Press the Enter key when you finish editing the label. You can clear the entire contents of a cell by clicking the cell and then pressing the Delete key on your keyboard.

FAQ How do I enter values?

A **value** is a number that you intend to use in a calculation and that is entered into a cell of a worksheet. Cells containing values can be used in formulas to calculate results. As mentioned on the previous page, numbers are meant to be used in calculations, so you should enter Social Security numbers, telephone numbers, and street addresses as labels, rather than as numbers.

Play It!

Figure 12-3

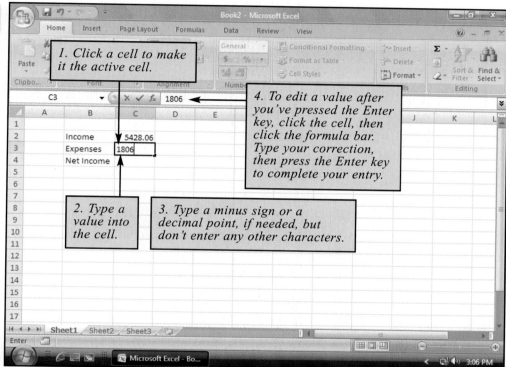

1. Click a cell to make it the active cell.

4. To edit a value after you've pressed the Enter key, click the cell, then click the formula bar. Type your correction, then press the Enter key to complete your entry.

2. Type a value into the cell.

3. Type a minus sign or a decimal point, if needed, but don't enter any other characters.

- Type a minus sign (-) before a number to enter a negative value. Although you can include the dollar sign and comma in values, it's best to just enter the unformatted number into a cell. You will learn how to format values in another chapter.

- After you've pressed the Enter key, you can edit a value just as you would edit a label—in the cell or in the formula bar.

- Excel makes assumptions about your entry while you are typing, and recognizes common combinations of numbers and punctuation as label data rather than as value data. If you want to specifically enter a number as a label, you can type an apostrophe (') before the number. For instance, type '555-1234 to enter the telephone number 555-1234 as a label.

- Values can be entered automatically using the fill handle and a technique called **drag-and-fill**. Enter a number in a cell and then point to the lower-right corner of the cell. The pointer changes to a black cross ➕ shape when you are in the right spot. Drag that pointer across or down several cells. After the cell selection is made, the 🔲 Auto Fill Options button is displayed. With the Auto Fill Options button, you can fill the selection with a series of numbers, the value of the initial cell with or without cell formatting, or cell formatting without a value.

- There are several other ways to drag-and-fill data, and you can use the Fill button in the Editing group on the Home tab. You can find more information about automatically filling cells in Excel Help.

FAQ How do I enter formulas?

A **formula** specifies how to add, subtract, multiply, divide, or otherwise calculate the values in worksheet cells. A formula always begins with an equal sign (=) and can use cell references that point to the contents of other cells. A **cell reference** is the column and row location of a cell. In the example below, the formula =C2-C3 subtracts the contents of cell C3 from the contents of cell C2 and displays the results in cell C4.

Figure 12-4

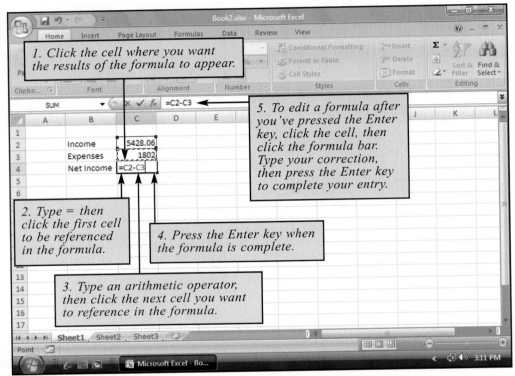

- The most common arithmetic operators are - (subtraction), + (addition), * (multiplication), / (division), % (percent), and ^ (exponent). Note that an asterisk (*) instead of the letter X is used for multiplication.

- The easiest way to create a formula is to use the pointer method. Basically, this method allows you to click cells for formulas instead of typing the cell reference. A rectangle of dashes around the selected cell is called a **marquee**. To continue creating your formula, type an arithmetic operator (+, -, *, /), then click the next cell you want to reference. Continue until the formula is complete, then press the Enter key.

- You can also type a formula directly into a cell. For example, you could type =B2*B3 and then press the Enter key to complete the formula. The problem with this method is that it's easy to make a mistake and type an incorrect cell reference.

- You can edit a formula after you've pressed the Enter key in the same way you would edit labels or values—in the cell or in the formula bar.

FAQ How do I create complex formulas?

A worksheet can be used for more than simple calculations. You can build complex formulas to calculate statistical, financial, and mathematical equations by using the usual arithmetic operators, parentheses, and a mixture of both values and cell references.

Figure 12–5

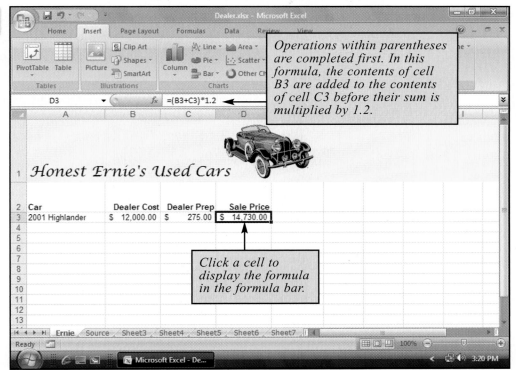

Operations within parentheses are completed first. In this formula, the contents of cell B3 are added to the contents of cell C3 before their sum is multiplied by 1.2.

Click a cell to display the formula in the formula bar.

- Use parentheses to make sure that arithmetic operations in a complex formula are executed in the correct order. If you don't use parentheses, Excel calculates the result using the standard mathematical order of operations, referred to as "mathematical precedence." Multiplication and division are performed first, then addition and subtraction. For example, if you enter the formula =B3+C3*1.2, Excel first multiplies the contents of cell C3 by 1.2, then adds the result of the calculation to the value in cell B3. By using parentheses, you can specify a different order for a calculation. For example, if you would like to add the contents of B3 and C3 before multiplying by 1.2, you would enter this formula: =(B3+C3)*1.2.

- Formulas can include values, cell references, or both. For example, if the total price of an item is displayed in cell C18, you could calculate a 6% sales tax using the formula =C18*.06. Or, you could put the sales tax percentage in cell C19, then calculate the sales tax using the formula =C18*C19. The result would be the same either way.

- You should be aware that cell references in formulas can lead to unexpected results when you copy or move the formulas. You'll learn more about this topic in another chapter.

FAQ How do I use functions?

In addition to writing your own formulas, you can use predefined formulas called **functions**. Excel includes many financial functions such as payments and net present value, mathematical and trigonometric functions such as absolute value and arctangent, and statistical functions such as average and normal distribution.

Avoid common errors when using formulas and functions by verifying that your formulas and functions reference the correct cells and data. A **circular reference**—a formula that references the cell in which the formula resides—can produce erroneous results and should be avoided.

Figure 12-6

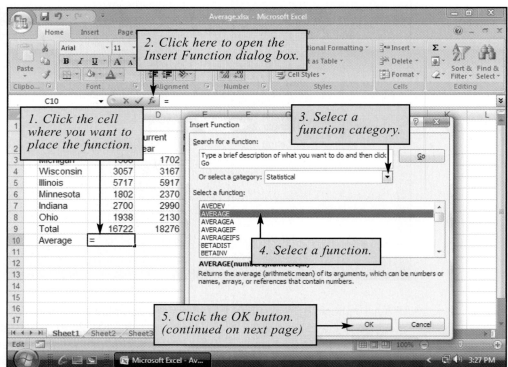

- You can use the Insert Function button to select a function from a list. Excel includes more than 250 functions from which you can choose. Commonly used functions, such as Sum, Average, Minimum, and Maximum, are located in the Statistical category.

- Another useful function is the Payment, or PMT, function, which calculates the payments for a loan. You can use the PMT function to calculate all types of loan payments, such as those for a car or for a house. Unfortunately, the PMT function is one of the more difficult functions to use, which is why it's covered in the Play It! on this page.

- Formulas can include multiple functions. For example, you could create a formula that uses both the Sum and the Average functions to get a total of the average values of a group of cells.

• How do I use functions? (continued)

After you select a function, you'll specify the arguments. An **argument** consists of values or cell references used to calculate the result of the function. For example, the Average function requires an argument consisting of a series of numbers or a series of cells. When you complete the Average function, the result is calculated as an average of the values in the cells you specified.

**Figure
12-7**

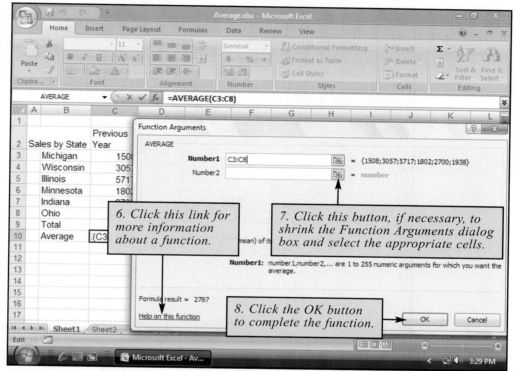

To select a range of cells for use as arguments in a function, click the top-left cell that contains data you want to use in the function, then drag down to the bottom-right cell. When you release the mouse button, the selected range of cells is displayed in the dialog box. Click the OK button to calculate the function.

Some functions use more than one argument and those arguments can be required or optional. The Payment (or PMT) function, for example, has three required arguments (Rate, Nper, and Pv) and two optional arguments (Fv and Type).

It can be difficult to determine how to enter the arguments for a function. For the PMT function, you have to divide the annual interest rate by 12 if you're using monthly payments. If you need help with the arguments for a function, click the *Help on this function* link.

Be careful when using functions you don't fully understand. If you're not sure how a function works, use the Excel Help window to find out more about it. When you use a new function, you should check the results with a calculator to make sure the function is working as you expected.

FAQ How do I use the AutoSum button?

Use the AutoSum button to quickly create a function to calculate the total of a column or row of cells. Excel examines the cells to the left of and above the current cell to determine which cells should be included in the total.

**Figure
12–8**

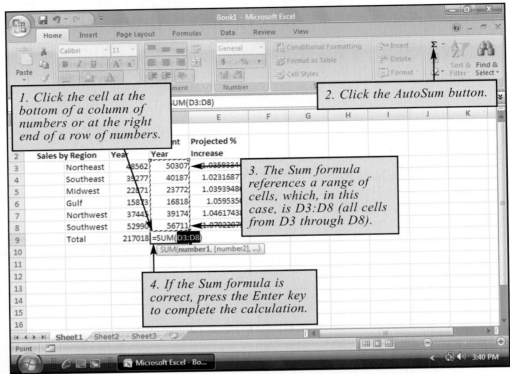

- The argument for the Sum function is typically a range or a series of adjacent cells.

- The AutoSum button usually does a good job of selecting the cells to be included in the function, but a blank cell or a cell containing a label can produce an incorrect answer. AutoSum works best if every cell in the row or column of cells contains a value.

- Be careful if you use the AutoSum button to calculate the sum of a column of cells with a number—such as 2007—as a column heading. If the heading has not been specifically formatted as a date, Excel includes it in the sum. Watch the marquee to be sure the correct range of cells is selected before you press the Enter key.

- If the AutoSum button does not automatically select the correct cells, press the Esc key to remove the function and create the Sum function manually. You can also drag across the correct range of cells, or hold down the Shift key while you use the arrow keys to select the correct range of cells. When the correct cells are selected, press the Enter key to complete the function.

QuickCheck A

1. The [_____] cell is the cell you can currently edit or modify.

2. B3:B12 is an example of a(n) [_____] of cells.

3. To edit a label, value, or formula after you've pressed the Enter key, click the cell, then click the [_____] bar.

4. The formula to subtract the contents of cell C3 from the contents of cell C2 is [_____] .

5. A(n) [_____] is a value or cell reference used to calculate the result of a function.

Check It!

QuickCheck B

Indicate the letter of the desktop element that best matches the following:

1. A cell containing a label [____]

2. A cell containing a value [____]

3. A cell containing a formula [____]

4. The AutoSum button [____]

5. The Insert Function button [____]

Check It!

CHAPTER **13**

Formatting a Worksheet

What's Inside and on the CD?

In this chapter, you'll learn how to format worksheets created with Microsoft Excel. Formatting is not just for looks—an effectively formatted worksheet is more approachable and helps readers understand the meaning of values and formulas presented in the worksheet. For example, an accountant might use a red font for negative values in a large worksheet so that possible losses are easier to spot. A quarterly banking statement might use a different colored border for each month to help readers recognize which transactions were made in a particular month.

In this chapter, you will learn that each type of data has special formatting characteristics that help to identify its purpose. Rather than typing dollar signs to identify financial values, for example, you will learn to format the values as currency data.

One of the most powerful advantages of using spreadsheet software for calculations is that you can easily make changes to the data in order to see how they affect results. You will learn how to copy and move data in a worksheet, and how the new location might change formulas and produce different results. Most importantly, this chapter explains how to avoid making incorrect modifications to values in a worksheet.

FAQ How do I add borders and background colors?

Borders and background colors define areas of a worksheet and call attention to important information. You can use the Font group on the Home tab and Format Cells dialog box to add borders and a colored background to one or more cells.

Figure 13-1

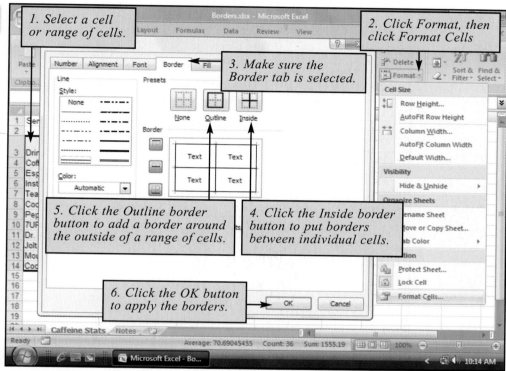

- To add borders around the outside and inside edges of selected cells, click both the Outline and Inside border buttons in the Presets section, as shown in the above figure. The Outline button puts a border around the outside edges of selected cells. The Inside button adds borders between individual cells.

- You can add and remove border lines by selecting any of the following border option buttons:

⊟	Top of range	⊞	Left of range
⊞	Inside horizontal lines	⊤	Inside vertical lines
⊟	Bottom of range	⊟	Right of range

- Line options allow you to select a decorative line style or to make all the border lines appear in a selected color.

- To add a colored background to the selected cell or cells, click the Fill tab. Select a color, then click the OK button to apply the background color.

- You can quickly add borders using the ⊞ Borders button in the Font group on the Home tab. However, this shortcut doesn't allow you to use all of the options that are only available in the Format Cells dialog box.

FAQ How do I format worksheet data?

You can use buttons in the Font group on the Home tab to select different font attributes for any data in worksheet cells. Values and formula results can be formatted with the same font attributes used to enhance the appearance of labels.

Play It!

Figure 13-2

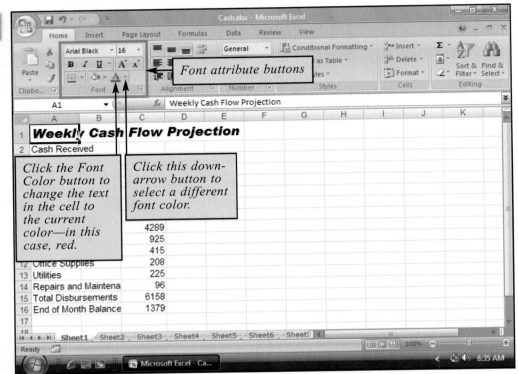

- You can apply multiple font attributes to any worksheet cell. Click the cell you want to format, then click as many font attribute buttons as you want. Click outside the cell to complete the process.

- To change the font for a range of cells, click the top-left cell, then drag the mouse to select the cells. Release the mouse button, then apply font formatting options to the selected cells.

- Font attributes are typically applied to the entire contents of a cell, but it is possible to change the font attributes for selected text inside a cell. For example, to display one of the words in a cell in bold text, type the contents of the cell, then click the formula bar. Use the mouse or the arrow keys to select one word within the cell, then click the Bold button. You can use the same process to apply different fonts and attributes such as italics, underlining, and font sizes.

- For more formatting options, click Format, then click Format Cells from the Cells group. You can also use the Format Cells Dialog Box Launcher from the Font group to display the Format Cells dialog box. Click the Font tab, if necessary. Select formatting options, such as superscript or subscript, then click the OK button to apply them.

FAQ How do I use the Format Cells dialog box?

In addition to font attributes, you can also apply number formats—currency, percent, commas, and decimals—to cells that contain values. The most commonly used number formats are available as buttons in the Number group on the Home tab. In addition, the Format Cells dialog box provides some special number formatting options that can improve the readability of a worksheet.

Play It!

Figure 13-3

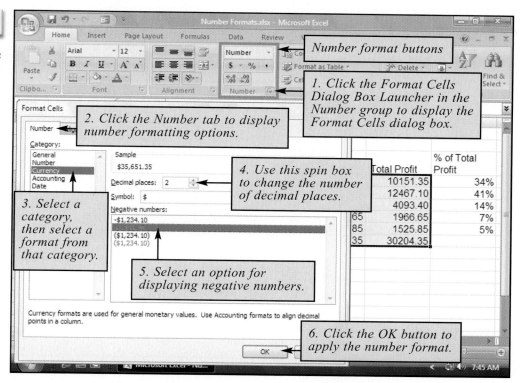

- The **$** Accounting Number Format button displays cell contents in your local currency format. For example, if your copy of Windows is configured for use in the U.S., the currency button displays cell contents as dollars and cents with a leading dollar sign ($) and two digits to the right of the decimal point.

- The **%** Percent Style button displays cell contents as a percentage, which means .35 is displayed as 35%.

- The **,** Comma Style button adds a comma to the values displayed in the cell. If your computer is configured for use in the U.S., the Comma Style button adds a comma every three digits to the left of the decimal point and displays two digits to the right of the decimal point.

- When you click the **.00** Decrease Decimal button, one less digit is displayed after the decimal point. When you click the **.00** Increase Decimal button, one more digit is displayed after the decimal point.

- To apply number formats to more than one cell, select a range of cells before you click any of the number format buttons or before you open the Format Cells dialog box.

FAQ How do I adjust column and row size?

If a column is too narrow, labels might be cut off and numbers are displayed as #####. Narrow columns allow you to fit more information on the screen or on the printed page, but you might need to adjust the width of some columns in your worksheet to make all of your worksheet data visible.

Play It!

Figure
13-4

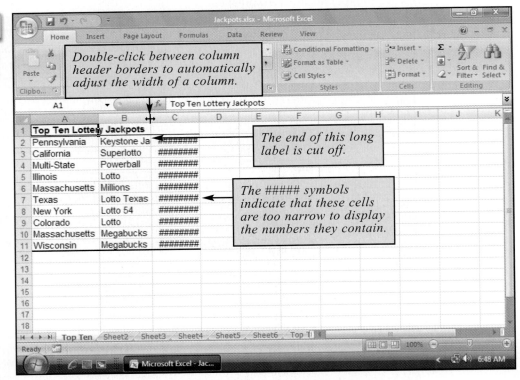

> *Double-click between column header borders to automatically adjust the width of a column.*

> *The end of this long label is cut off.*

> *The ##### symbols indicate that these cells are too narrow to display the numbers they contain.*

- To change the width of a cell, you must increase the width of the entire column. You can't make one cell in a column wider without affecting the other cells in that column.

- To manually adjust the width of a column, position the pointer over the vertical line between two column headings so that the pointer changes to a ✛ shape. Press and hold the left mouse button while you drag the vertical line left or right to manually adjust the width of the column.

- Excel automatically adjusts the height and width of selected cells when you use the AutoFit command located on the Home tab's Format button.

- If a label is too long to fit into a cell, it extends into the next cell on the right, if that cell is empty. If the cell on the right contains data, the end of the label is cut off.

- If a value is too long to fit into a cell, Excel displays a series of # characters in the cell. This is a signal that the cell contains a value that cannot fit within the current cell width. To see the number, simply increase the column width.

FAQ How do I center and align cell contents?

By default, labels are aligned on the left edge of a cell while values and formulas are aligned on the right edge of a cell. Unfortunately, this means that a label at the top of a column of numbers is not aligned with numbers in the rest of the column. Typically, you'll want to center or right-align the headings for columns of numbers.

Figure 13–5

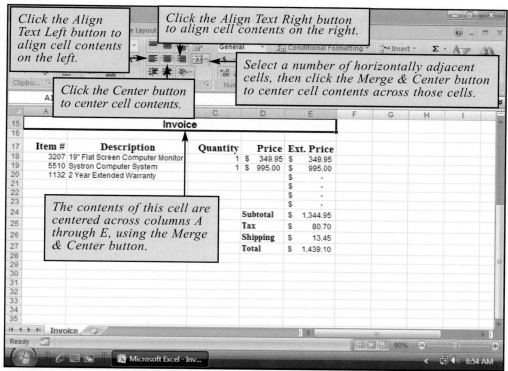

Click the Align Text Left button to align cell contents on the left.

Click the Align Text Right button to align cell contents on the right.

Select a number of horizontally adjacent cells, then click the Merge & Center button to center cell contents across those cells.

Click the Center button to center cell contents.

The contents of this cell are centered across columns A through E, using the Merge & Center button.

- If a cell containing label data is a column heading, select the cell and click the Align Text Right button in the Alignment group on the Home tab to move the label to the right side of the cell so that it aligns with the column of numbers.

- To change the alignment of a range of cells, select the range of cells, then click the desired alignment button from the Alignment group on the Home tab.

- To quickly select all cells in a column, click the column header at the top of the column. To select all cells in a row, click the row header on the left side of the row.

- Sometimes you'll want to center a label across a number of columns. In the figure above, the title "Invoice" is centered across columns A through E. To center text across columns, select the range of cells to be merged, then click the Merge & Center button in the Alignment group on the Home tab.

- To merge a range of cells in a column, select the range of cells, then click the Merge & Center button in the Alignment group on the Home tab. The down-arrow button next to the Merge & Center button allows you to unmerge cells as well as merge without centering.

FAQ What happens when I copy and move cells?

You can use the Cut, Copy, and Paste buttons in the Clipboard group on the Home tab to copy and move cell contents to a different worksheet location. Label data is copied or moved without changing. If you copy and paste cells that contain a formula, the copied formula is modified to work in the new location. A cell reference that changes when a formula is copied or moved is called a **relative reference**. Excel treats all cell references as relative references unless you specify otherwise.

Figure 13–6

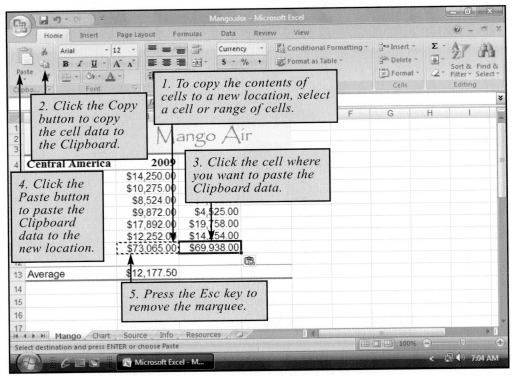

1. To copy the contents of cells to a new location, select a cell or range of cells.

2. Click the Copy button to copy the cell data to the Clipboard.

3. Click the cell where you want to paste the Clipboard data.

4. Click the Paste button to paste the Clipboard data to the new location.

5. Press the Esc key to remove the marquee.

- To move the data in cells, select the cells, then click the Cut button. Click the cell where you want to paste the data, then click the Paste button. The data is moved from the original location to the new location.

- If you copy or move the data in a range of cells, the pasted data is positioned below and to the right of the active cell. In other words, click the cell in the top-left corner of the data's new location.

- A formula that contains a relative reference changes when the formula is copied or moved. For example, assume cell C4 contains the formula =C2+C3. You then copy and paste that formula to cell F4. The formula will be changed to =F2+F3. The references C2 and C3 in the original formula were relative references. When the formula was originally located in cell C4, it actually meant =(the contents of the cell two rows up)+(the contents of the cell one row up). When you copy the formula to cell F4, Excel adjusts the formula so that it retains the same relative references. When you paste the formula into cell F4, it becomes =F2+F3.

- Be careful when pasting, moving, and copying the contents of cells so that you maintain working formulas. For example, do not paste a value into a cell where a formula belongs.

FAQ When should I use absolute references?

Most of the time, you want Excel to use relative references; but in some situations, cell references should not be modified when moved to a new location. An **absolute reference** does not change, and will always refer to the same cell, even after the formula is copied or moved.

Figure 13–7

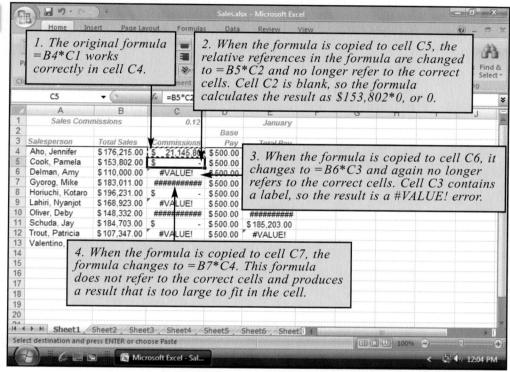

- In the example above, cell C1 contains a commission rate. When you copy the formula in cell C4 to cell C5, the original formula =B4*C1 is changed to =B5*C2. The B5 part is fine, but C2 is an empty cell. The formula should still refer to the commission rate in cell C1.

- To create an absolute reference, insert a dollar sign ($) before the column reference and another dollar sign before the row reference. In the example above, you would modify the original formula to read =B4*$C$1. Using an absolute reference, no matter where the formula moves, Excel must always refer to the contents of cell C1 for the second part of the formula. When you copy the formula =B4*$C$1 to cell C5, the formula is changed to =B5*$C$1. The absolute cell reference is protected by the $ sign and will not be modified or adjusted.

- If you want to use an absolute reference in a formula, you can start typing, then press the F4 key after you click a cell to add it to the formula. Pressing the F4 key changes a cell reference to an absolute reference.

- You can also create mixed references by combining references so that only one of the column or row references is absolute. For example, $C1 creates an absolute column and a relative row reference. C$1 creates a relative column and an absolute row reference. The absolute identifier will not change, but the relative identifier will.

FAQ How do I delete and insert rows and columns?

It is easy to delete a row, or insert a blank row between rows that already contain data. You can also insert and delete columns. Excel even modifies your formulas as needed to make sure they refer to the correct cells each time you insert a new row.

Figure 13-8

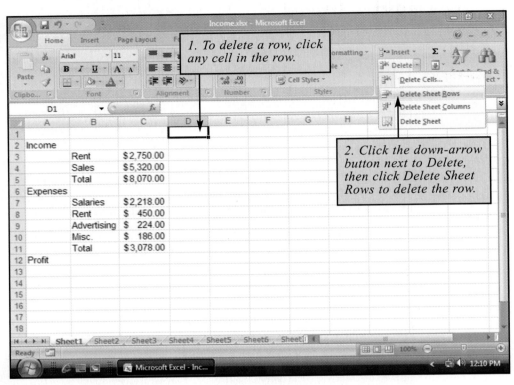

- To insert a row, click any cell. You can also select a row by clicking the row identifier button on the left side of the window. Click the down-arrow button next to Insert in the Cells group, then click Insert Sheet Rows. The new row is inserted above the selected row.

- To insert more than one row at a time, drag down over the number of rows you want to insert. Click the down-arrow button next to Insert in the Cells group, then click Insert Sheet Rows to insert the new rows.

- To delete more than one row at a time, drag down over the rows you want to delete. Click the down-arrow button next to Delete in the Cells group, then click Delete Sheet Rows to delete the rows.

- Use the same procedures to insert and delete columns. To insert one or more columns, select the column or columns, click the down-arrow button next to Insert in the Cells group, then click Insert Sheet Columns. To delete one or more columns, select the column or columns, click the down-arrow button next to Delete in the Cells group, then click Delete Sheet Columns.

- As you insert and delete rows and columns, Excel adjusts relative cell references in formulas to keep them accurate. For example, the formula =C8+G8 changes to =C8+F8 if the original column D is deleted. In the same way, the formula =C8+G8 changes to =C7+G7 if row 6 is deleted.

FAQ Can I use styles?

As with Microsoft Word, Excel allows you to work with styles. You can use predefined styles or create custom styles. Predefined styles are built into the software, and include formats for displaying currency, percentages, and general numbers. You can also create your own styles to enhance the appearance of your worksheet.

Figure 13-9

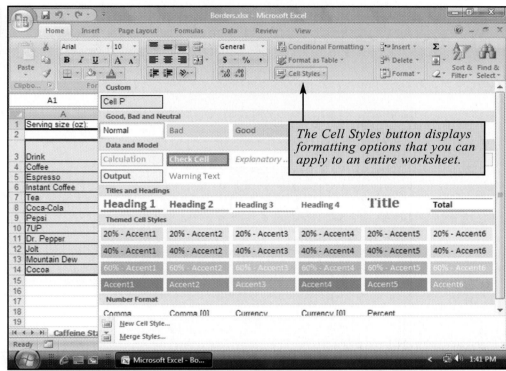

The Cell Styles button displays formatting options that you can apply to an entire worksheet.

- The $, % , and ʼ buttons in the Number group automatically format a cell or group of cells with a predefined style. Click Cell Styles in the Styles group, right-click the desired style from the Number Format section, then click Modify to redefine the default setting.

- Styles include text formatting, such as font, size, and color, as well as numeric formatting, such as comma placement, number of decimal points, and the currency symbol.

- You can create your own styles for numbers or text. Click Cell Styles in the Styles group, then click New Cell Style. Type the new style name. If you want to modify characteristics of the new style, click the Format button to open the Format Cells dialog box. Click the OK button to accept the changes in the Format Cells dialog box, then click the OK button in the Style dialog box to create the style.

- The Format Painter button allows you to copy and paste formats from one cell to another. Click the cell containing the formats you want to copy, then click the Format Painter button in the Clipboard group. Click the cell where you want to apply the formats.

- The Styles group includes a variety of predefined formats designed to format entire worksheets or sections of worksheets. Click either the *Cell Styles* or *Format as Table* button in the Styles group to view available formats.

- The Hide function can be used to hide rows or columns you don't want displayed. To hide a block of rows or columns, first select the rows or columns to be hidden. Right-click the highlighted area, then select Hide.

- To display rows or columns that were previously hidden, select the rows or columns that border the hidden section. Right-click, then choose Unhide.

FAQ How do I manage multiple worksheets?

A workbook—sometimes called a "3D workbook"—is a collection of worksheets. Workbooks allow you to group related worksheets together in one file, and easily navigate from one worksheet to another. Worksheets in a workbook can access data from other worksheets in the workbook; for example, a workbook might contain a Quarterly Report worksheet, which accesses totals calculated from January, February, and March worksheets.

Figure 13-10

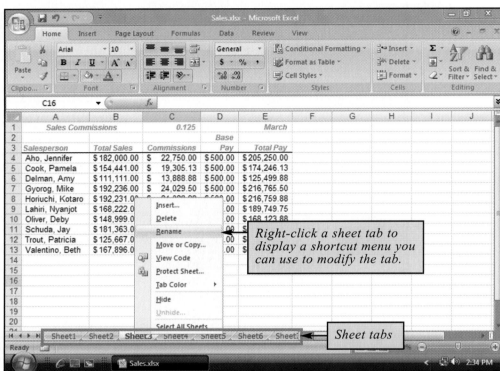

- The default workbook contains three worksheets, titled Sheet1, Sheet2, and Sheet3. Click the tabs at the bottom of the screen to navigate through the worksheets.

- You can rename worksheets, change the color of the tabs, or change the order of the worksheets by right-clicking a worksheet tab and making a selection from the shortcut menu.

- Insert a new worksheet by right-clicking the tab for the worksheet that should immediately follow the new worksheet. Select Insert from the shortcut menu, then make a selection from the Insert dialog box. You can insert a new worksheet at the end of the worksheet tabs by clicking the Insert Worksheet button after the final worksheet.

- Delete an existing worksheet by right-clicking the worksheet's tab and clicking Delete.

- The Move/Copy option allows you to change the order of worksheets. For example, if you want to insert a new worksheet in front of Sheet1, simply insert the sheet after any tab, then use the Move/Copy option to position it as the first worksheet.

- To reference data from other worksheets, include the tab name before the row letter and column number. For example, the reference Sheet3!A1 indicates Column A, Row 1, on the worksheet called Sheet3. You can also reference data in other worksheets by navigating to the worksheet and clicking the desired cell while entering a formula or function.

QuickCheck A

1. True or false? When the contents of a cell are displayed as #####, that cell contains a number that is too long to display in the cell. [＿＿＿＿＿]

2. To center a label across several cells, select the horizontally adjacent cells, then click the [＿＿＿＿＿＿＿＿] & Center button.

3. A(n) [＿＿＿＿＿＿＿＿] reference is a cell reference that will be modified if the formula is copied or moved to a new cell.

4. A(n) [＿＿＿＿＿＿＿＿] reference is a cell reference that will not be modified if the formula is copied or moved to a new cell.

5. To write the formula =B2*D6 so that it always refers to cell D6, even when moved or copied, you would change the formula to [＿＿＿＿＿＿＿＿] .

Check It!

QuickCheck B

Indicate the letter of the desktop element that best matches the following:

1. The Accounting Number Format button [＿＿＿]

2. The Merge & Center button [＿＿＿]

3. A cell formatted in the Currency style [＿＿＿]

4. A cell formatted in the Percent style [＿＿＿]

5. The Decrease Decimal button [＿＿＿]

Check It!

CHAPTER **14** Finalizing a Worksheet

What's Inside and on the CD?

In this chapter, you'll learn how to finalize your worksheets by sorting data, creating charts, adding graphics, checking spelling, and testing formulas. You'll also learn how to prepare your worksheets for printing by adding page breaks, headers and footers, and gridlines. As an added bonus, you'll find out how to turn your worksheets into Web pages.

FAQ Can I sort data in a worksheet?

Excel provides tools that allow you to sort data in ascending or descending order. Data sorted in ascending order will be arranged in alphabetical order—labels that start with A will be positioned above those that start with B. Data sorted in descending order will be arranged in reverse alphabetical order—labels that start with Z will be positioned above those that start with Y.

Play It!

Figure 14-1

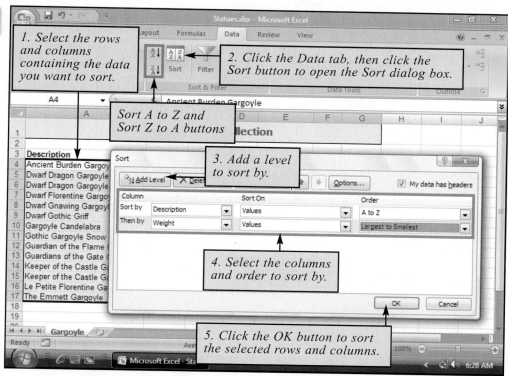

* It's a good idea to save your worksheet before performing a sort, just in case you forget to select all the necessary columns and end up scrambling your data.

* It is essential that you select all columns of related data. For example, if column A contains the names of salespeople and column B contains the year-to-date sales for each person, you must select all cells in columns A and B before performing the sort. If you don't, your data will become scrambled, and the names will no longer be associated with the correct year-to-date sales numbers.

* If you forget to select all columns before sorting, click the Undo button to undo the sort. Check the data carefully to make sure each row still contains the correct data, then select all columns of data and try the sort again.

* If you just want to sort by the data in the first column, you can use the ▲↓ Sort A to Z or ▼↓ Sort Z to A buttons in the Sort & Filter group on the Data tab.

* If you want to sort by a column other than the first column, or if you want to sort by several columns, use the procedure shown in Figure 14-1. If you need to perform a multilevel sort, designate the first column in the *Sort by* box. Add additional levels with the *Add Level* button and designate the columns from the *Then by* list. You can set each level of the sort for either ascending or descending order. Click the OK button to apply the sort.

FAQ How do I create a chart?

You can use the Charts group on the Insert tab to chart or graph data in your worksheet. You should pick a chart type that suits the data. A **line chart** is used to show data that changes over time. A **pie chart** illustrates the proportion of parts to a whole. A **bar chart** (sometimes called a "column chart") is used to show comparisons.

Figure
14-2

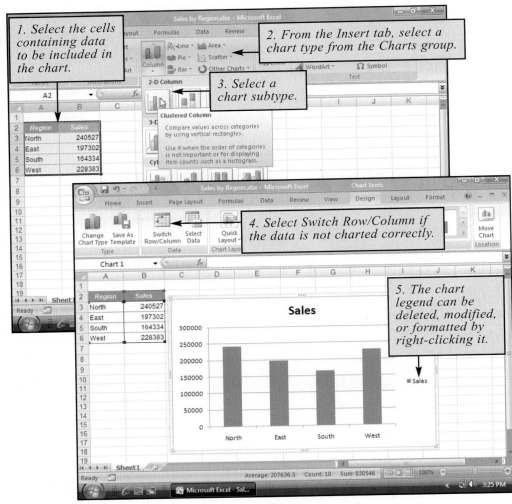

1. *Select the cells containing data to be included in the chart.*

2. *From the Insert tab, select a chart type from the Charts group.*

3. *Select a chart subtype.*

4. *Select Switch Row/Column if the data is not charted correctly.*

5. *The chart legend can be deleted, modified, or formatted by right-clicking it.*

- When selecting the cells for a chart, include the cells that contain labels and they will be used to identify the lines, columns, or pie slices on the chart.

- If you are not certain which chart type to use, hover the pointer over any of the chart buttons to display a description and usage recommendation.

- If the chart doesn't seem to make sense, make sure the chart is selected and try clicking the Switch Row/Column button in the Data group. This button swaps the data plotted on the horizontal axis with the data plotted on the vertical axis.

- By default, the chart is inserted into the current worksheet. You can move the chart with the Move Chart button on the Design tab.

- When a chart is selected, you can move it or resize it by dragging the sizing handles.

FAQ How do I modify a chart?

Excel creates a chart based on the data and labels you select from a worksheet. You can modify this basic chart by changing the chart type and adjusting the chart data.

When making changes to a chart, make sure the chart is selected so that Excel displays all of the charting tabs, including Design, Layout, and Format.

PlayIt!

Figure 14-3

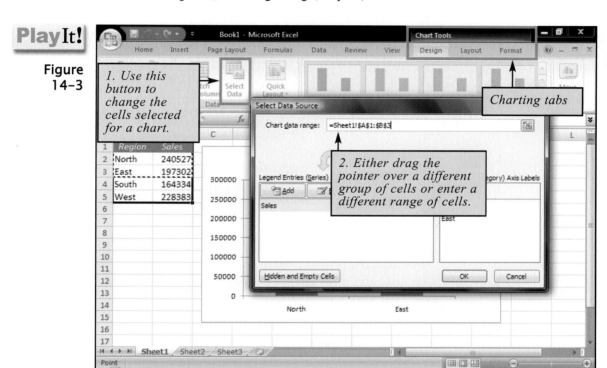

To select a different chart type, select the Design tab, and then click the Change Chart Type button.

To select a different range of cells to be charted, click the Select Data button from the Design tab. You can then drag over the cells directly in the worksheet, or you can type a range into the Chart data range box.

If you change the data in a worksheet cell, Excel updates the chart immediately after you press the Enter key.

• How do I modify a chart? (continued)

When you're satisfied that your chart displays the right data using a meaningful chart type, you can turn your focus to improving the readability and appearance of the chart.

In general, most modifications begin by right-clicking the chart element you want to change. Excel displays a shortcut menu that contains options you can use to modify the chart element you've selected.

Figure 14–4

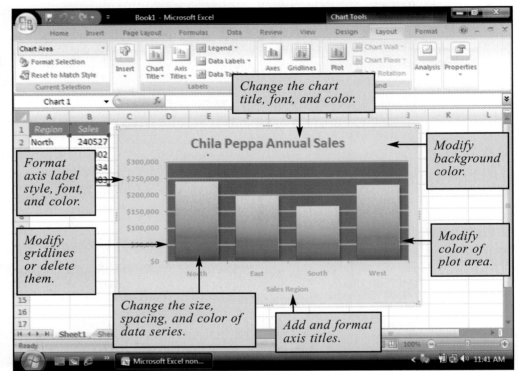

- Label formats on charts can be different from those in the worksheet cells. In the example above, sales data such as 240527 in the cells was unformatted, whereas corresponding data on the vertical axis is formatted for currency style as $250,000.

- For readability, consider changing the units used for axis labels. In the example above, the vertical axis uses single units and displays lots of zeros. If you change the units to thousands, Excel displays $300 instead of $300,000 and adds the word "Thousands" as a vertical axis label.

- Excel includes a huge variety of colors, patterns, and gradients that can be applied to backgrounds, plot areas, gridlines, and data series. Use special effects sparingly to avoid creating charts that are distracting rather than informative.

FAQ Can I add graphics to a worksheet?

Worksheet graphics can be used to highlight important sections, add interest or pizzazz to otherwise dull pages, or graphically illustrate spreadsheet data. Vector drawings can be created using Excel's drawing tools. Photographs or clip art can be inserted from a file or imported directly from imaging devices, such as scanners and digital cameras.

Figure 14–5

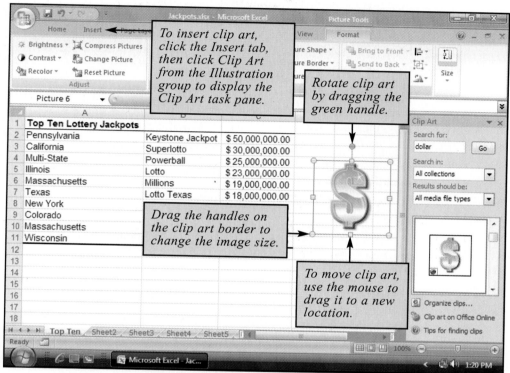

- To insert clip art, click the cell where you wish to place the graphic. Click the Insert tab, then click Clip Art in the Illustrations group. When the Clip Art task pane appears, enter a keyword for the type of clip art you would like to use in the *Search for* text box, then click Go. Choose an image from the available pictures, then close the Clip Art task pane.

- Graphics can be resized using the round "handles" that appear on the edges of a selected graphic. For example, to enlarge a graphic, first select it by clicking anywhere on the graphic. Drag the handle in the bottom-right corner down and to the right.

- To move a graphic, click the graphic to select it, then hold the mouse button down while dragging it to the new location.

- The round, green handle that appears at the top of a graphic allows you to rotate the graphic. To rotate a graphic, click to select it, then drag the green rotate handle right or left.

- The Shapes tools allow you to draw simple lines and shapes. To draw an arrow, click the Insert tab, then click Shapes in the Illustrations group. Select Arrow from the Lines group. Click the worksheet cell where you would like the arrow to start, and then drag to "draw" the arrow.

- The SmartArt button in the Illustrations group on the Insert tab allows you to insert professionally designed visual aids into your worksheet. To insert SmartArt, click the SmartArt button from the Illustrations group on the Insert tab, select the shape you want to insert, and then click the OK button. Drag the shape to the location on the worksheet where you would like the shape to be positioned.

FAQ How do I check spelling in a worksheet?

Excel can check the spelling of all labels in a worksheet. Unlike Word, however, Excel doesn't show misspelled words with wavy red underlines. Excel also doesn't provide a grammar checker. So it is important for you to proofread your worksheets for grammar errors and spelling errors not caught by the spelling checker.

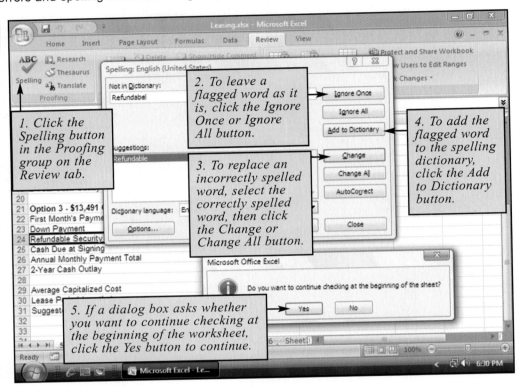

Play It!

Figure 14–6

1. Click the Spelling button in the Proofing group on the Review tab.

2. To leave a flagged word as it is, click the Ignore Once or Ignore All button.

3. To replace an incorrectly spelled word, select the correctly spelled word, then click the Change or Change All button.

4. To add the flagged word to the spelling dictionary, click the Add to Dictionary button.

5. If a dialog box asks whether you want to continue checking at the beginning of the worksheet, click the Yes button to continue.

- You can begin to check the spelling with any cell selected. However, if you make cell A1 the active cell, you will avoid the question displayed in Step 5 above.

- If the correct spelling appears in the Suggestions list, click to select it, then click the Change button to correct the misspelled word.

- If no suggested spellings are displayed, click the *Not in Dictionary* text box, then type the correct word. Click the Change button to replace the misspelled word.

- If you're sure the word is spelled correctly, click the Ignore Once button to ignore this occurrence of the word. Sometimes a word—for example, a person's name—is not recognized by Excel. Click the Ignore All button if you want to ignore all other occurrences of this word throughout the entire worksheet.

- If the word is one you use frequently, click the Add to Dictionary button to add the current word to the spelling dictionary. For example, adding the city name "Ishpeming" to the Excel dictionary stops the spelling tool from identifying the name of this city as a misspelled word.

FAQ How do I test my worksheet?

You should always test your worksheets before relying on the results. Don't assume the result is correct just because it's generated by a computer. Your computer is almost certainly returning the correct results for the formulas and data you've entered, but it is possible you might have entered the wrong value in a cell, used the wrong cell reference in a formula, or made some other mistake in a formula.

Play It!

Figure 14–7

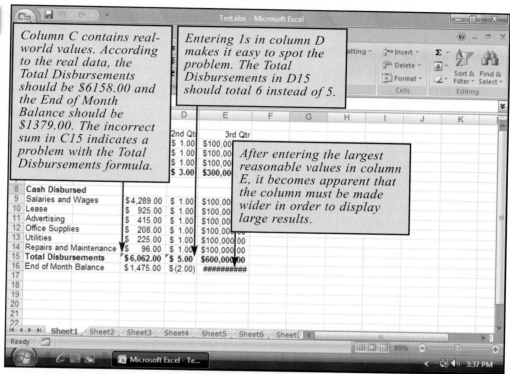

Column C contains real-world values. According to the real data, the Total Disbursements should be $6158.00 and the End of Month Balance should be $1379.00. The incorrect sum in C15 indicates a problem with the Total Disbursements formula.

Entering 1s in column D makes it easy to spot the problem. The Total Disbursements in D15 should total 6 instead of 5.

After entering the largest reasonable values in column E, it becomes apparent that the column must be made wider in order to display large results.

- It's a good idea to use the Save As option to rename and save an extra copy of your worksheet before testing, just in case your test significantly changes the worksheet.

- One way to test your worksheet is to enter a series of consistent and easily verified values, such as 1 or 10, into the data cells. If you enter 1s, you can quickly check the calculated results in your head and spot potential formula errors.

- Another way to test your worksheet is to enter a set of real-world values for which you already know the results. Compare the calculated result from the worksheet with the real-world result to make sure the worksheet is returning correct results. Testing with real data also helps identify problems such as columns that are too narrow to hold calculated results.

- It is also a good idea to test your worksheet by entering the largest and smallest values that would reasonably be expected in normal use of your worksheet. Small values, including zero, can lead to errors such as division by zero. The use of large values can lead to results that do not fit into the cell where the answer is to be displayed. In such a case, you'll need to make those columns wider.

FAQ How do I use Print Preview and Page Setup?

Excel's Print Preview window allows you to see how a worksheet will look when it is printed. To display the Print Preview window, click the Microsoft Office button, point to Print, then click Print Preview. You can also open the Print Preview window by clicking the Preview button on the Print dialog box. Most experienced worksheet designers use the Print Preview window in the final stages of worksheet development. They look at the default print format, and then refine it by adjusting margins, adding headers, and specifying whether to fit the worksheet on a single page or distribute it over multiple pages.

Figure 14–8

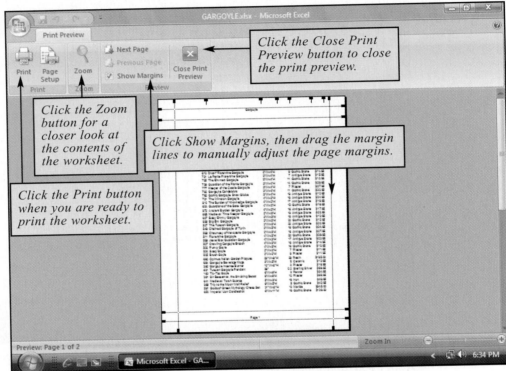

Click the Close Print Preview button to close the print preview.

Click the Zoom button for a closer look at the contents of the worksheet.

Click Show Margins, then drag the margin lines to manually adjust the page margins.

Click the Print button when you are ready to print the worksheet.

- The Zoom button switches between a close-up and a normal view. Just click the Zoom button again to switch back to the previous view. It's a good idea to zoom in to look for cells that contain #####, indicating a column that needs to be wider.

- To adjust margins, click the Show Margins check box. Position the pointer over a margin line until it changes to a ✛ shape or a ✛ shape, drag that margin line to its new position, then release the mouse button. You can also set margins using the Page Setup dialog box.

- Notice that there are two margin lines at the top and bottom of the page. The outside top and bottom lines control the location of the header and footer. The inside lines control the placement of worksheet data.

- If you're not satisfied with the appearance of the worksheet in the Print Preview window, click the Page Setup button to display the Page Setup dialog box. You will find more options there for controlling the worksheet's printed format.

How do I use Print Preview and Page Setup? (continued)

Excel's Page Setup dialog box allows you to control the orientation and structure for printed worksheet pages. Use this feature along with the Print Preview window before you print a worksheet. You can access the Page Setup dialog box by clicking the Page Setup button from the Print Preview window. You can also click the Page Layout tab, then click the Page Setup Dialog Box Launcher in the Page Setup group. Settings you make with the Page Setup dialog box are saved when you save the worksheet.

Figure 14-9

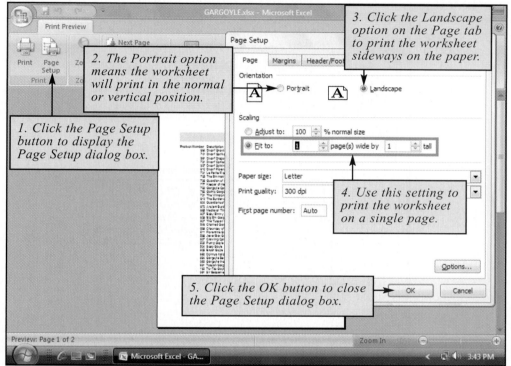

- The Page tab in the Page Setup dialog box contains handy settings for worksheet orientation and scaling. **Portrait orientation** prints a worksheet on a vertically oriented page. **Landscape orientation** prints a worksheet on the page sideways. You can use the Scaling options to adjust a worksheet's overall size or force it to fit the width of a single page. Printing a large worksheet on a single page makes it easier to read, as long as the font is legible. To cancel scaling, click the *Adjust to* option button and change the corresponding value to 100% normal size.

- The Margins tab in the Page Setup dialog box provides an alternative to the Print Preview window for specifying margin settings.

- The Header/Footer tab in the Page Setup dialog box allows you to add the worksheet title, date, and page numbers to the top or bottom of each page.

- The Sheet tab in the Page Setup dialog box allows you to specify a section of a worksheet to print—useful for printing a selected section of a large worksheet. The Sheet tab also allows you to specify whether you want to print gridlines or row and column headings. **Gridlines**—the lines that separate one cell from another—can be printed to create visual boundaries for rows and columns. Row and column headings are the column letters and row numbers. Printouts that include gridlines and row/column headings can be useful when you want to show the structure of a worksheet.

FAQ How do I add headers and footers to a worksheet?

As in Microsoft Word, Excel worksheets can contain headers and footers. A header is text that appears at the top of every page. A footer is text that appears at the bottom of every page. Excel includes predefined headers and footers that contain information such as the title of the worksheet, the date, and the page number. You can also create your own headers and footers.

Figure 14–10

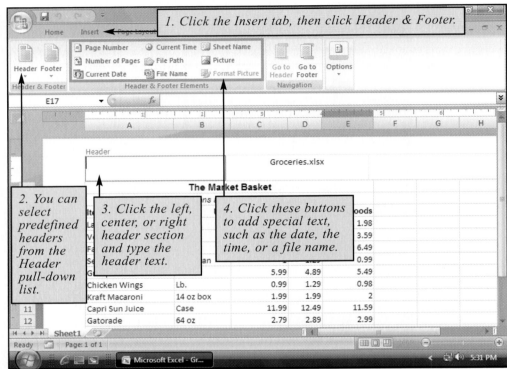

- Footers work just like headers—simply select the appropriate footer option.

- Header and footer options are available on the Header/Footer tab in the Page Setup dialog box. The custom Header and Footer dialog boxes contain buttons that insert commonly used elements in the header or footer. To use these buttons:

  A   Select the text, then click this button to display the Font dialog box to format the header text.

  Click this button to insert page numbers.

  Click this button to insert the total number of pages.

  Click this button to insert the current date.

  Click this button to insert the current time.

  Click this button to insert the file path (drive letter and folders).

  Click this button to insert the name of the file.

  Click this button to insert the name of the worksheet tab.

  Click this button to insert a picture.

  Click this button to format the picture you inserted.

FAQ How do I set up a multipage worksheet?

Large worksheets sometimes require additional setup so that they print correctly on multiple pages. Before printing a multipage worksheet, use the Page Break Preview to examine page breaks and modify them to arrange data logically on each page. It is also good practice to include row and column labels on every printed page to help readers identify data in rows and columns after they read past page 1. To save time collating, you can use the Page Setup dialog box to specify the order in which multipage worksheets print.

Figure 14-11

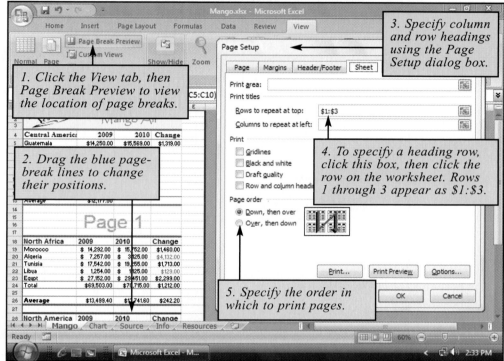

3. *Specify column and row headings using the Page Setup dialog box.*

1. *Click the View tab, then Page Break Preview to view the location of page breaks.*

2. *Drag the blue page-break lines to change their positions.*

4. *To specify a heading row, click this box, then click the row on the worksheet. Rows 1 through 3 appear as $1:$3.*

5. *Specify the order in which to print pages.*

- To view page breaks, click the View tab, then click Page Break Preview in the Workbook Views group. Click and drag the blue page break lines to change their locations.

- To insert a new page break, click a location for the new page break. Click the Page Layout tab, click Breaks in the Page Setup group, then click Insert Page Break.

- To exit the Page Break View, click the View tab, then click Normal.

- To include column or row labels on every page, open the Page Setup dialog box using the Page Setup Dialog Box Launcher from the Page Setup group on the Page Layout tab. On the Sheet tab, use the *Print titles* text boxes to specify the row and column that contain headings.

- To specify the order in which pages of a multipage worksheet are printed, use the Sheet tab of the Page Setup dialog box. In the Page Order section, choose *Down, then over* or *Over, then down.*

FAQ How do I print a worksheet?

Use the Print dialog box to print a single copy of the current worksheet, to print multiple copies, to designate selected pages, or to use advanced print options. For example, you can print all the worksheets that make up a workbook. The default setting prints only the current worksheet.

Figure 14-12

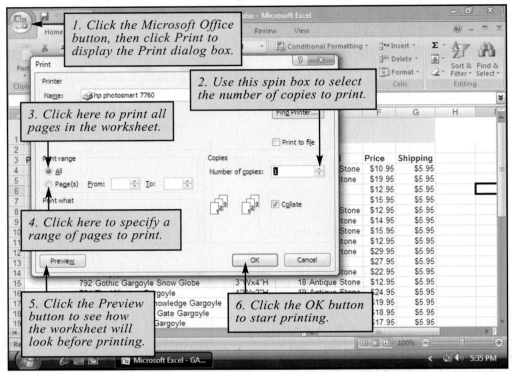

1. Click the Microsoft Office button, then click Print to display the Print dialog box.

2. Use this spin box to select the number of copies to print.

3. Click here to print all pages in the worksheet.

4. Click here to specify a range of pages to print.

5. Click the Preview button to see how the worksheet will look before printing.

6. Click the OK button to start printing.

- Determine what you want to print before opening the Print dialog box. By default, Excel prints the entire active worksheet. If you want to print only a section of the worksheet, select the range of cells before you click the Microsoft Office button and select Print. You can then simply click the *Selection* option in the *Print what* section of the dialog box.

- To print only the current worksheet, click the *Active sheet(s)* option in the *Print what* section of the dialog box.

- To print all worksheets in the current workbook, click the *Entire workbook* option in the *Print what* section of the dialog box.

- Click the Preview button to see how the worksheet or workbook will look when printed.

- If your worksheet doesn't print, check that the printer is online, and make sure you have specified the correct printer in the Print dialog box.

FAQ How do I save a worksheet as a Web page?

You can save your worksheet as a Web page that you can post on the Internet. This Excel feature provides an easy way to make your worksheet data accessible to a large number of people without having to send each person a printed copy of the worksheet.

Figure 14–13

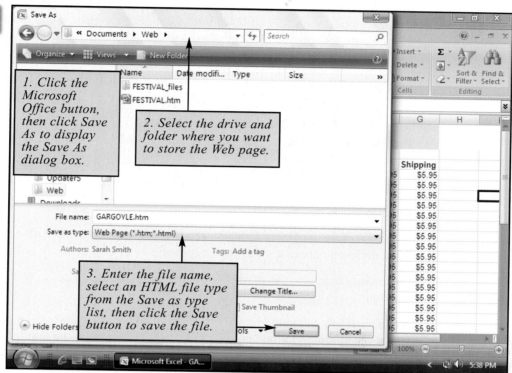

1. Click the Microsoft Office button, then click Save As to display the Save As dialog box.

2. Select the drive and folder where you want to store the Web page.

3. Enter the file name, select an HTML file type from the Save as type list, then click the Save button to save the file.

- Before you save a worksheet as a Web page, it's a good idea to save it in normal Excel .xlsx format.

- Tables are a valuable formatting tool for creating Web pages. You can use Excel to create a table for this purpose. First, select the range of cells you want to include in the table, then follow the same steps to save as a Web page. In the Save As dialog box, click the Selection option, choose the HTML file type, name your file, and click Save.

- Some formatting options available in Excel cannot be duplicated in a Web page. If a worksheet contains formatting that isn't available in HTML, you'll be notified of the problem areas and will have the option of canceling or continuing with the save.

- Not all worksheets convert successfully to Web pages, so you should preview your worksheet in a Web browser to make sure the conversion is acceptable before you post your worksheet Web pages on the Internet.

FAQ What makes a good worksheet?

Well-organized and well-formatted worksheets present data accurately, concisely, and in a format that is easy to understand. Consider the following recommendations for creating effective worksheets and avoiding common design errors.

- When deciding whether to put your data into rows or columns, structure your data so that the longest data sets go down the screen. For example, if you have 100 years of climate data for each of 12 months, put the labels for the years down the left side of the worksheet, and place the labels for each month across the top.

- Arrange the information on your worksheet so it reads from left to right and top to bottom. Organize the data into rows and columns. Use cells outside of the main data area to hold constants, such as sales tax rate, that are referenced by multiple formulas.

- Provide meaningful labels for all data. Labels should be spelled correctly and use consistent capitalization.

- Make sure your data is entered accurately.

- Enter formulas and functions carefully and test them for accuracy.

- Avoid the mistake of incorporating cells that contain labels into mathematical formulas, as sometimes happens when you copy formulas or fill a series of cells with a formula.

- Avoid circular references in which a formula references the cell in which the formula is entered.

- Make sure you understand the rules of mathematical precedence (i.e., multiplication and division are performed before addition and subtraction) so that formulas produce the results you intended; use parentheses to indicate the parts of formulas to be calculated first.

- Use absolute and relative references appropriately. In formulas, refer to cells that hold the data, rather than entering the data itself. For example, suppose cell B12 holds the total price of merchandise in a buyer's shopping cart. When calculating sales tax for a purchase, instead of using the tax rate directly in a formula like =.04*B12, place the sales tax rate into a cell such as D3. The formula to calculate sales tax becomes =D3*B12.

- Avoid using too many fonts, font sizes, and colors in a worksheet, but do use font attributes to highlight the most important data on your worksheet, typically totals and other summary data. By convention, red is the color used for negative values, overdrafts, and deficits.

- Format numbers for easy reading. For example, use commas in numbers and currency symbols for cells that hold numbers pertaining to money.

- Use consistent formats for similar data. For example, format all currency using the same number of decimal places and comma placement.

- Format cells so that data fits into them rather than spilling into neighboring cells. Blank cells should look blank so that cells holding data can be clearly identified. The exception to this rule is for worksheet titles that can be allowed to stretch over several cells.

- Add documentation as necessary, especially if other people will be entering data or modifying the worksheet.

QuickCheck A

1. True or false? Excel displays a wavy red underline under words that might be misspelled.

2. If the labels apple, banana, and peach are sorted in descending order, which label would be at the top of the sorted list?

3. True or false? Spreadsheet software always calculates correctly, so it's not necessary to test your worksheets before using them.

4. Use a(n) [   ] chart to show proportions of a part to a whole.

5. True or false? Excel includes a feature that fits a worksheet onto a single page of paper when printed.

Check It!

QuickCheck B

Indicate the letter of the desktop element that best matches the following:

1. The Spelling button

2. The sort ascending button

3. The Clip Art button

4. The button used to add page numbers

5. A column that is good for testing data because it contains easily verified values

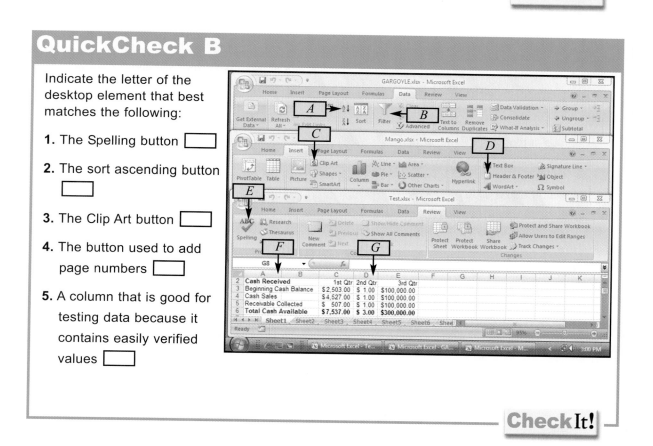

Check It!

CHAPTER **15**

Creating a Presentation

What's Inside and on the CD?

Microsoft PowerPoint is the component of Microsoft Office best suited for creating visual backdrops for speeches and oral presentations. As presentation software, Microsoft PowerPoint provides a set of tools to help you script, organize, and display a presentation.

A **PowerPoint presentation** consists of a number of slides. Each **slide** contains objects such as titles, items in a bulleted list, graphics, and charts. Slides can even contain multimedia elements, such as video clips and sound bytes. Typically, slides are presented with a computer and a projection device. PowerPoint presentations can also be printed on transparent sheets for use with an overhead projector, printed on paper for handouts, or converted to Web pages for display on the Internet.

Good graphic design makes slides visually compelling and presentations easy to understand. A few simple bullets can be used to list key concepts. Numbered lists can present the steps in a process. Tables, charts, and graphics can simplify complex ideas and present numerical or statistical data creatively. To design effective slides, avoid clutter and unnecessary graphical elements. Put common elements, such as the title of the presentation or the name of the author, on each slide to create consistency from slide to slide.

FAQ What's in the PowerPoint window?

Microsoft PowerPoint creates a slide show that can be presented with a computer and a projection device, printed on transparency film, or converted to HTML and viewed through a Web browser. To create useful handouts for distribution to an audience, slides can be printed on paper in a variety of layouts.

To start PowerPoint, click Start, point to All Programs, click Microsoft Office, then click Microsoft Office PowerPoint 2007. The PowerPoint window includes several work areas, called "panes," in addition to controls on the ribbon, scroll bars, and status bar.

Figure 15-1

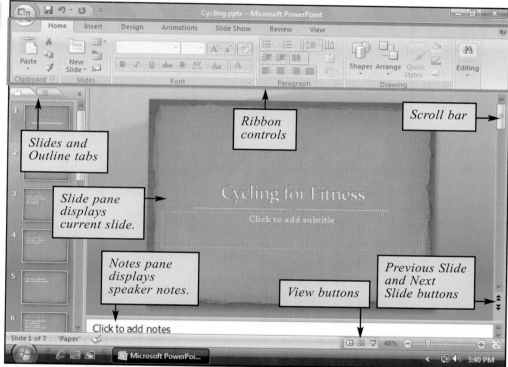

• When a presentation is open in Normal view, the current slide is displayed in the Slide pane of the PowerPoint window, the Slides and Outline tabs are shown in the left pane, and the Notes pane near the bottom of the window provides a place to type speaker notes.

• Use the scroll bar or the ⬆ Previous Slide and ⬇ Next Slide buttons to move from one slide to another in Normal view.

FAQ How do I create a presentation?

You can create a presentation by selecting a theme or template. You can also create a blank presentation, which allows you to fully customize the slide components.

A **theme** is a collection of professionally selected slide color schemes, fonts, graphic accents, and background colors. All the slides in a presentation should have a similar look, or design. Once you select a theme, PowerPoint automatically applies it to every slide in your presentation.

Figure 15–2

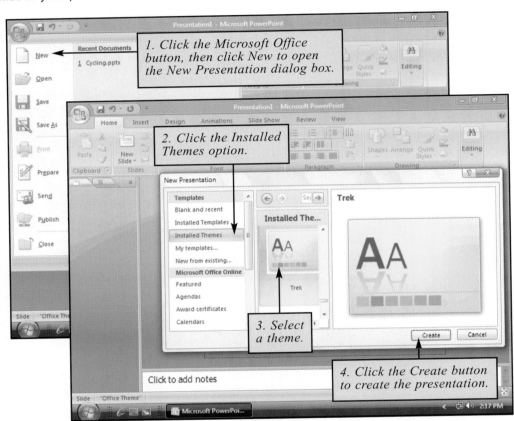

- When you create a new presentation, a Title Slide is generated for you. You can select other layouts from the Layout button in the Slides group on the Home tab.

- It's a good idea to save your presentation as soon as you have created the first slide. PowerPoint presentations are saved with a .pptx extension. As you are building the presentation, you should save frequently. When you save a presentation, all slides in the presentation are saved in the same file.

- If you change your mind about the theme you selected for a presentation, you can change it by clicking the Design tab. Click any theme from the Themes group to apply the new theme to all slides in the presentation. You can also apply a theme to just one slide or to a group of slides by selecting the slide(s), right-clicking a theme in the Themes group, then selecting Apply to Selected Slides. All formatting applied before you change the theme is replaced with the new design.

- Change the background color of a slide by clicking the Design tab, selecting Background Styles from the Background group, then selecting a style from the drop-down list. Additional background formatting is available from the Format Background option in the drop-down list.

FAQ How do I add a slide?

The New Slide button adds a slide to your presentation. When you add a slide, PowerPoint gives you a choice of slide layouts. Most slide layouts include at least one placeholder, in which you can enter text or graphics. You'll typically use the Title Slide layout for the first slide in your presentation. Other slide layouts are set up for arranging bulleted lists, graphics, charts, tables, clip art, and videos.

Figure 15-3

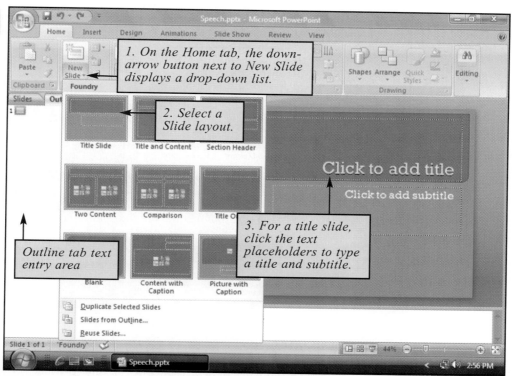

1. On the Home tab, the down-arrow button next to New Slide displays a drop-down list.

2. Select a Slide layout.

3. For a title slide, click the text placeholders to type a title and subtitle.

Outline tab text entry area

- If you don't like the predefined slide layouts, you can use the Blank layout and then use buttons on the Insert tab to add placeholders for text boxes, pictures, clip art, photos, shapes, or charts. For example, click the ▣ Text Box button in the Text group, then drag across a section of the slide to create a text placeholder. Click inside the placeholder, then type your text.

- You can resize any placeholder or any slide object by using its sizing handles—the small circles and squares that appear on the object's borders.

- In addition to entering text into placeholders, you can enter text for slides in the Outline tab entry area whenever the slide show is displayed in Normal view. You can edit this text, much like working with a word processor, using the editing keys. You can also rearrange items by dragging them to new locations in the outline.

FAQ How do I add a bulleted list?

When you want to present a list of bulleted or numbered points, use one of PowerPoint's title and content layouts, such as *Title and Content*, *Two Content*, or *Comparison*. Bulleted lists focus the audience's attention on each point you are making. Each bullet should be a brief summary of what you are saying. Numbered lists help the audience to focus on sequences, priorities, and rankings.

Figure 15-4

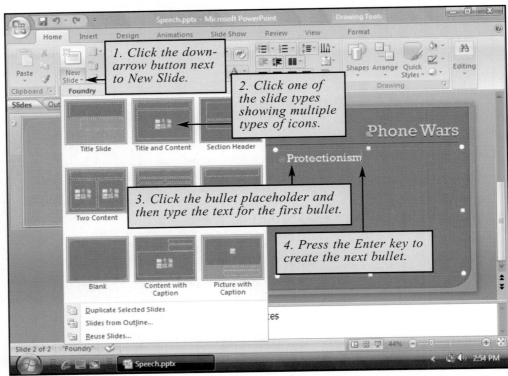

- When you use the Title and Content layout, the text is formatted as a bulleted list in the Content area. If you do not want the text bulleted, you can click the ⊞ Bullets button in the Paragraph group on the Home tab to remove them.

- If you would like the list numbered, use the ⊞ Numbering button.

- Press the Enter key after typing each item in a list. Each time you press the Enter key, PowerPoint generates a new bullet or number. After you type the last item in the list, press the Enter key. Click the Bullets button in the Paragraph group to stop generating bullets. Or, click the Numbering button to stop generating numbers.

- You can press the Backspace key to remove a bullet or number.

- To create sub-bullets, use the ⊞ Increase List Level button in the Paragraph group on the Home tab.

- You can add animation effects to a bulleted list to make the bulleted items appear one by one. You'll learn how to do this in the next chapter.

- Bullets are an effective overview or summary, but limit their use to a maximum of five to seven per slide.

FAQ How do I add a graphic?

You can add visual interest to your slides with graphics. The easiest way to add a slide with a graphic is to select a slide layout with content in the New Slide drop-down list. After adding the slide, you'll replace the Picture, Clip Art, or SmartArt placeholder with the graphic you want to use.

Play It!

Figure 15–5

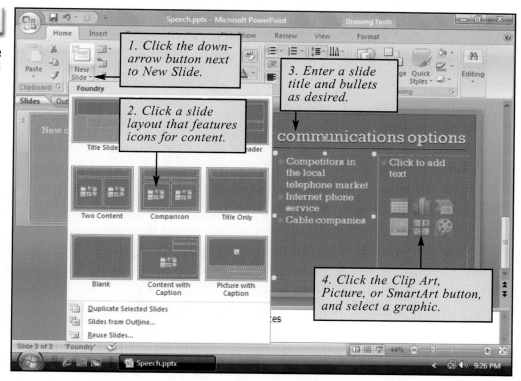

- To add clip art, click the ⊞ Clip Art icon. The Clip Art task pane opens. Click any graphic to select it. The graphic is inserted in the slide, replacing the placeholder.

- The Clip Art task pane includes a search tool to look for clip art. Enter a search specification in the *Search for* text box, then click the Go button.

- To add a photo or scanned image instead of clip art, click the ▣ Insert Picture from File icon displayed in the slide's placeholder. When the Insert Picture dialog box appears, use it to specify the picture's device, folder, and file name.

- SmartArt is a collection of graphical templates that can be used to depict organizational charts and processes. They can also provide a visually interesting backdrop for slide text and offer a modern alternative to the use of bullets. Clicking the SmartArt icon displays PowerPoint's roster of SmartArt designs.

- Click any picture, clip art, or SmartArt and use the sizing handles to change its position or size.

- To delete a graphic, select it, then press the Delete key.

- You can insert pictures, clip art, or SmartArt into any slide layout, even if it doesn't contain a graphic placeholder. Click the Insert tab; click Picture, Clip Art, or SmartArt from the Illustrations group; then select a graphic. Use the sizing handles to position and size the graphic.

FAQ How do I add a chart?

PowerPoint provides several slide layouts containing chart placeholders. You can use the Insert Chart icon to add a bar chart, line chart, or pie chart. The chart comes complete with sample data in a datasheet, which you'll change to reflect the data you want to display on your chart. Some slide layouts provide an area for a large chart, while others are designed to accommodate a smaller chart plus bullets or other text.

Figure 15–6

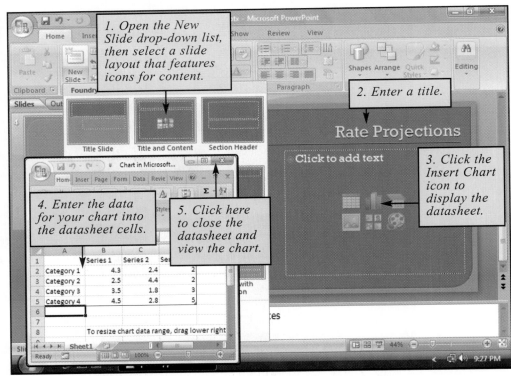

- You'll need to change the table of sample data by entering your own column headings, row labels, and data values. Click each cell containing sample data and replace it with your own labels or numbers.

- If you want to delete sample data in the datasheet's columns or rows, select the cells, then press the Delete key.

- Use the scroll bars to view additional rows and columns.

- If you want to move data, select the cells, then right-click to display the shortcut menu. Click Cut, then right-click the cell where you want to move the data. Click Paste on the shortcut menu.

- To insert a row, right-click the cell where you want the row inserted. Click Insert on the shortcut menu, then select Table Rows Above. The steps to insert a column are similar to inserting a row. The steps to delete a row or column are similar to the steps to insert them, except you use the Delete option on the shortcut menu.

FAQ How do I add a table?

You can add a table to a slide if you want to display text or graphics arranged in columns and rows. Select the Table icon on any new slide layout to specify the number of columns and rows for your table. A blank table is displayed, and you can enter data into each cell.

Play It!

Figure 15-7

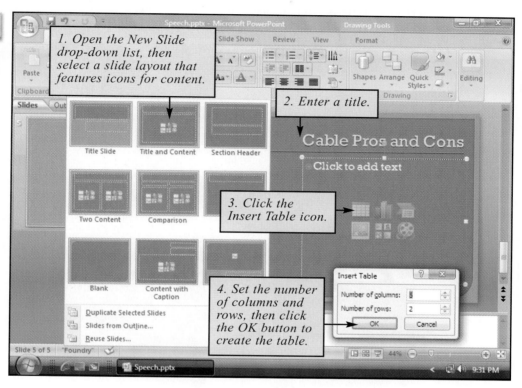

- When a table is inserted into a slide, the Table Tools Design and Layout contextual tabs appear. Using the buttons on these tabs, you can format table borders, add color shading to cells, and adjust the alignment of text in cells.

- To add text to a cell, click inside the cell, then type the text. You can edit and format text inside a table the same way as other slide text. You will learn more about formatting text in the next chapter.

- To add a graphic to a cell, click the cell, then click the Insert tab. Select Picture or Clip Art from the Illustrations group, depending on the type of graphic you want to insert.

- To adjust the height or width of cells, position the pointer over one of the dividing lines between cells. When the pointer changes to a ✛ or ✚ shape, drag the dividing line to the correct position.

- To insert rows, click the cell where you want to insert a row, then click either Insert Above or Insert Below from the Rows & Columns group on the Table Tools Layout contextual tab. The steps to insert a column are similar to the steps for inserting a row, except you click either Insert Left or Insert Right. The steps to delete a row or column are similar to the steps to insert them, except you use the Delete option from the Rows & Columns group on the Table Tools Layout contextual tab.

FAQ How do I work with multimedia elements such as videos?

You can launch an audio clip or video segment from a PowerPoint slide. Audio clips are most frequently added to slides as sound effects, a process covered in the next chapter. Videos are called "movies" in PowerPoint jargon. You can easily insert movies stored in ASF, AVI, MPEG, and WMV formats. PowerPoint does not support clips from video DVDs, such as commercial films. Special steps are required to incorporate Flash movies and QuickTime moves. Refer to PowerPoint Help for details.

Figure 15-8

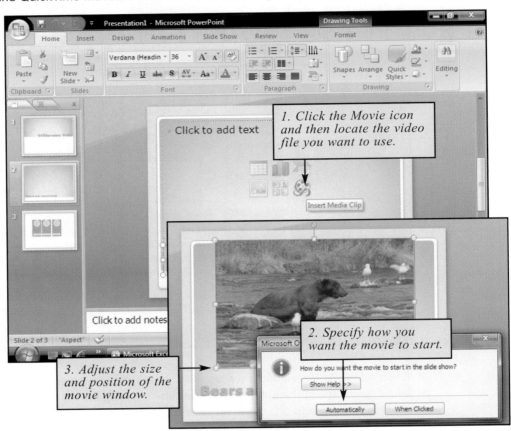

- To stop a movie during a presentation, simply click it.

- PowerPoint offers a set of Movie Tools for adjusting the way movies appear on slides and play during presentations. To access Movie Tools, click the movie window and then select the Options tab.

- Movies play within the movie window displayed on the slide. You can change the size of the movie window by dragging its sizing handles.

- You can configure a movie to fill the screen when it plays, regardless of its size on the slide. Select the Play Full Screen box on the Options tab.

- You can hide the movie window so it does not appear on a slide during the presentation, but still plays automatically when you reach the slide. Use the Options tab to select Hide During Show and Play Full Screen.

- Additional settings on the Options tab allow you to set a movie to loop until you stop it or rewind after it is played.

FAQ Can slides include Web links?

PowerPoint slides can display several types of links, including links to Web sites. If you want to link live to a Web site during a presentation, simply add the Web site's URL to create a hyperlink on a slide. Clicking the hyperlink automatically opens a browser and displays the specified Web page. Just make sure the computer at your presentation site has an Internet connection.

In addition to Web links, you can create links to other slides in your presentation so that you can quickly skip ahead or backtrack. You can also create links to slides in different presentations, to e-mail addresses, or to various files.

Figure 15-9

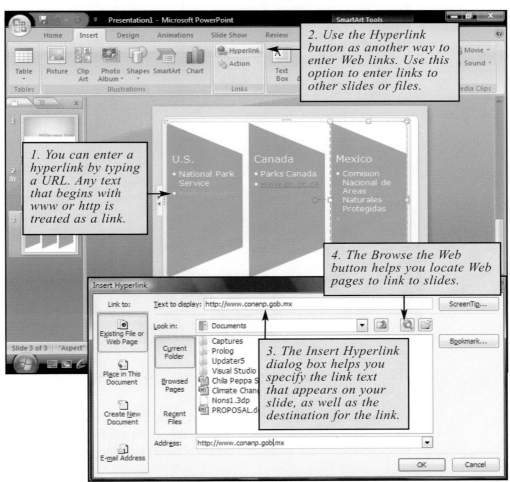

• When the Insert Hyperlink dialog box is open, you can click the 🔍 Browse the Web button to find a Web page and insert its URL. Using this method, you don't have to type in lengthy URLs.

• Make sure to test hyperlinks before giving your presentation to make sure they work correctly.

FAQ How do I view a slide show?

When you build a presentation, your screen contains the ribbon and other objects that should not be displayed when you deliver your presentation to an audience. In this chapter, you have seen how to create and modify a presentation in the Normal view. When you are ready to see how your slides will look to your audience, switch to the **Slide Show view**, which maximizes the slide pane so it fills the screen.

Figure 15-10

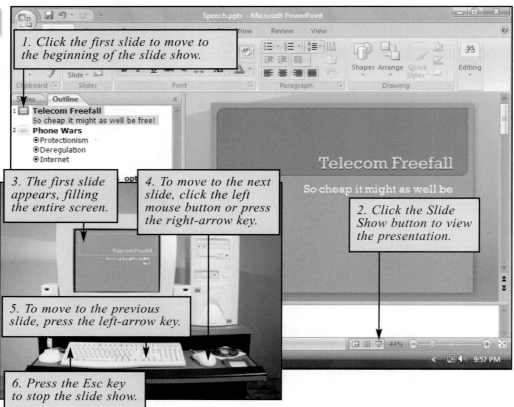

1. Click the first slide to move to the beginning of the slide show.

2. Click the Slide Show button to view the presentation.

3. The first slide appears, filling the entire screen.

4. To move to the next slide, click the left mouse button or press the right-arrow key.

5. To move to the previous slide, press the left-arrow key.

6. Press the Esc key to stop the slide show.

- The slide show starts with the current slide, so it's important to move to the first slide before starting your presentation.

- You can use the buttons in the lower-left corner of the slide to navigate through the slides as well as add or view Speaker notes, write on the slide with the PowerPoint pen or highlighter, or switch to another program during the slide presentation.

- During a presentation, you can navigate through the slides in several ways. For instance, you can press the left mouse button or the right-arrow key to display the next slide or the next bullet. Press the left-arrow key or the P key to move to the previous slide or the previous bullet.

- Right-click a slide to display a shortcut menu that allows you to select a specific slide to display. Click Previous on the shortcut menu to go back one slide.

- Press the Esc key to cancel the slide show and return to the PowerPoint application.

- Before presenting to an audience, be sure to familiarize yourself with the content of each slide. Then, practice the timing of your presentation.

QuickCheck A

1. Microsoft PowerPoint is an example of [＿＿＿＿＿＿＿＿＿] software.

2. After adding a slide, you click the title text [＿＿＿＿＿＿＿＿＿] to replace it with your own title.

3. To add a new bullet to a bulleted list, press the [＿＿＿＿＿] key at the end of the previous bullet.

4. When you add a(n) [＿＿＿＿＿＿＿] to a presentation, you specify the number of rows and columns that will be displayed on the slide.

5. Before displaying a presentation, you should move to the [＿＿＿＿＿＿＿＿] slide in the presentation.

Check It!

QuickCheck B

Indicate the letter of the desktop element that best matches the following:

1. The New Slide button [＿＿＿]

2. The Title Slide layout [＿＿＿]

3. The Normal view button [＿＿＿]

4. The Slide Show button [＿＿＿]

5. The Insert Chart button [＿＿＿]

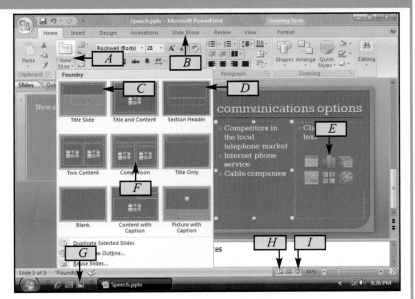

Check It!

Finalizing a Presentation

What's Inside and on the CD?

In this chapter, you'll learn how to use the different views included with Microsoft PowerPoint. In addition, you'll learn formatting techniques, as well as how to add animation and other visual effects to your slides. To finalize presentations, you'll learn how to print your presentation script, create handouts for your audience, save your presentation as Web pages, and use an overhead projector if a computer projection device is not available.

FAQ How do I use the Normal view?

Microsoft PowerPoint provides different views you can use to build, modify, and display your presentation. Most of the time, you will work in Normal view. To change views, click the View buttons at the bottom of the PowerPoint window.

Play It!

Figure 16–1

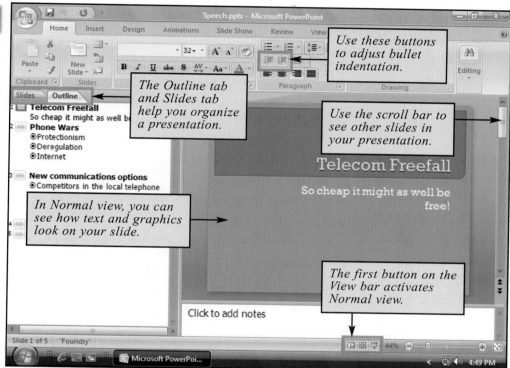

- In  Normal view, you can work in any of the three panes—the Slide pane, the Notes pane, or the Outline/Slides tab pane. Normal view is convenient for building the basic structure of your presentation and for adding speaker notes.

- To work effectively on all the slides' contents, use the Outline tab. After you create most of the slides in a presentation, the Outline tab is useful for revising and rearranging the contents of your presentation. Use the ▤ Increase List Level button to indent a bullet, or use the ▤ Decrease List Level button to return a bullet to its previous level.

- When you are satisfied with the order of the content in your presentation, use the Slides tab to add graphics and visual effects to one slide at a time. You can navigate to and work on other slides by clicking the slide icons in the Slides tab or by using the scroll bar on the right side of the PowerPoint window.

FAQ How do I use the Slide Sorter view?

Slide Sorter view allows you to view miniaturized versions of all the slides in a presentation. In this view, it is easy to rearrange slides as needed. You can add special effects to your presentation by using the Animations tab on the ribbon.

**Figure
16-2**

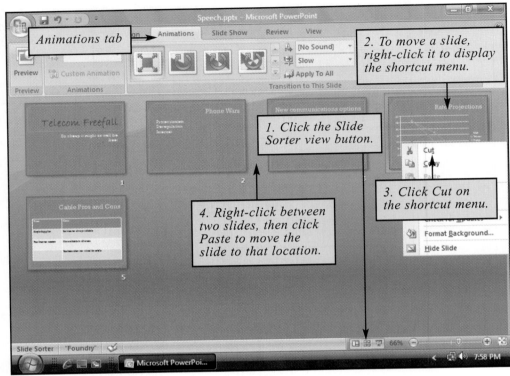

- You can use the drag-and-drop method to move a slide. Select the slide, then drag it to a new location. PowerPoint displays a vertical line between slides to indicate the proposed position before you release the mouse button.

- To delete a slide, right-click the slide to display the shortcut menu, then click Delete Slide. You can also select a slide, then press the Delete key on your keyboard.

- You can duplicate a slide in several ways. You can use the Copy and Paste buttons on the Home tab. You can right-click a slide and use the shortcut menu's Copy and Paste options. You can also click the down-arrow button next to the New Slide button on the Home tab, then select Duplicate Selected Slides. Before using any of these methods, click the slide you want to duplicate.

- You can hide a slide so that it won't appear when you show the presentation. While in Slide Sorter or Normal view, right-click the slide, and then click Hide Slide on the shortcut menu. Repeat this procedure when you want to make the slide visible again. Hiding slides can be handy when you would like to give a shortened version of your presentation. Rather than showing slides without commenting on them, you can just hide the slides you won't have time to discuss.

FAQ How do I add transitions?

A **transition** is an effect that specifies how a slide replaces the previous slide during a presentation. Transitions include fades, wipes, and other effects. You can also select sound effects to go along with each transition. If you do not specify a transition, a new slide replaces the entire current slide all at once. Carefully selected transitions can make a presentation more interesting and help the audience pay attention, but overuse of transitions can become irritating and distract attention from the content of your presentation.

Play It!

Figure 16-3

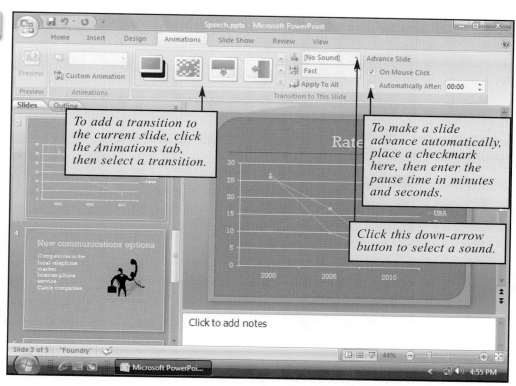

To add a transition to the current slide, click the Animations tab, then select a transition.

To make a slide advance automatically, place a checkmark here, then enter the pause time in minutes and seconds.

Click this down-arrow button to select a sound.

- After you apply a transition, it is indicated by an ☆ Animation icon. You can see the icon on the Slides tab (Normal view) or in Slide Sorter view. While developing your slide show, you can click the icon any time you want to see how the transition looks.

- You can change a transition by selecting a slide, clicking the Animations tab, then selecting a different transition from the Transition to This Slide group.

- In Slide Show view, a presentation advances from one slide to the next when you click the mouse or press a key. If you want a slide to advance automatically after a specified period of time, click the Automatically After check box in the Transition to This Slide group on the Animations tab. Use the spin box to set the display time. The time is displayed as mm:ss, where the first two digits represent the number of minutes and the last two digits represent the number of seconds. To force the slide to advance after 1 minute and 30 seconds, for example, enter 01:30 in the Automatically After spin box.

FAQ How do I format text on a slide?

PowerPoint includes themes preformatted with fonts and font sizes specially selected to complement the background design. In most cases, these fonts work well; but sometimes you'll find it necessary to modify font attributes.

Figure 16-4

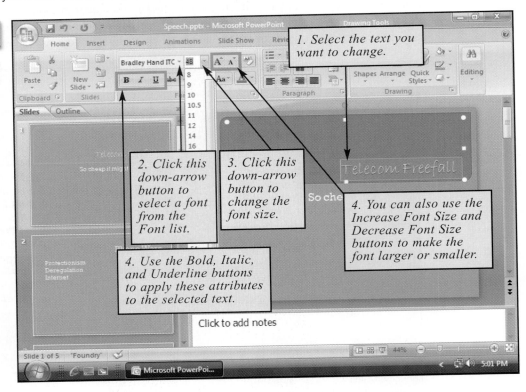

- For more font options, select the text, then click the Font Dialog Box Launcher in the Font group on the Home tab. Select the desired font, font style, size, color, and effect, then click the OK button to apply the font changes.

- When you select font sizes, you should consider the size of your presentation venue and use fonts that are visible even from the back of the room. When using a large font, you might have to use fewer words on each slide.

- You also should consider the lighting in the room in which your presentation will be given. In a brightly lit room, slides are easier to read if you use a dark font color on a light background. In a dark room, you should use a dark background with light font colors. You can experiment with font colors to find the combination that works best in the room in which you deliver the presentation.

- You can change the font attributes for all the slides in your presentation at the same time by using the slide master. The **slide master** is a template you can modify to create a consistent look for your presentation. Click the View tab, then click Slide Master from the Presentation Views group. Select the text styles you want to modify, then change the font attributes using the Font dialog box. To close the slide master, click Close Master View on the Slide Master tab. Use the Slide Sorter view to verify that the new font attributes are applied to the text on all the slides in your presentation.

FAQ How do I add animation effects to a bulleted list?

The Animations tab provides options for adding animation effects and sounds to items on a slide. **Animation effects** are typically used to draw attention to bullets as they appear on the slide during a presentation. For example, each bulleted item can "fly" in from the side when you click the mouse button. Animation effects can also be accompanied by sound effects to draw attention to each new bullet. You can use the Custom Animation task pane to add effects to bullets.

Play It!

Figure 16–5

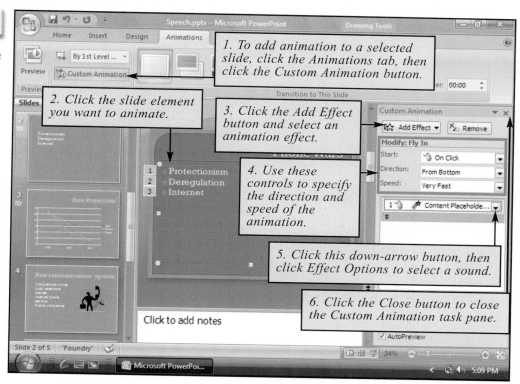

1. To add animation to a selected slide, click the Animations tab, then click the Custom Animation button.

2. Click the slide element you want to animate.

3. Click the Add Effect button and select an animation effect.

4. Use these controls to specify the direction and speed of the animation.

5. Click this down-arrow button, then click Effect Options to select a sound.

6. Click the Close button to close the Custom Animation task pane.

• You can apply animation effects to any slide element, including text, graphics, charts, and tables. After you apply an animation effect, you can test it by clicking the ⭐ Animation icon next to the slide. You can also select the slide and then switch to Slide Show view.

• After selecting Effect Options, you can use the *After animation* option to indicate whether the object should change to a different color or disappear after animation. For example, you can change a bullet to a light font color just before the next bullet appears. The new bullet in a darker font will then become the focus.

• Use sounds sparingly—a sound effect can be humorous and effective the first time it's used, but the effect can become less amusing after 10 or 20 slides. If you use sounds for a presentation, make sure your presentation equipment includes a sound system with adequate volume for your audience.

FAQ How do I check spelling in a presentation?

PowerPoint's spelling checker is very similar to the one you use in Word. It provides an inline spelling checker that automatically indicates possible spelling errors with wavy red lines. As with Word, simply right-click a word marked with a wavy red line to view a list of correctly spelled alternatives. You can also use the Spelling button on the Review tab to manually initiate a spelling check of an entire presentation.

**Figure
16-6**

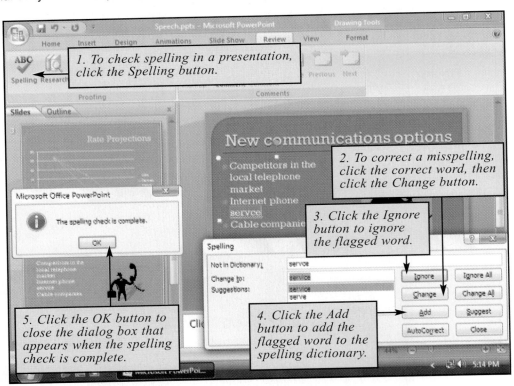

- Don't worry—the wavy red lines do not appear in Slide Show view when you display a presentation.

- You should always check spelling in a presentation before you save the final version. Misspellings can make your audience doubt the accuracy and validity of your statements.

- PowerPoint does not include a grammar checker, so make sure you proofread your presentation to eliminate grammar errors. Bulleted items are usually sentence fragments, but sometimes complete sentences are more appropriate. You should try to be consistent on each slide, using either complete sentences or only phrases.

- PowerPoint's AutoCorrect feature can automatically correct common typing errors as you work. Click the Microsoft Office button, the PowerPoint Options button, the Proofing tab, then click the AutoCorrect Options button. In the AutoCorrect dialog box, select any options that are useful to you. Options include automatically capitalizing the first word in a sentence and the names of days, changing two capital letters at the beginning of a word to a single capital letter, and correcting capitalization errors caused by accidental use of the Caps Lock key.

FAQ How do I add and print speaker notes?

You can prepare and print **speaker notes** that remind you what to say about each slide. Because speaker notes also contain printed versions of each slide, you won't have to keep looking back at the projected slides. This feature allows you to maintain better eye contact and rapport with the audience.

Figure 16-7

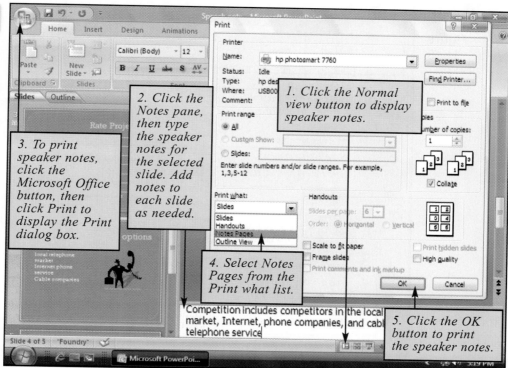

- Speaker notes shouldn't include the exact text that appears on the slide. Use speaker notes for any additional comments you want to make.

- To print speaker notes, click the Microsoft Office button, then click Print. Select Notes Pages from the *Print what* section of the Print dialog box. Click the OK button to print the speaker notes.

- Speaker notes can be included as part of a presentation viewed in a Web browser. This feature can be useful for sharing your presentation and comments with others who could not attend the actual presentation. You will learn how to save the slides in your presentation as Web pages later in this chapter.

FAQ How do I print handouts?

Handouts help your audience remember the content of your presentation. Microsoft PowerPoint offers several print layouts for handouts. Choose the one that best fits the content and number of slides in your presentation.

Figure 16-8

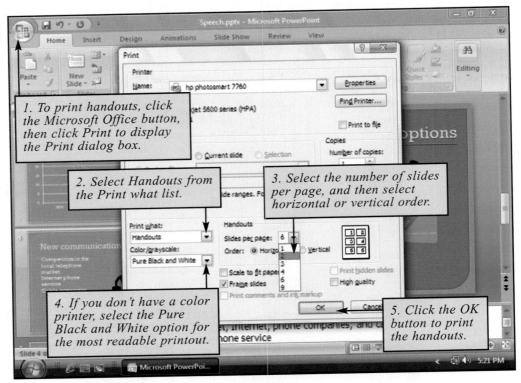

1. To print handouts, click the Microsoft Office button, then click Print to display the Print dialog box.

2. Select Handouts from the Print what list.

3. Select the number of slides per page, and then select horizontal or vertical order.

4. If you don't have a color printer, select the Pure Black and White option for the most readable printout.

5. Click the OK button to print the handouts.

- If your presentation is brief, you can print two or three slides per page for handouts. The two-slide layout prints each slide on one-half of the page. It is appropriate to use this layout when the graphics and bullets on the slides include most of the details of your presentation content. The three-slide layout prints blank lines to the right of each slide. It is appropriate to use this layout when you expect your audience to write notes about each slide.

- You can save paper by printing four to nine slides per page. You can select either horizontal or vertical order for all of these print layouts. Horizontal order prints multiple slides (in order) across the page; vertical order prints the slides (in order) down the page. The Handouts section of the Print dialog box provides a preview of the selected order.

- The biggest advantage of using a PowerPoint presentation is the variety of colors and graphics you can use to enhance your slides. Your handouts can be printed in black and white, or in color, depending on your printer. Select the Pure Black and White option to convert the colors in your slides to the most readable grayscales for a black and white printer.

- The *Frame slides* option gives your handouts a professional look by drawing a thin black line around each slide.

- You can print a text-only version of your presentation by selecting Outline View from the *Print what* list. This handout is useful for very long presentations that include a number of bulleted items. Graphics do not print in the Outline View version.

FAQ How do I save a presentation as Web pages?

If you convert your presentation to Web pages, people who missed it or didn't take notes can later view it on the Web.

It's easy to save your presentation as Web pages. The converted presentation can be viewed over the Internet using a standard Web browser. Each slide appears as a separate Web page with navigation tools to move from slide to slide.

Figure 16–9

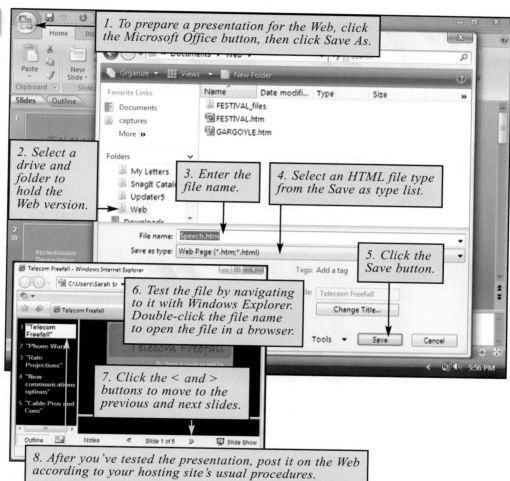

1. To prepare a presentation for the Web, click the Microsoft Office button, then click Save As.

2. Select a drive and folder to hold the Web version.

3. Enter the file name.

4. Select an HTML file type from the Save as type list.

5. Click the Save button.

6. Test the file by navigating to it with Windows Explorer. Double-click the file name to open the file in a browser.

7. Click the < and > buttons to move to the previous and next slides.

8. After you've tested the presentation, post it on the Web according to your hosting site's usual procedures.

- If your slides are posted on the Web, during your presentation you might display a slide with the Web site address so that interested audience members can later review the presentation there.

- In the *Save as type* box, use Microsoft's Single File Web Page (*.mht, *.mhtml) format or select the Web page (*.htm, *.html) format.

- PowerPoint is useful for converting a presentation to Web pages, but some slide features cannot be duplicated. For instance, a viewer who is looking at the Web presentation might not see transitions and animation effects. If a presentation contains formatting that cannot be duplicated in Web pages, you'll be notified of the problem areas and will have the option of canceling or continuing with the save.

- You should preview your presentation in a Web browser to see how it will actually look on the Web. If you're not satisfied with the Web version, refer to *Web presentations* in PowerPoint Help.

FAQ Can I show my presentation with an overhead projector?

Typically, you'll connect your computer to a projection device, then display the presentation directly from PowerPoint. However, sometimes you won't have access to a computer and projection device, which means you might have to display your presentation the old-fashioned way—with transparency film and an overhead projector. You'll lose the transitions, animations, and sound effects, but at least you'll be able to display the content of your PowerPoint slides while you make your comments.

Figure 16–10

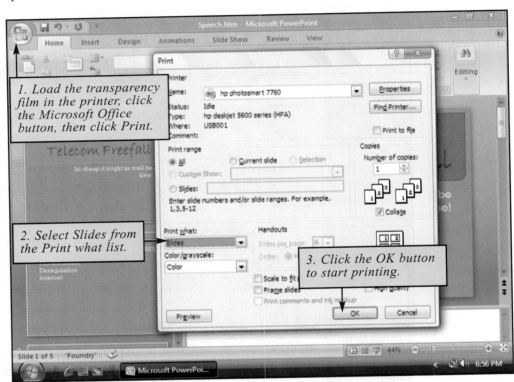

1. Load the transparency film in the printer, click the Microsoft Office button, then click Print.

2. Select Slides from the Print what list.

3. Click the OK button to start printing.

- You can purchase transparency film from an office supply store. The type of film you purchase depends on whether you are printing on a laser printer or an ink jet printer. Read the packaging carefully to make sure you buy the right kind of transparency film.

- If your printer allows it, you can put transparency film into the paper feeder and print directly onto the transparencies. However, you might have to print on regular paper and use a xerographic copier to create the transparencies. Read your printer manual for details.

- A color printer that accepts transparency film can be used to create color transparencies. If you don't have access to a color printer, you should select the Pure Black and White option in the Print dialog box to create slides with the most readable grayscales your black and white printer can produce.

QuickCheck A

1. [_____] notes help you remember what to say when each slide is displayed during a presentation.

2. A(n) [_____] effect controls the way bullets appear in a bulleted list.

3. A(n) [_____] controls the way a slide replaces the previous slide during a presentation.

4. True or false? Transparencies can only be used to display black and white versions of the slides in a PowerPoint presentation. [_____]

5. If you're going to put your presentation on the Web, you should always include a slide with the [_____] where the presentation will be located.

Check It!

QuickCheck B

Indicate the letter of the desktop element that best matches the following:

1. The Slide Sorter view button [____]

2. The Increase List Level button [____]

3. The Increase Font Size button [____]

4. The Slide Show view button [____]

5. The Normal view button [____]

Check It!

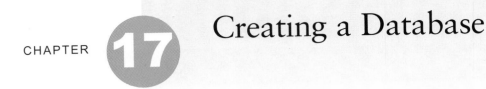

CHAPTER **17**

Creating a Database

What's Inside and on the CD?

Microsoft Access is the component of the Microsoft Office suite best suited for working with large collections of data called databases. As database software, Microsoft Access provides a powerful set of tools for entering and updating information, deleting information, sorting data, searching for specific data, and creating reports.

The databases you create with Access are technically referred to as "relational databases." A **relational database** contains data organized into easy-to-visualize tables. A table is composed of fields and records. A **record** contains information about a single "entity" in the database—a person, place, event, or thing. A **field** contains a single unit of information, such as a name, birth date, or ZIP code.

A relational database can contain more than one table and you can define relationships between these tables so that they can be used in conjunction with each other. For example, a video store database might include a table of movies and a table of customers. Suppose a customer checks out one of the *Star Wars* movies. If the movie is not returned by its due date, the relationship between the movie and customer tables allows the clerk to contact the appropriate customer about returning the movie. The customer number, which was entered in the *Star Wars* record when the movie was checked out, acts as a link to the customer table that displays the customer's address, phone number, and credit card billing information.

FAQ How is data organized in a database?

Because it's useful for organizing many types of data, database software, such as Microsoft Access, can be complex. A few simple concepts, however, should provide you with the background necessary to start working with this important data management tool. An Access database consists of tables. Each table is similar to a stack of index cards. Each card in the stack has the same kind of data written on it, which relates to a single entity. A database record is equivalent to one index card, as shown below.

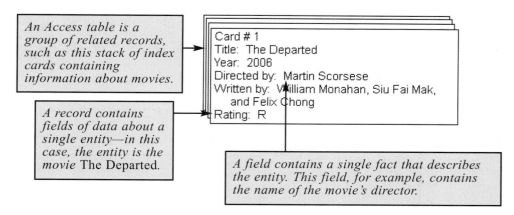

An Access table is a group of related records, such as this stack of index cards containing information about movies.

Card # 1
Title: The Departed
Year: 2006
Directed by: Martin Scorsese
Written by: William Monahan, Siu Fai Mak, and Felix Chong
Rating: R

A record contains fields of data about a single entity—in this case, the entity is the movie The Departed.

A field contains a single fact that describes the entity. This field, for example, contains the name of the movie's director.

The data in a database can be displayed in different ways. Most of the time, you'll work with the data arranged in a table, such as the one shown below. Data arranged in this way uses the same records and fields as the index cards shown above—it just looks different because of its arrangement. In the figure below, each row contains one record, equivalent to one index card. Each cell in a row contains the data for one field. The table includes all fields in all rows—equivalent to the entire stack of index cards.

Play It!

Figure 17-1

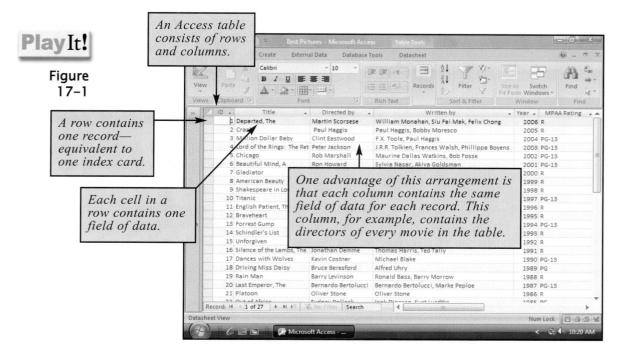

An Access table consists of rows and columns.

A row contains one record—equivalent to one index card.

Each cell in a row contains one field of data.

One advantage of this arrangement is that each column contains the same field of data for each record. This column, for example, contains the directors of every movie in the table.

FAQ What's in the Access window?

To start Access, click Start, point to All Programs, click Microsoft Office, then click Microsoft Office Access 2007. Unlike other Microsoft Office applications, Access doesn't automatically display an empty workspace when you start the program. When you start Access, the Getting Started with Microsoft Office Access window appears. You can use this window to connect to Microsoft Office Online, search for an existing file, create a new database, or open an existing database.

Figure 17–2

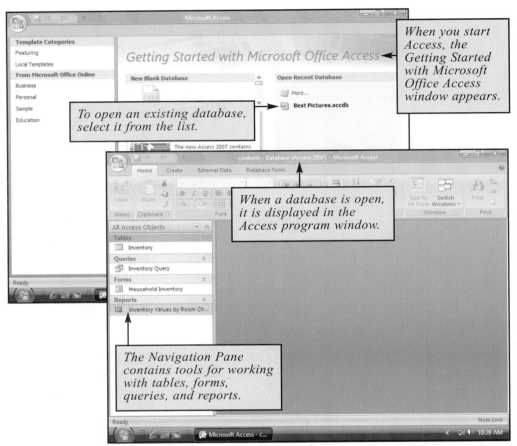

When you start Access, the Getting Started with Microsoft Office Access window appears.

To open an existing database, select it from the list.

When a database is open, it is displayed in the Access program window.

The Navigation Pane contains tools for working with tables, forms, queries, and reports.

- When you work with Access, you typically will not create a new database each time you use the program. Instead, you'll open an existing database in order to add to, or edit, the data it contains.

- As you've learned in previous chapters, documents and spreadsheets appear on-screen similar to the way they will look when printed. Databases are different—their data can be displayed and manipulated in many different ways.

- Access provides several tools you can use to create, modify, and display data in the database. These tools are contained in the Navigation Pane on the left side of the database window. In this chapter, you'll learn how to use these tools to create tables and simple queries. In the next chapter, you'll learn how to use additional tools to create simple forms and reports.

- Access also offers many different ways to use each of the tools. You should remember that Access is complex software. In order to simplify your introduction to Access, you will learn some basic ways to use the most common tools.

FAQ How do I create a new database or open an existing database?

Creating a database is different from creating a document, worksheet, or presentation. With Word, for example, you typically enter text into a new document before you save it. With Access, first you save an empty database, then you create the elements that make up the database. These elements include tables, reports, forms, and queries.

Play It!

Figure 17-3

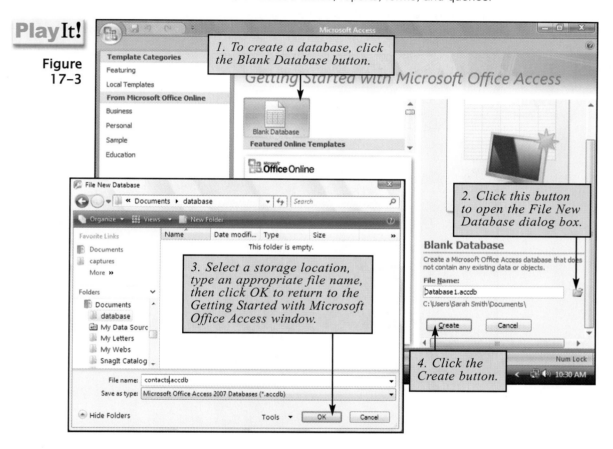

1. To create a database, click the Blank Database button.

2. Click this button to open the File New Database dialog box.

3. Select a storage location, type an appropriate file name, then click OK to return to the Getting Started with Microsoft Office Access window.

4. Click the Create button.

- You only have to save a database once, when you first create it. As you add or change data in the database, the changes are automatically saved in the database file. When you're finished using the database, you just close it—there's no need to take an extra step to save the data because all changes are saved as you make them.

- If you have already created a database, select the name of the database from the Getting Started with Microsoft Office Access window.

- To open a database, you can use the Open Recent Database list or the ☞ More link on the Getting Started with Microsoft Office Access window. Select the appropriate storage device and file name, then click the Open button.

FAQ How do I create a table using a Table Template?

Before you can enter data in a database, you must specify the structure of the tables, records, and fields in your database. A table contains records. Each record consists of one or more fields, and each field contains a particular type of data, such as a name or date. When Access creates a new database, it creates an empty table called Table1 for you to modify. Table Templates make it easy to create tables for common business and personal databases. Table Templates also help you select and define fields.

Figure 17–4

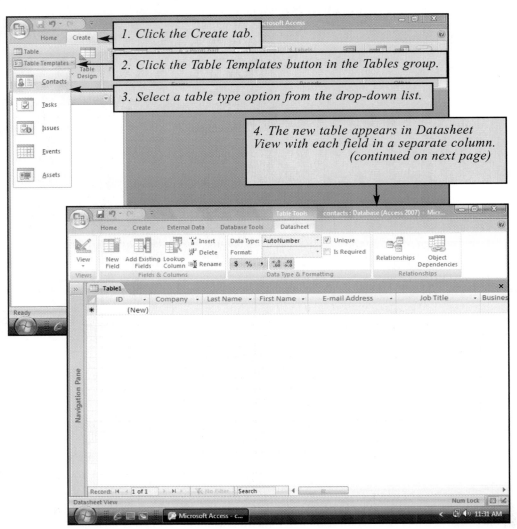

1. *Click the Create tab.*

2. *Click the Table Templates button in the Tables group.*

3. *Select a table type option from the drop-down list.*

4. *The new table appears in Datasheet View with each field in a separate column.*
(continued on next page)

- Access includes sample tables for common business and personal databases. Select the most appropriate table type from the Table Templates list.

- The sample tables include many fields, and some might not be necessary for your database. These fields can be deleted, as explained on the next page.

• **How do I create a table using a Table Template? (continued)**

Figure 17-5

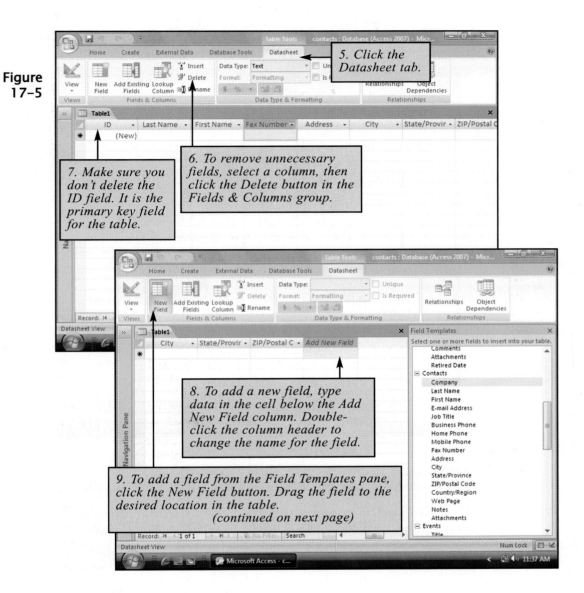

5. *Click the Datasheet tab.*

7. *Make sure you don't delete the ID field. It is the primary key field for the table.*

6. *To remove unnecessary fields, select a column, then click the Delete button in the Fields & Columns group.*

8. *To add a new field, type data in the cell below the Add New Field column. Double-click the column header to change the name for the field.*

9. *To add a field from the Field Templates pane, click the New Field button. Drag the field to the desired location in the table.*
(continued on next page)

• A **primary key** is a field that uniquely identifies each record. It's very important that no two records are ever assigned the same value for this unique field. For this reason, it's usually best to have Access create the primary key. Access is then responsible for assigning a unique value to each record. As an alternative, you can select your own primary key. For example, you could use each contact's Social Security number as the primary key. To modify the primary key field, you will need to be in Design View. You'll learn more about Design View later in this chapter.

• How do I create a table using a Table Template? (continued)

When you're satisfied with the fields you've selected, it is a good idea to save the table before entering data.

Figure 17–6

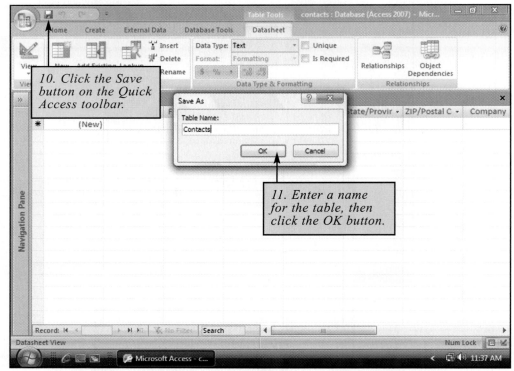

10. Click the Save button on the Quick Access toolbar.

11. Enter a name for the table, then click the OK button.

• Give the table a unique name so that you can identify it easily. You don't have to save it again when you exit Access—just close the Access program window when you're through.

• The name you enter when you save the table is the name for the table, which is not necessarily the same as the name for the database. For example, a database called Contacts.accdb might have tables called Contacts, Meetings, and so on. All tables in the database are stored in the same database file.

• If you are saving on a floppy disk or USB flash drive, do not remove it from the computer until the Access window closes. If you remove it too soon, your database file might become corrupted and some of your data could be lost.

• To open the database the next time you start Access, click the file name from the Getting Started with Microsoft Office Access window or click the More link to display the Open dialog box.

FAQ How do I enter and edit data in a table?

Once you've defined the fields for a table, you can enter data. If you have just created a table using a Table Template, the table is open. If the table is not open, double-click the name of the table in the Navigation Pane. Access displays an empty record into which you can begin to enter data.

Figure 17-7

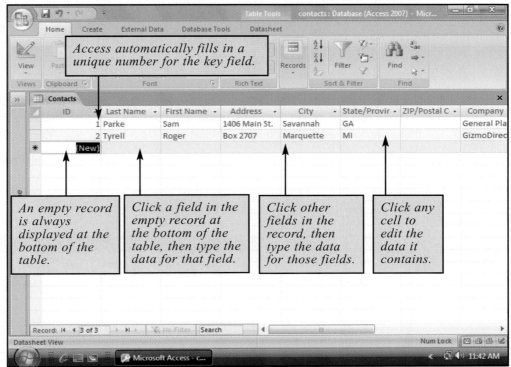

Access automatically fills in a unique number for the key field.

An empty record is always displayed at the bottom of the table.

Click a field in the empty record at the bottom of the table, then type the data for that field.

Click other fields in the record, then type the data for those fields.

Click any cell to edit the data it contains.

- An empty record is always displayed at the bottom of a table. Each time you enter data into that empty record, a new empty record appears.

- Be careful to enter data in a consistent manner. For example, don't use inconsistent entries, such as MI and Michigan, in the same database. If you're entering state names, always use either the state abbreviation or the entire state name. Later, when the database contains many records, it will be easier to locate the records if the data has been entered consistently. In this example, if you ask the database to list all of the contacts in the state of "MI," any records for contacts in "Michigan" might not be included in the list.

- To edit data, click the cell containing the data. Use the left-arrow and right-arrow keys to move the insertion point within the field. Use the Backspace and Delete keys to delete text to the left or to the right of the insertion point, respectively.

- To delete an entire record, right-click the row header containing the record. Click Delete Record on the shortcut menu, then click the Yes button.

FAQ Can I import data into a database?

As an alternative to typing data into a database table, you can import data from files created with other software, including worksheets created with Excel, databases created with older versions of Access, and e-mail address books created with Outlook. You can also import comma-delimited files created with a word processor or exported from other software.

A **comma-delimited file**, sometimes referred to as a **CSV file** (comma-separated values), is simply data separated by commas similar to the following:

Stray Cat Blues,The Rolling Stones,4:37,Classic Rock
Buenos Aires,Madonna,4:09,Soundtrack
Over the Rainbow,Jason Castro,3:30,Folk

Many software applications offer an export option that creates a comma-delimited file. You can use the export option to create a file that can then be imported into Access. Import options are listed on Access's External Data tab.

Suppose you have a list of classic albums that you're planning to sell on eBay. The list has become so large that you want to manage it in Access. To import the list, begin by selecting *Import text file* from the External Data tab and then select the file that currently holds the music list.

Figure 17–8

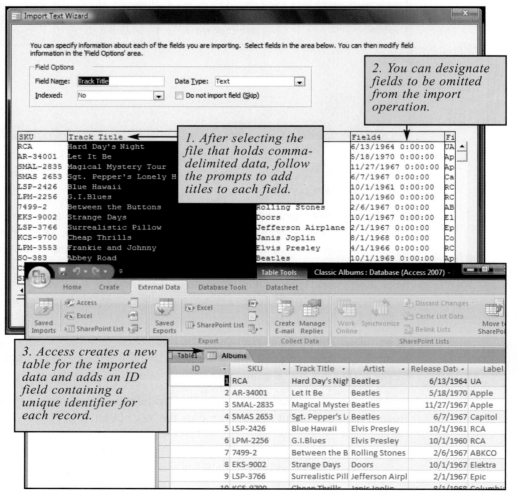

FAQ How do I create a table in Design View?

If the sample tables offered in the Table Templates list don't meet your needs, you can create your own table using Design View. This option requires just a bit more planning because you must specify a data type for each field. A **data type** determines what kind of data can be entered into a field.

Play It!

Figure
17–9

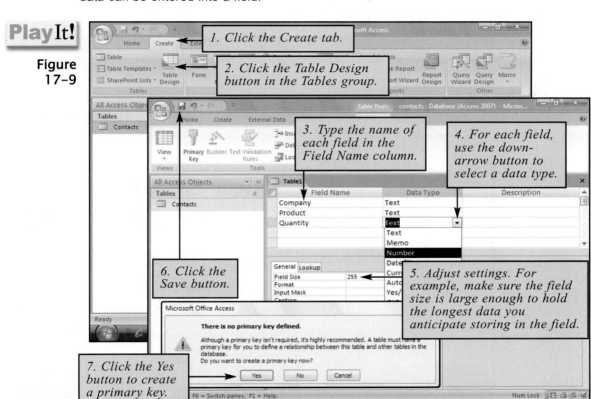

1. Click the Create tab.

2. Click the Table Design button in the Tables group.

3. Type the name of each field in the Field Name column.

4. For each field, use the down-arrow button to select a data type.

6. Click the Save button.

5. Adjust settings. For example, make sure the field size is large enough to hold the longest data you anticipate storing in the field.

7. Click the Yes button to create a primary key.

- Use the **Text data type** for fields that contain words and symbols of up to 255 characters in length.

- Use the **Memo data type** for fields that contain variable length data, such as comments, notes, and reviews.

- Use the **Number data type** for fields that contain numeric data. Don't use the Number data type for data that looks like a number, but that will never be calculated. For example, the data type for telephone numbers should be defined as Text.

- Use the **Date/Time data type** for dates and times. This special data type makes it much easier, for example, to determine if one date occurs before or after another date.

- When you allow Access to define the primary key, the ID field is created using the **AutoNumber data type**. A unique number is automatically entered in this field as you enter each new record.

- The **Yes/No data type** can be useful for fields designed to hold simple Yes/No or True/False data. For example, you might use a Yes/No data type for the field "Subtitled?"

- When you have defined all the fields, save and then close the Table window to begin entering data into your new table.

FAQ How do I work with tables?

Working with the data in an Access table has similarities to working with data in an Excel worksheet. You can add, delete, move, and sort data, as well as search for specific data items. Controls for these operations are on the ribbon, but they can also be accessed by right-clicking the column or row you want to work with. Remember that rows represent records and columns represent fields.

Figure 17–10

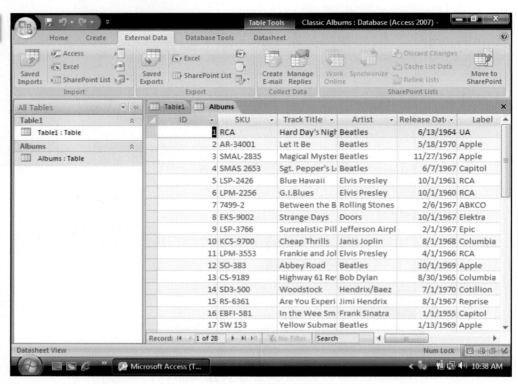

- **Modify data.** Click the field you'd like to modify. Use the Backspace, Delete, and typing keys to change the data. Press the Enter key to complete the modification.

- **Insert a record.** Scroll to the bottom of the database (or on the Home tab, click the Records button) and then click New. New records are always added at the end of the database.

- **Delete a record.** Right-click the light-blue box on the left side of the record you want to delete. Select Delete Record from the shortcut menu.

- **Move a field.** Select the column or columns that you want to move. Drag the column horizontally to the desired location.

- **Hide a field.** Right-click the column title and select Hide Columns from the shortcut menu.

- **Sort records.** Right-click the column that holds data you want to use as the sort key; for example, click the LastName field if you would like all the records sorted according to last name. From the shortcut menu, select either Sort A to Z or Sort Z to A.

- **Search.** Right-click the title of the column that is likely to hold the data you seek. Select Find from the shortcut menu. Enter the data you seek in the Find and Replace dialog box. Click the Find Next button.

FAQ How do I create a query using a Wizard?

After you have organized your data into one or more tables, you can manipulate the data in many ways. For example, you can search a company database for all customers in a specific state or search an inventory database for all products that cost more than $10. You can create a **query** to search your database for records that contain particular data. A query contains criteria that specify what you would like to find. You can also use a query to display some, but not all, of the fields in a table. The Query Wizard offers a quick way to create simple queries and use them to locate data.

Figure 17–11

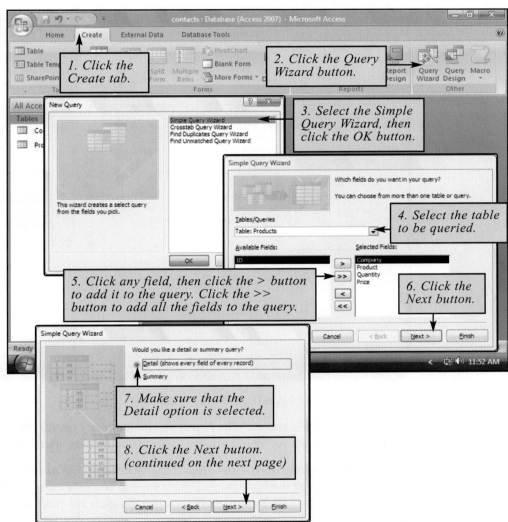

Simple Query Wizard - Which fields do you want in your query?

- The fields you select in this step will be included in the query results. Click a field, then click the `>` button to add an individual field. Click the `>>` button to add all fields. Click the `<` button to remove a field from the query. Click the `<<` button to remove all fields.

Simple Query Wizard - Would you like a detail or summary query?

- Selecting the Detail option shows all of the specified fields for the records, whereas selecting the Summary option only displays how many records match your criteria.

• **How do I create a query using a Wizard? (continued)**

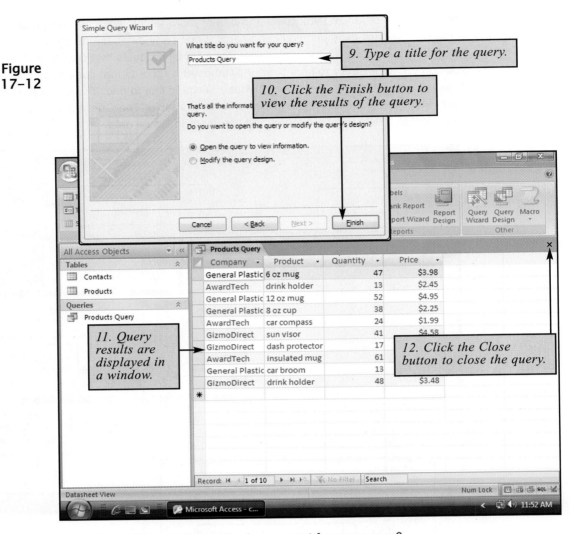

Figure
17-12

Simple Query Wizard - What title do you want for your query?

• After you enter a title and click the Finish button, the query results appear in a new window. In this example, results show data for the four fields specified by the query.

• To further refine a search, you can specify **query criteria**. For example, instead of a query that returns all the records, you might want to see only those records for products that cost more than $10. To add query criteria, right-click the query tab at the top of the window, then click Design View on the shortcut menu. Type >10 in the criteria row under the Price field. Click the ⏹ Run button in the Results group on the Query Tools Design contextual tab to display the query results. Records that match the criteria are displayed in the query results window.

• When you close the query window after viewing the results of a query, you'll see a message asking *Do you want to save changes to the design of query 'Query Name'?* Click Yes if you would like to use the same query criteria every time you use this query.

• After a query is saved, you can run it repeatedly to display all the records—including new and updated data—that match the criteria you've specified.

QuickCheck A

1. True or false? A relational database contains information that is organized into tables containing columns and rows. ▢

2. A(n) ▢ contains a single piece of information, such as a name or ZIP code.

3. A(n) ▢ contains fields of information about a single entity in the database, such as a person, event, or thing.

4. True or false? Each time you enter new data into a database table, you must save the table. ▢

5. A(n) ▢ contains criteria that specify the data you want to find in a database.

Check It!

QuickCheck B

Indicate the letter of the desktop element that best matches the following:

1. A text field ▢

2. A number field ▢

3. A primary key field ▢

4. A currency field ▢

5. A blank field in a new record ▢

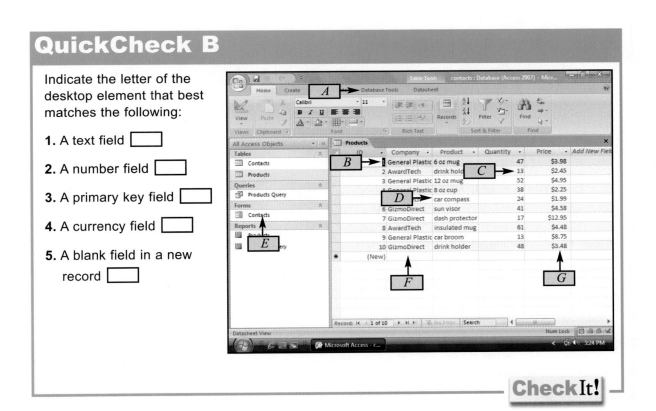

Check It!

CHAPTER **18**

Finalizing a Database

What's Inside and on the CD?

In this chapter, you'll learn how to manipulate a database to create forms, generate reports, print reports, and convert reports into Web pages.

A **form** allows you to customize the way Access displays records by selecting particular fields, specifying the field order, and adding descriptive field labels. Forms are designed to simplify the data entry process by making each screen-based record look like a printed form.

A **database report** is typically a printed document containing data selected from a database. Like a query, a report can be based on criteria that determine which data is included in the report. Reports can be formatted in various ways. Many reports are formatted in columns, with headings at the top of each column and data from each record displayed below each heading. Reports also often include totals and subtotals. In addition to printing reports, Microsoft Access makes it easy to export reports to Web pages.

FAQ How do I create a form using a Wizard?

You can organize your data into rows and columns using a table, which is the best way to view the data contained in a large number of records. Another way to display your data is with a form. A form allows you to view your data one record at a time, with the fields of each record arranged on your computer screen as they might be arranged on a printed form. The Form Wizard helps you design an on-screen form in which you can enter and manipulate data for each record of a database.

Figure 18-1

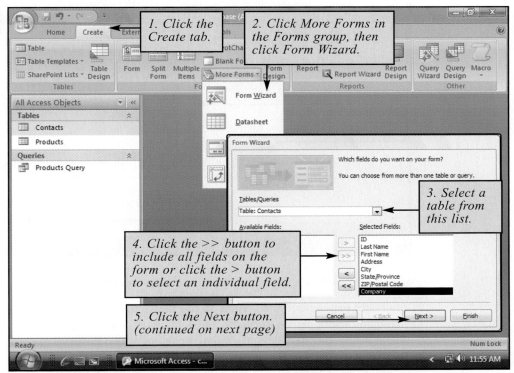

Form Wizard - Which fields do you want on your form?

- Most of the time, you'll want to include all fields on the form. To do so, click the >> button.

- As an alternative, you can select individual fields. For example, if you are going to enter specific data, such as today's purchases, you might use a form that shows only ID, FirstName, and LastName, along with a field for the purchase amount. You don't need to see the contact's address information while you are entering purchase data. To select a specific field, click it, then click the > button. Repeat these steps for each field you want to include on the form.

- You can remove an individual field from the Selected Fields list by clicking the < button.

● **How do I create a form using a Wizard? (continued)**

Figure 18-2

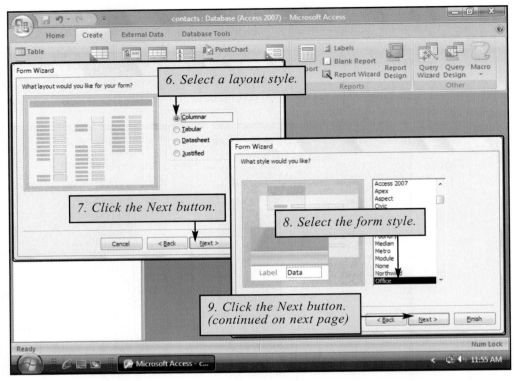

Form Wizard - What layout would you like for your form?

● You might experiment with layouts to see how they work for different types of data. The Columnar layout places labels next to fields, and lists the fields in columns. The Tabular layout places field labels at the top of a column, which makes it appear like a table. The Datasheet layout resembles a spreadsheet, with cells for entering data. The Justified layout displays fields across the screen in rows, with a label above each field.

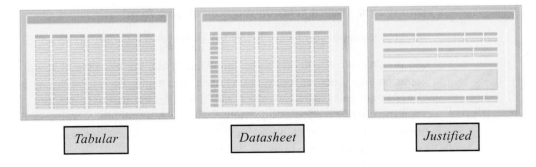

Tabular   *Datasheet*   *Justified*

Form Wizard - What style would you like?

● The form style determines the font, font color, and background for the form. Choose a style that seems appropriate for your data. The preview area to the left of the list of styles is useful for selecting a form style. The available styles are similar to the themes available in the other Office 2007 applications.

• How do I create a form using a Wizard? (continued)

Figure 18-3

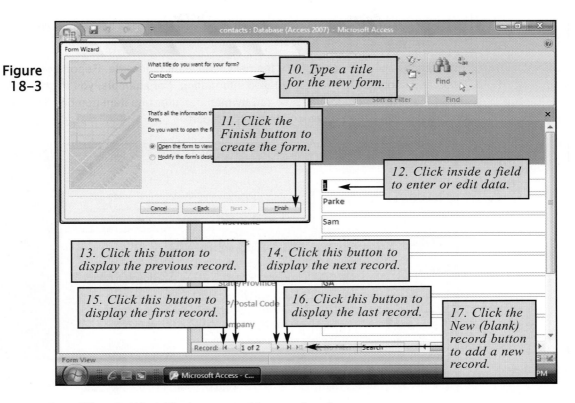

Form Wizard - What title do you want for your form?

- After you enter a title, the Form Wizard closes and the first record is displayed in the new form. You can now use the form to view, edit, or add records to the table. Use the navigation controls (see Steps 13 through 17 in Figure 18-3 above) to move from one record to the next and to add new records to the database.

- Forms that you create are automatically saved in the database file, so you don't have to save a form separately. Changes you make to data while using a form automatically update the corresponding table in your database.

- You can modify the design and layout of any form by switching to Design View. To switch to Design View, right-click the tab at the top of the form window and then click Design View on the shortcut menu.

- You can use tools on the Form Design Tools tabs to apply additional formatting to the form. You can change the form layout from Tabular to Stacked using the buttons in the Control Layout group. If you want more control over the layout of the controls on the form, you can remove the Tabular or Stacked layout from a control or an entire form with the Remove button in the Control Layout group.

- Click any label to edit it. To move a label and the associated data field, click to select the object, move the pointer over the edge of the object until the pointer changes to a ✛ shape, then drag the label and data field to a new location. To delete a label and data field from the form, right-click the label, then click Cut on the shortcut menu.

- As you become more familiar with Access, you might eventually want to create forms using Design View. Start with a blank form, then add labels and controls. Design View provides maximum flexibility for designing a form, but requires more time on your part.

FAQ How do I create a report using a Wizard?

When you want to create a polished printout of some or all of the data in your Access database, you can create a report.

To create a report, simply specify the fields you want to include. Reports often include totals and subtotals as well as detailed information. For example, you might create a report that lists inventory items sorted by manufacturer and item number. The Report Wizard simplifies the process of creating a report.

Figure 18-4

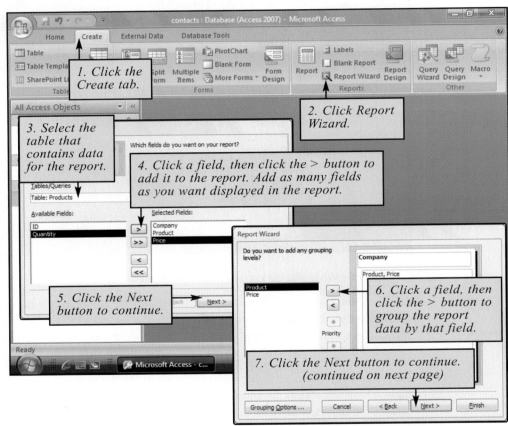

Report Wizard - Which fields do you want on your report?

- To add individual fields to the report, click a field, then click the `>` button. Click the `>>` button to add all available fields to the report.

Report Wizard - Do you want to add any grouping levels?

- When you add a grouping level, records are sorted according to entries in the group field. You can add several grouping levels to a report. For example, you might group a list of products by the manufacturer, then group them by item number. Grouping also helps arrange data when you want to produce a report containing subtotals.

• How do I create a report using a Wizard? (continued)

Figure 18–5

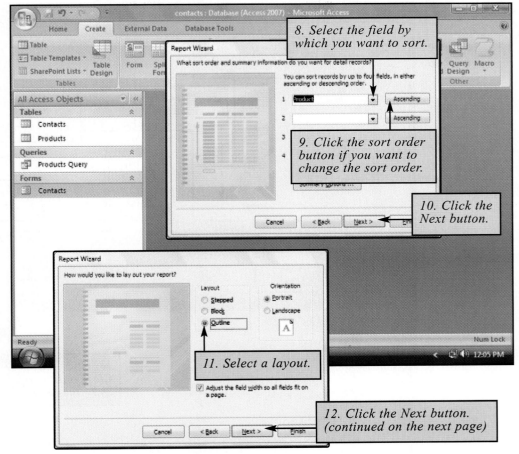

Report Wizard - What sort order and summary information do you want for detail records?

• To sort records within a group, click the down-arrow button and select the field by which you want to sort.

• Click the [Ascending] button to sort from A to Z or from low to high. Click the [Descending] button to sort from Z to A or high to low.

Report Wizard - How would you like to lay out your report?

• Select an option button in the Layout section. The preview area helps you select a layout.

• How do I create a report using a Wizard? (continued)

Figure 18–6

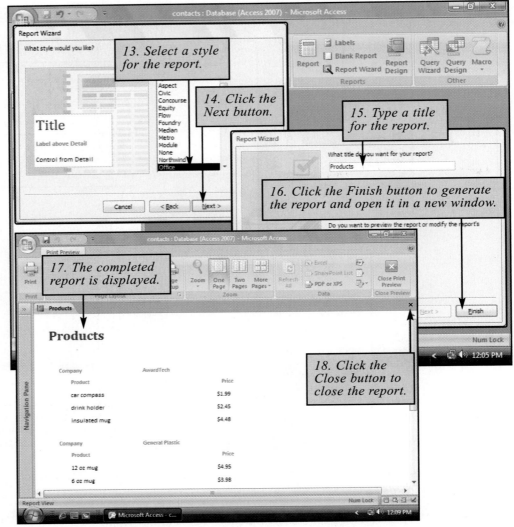

Report Wizard - What style would you like?

• Select the style that seems most suitable for your report. The preview area to the left of the list of styles is useful for selecting a report style.

Report Wizard - What title do you want for your report?

• Type a report name, which is used to identify the report so that you can open it in the future. The report layout is automatically saved in the database file along with the tables, queries, and forms that you have already created.

• When you click the Finish button, the report is displayed in a window. Use the vertical and horizontal scroll bars to view parts of the report that are not initially visible.

• You can modify the report layout at any time. Right-click the report name in the Navigation Pane. Click Design View from the shortcut menu. You can use the options on the Report Design Tools tabs to modify the report. Select an object on the report, then use the sizing handles to adjust their size. To move an object, click the object to select it, move the pointer over the edge of the object until the pointer changes to a ✛ shape, then drag the object to a new location.

FAQ How do I print a report?

Each time you display or print a report, the contents of the report are automatically updated to reflect the current data stored in the database. For example, suppose that you print a report today. Over the next week, you add and change data in the database. If you display or print the report next week, it will include all of the updated data.

Play It!

Figure 18-7

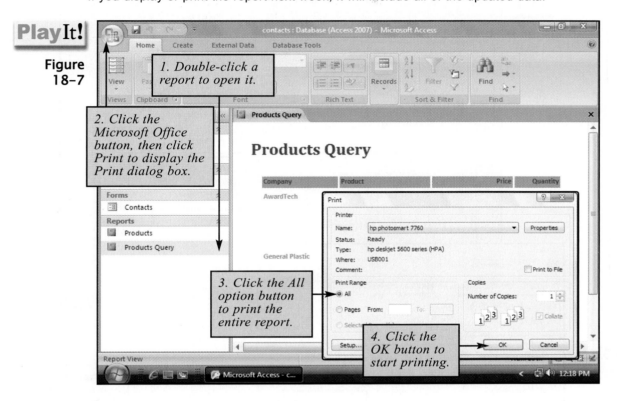

1. Double-click a report to open it.

2. Click the Microsoft Office button, then click Print to display the Print dialog box.

3. Click the All option button to print the entire report.

4. Click the OK button to start printing.

- The data in a printed report is a "snapshot" that shows the status of your database at a particular point in time. When you edit or add data to the database, your report includes new and revised data. It is a good idea to include the date the report was printed on all pages to help readers determine if the data is current.

- To add the date or time as a report header, right-click the report name in the Navigation Pane, then click Design View on the shortcut menu. Click the Date & Time button in the Design tab. Select the date and time formats, then click the OK button. You can move the date and time fields to any location on the report. Select both fields by holding down the Shift key while you click each field. Move the pointer over the edge of the fields until the pointer changes to a ✛ shape, then drag the fields to the desired location in the report.

Figure 18-8

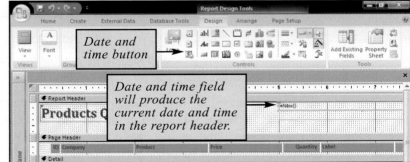

Date and time button

Date and time field will produce the current date and time in the report header.

FAQ How do I save a report as a Web page?

Once you've created a report, you can print it or post it on the Web. As with other Web pages, your report must be in HTML format to be accessible to Web browsers.

Figure 18-9

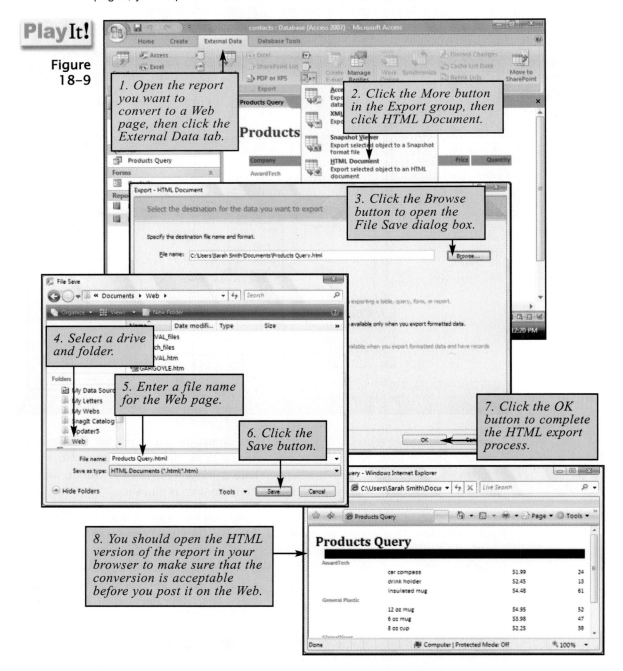

1. Open the report you want to convert to a Web page, then click the External Data tab.

2. Click the More button in the Export group, then click HTML Document.

3. Click the Browse button to open the File Save dialog box.

4. Select a drive and folder.

5. Enter a file name for the Web page.

6. Click the Save button.

7. Click the OK button to complete the HTML export process.

8. You should open the HTML version of the report in your browser to make sure that the conversion is acceptable before you post it on the Web.

• Use a Web browser to preview the report as a Web page. Microsoft Access usually does a fairly good job when converting reports to Web pages, but you should check to make sure that the report layout and data appear to be correct.

• As the data in your database changes, the Web page version of the report will become increasingly out of date. Periodically, you should open the report and export it again as a Web page. This action ensures that all new data is included in the Web-based version of the report.

FAQ Do I need to specify relationships?

In a relational database, tables can be related to each other and you can use that feature to make data management more efficient. For example, suppose that you operate a small eBay store selling gargoyle merchandise. You maintain an Access database to keep track of your merchandise. You also would like to keep track of orders.

You quickly realize that it doesn't make sense to add fields for customer names and addresses to your table of merchandise. You also realize that because a customer can order more than one item at a time, you need some way to include several items on an order. To handle orders, you can create two additional tables, one table with information about who placed the order and one table for the items on each order. You can create links between the data in the three tables to view the data as a single order form showing all the details about the customer and ordered items.

In database terminology a link between two tables is called a **relationship**. There are several types of relationships. In a **one-to-many relationship**, one record from a table is related to many records in another table, as when one order contains many items purchased by a customer.

In a **many-to-many relationship**, a record in one table can be related to several records in another table and vice versa. This complex relationship exists between movies and actors. One movie can have many actors, but any of those actors can also have roles in many other movies. A **one-to-one relationship** means that a record in one table is related to only one record in another table. This type of relationship is rare in the world of databases.

You can use the Relationships group on the Database Tools tab to create, view, and modify relationships between the tables in a database. Projects AC-6, AC-7, and AC-8 provide additional information about setting up and maintaining relationships within the tables of a database.

Figure 18–10

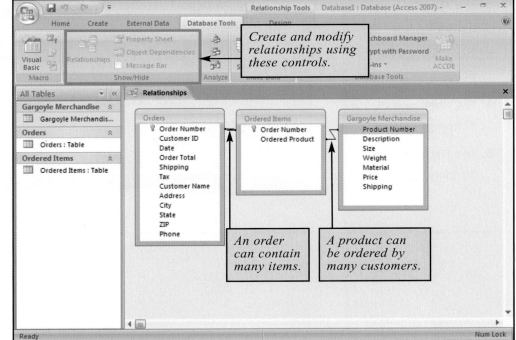

Create and modify relationships using these controls.

An order can contain many items.

A product can be ordered by many customers.

QuickCheck A

1. A(n) [＿＿＿＿＿＿] allows you to display one record at a time, rather than an entire table of data.

2. A(n) [＿＿＿＿＿＿] is typically a formatted printout of some or all of the data contained in a database.

3. True or false? You can use a form to view, edit, and add data to a table. [＿＿＿＿]

4. True or false? Reports are updated each time you display them. [＿＿＿＿]

5. True or false? Access automatically updates the data in Web pages every time you print a report. [＿＿＿＿]

CheckIt!

QuickCheck B

Indicate the letter of the desktop element that best matches the following:

1. A text field [＿＿＿]

2. The New (blank) record button [＿＿＿]

3. The First record button [＿＿＿]

4. The Last record button [＿＿＿]

5. The Next record button [＿＿＿]

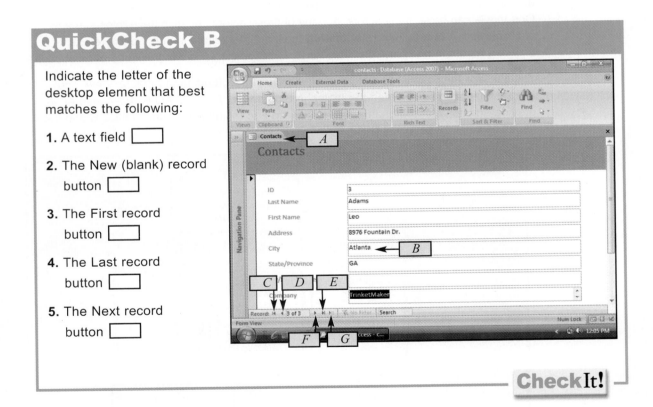

CheckIt!

Section III
Online Connections

When you complete Section III, click the **Get It?** button while using the BookOnCD to take a Practice test.

CHAPTER 19

Networks

What's Inside and on the CD?

Today networks are everywhere. Businesses, educational organizations, and government agencies all use computer networks to share information and resources. Home networks and public networks in coffee shops, airports, and other public places provide access to the largest network in existence—the Internet.

In this chapter, you'll learn basic network terminology, learn to identify network components, and learn about the advantages and disadvantages of networks.

FAQ What is a network?

A **network** is any collection of devices with the ability to communicate with each other. Today, telephone, cellular phone, cable television, satellite television, and computer networks criss-cross the globe and offer unprecedented access to information, people, and events. These networks carry a mix of conversations, documents, photos, music, videos, and databases originating from computers, fax machines, telephones, cell phone cameras, and other devices.

A computer network consists of two or more computers connected in a way that allows information and devices to be shared. You can access computer networks using a personal computer, PDA, cell phone, computer game system, or other network-ready digital device. A **communications protocol** is a set of rules for efficiently transmitting data from one network device to another. Protocols allow diverse devices, such as computers, PDAs, and cell phones, to communicate with each other. Communications protocols are also one of the factors that characterize various types of network standards, such as Ethernet, Wi-Fi, and Bluetooth.

Figure 19-1

Ethernet is a popular network standard for businesses, school computer labs, and home networks. Ethernet is a wired network technology, requiring a cable to connect network devices.

Wi-Fi (or "WiFi") is a popular type of wireless network. Pronounced "Why Fhy," this type of network transmits data from one device to another using radio waves (also called "RF signals"). You're likely to encounter Wi-Fi networks in coffee shops, airports, and other public places. Wi-Fi is also a popular alternative to Ethernet for home, school, and business networks. Wi-Fi and Ethernet can coexist, too, so some networks include wireless and wired devices.

Bluetooth is another wireless network technology, but reserved for short-range applications, such as transferring data between a mobile phone and a headset, between a PDA and a computer, or between a mouse and a computer. An important use of Bluetooth is to synchronize the data in a PDA's address book with the address book on a personal computer.

A computer network can be as small as two PCs in a dorm room sharing a printer, or as large as the global Internet. A computer network can be categorized as a LAN or WAN.

A **local area network** (LAN) typically connects personal computers within a very limited geographical area—usually a single building. Home networks and computer labs are classified as LANs. A **wide area network** (WAN) covers a large geographical area and typically consists of several smaller networks, which might use different computer platforms and network technologies. Networks for nationwide banks and multi-location superstores can be classified as WANs. The Internet is the world's largest WAN.

An **intranet** is a private LAN that uses Internet technology. Whereas the Internet is open to the public, an intranet is typically maintained by a private business or organization, and access is limited to employees. Intranets are commonly used in business situations to circulate and store internal documents. A private intranet can be expanded into an **extranet** that uses public telephone and computer networks to share data with external suppliers, vendors, and customers.

FAQ What are the components of a local area network?

Network components include computers and peripheral devices used for input and output, specialized computers used to store and distribute data, network devices that handle communications between devices, and communications software that manages network protocols.

You can think of a network as a spiderweb with many interconnecting points. Each connection point on a network is referred to as a **node**. A network node typically contains a computer, but could also contain a peripheral device, network communication device, home entertainment equipment, or network-ready printer. A typical local area network might include components like those in Figure 19-2.

Figure 19–2

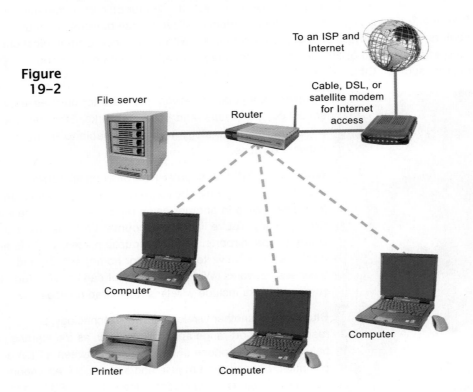

To connect to a LAN, a device requires network circuitry designed to handle incoming and outgoing network data. Circuitry for Ethernet or Wi-Fi networking is incorporated into the motherboard of most personal computers. Network circuitry can also be added to a computer's expansion slot or USB port with a network adapter.

An **Ethernet adapter** (also referred to as a "network interface card" or "NIC") connects a computer to network cabling. The cable is similar to a standard telephone cable, but has a slightly larger plastic snap-in plug.

A **Wi-Fi adapter** transmits wireless signals. Some wireless devices have an antenna for transmitting and receiving data, but many wireless devices, such as notebook computers, have no visible antenna. To determine if a device is equipped for wireless networking, check the manufacturer's specifications or look for communications software.

● What are the components of a local area network? (continued)

Network adapters supply the hardware for controlling incoming and outgoing data, but communications software is also required. **Communications software**, supplied with a computer operating system or built into a digital device, formats and packages data for transport. Windows Vista provides communications software through the Network and Sharing Center.

**Figure
19-3**

For some network configurations, computers with network adapters and software are all that's necessary for exchanging data. Within an **ad hoc network**, network data can travel directly from one device to another. For example, a wireless network could be set up so that computers transmit data directly to each other.

More typically, however, computer networks incorporate some type of centralized device to handle communications. Devices used for this purpose include hubs, switches, bridges, and wireless access points, but most LANs today use a router.

A **router** is a device that links two or more nodes of a network and is able to ship data from one network to another. Routers are handy for exchanging data between computers within a local area network and for connecting to the Internet. In a network configured with a router, all network data travels to the router before continuing to its destination.

Routers and network adapters are designed for specific network standards. For example, Ethernet standards include Fast Ethernet and Gigabit Ethernet. Wi-Fi standards include 802.11a, 802.11g, and 802.11n. When setting up a local area network or expanding it, make sure all your network equipment works with the same standards.

**Figure
19-4**

Many routers can accept wireless and wired connections. This router's antenna transmits signals to Wi-Fi devices. Its four wired ports can connect to Ethernet devices, and the wired uplink port (white cable) can connect to a modem for Internet access.

FAQ What are the roles of clients and servers on a network?

Network devices can function as clients or as servers. A **network server** is a computer that provides services to other computers called **clients**. For example, you might use your computer—the client—to access a file server on your school network and download a copy of a course syllabus. You might use a client computer at work to access an e-mail server that stores your messages and transfers them to your computer when you log in. Your school might give your client computer access to an application server that runs software to get you enrolled in courses for next semester.

In the past, network servers were typically mainframes or minicomputers. Today, servers can also be powerful personal computers running Windows, Linux, or Mac OS. Network servers are often dedicated to the task they perform, which means that they are not typically used for everyday computer tasks.

Networks that include one or more servers can operate in **client/server mode**, which you can envision as a hierarchical structure with servers at the top of the hierarchy. Your client computer requests a file, e-mail, or other service from a server. If your client is authorized to receive the service, based on sharing, permissions, and user rights, the server complies with the client's request.

Figure 19-5

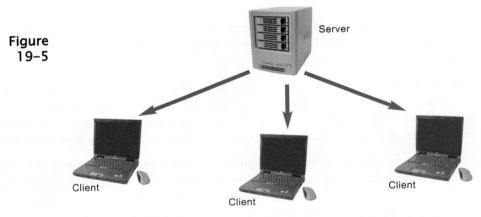

In client-server mode, client computers use locally installed client software such as a browser or e-mail package to access a server.

Not all data exchanges take place between a client and a server. Files and applications can be exchanged among computers operating in **peer-to-peer mode** (sometimes referred to as "P2P"). In this mode, computers share responsibility for processing, storage, printing, and communications tasks. Popular file sharing applications such as Gnutella, Kazaa, and BitTorrent operate in peer-to-peer mode.

Figure 19-6

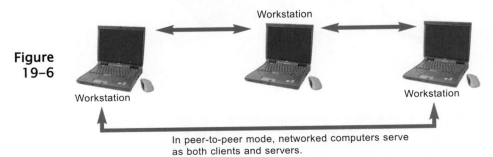

In peer-to-peer mode, networked computers serve as both clients and servers.

FAQ How does the Internet work?

The Internet is a global network that connects millions of smaller networks, computers, and other devices that exchange data using a standard protocol called **TCP/IP**. TCP/IP also divides documents, e-mail messages, photos, and other digital files into standard-sized packets of data, which are shuttled to routers and on to their destination.

The Internet is not owned or operated by any single corporation or government. Instead, it has grown over time in a somewhat haphazard configuration as networks connected to other networks and to the Internet backbone.

The **Internet backbone** is a network of high-capacity communications links that provide the main routes for data traffic across the Internet. At one time, the topology of the Internet backbone and interconnected networks might have resembled a spine with ribs connected along its length. Today, however, it more resembles a map of interstate highways with many junctures and redundant routes.

The Internet backbone is maintained by **network service providers** (NSPs) such as AT&T, British Telecom, Sprint, and Verizon. NSP equipment and links are tied together by **network access points** (NAPs), so that, for example, data can begin its journey on a Verizon link and then cross over to a Sprint link, if necessary, to reach its destination. NSPs supply Internet connections to large Internet service providers, such as EarthLink, AOL, and Comcast. An **Internet service provider** (ISP) is a company that offers Internet access to individuals, businesses, and smaller ISPs.

Play It!

Figure 19–7

Every device on the Internet has a unique **IP address** (also called an "Internet address") that identifies it in the same way that a street address identifies the location of a house. When your computer is connected to any network that uses Internet protocols, it also has an IP address, which is attached to every packet of data you send or receive.

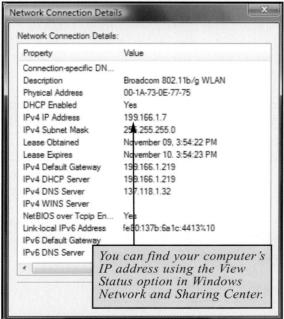

You can find your computer's IP address using the View Status option in Windows Network and Sharing Center.

IPv4 (Internet Protocol version 4) addresses, such as 204.127.129.1, are divided by periods into four segments called **octets**. Longer **IPv6** addresses, such as 2001:0db8:85a3:0000:0000:8a2e:0370:7334, are divided by colons into eight segments.

A computer can have a permanently assigned **static IP address** or a temporarily assigned **dynamic IP address**. Typically ISPs, Web sites, Web hosting services, and e-mail servers that always need to be at the same address require static IP address. Most other network users have dynamic IP addresses.

Your computer can be assigned an IP address by a network administrator or ISP. IP addresses can also be assigned by **DHCP** (Dynamic Host Configuration Protocol) servers. You can find the IP address for your computer by using online tools or the Network and Sharing Center in Windows Vista.

• How does the Internet work? (continued)

Although IP addresses work for communication between computers, people find it difficult to remember long strings of numbers. Therefore, many Internet servers also have an easy-to-remember name, such as *nike.com*. The official term for this name is *fully qualified domain name (FQDN)*, but most people just refer to it as a **domain name**. By convention, you should type domain names using all lowercase letters.

A domain name is a key component of e-mail addresses and Web site addresses. It is the e-mail server name in an e-mail address and the Web server name in a Web address. For example, in the Web address *www.msu.edu/infotech*, the domain name is *msu.edu*.

A domain name ends with an extension, such as .com or .org, that indicates its **top-level domain**. For example, in the domain name *msu.edu*, *edu* indicates that the computer is maintained by an educational institution. Country codes serve as top-level domains. For example, Canada's top-level domain is ca; the United Kingdom's is uk; Australia's is au. Some of the most commonly used top-level domains are listed in the table below.

Figure 19–8

Domain	Description
biz	Unrestricted use; usually for commercial businesses
com	Unrestricted use; usually for commercial businesses
edu	Restricted to North American educational institutions
gov	Restricted to U.S. government agencies
info	Unrestricted use
int	Restricted to organizations established by international treaties
mil	Restricted to U.S. military agencies
net	Unrestricted use; traditionally for Internet administrative organizations
org	Unrestricted use; traditionally for professional and nonprofit organizations

An organization called **ICANN** (Internet Corporation for Assigned Names and Numbers) is recognized by the United States and other governments as the global organization that coordinates technical management of the Internet's Domain Name System. It supervises several for-profit accredited domain registrars, which handle domain name requests. Domain names can be registered for a small annual fee—currently between U.S.$5 and U.S.$50, depending on the registration service.

Figure 19–9

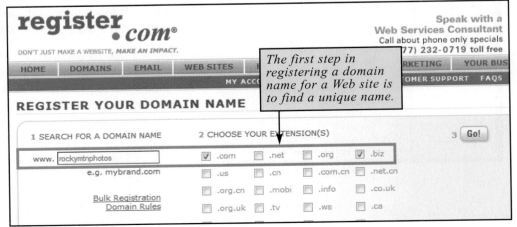

The first step in registering a domain name for a Web site is to find a unique name.

FAQ How do I connect my computer to the Internet?

Computers can be connected to the Internet through telephone lines, cable television systems, satellites, cellular networks, wireless hotspots, and local area networks. Internet services vary in cost, speed, and reliability.

The capacity of an Internet connection is sometimes referred to as **bandwidth** and can be measured in bits per second. The slowest connections transmit a mere 56 Kbps (56 thousand bits per second), whereas fast connections, called **broadband**, blaze away at 6 Mbps (6 *million* bits per second) or more. Capacity is related to speed, and often the two are used interchangeably, though technically speeds would be measured in milliseconds (ms). Higher capacity and faster speeds are better if you want to play online games, use voice over IP, participate in Web conferences, or watch online videos.

Some Internet services offer **symmetrical connections**, in which data travels **upstream** from your computer to the Internet at the same speed as data traveling **downstream** from the Internet to your computer. However, **asymmetrical connections** are more common, with data traveling faster downstream than upstream. When using an asymmetric connection, for example, uploading a video typically requires more time than downloading it.

Internet connections are classified as **always-on connections** if they remain active even when you are not online. With an always-on connection, your IP address can remain the same for days, weeks, or even months. However, an active connection makes your computer more vulnerable to intrusions.

Cable Internet service is a means of distributing broadband Internet access over the same infrastructure that offers cable television service. Local and national cable companies, such as Comcast, Cox Communications, and Charter Communications, offer cable Internet service for a monthly subscription. Of all Internet services, cable Internet currently offers the fastest access speeds. However, advertised speeds are usually for downstream data transfer. Upstream speeds might be much slower. Cable Internet service uses a cable modem to transfer data from your computer to your home cable connection and then to the Internet.

DSL (digital subscriber line) is a broadband, Internet access technology that works over standard phone lines. It offers fast, affordable connections. DSL is available from local telephone companies and third-party DSL providers. DSL services can be symmetrical or asymmetrical. If you need lots of upstream speed, a symmetrical DSL connection could be the best choice. You can contact your telephone company to find out whether DSL is available in your area.

Dial-up Internet service uses a **voiceband modem** and telephone lines to transport data between your computer and an ISP. The modem converts digital data that originates on your computer into an analog signal that can travel over the same frequencies as voices carrying on a telephone conversation. Many ISPs, including AT&T, AOL, and EarthLink, offer dial-up Internet access. The service typically costs less than U.S.$10 per month, but access speed is slow. Dial-up connections are not suitable for playing online games, teleconferencing, using Voice over IP, or watching videos that stream down from the Web. Even downloading software and operating system updates can take hours on a dial-up connection.

Satellite Internet service distributes broadband asymmetric Internet access by broadcasting signals to and from a personal satellite dish. In many rural areas, satellite Internet service is the only alternative to dial-up access. Unfortunately, susceptibility to bad weather makes it less reliable than cable-based services. In addition, the time required for a signal to travel to a satellite makes this type of connection too slow for online gaming.

● **How do I connect my computer to the Internet? (continued)**

Alternative wireless technologies, such as WiMAX and mobile broadband, transmit data from your computer to a nearby communications tower, which then links to the Internet. These services are offered by wireless Internet service providers and cellular phone service providers. Speed and reliability of these connections can deteriorate as the distance to the tower increases. Signals can be disrupted by interference from electrical appliances and environmental factors such as hills, valleys, trees, brick walls, and concrete floors.

Local area networks also provide Internet access. Typically, the LAN's router is connected to a cable Internet or DSL provider and can pass the service along to any of the computers connected to the LAN. Many home networks are configured to allow one Internet connection to be shared by multiple computers.

Wi-Fi hotspots offer public Internet access from coffee shops, airports, hotels, libraries, school campuses, and many other locations. A Wi-Fi hotspot is basically a wireless local area network that provides access to guests using notebook computers, PDAs, or other mobile devices. Some hotspots are free, whereas others require guests to register, pay a fee, and obtain a user ID and password to log in. Many hotspots are unsecured, so legitimate users should be cautious about sending and receiving sensitive data from hotspots.

So many factors affect the speed of an Internet connection that you shouldn't be surprised if your connection speed varies from one day to the next. In addition to environmental factors that affect the speed of wireless connections, factors that can slow down a connection include the number of users logged in to your Internet service, and the amount of traffic that's circulating on the Internet, rerouting caused by equipment failures, power outages that affect the Internet backbone, and bottlenecks caused by viruses. You can check the speed of your Internet connection at any time by using tools such as Ping or Speedtest.net.

PlayIt!

Figure 19-10

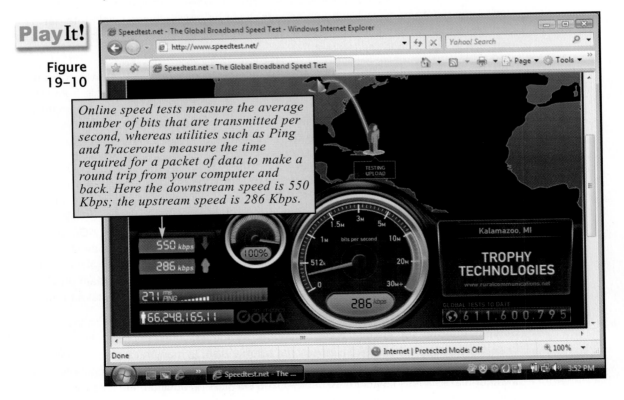

Online speed tests measure the average number of bits that are transmitted per second, whereas utilities such as Ping and Traceroute measure the time required for a packet of data to make a round trip from your computer and back. Here the downstream speed is 550 Kbps; the upstream speed is 286 Kbps.

FAQ What are the advantages of networks?

The Internet is the most visible network, but many smaller computer networks operate "behind the scenes" to facilitate everyday tasks. A global network of ATMs allows you to access your bank account and withdraw money from almost any location on earth. Every day, computer networks manage millions of transactions, such as credit card approvals and point of sale purchases. Industrial networks control assembly lines in vacuum cleaner factories and optimize the work of heavy equipment in mining operations. Even cars include on-board computers that access remote networks to give you immediate help in emergencies.

In general, the advantages of networks include cost savings, centralized control, increased productivity, convenience, and increased opportunities for communications and collaboration.

- Sharing networked hardware can reduce costs. In an office environment, for example, a single color printer can be purchased and attached to a network, instead of the expensive alternative of purchasing color printers for every employee who wants to generate color printouts. Home and business networks can allow multiple users to access Internet services through a single Internet connection.

- Sharing networked software can also reduce costs. Although purchasing and installing a single software copy for an entire network might be technically possible, it is typically not allowed under the terms of a single-user license agreement. However, software site licenses for network use are typically less expensive than purchasing single-user versions of a product for each network user.

- Networks can provide access to a wide range of services and specialized peripheral devices. Networked peripheral devices, such as scanners, photo printers, plotters, high-capacity storage devices, and computer-aided manufacturing (CAM) equipment, can be accessed by any authorized network user.

- Sharing data on a network is easy. To transfer data between standalone computers, a file is usually copied to some type of removable storage media, which is carried to the other computer where it is copied onto the hard disk. Networks can provide authorized users with convenient access to data stored on network servers or clients.

- In business environments, networks provide a means to monitor and control many aspects of the enterprise. In many cases, software updates can be made in a central location, rather than on individual computers—a process that saves time and encourages the use of a standard set of tools. Networks can be centrally monitored for security breaches and important servers can be maintained by trained professionals.

- Networks are convenient, which translates to increased productivity. They reduce the overhead of telephone tag and eliminate convoluted procedures for obtaining information by making access to data in files and databases more immediate.

- Networks enable people to work together regardless of time and place. Using groupware and other specialized network application software, several people can work together on a project, collaborate on a single document, communicate via e-mail and instant messaging, and participate in online conferences and Webcasts. More information on this topic is supplied in the next FAQ.

FAQ How do networks facilitate communication and collaboration?

E-mail is one of the most well-known network-based tools, but many other tools operate on LANs, cellular networks, and the Internet. You'll read more about e-mail in later chapters, but the following communication and collaboration tools have their own unique uses.

Message boards, **online bulletin boards**, and **newsgroups** were three of the first technologies for communicating and collaborating online. Although dwindling in popularity, they typically offer a place where participants can post a message, which is read and responded to by other participants who log in later. Newsgroups and boards usually focus on a specific topic and participants are required to subscribe to the group before they can log in. Abuse of these venues led to the need for moderators to filter out postings that wander off topic.

File Transfer Protocol (FTP) is an established technology for exchanging files, particularly those that are a bit too large to be sent as e-mail attachments. Files are uploaded to an FTP server, where they are cataloged, stored, and available for download. Access to an FTP server usually requires a user ID and password, plus FTP client software.

Voice over IP (VoIP) carries voice conversations over a computer network. VoIP software installed locally converts audio signals into digital data, divides it into packets, and ships it over the Internet, through numerous routers to a specified destination where the packets are assembled into a coherent audio stream—all in less than a second. Although the technology sounds a bit complex, VoIP call quality is similar to that of a cell phone and offers substantial cost savings over cellular or land-line phone service.

Instant messaging (IM) is a form of quick communication in which a message is typed, sent to one or more people, and received instantly. IM is typically computer-based and requires access to a network-based IM server that tracks who is logged in and delivers messages. Senders and recipients typically are both online during the exchange. Instant messaging is used in social and business situations. Also referred to as "online chat," IM offers quick response to questions and allows people to coordinate activities and send short informational messages without getting involved with extended verbal communications.

Figure 19–11

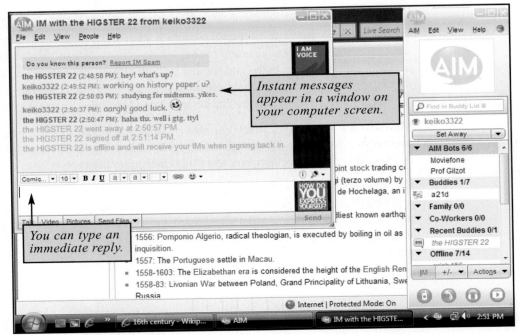

Instant messages appear in a window on your computer screen.

You can type an immediate reply.

How do networks facilitate communication and collaboration? (continued)

Text messaging (TM) refers to exchanging short messages usually sent over a mobile phone service and entered by means of a cell phone keypad. Text messaging is also called "texting" or "SMS" (Short Message Service). Text messaging is an asynchronous service; messages are delivered to a mobile device where they are stored until viewed. Originally, messages were limited to 160 characters; but some TM services allow messages up to 3,000 characters and support graphics, audio, video, and Web links. In addition to its popularity for communicating with friends and colleagues, text messaging is used extensively to collect opinions and "votes" for reality shows such as American Idol. It is used in political campaigns to connect with voters. However, TM has also been misused for cheating on exams, and texting while driving can pose a public safety problem.

Web conferencing and **video conferencing** technologies allow participants at two or more locations to interact through two-way video carried over the Internet or over the telephone system. Video conferencing applications offer substantial cost savings for business meetings, distance education, legal proceedings, and telemedicine because participants are spared the cost of travel. Conferencing software is usually installed locally, but mediated through a Web-based subscription service.

Chat rooms, sometimes referred to as "online forums," provide an online environment in which a group of participants share text-based information. Pioneered by AOL and similar services, chat rooms were an early form of social networking where people met and interacted in cyberspace. The popularity of chat rooms is declining as more sophisticated online environments for social networking have become available.

Figure 19–12

Social networking sites are based on profiles, contacts and referrals.

Social networking is a term that commonly refers to participation at Web sites designed to facilitate online communities of people who have similar interests. Typically a participant uses tools supplied at the social networking site to create a profile that includes information about schools attended, hometown, friends, hobbies, and interests. A built-in referral system helps participants contact other participants with similar interests. Popular social networking sites such as Facebook and MySpace were originally designed to help people get in contact with old friends and schoolmates; but today social networking sites play a wider role that can encompass distance education, marketing, and job searches. Participants at social networking sites do need to carefully consider the amount of personal information they want to reveal and its effect on their privacy.

A **blog** (short for "Web log") is a series of entries posted online similar to the entries in a diary or commentary expressed in a daily editorial column. Blogs are typically text-based, though videoblogs (vlogs) and photoblogs also exist. Software to create a blog using your computer or smart phone is free and readily available. The majority of blogs are personal and typically recount significant life events or opinions. These blogs often remain private, but many are open to the public. Blogs intended for public access sometimes focus on a particular topic; political, travel, and fashion blogs are popular. Blogs are responsible for a surge in citizen journalists, who now have access to a public forum but are sometimes less rigorous than professional journalists when it comes to checking facts.

FAQ How do I choose the right communications tools?

Networks can increase the speed of communication and reduce its cost. They provide local and remote access from computers, cell phones, and other devices. Network-based communications tools can be used in creative ways to facilitate group collaboration: for example, a project team can use e-mail to exchange schedules, instant messaging to get quick answers, teleconferencing for periodic meetings, and collaborative online tools, such as Web apps, for commenting on documents. When selecting one or more tools for a task, keep in mind the following factors.

Media. Most networks support text, audio, graphical, and video communications. However, the software you select might limit your media options. For example, the software you use for instant messaging might limit you to text messages. If you would like to share videos with friends or coworkers, you might consider a social networking site or videoblog.

Audience. Communications applications make it easy to send, post, forward, and route messages, but the tool you use affects the audience you can reach. E-mail and instant messaging reach private venues for one-to-one or one-to-many correspondence with people designated in your address book. Reaching a wider public, however, requires posting to a bulletin board, message board, chat room, social networking site, blog, or RSS feed. You can envision **RSS** (Really Simple Syndication) as a blog that subscribers receive automatically when updates are posted. RSS allows individuals or groups to publish information such as press releases, political commentary, sports news, and real estate listings.

Confidentiality. Many communications tools have the ability to track and record the history of a communication thread. E-mail software typically incorporates the text of the original message in the context of the reply. Instant messaging systems usually maintain a running log of messages sent and received during a session. Bulletin boards, online forums, message boards, and chat rooms maintain a transcript of posted material. Social networking sites may store your profile even after you take it offline. In most situations, a record of communication is useful, but participants should understand how long records are maintained and who can view those records.

Community. Networks can contribute to community building. Social networking sites and chat rooms bring together people with similar interests. They can also be used in businesses. For example, when teams from several locations work together on a project, team members can be encouraged to post photos and short biographies to personalize their interactions with other team members.

Convenience. **Synchronous communications** require that participants are online during an exchange. The advantage is immediate response, but the requirement to schedule meetings can be inconvenient. **Asynchronous communications**, such as e-mail, newsgroups, and social networking, allow participants to send and receive messages at their convenience. They do so, however, knowing that they have to wait for a response.

Overhead. When communicating and exchanging data, participants are identified by a unique address, number, or ID. For example, e-mail addresses are also used for instant messaging, whereas phone numbers are used when communicating over cell phones, placing calls on land lines, using Voice over IP, and sending text messages. Social networking sites, chat rooms, and other online forums usually require participants to register and use a password to log in. Managing multiple logins can become cumbersome, so carefully consider other options before selecting a tool that requires you or your teammates to create yet another set of user IDs and passwords.

FAQ Do networks have disadvantages?

The primary disadvantage of networks is their vulnerability to unauthorized access. Whereas a standalone computer is vulnerable to on-premises theft or access, network computers are vulnerable to unauthorized access from many sources and locations.

Through unauthorized use of a network client, intruders can access data stored on a network server or other clients. Networks connected to the Internet are vulnerable to intrusions from remote computers in distant states, provinces, or countries.

Networks are also more vulnerable than standalone computers to malicious code. Whereas the most prevalent threat to standalone computers is disk-borne viruses, networks are susceptible to an ever increasing number of attacks from malicious software that autonomously trolls networks looking for unprotected computers.

Organizations typically employ a **network administrator** to create network policies, supervise network maintenance, and implement security. Fundamental network security principles include the following:

Figure 19–13

Logging into a network is sometimes an additional step after logging into Windows.

- Grant access only to authorized users.

- Use authentication procedures, based on passwords, fingerprint scans, or other biometric data, to screen out unauthorized users.

- Install protective technology such as firewalls and proxy servers to act as deterrents to viruses, worms, and other malicious programs.

- Monitor the network for unusual traffic that might indicate a security breach.

Compared to wired networks, wireless networks are much more susceptible to unauthorized access and use. To join a wired network, you have to gain physical access to the router and plug in a cable. To access many wireless networks, you simply boot up a wireless-enabled device such as a notebook computer within range of the wireless router.

Preventing Wi-Fi signal interception is difficult, but encrypting transmitted data makes it useless to intruders. Wireless encryption scrambles the data transmitted between wireless devices and then unscrambles the data only on devices that have a valid encryption key. Several wireless encryption technologies such as WEP (Wired Equivalent Privacy), WPA (Wi-Fi Protected Access), and PSK (pre-shared key) are discussed in Chapter 22.

Although security tops the list of network disadvantages, another drawback is loss of autonomy, especially in an organizational setting. With centralized network control, individuals may lose the freedom to select software and access information. Business networks and school labs are often locked down to prevent unauthorized installation of software. Business policies might discourage personal use of workplace computers, prohibiting use of personal e-mail accounts and access to online shopping, sports scores, or similar non-business information.

• Do networks have disadvantages? (continued)

The characteristics of networks that make them convenient for sharing data also make them a potential privacy risk. When corporate databases are compromised, sensitive data pertaining to individuals can fall into the wrong hands. Organizations take steps to secure their networks, but even the best security plans sometimes fail and consumers need to remain vigilant about personal data.

Networks themselves sometimes fail and cut off users from important services, such as e-mail and Internet access. Network-wide system failures can occur on a local area network or on sections of the Internet backbone. The distributed architecture of the Internet helps to keep data flowing over alternative routes, but rerouted data can get delayed as it waits to get through overburdened routers.

Home networks face many of the same threats as larger networks, but typically do not have the resources of an experienced network administrator or sophisticated network monitoring software. Home networks can be protected. Detailed security procedures for personal computers are presented in later chapters, but in general network security includes the following steps:

• Make sure that all network computers require user IDs and passwords.

• Install antivirus software on all computers and keep it updated.

• Activate the firewall software provided by your operating system.

• Activate encryption on wireless networks.

• Install operating system updates as they become available.

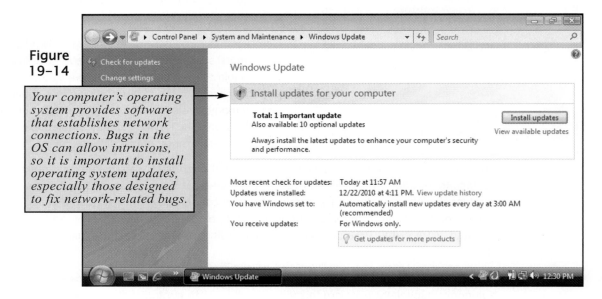

Figure 19-14

Your computer's operating system provides software that establishes network connections. Bugs in the OS can allow intrusions, so it is important to install operating system updates, especially those designed to fix network-related bugs.

Most computer owners are enthusiastic about the benefits provided by networks and believe that those benefits outweigh the risks of intrusions and viruses—especially if their computers can be protected by security aids, such as antivirus software and personal firewall software.

QuickCheck A

1. A communications [   ] is a set of rules implemented by telecommunications software that is typically supplied with your computer's operating system.

2. [   ] is the transmission capacity of a communications channel.

3. A device called a [   ] links two or more nodes of a network and can also link to the Internet.

4. The Internet is a collection of networks tied together by high-speed communications links called the Internet [   ] .

5. [   ] communications require that participants are online during an exchange.

Check It!

QuickCheck B

Indicate the letter of the network element that best matches the following:

1. A peer-to-peer network [   ]

2. A server [   ]

3. A peer [   ]

4. A client [   ]

5. A client/server network [   ]

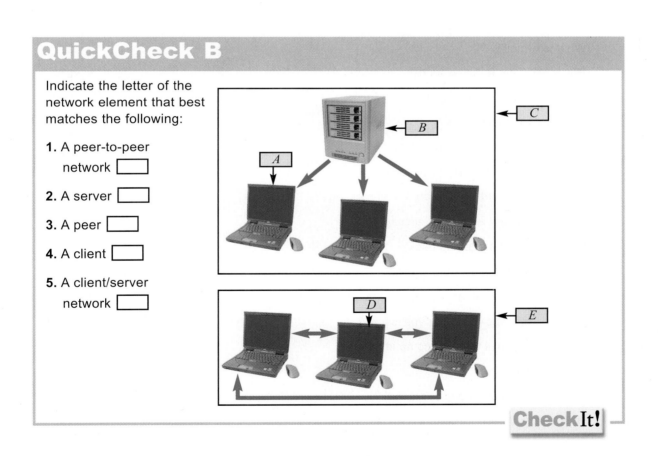

Check It!

CHAPTER **20**

Working with E-mail

Billions of messages speed over the Internet every day. Electronic mail, which is usually abbreviated as "e-mail" or "email," has become an essential element of modern life. It has become enormously popular because it is inexpensive and easy to use, delivers messages in a matter of minutes, and lets you broadcast the same message simultaneously to more than one person.

In the workplace, e-mail allows people in diverse locations to collaborate on projects and share ideas. Students use e-mail to communicate with instructors, submit assignments, and chat with other students. Home-based computer owners take advantage of e-mail to keep in touch with friends and relatives.

In this chapter, you'll learn the basics of e-mail. You'll also learn how to use an electronic address book, organize your e-mail messages, and maintain tight e-mail security.

FAQ What is e-mail?

E-mail is an electronic version of the postal system that transmits messages from one computer to another, usually over the Internet. The term "e-mail" can refer to a single message or to the entire system of computers and software that transmits, receives, and stores e-mail messages.

An **e-mail message** is an electronic document transmitted over a computer network. E-mail messages arrive in your electronic **Inbox** where they can be stored for later use, forwarded to individuals or groups, and organized to create electronic "paper trails" that provide a record of messages and their replies. As you compose e-mail messages, they can be stored in an **Outbox** until you are ready to send them. Once messages are sent, a copy is usually stored in a folder called "Sent Mail."

E-mail messages have a standard format that consists of two major sections: a header and body. An **e-mail header** is divided into fields that contain the sender's e-mail address, the recipient's address, a one-line summary of the message, and the date and time the message was written. Additional fields can contain addresses for sending copies, priority levels, and tracking information. The body of an e-mail message contains the message itself and the data for any photos or supplementary files that are attached to the e-mail message. Figure 20-1 illustrates the main parts of an e-mail message.

Figure 20-1

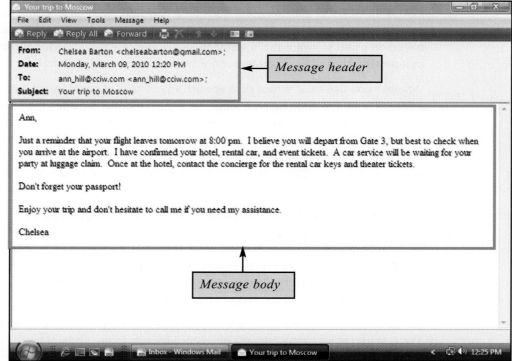

• **What is e-mail?** (continued)

The computers and software that provide e-mail services form an **e-mail system**. At the heart of a typical e-mail system is an **e-mail server**—a computer that essentially acts as a central post office for a group of people. E-mail servers run special e-mail server software, which provides an electronic mailbox for each person, sorts incoming messages into these mailboxes, and routes outgoing mail over the Internet to other e-mail servers. To use an e-mail system, you need an Internet connection, an e-mail account, and software to compose e-mail messages.

Internet connection. As you learned in earlier chapters, Internet connections are available from telephone, cable, satellite, and cellular service providers. Wi-Fi hotspots and local area networks at home, school, or work can also provide Internet access. Any of these connections work for e-mail, though a dial-up connection will respond slowly when sending or receiving messages with photos or other large files attached.

E-mail account. Obtaining an e-mail account gets your electronic mailbox set up on an e-mail server. Your ISP typically plays the role of postmaster, sets up your e-mail account, and provides you with e-mail software. You can also obtain an e-mail account from a Web-based e-mail service, such as Hotmail, Gmail, or Yahoo!.

E-mail software. The software you use to send, receive, and manage messages is called **e-mail client software**. It is available for computers, mobile phones, and PDAs. It can be installed on a local device such as a computer hard disk, stored as a portable app on a USB flash drive, or accessed from the Web through a browser. E-mail systems based on client software that's installed locally are referred to as **local e-mail**. Systems that provide access to e-mail through a browser are called **Webmail**.

Whether you use local e-mail or Webmail, your e-mail account has a unique **e-mail address**. Like the address on a letter, an e-mail address provides the information necessary to route messages to a specified mailbox. An e-mail address typically consists of a user ID (also called a "username"), followed by the @ sign and the name of the e-mail server that manages the user's electronic post office box. For example, the e-mail address john_smith@mtc.com refers to the e-mail account for John Smith on the e-mail server named mtc.com.

In order for e-mail to be routed correctly, each e-mail address must be unique. Gmail can have only one JohnSmith user ID, which explains the existence of e-mail addresses such as JohnSmith256@gmail.com and JSmithTraverseCity@gmail.com. You can, however, use the same user ID for e-mail accounts on different servers. For example, AlexV@msu.edu and AlexV@Hotmail.com are perfectly acceptable for a student who has e-mail accounts on a school server and at Hotmail.

E-mail addresses can sometimes tell you a bit about the person who holds the account. The first part of an e-mail address often corresponds to the account holder's name, nickname, or online persona. For example, the address cat_lover32@hotmail.com probably belongs to a person who likes cats.

The second part of an e-mail address is the e-mail server's domain name, which can provide information about the account holder's job or school. An account for jwatson@ibm.com probably belongs to an IBM employee. An account for rbutler@uga.edu probably belongs to a student at the University of Georgia. An account for gijoe@centcom.mil might belong to a member of the U.S. military.

FAQ How does local e-mail work?

When you use local e-mail, an e-mail server stores your incoming messages until you launch your e-mail client and get your mail. Messages are then downloaded to a folder on a local storage device that serves as your e-mail Inbox. Once the messages are stored on your computer, the e-mail server removes them from your server-based mailbox.

Using your e-mail client, you can read your mail at your leisure. You can also compose new mail and reply to messages. This outgoing mail can be temporarily stored in an Outbox or it can be sent immediately.

The protocol POP3 (Post Office Protocol version 3) is typically used to manage your incoming mail, whereas SMTP (Simple Mail Transfer Protocol) handles outgoing mail. Keep these two protocols in mind when setting up local e-mail, because the server you specify for outgoing mail might be different than the server for incoming mail.

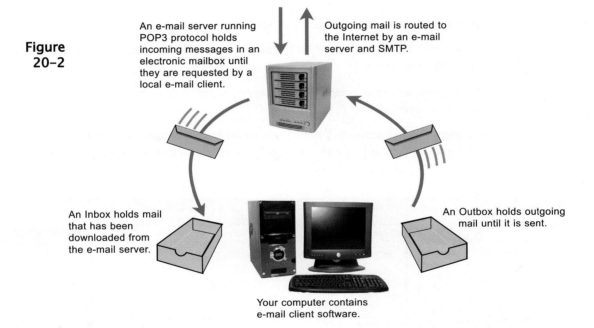

Figure 20-2

An e-mail server running POP3 protocol holds incoming messages in an electronic mailbox until they are requested by a local e-mail client.

Outgoing mail is routed to the Internet by an e-mail server and SMTP.

An Inbox holds mail that has been downloaded from the e-mail server.

An Outbox holds outgoing mail until it is sent.

Your computer contains e-mail client software.

Because local e-mail stores your Inbox and Outbox on your computer, you can compose and read mail offline. You are required to go online only to transfer outgoing mail from your Inbox to the e-mail server, and to receive incoming messages. On a slow dial-up connection or in situations where you are charged for dial-up service by the minute, local e-mail might be preferable to Webmail.

Local mail also works well with broadband always-on connections, such as DSL, cable Internet, or satellite Internet. When using these connections, you can remain online throughout the entire process of collecting, reading, and sending mail. By configuring your e-mail client to send messages immediately, messages can be sent as they are composed instead of remaining in your Outbox and sent as a batch.

The major advantage of local mail is control. Once your messages are transferred to your computer's hard disk, you can control access to them. With this control, however, comes the responsibility for maintaining backups of your important e-mail messages.

FAQ How do I set up local e-mail?

To set up local e-mail, the first step is selecting a local e-mail client. Microsoft Outlook is one of the most popular e-mail clients. Its pared down cousin, Windows Mail, is included with Windows Vista, and Outlook Express is included free with Windows XP. Thunderbird, a free open source e-mail client, is another popular alternative and several other very serviceable e-mail clients are available as shareware. Some ISPs, such as AOL, provide special proprietary e-mail client software that's required for using their e-mail systems. Other ISPs allow you to use the e-mail client of your choice.

After installing an e-mail client, you can configure it for the e-mail service you're using. Your e-mail provider usually supplies the information needed for this task. That information can include the following:

- Your e-mail user ID, which is the first part of your e-mail address (For example in AlexHamilton@gsu.edu, the user ID is AlexHamilton.)

- Your e-mail password, if required to access the e-mail server

- An address for the outgoing (SMTP) server, typically something like mail.viserver.net or smtp.mailisus.com

- An address for the incoming (POP3) server, typically something like mail.gsu.edu or pop.mailserver.net

To configure your local e-mail client, look for an Accounts option on the Tools menu. Figure 20-3 shows how to set up an account and the tour provides an overview of local e-mail.

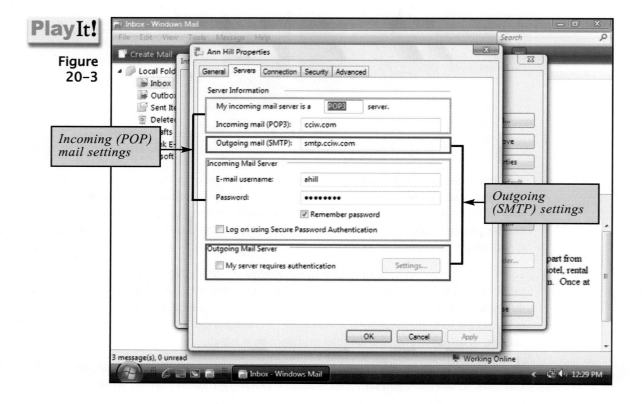

PlayIt!

Figure 20–3

Incoming (POP) mail settings

Outgoing (SMTP) settings

FAQ How does Webmail work?

Webmail is typically a free service accessed using a browser. Some Webmail services also can be accessed using a local e-mail client, such as Microsoft Outlook, but that configuration would be the exception rather than the rule.

In a classic Webmail configuration, your Inbox is stored on the Web; and because messages are sent immediately, an Outbox is not needed. When you want to read or send mail, use a browser to go to your e-mail provider's Web site and log in. The controls for reading, composing, and managing messages are all presented in the browser window. While reading and composing mail, you typically must remain online. Figure 20-4 illustrates how Webmail works.

Figure 20-4

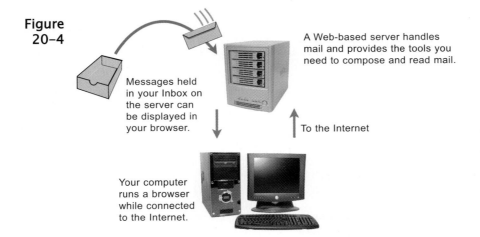

A Web-based server handles mail and provides the tools you need to compose and read mail.

Messages held in your Inbox on the server can be displayed in your browser.

To the Internet

Your computer runs a browser while connected to the Internet.

Webmail can also be accessed from mobile devices when your computer is not handy. If you opt to use mobile mail, read the options offered by your e-mail service provider and make sure you understand how to sync your mobile e-mail with the mail you view on your computer so that you don't miss an important message.

Free Webmail is supported by advertising, so expect to see advertisements. Today's sophisticated ad servers can search the content of an incoming message looking for keywords and then use them to display targeted ads in your e-mail window. For example, suppose you receive an e-mail message about a trip to Moscow. When viewing the message, you'll also be presented with ads about Moscow hotels, flights to Moscow, and similar promotions. Some Webmail services offer an ad-free option for a monthly fee.

Webmail is ideal for people who travel because accounts can be accessed from any computer connected to the Internet. Accessing e-mail from a public computer can be a security risk, however. If possible, reboot the computer before logging into your e-mail account. Avoid entering sensitive information, such as your credit card number, in case your keystrokes are being monitored by malicious software lurking on the public computer. Be sure to log off when your session is finished. Log out of Windows and shut down the computer if you are allowed to do so.

Even when accessing Webmail from your home, security can be an issue. Unfortunately, Webmail services are the target of many malicious exploits, which can work their way into your computer through various security holes. When using Webmail, your computer must be protected by security software, and your computer will be more secure if you log out of your e-mail account when you are not using it.

FAQ How do I get a Webmail account?

Getting a Webmail account is an automated process that you can complete online. Begin by using a browser to access a Webmail site such as www.gmail.com, www.hotmail.com, or www.yahoomail.com. Selecting the Sign Up or Register option produces an on-screen form like the one shown below. When you submit the completed form, your e-mail account is created and ready for immediate use.

Figure 20–5

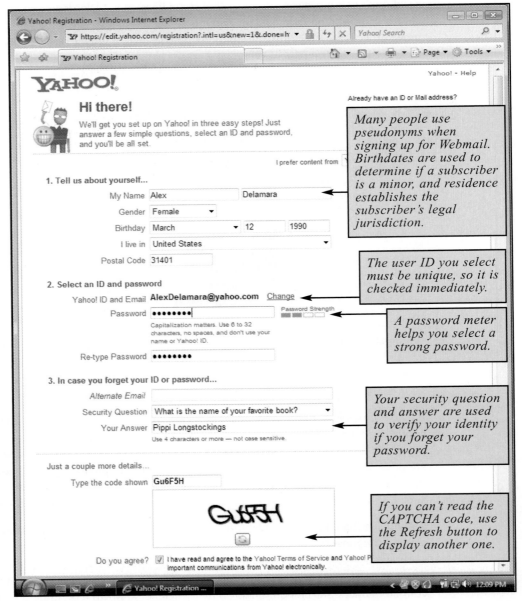

Most Webmail services display a goofy looking code called a **CAPTCHA** that you have to type in at the end of the registration process. Captchas are designed to block automated computer bots from creating e-mail accounts that are subsequently used for sending unsolicited e-mail called "spam."

FAQ How do I write an e-mail message?

When you want to compose a message, look for a toolbar button or link labeled "Create Mail" or "Compose Mail." Enter the recipient's address in the To: box. If you want to send a copy of the message to other people, you can include their e-mail addresses in the Cc: box. Use the Subject box for a brief description of the message.

Most e-mail clients provide a sort of mini word processor for composing e-mail messages. You can type your message, edit it, and even check your spelling. Depending upon your e-mail settings, clicking the Send button either sends the message immediately or places the message in your Outbox to be sent the next time you send and receive a batch of messages.

Figure 20-6

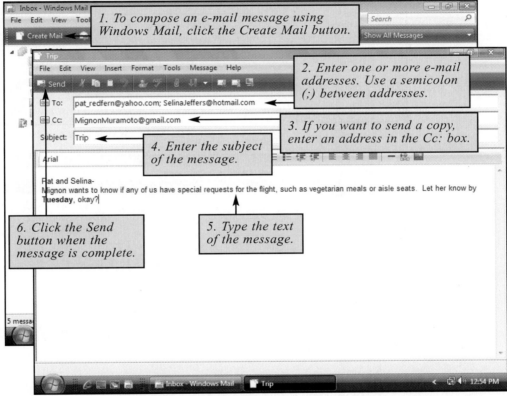

- As you enter text, use the mouse or arrow keys to move the insertion point. Use the Backspace key to delete the character to the left of the insertion point. Use the Delete key to delete characters to the right of the insertion point.

- As when you use word processing software, only press the Enter key at the end of a paragraph.

- To send messages to more than one address, enter additional addresses in the To: box. You can use the Cc: box to "copy" a message to people who might be interested in the information, but who do not necessarily need to act on it. Remember that the message recipient will receive a header that lists all the other recipients. To hide the recipient list, enter additional recipients in the Bcc: box instead of the To: box or Cc: box.

- Most e-mail clients support formatted text, such as bold and italics. If you prefer the additional security offered by plain text messages that cannot carry malicious scripts, look for an ASCII, or plain text configuration option.

FAQ How do I read and reply to an e-mail message?

When new mail messages arrive, you'll want to read them and perhaps reply to some of them. To read a message using Windows Mail, click the message in the Inbox list. To respond to the message, click the Reply button, then type your response. To respond to everyone who received the message, click the *Reply All* button, then type your response.

Play It!

Figure 20-7

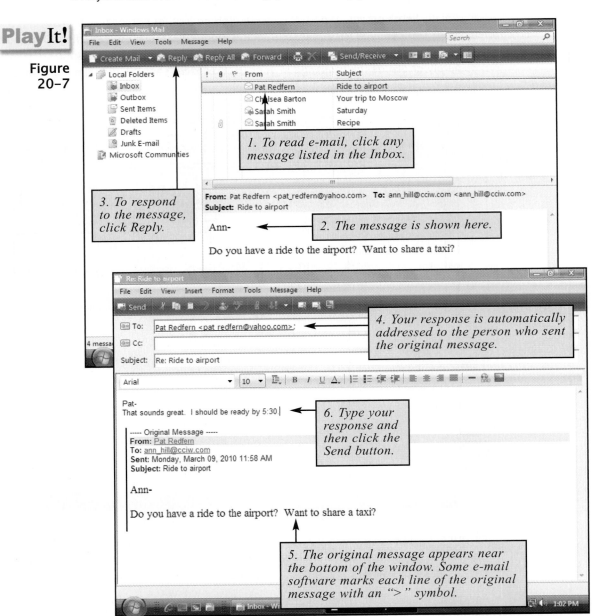

• If you want to respond to a number of points from the original message, the first line of your message might say, "See my comments below." Then, you can scroll down and intersperse your comments within the text of the original message. You can use an alternative font color or style to differentiate your comments from the original message.

FAQ How do I forward an e-mail message?

After you receive an e-mail message, you can pass the message on to other people—a process called "forwarding." You might use forwarding if you receive a message that should be handled by someone else.

When you initiate the forwarding process, the original message is copied into a new message window, complete with the address of the original sender. You can then enter the address of the person to whom you are forwarding the message. You can also add text to the forwarded message to explain why you are passing it along. Some e-mail software allows you to alter the text of the original message before you forward it. Because a message can be altered before being forwarded, you should be aware that forwarded messages you receive might not be entirely accurate versions of the original messages.

To forward a message using Windows Mail, click the message, then click the Forward button. Enter the address of the person to whom you want to forward the message, then click Send to send the message.

Figure 20–8

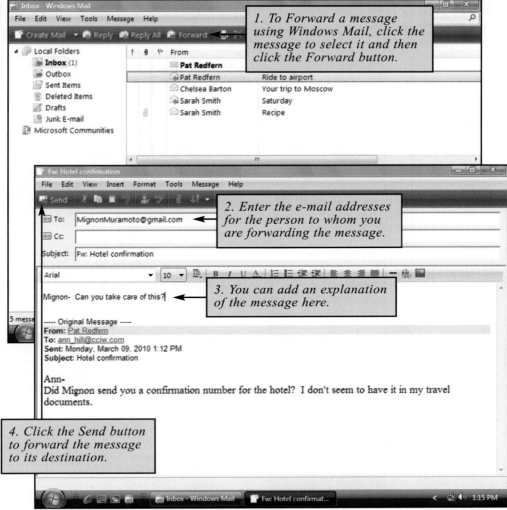

1. To Forward a message using Windows Mail, click the message to select it and then click the Forward button.

2. Enter the e-mail addresses for the person to whom you are forwarding the message.

3. You can add an explanation of the message here.

4. Click the Send button to forward the message to its destination.

FAQ How do I use the address book?

An **e-mail address book** contains a list of e-mail addresses for individuals and groups. Addresses can be manually entered, but you can also add an address by clicking the address in messages you receive. When addressing mail, simply type the first few characters of any address in the address book and your e-mail software will complete the entry for you.

A **mail group** or "mailing list" is a list of e-mail addresses stored under a unique title. Groups are easy to set up and handy to use as mailing lists when you frequently send the same message to the same group of people.

Most address books include fields for expanded contact information, such as telephone numbers, mailing addresses, fax numbers, and company affiliations. The extent of these fields depends on the e-mail software; local clients tend to offer more comprehensive address book features than Webmail. Make sure to keep your address book current by removing outdated addresses and duplicates.

Figure 20–9

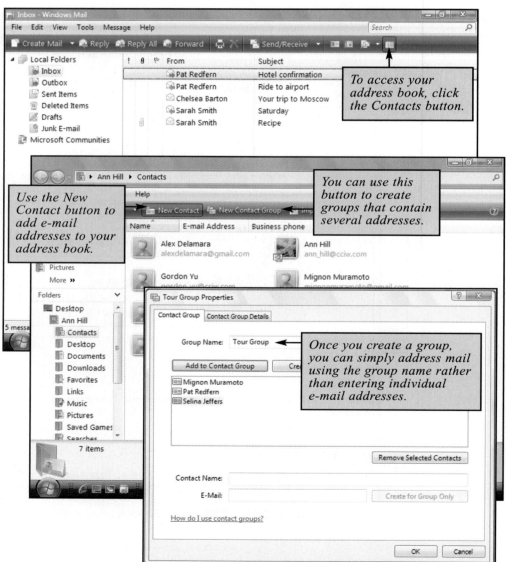

To access your address book, click the Contacts button.

Use the New Contact button to add e-mail addresses to your address book.

You can use this button to create groups that contain several addresses.

Once you create a group, you can simply address mail using the group name rather than entering individual e-mail addresses.

FAQ How do I send e-mail attachments?

An **e-mail attachment** is a file, such as a document, photo, music clip, or spreadsheet, that is attached to and sent along with an e-mail message. Attachments allow you to quickly, easily, and immediately share files with others.

PlayIt!

Figure 20-10

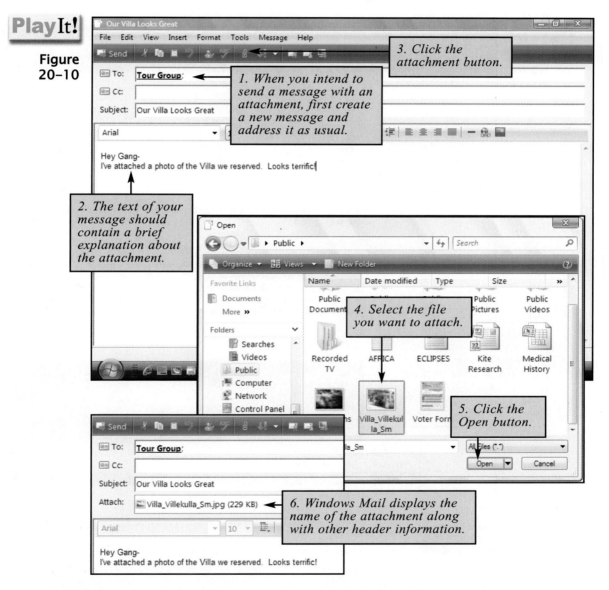

1. When you intend to send a message with an attachment, first create a new message and address it as usual.

2. The text of your message should contain a brief explanation about the attachment.

3. Click the attachment button.

4. Select the file you want to attach.

5. Click the Open button.

6. Windows Mail displays the name of the attachment along with other header information.

- The files used for e-mail attachments can be stored on your computer's hard disk or another storage device; your e-mail software uploads them automatically to the mail server.

- Consider zipping large files before you attach them. Zipping files makes them smaller and reduces transfer time. Use a compression utility, such as WinZip, to reduce the size of the file. The recipient will have to "unzip" the file to return it to its original size.

- As an alternative to attachments, you can use Web links simply by typing a Web site address in the body of an e-mail message. Your mail recipient can click this link to connect to the Web site and view the material. This method works well for sharing large images you've posted on a Web site and for information that changes frequently.

FAQ How do I view, save, and delete e-mail attachments?

Various e-mail clients work with attachments in different ways. Usually a simple click displays an e-mail attachment as long as your computer has the software necessary to open it. If you receive an attachment stored in an uncommon file type, you might have to search for its file extension on the Web to discover the software needed to open it.

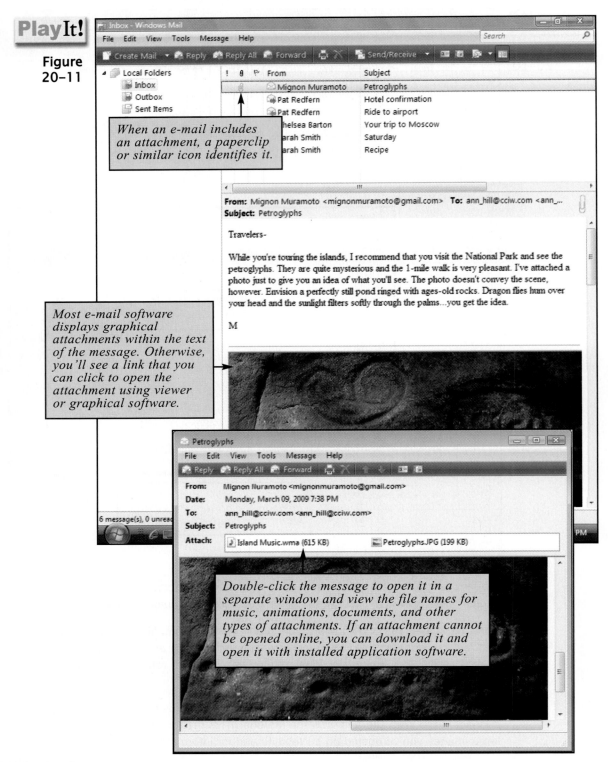

Figure 20–11

When an e-mail includes an attachment, a paperclip or similar icon identifies it.

Most e-mail software displays graphical attachments within the text of the message. Otherwise, you'll see a link that you can click to open the attachment using viewer or graphical software.

Double-click the message to open it in a separate window and view the file names for music, animations, documents, and other types of attachments. If an attachment cannot be opened online, you can download it and open it with installed application software.

• How do I view, save, and delete e-mail attachments? (continued)

You can save an attachment on your hard disk for later use. The steps for doing so depend on the e-mail client you're using. In general, Webmail attachments are downloaded from the mail server if and when you save them. Attachments to local mail are stored in a temporary folder on your computer's hard disk; the process of saving an attachment moves it to one of your personal folders.

Figure 20-12

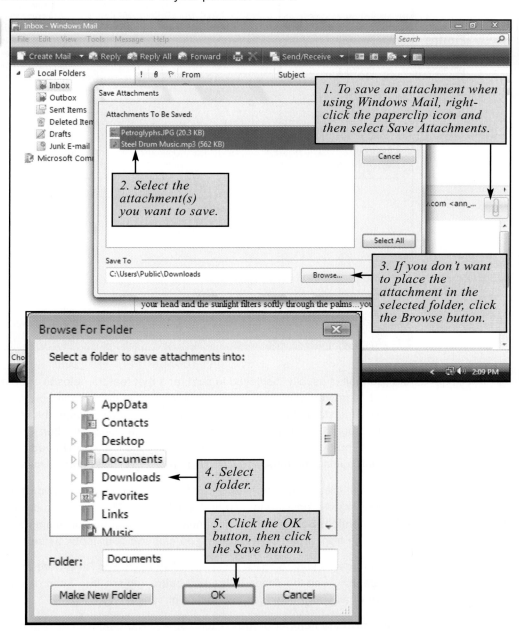

1. To save an attachment when using Windows Mail, right-click the paperclip icon and then select Save Attachments.

2. Select the attachment(s) you want to save.

3. If you don't want to place the attachment in the selected folder, click the Browse button.

4. Select a folder.

5. Click the OK button, then click the Save button.

• Some e-mail systems allow you to delete e-mail attachments but leave the text of the message in your Inbox. Deleting attachments frees up hard disk space, but allows you to keep the message for further reference.

• If your antivirus software is not checking attachments as they arrive, you should save suspicious attachments on your disk before opening them. Once saved, you can use antivirus software to check the files for viruses.

FAQ How do I manage my e-mail messages?

E-mail software includes tools for organizing messages so that information they contain is easy to find. Sifting through thousands of messages in an unorganized Inbox is inefficient, so it pays to learn how to use the organizational tools your e-mail client offers.

Figure 20–13

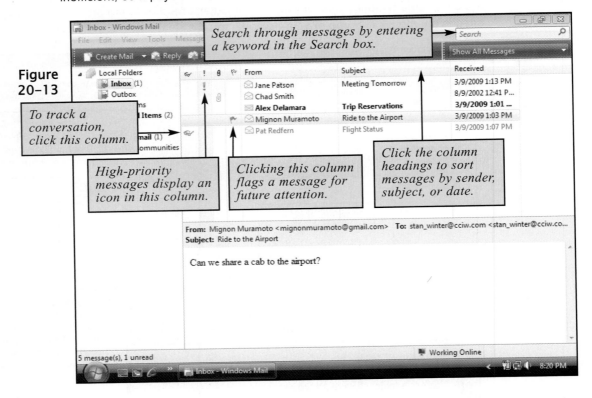

Search through messages by entering a keyword in the Search box.

To track a conversation, click this column.

High-priority messages display an icon in this column.

Clicking this column flags a message for future attention.

Click the column headings to sort messages by sender, subject, or date.

- Unread mail is usually displayed in bold, and that feature helps to ensure that you've not missed an important message. Once you open a message, the bold font is removed and the message status becomes "read." You can manually change the read/unread status of a message. The most typical use of this feature would be when you've read a message, but want to respond to it later. Using the Mark As Unread option reinstates the bold font, putting the message visually in a category with unread messages.

- Your e-mail client might provide a way to prioritize messages, allowing you to deal with the most urgent correspondence first. Clicking the "Flag" column marks a message for future attention. Sometimes sorting messages is useful. For example, when looking for a message from a particular person, you can sort your Inbox by sender.

- A more targeted way to find a message is by searching for a word or phrase. For a quick search, limit the scope to the text in the subject line. Searching through the entire content of all your messages can take a bit longer.

- To minimize the number of messages you have to deal with, delete mail that you don't need to keep. Find out if your e-mail client is able to restore deleted mail in case you inadvertently delete a valuable message. You might want to delete messages containing sensitive information, especially if you are using Webmail. Before doing so, consider if you want to save the message as a standalone file on your computer's hard disk. When using Windows Mail, you can save a message as a standalone file using the Save As option on the File menu.

● How do I manage my e-mail messages? (continued)

An **e-mail thread** (sometimes referred to as a "conversation") consists of an original message and all of the replies and forwards that stem from it. The ability to pull up all the messages that pertain to a thread can be handy. Some e-mail packages automatically track threads according to the subject line. Other e-mail packages allow you to designate labels, such as "Caribbean Trip," for similar messages. You can then use filters to display messages with the same labels.

Figure 20-14

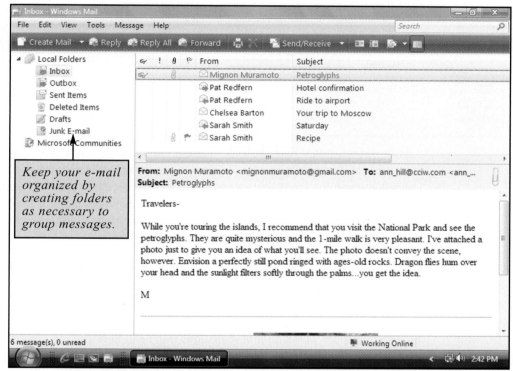

Keep your e-mail organized by creating folders as necessary to group messages.

● Most e-mail clients offer several predefined folders, such as Inbox, Drafts, Sent Mail, Spam, and Trash. You should periodically empty or purge the contents of the Spam and Trash folders if that task is not automated.

● Most e-mail clients allow you to create additional folders or subfolders to group messages. For example, you might create a folder to hold messages that pertain to an ongoing project. You can manually move messages from your Inbox into a folder using the procedure specified by your e-mail client. Instead of manually moving messages, your e-mail client might allow you to create rules or filters for distributing messages into appropriate folders based on the sender or message subject line.

● You can also use folders for archiving mail. For example, at six month intervals, you can move all the mail out of your Inbox and into a folder with a title such as *Mail January-June 2010*. Moving a batch of messages to a secondary folder reduces the size of your Inbox and reduces the possibility that it will become corrupted.

FAQ What other e-mail features come in handy?

Many e-mail clients offer advanced features, such as the ability to use and display tables, graphics, links, and other advanced formatting. Depending on your e-mail system and software, you might be able to use all or some of the features described below.

Autoforward. Autoforwarding allows you to forward messages to other e-mail addresses automatically. Use autoforwarding to forward messages to coworkers, friends, or other contacts who must be kept in the loop.

Figure 20–15

Autoreply. Most e-mail clients can be configured to automatically reply to e-mail messages, a feature sometimes referred to as "out of office response." Use this feature when you are away from your computer for extended periods of time—for example, when you are on vacation.

E-mail tracking. You can ask to be notified if a message has been received by using a **return receipt**. When a message carries a return receipt, you receive an automated reply indicating when the message was received. A read receipt works in a similar way, but indicates when the message was actually opened by its recipient. E-mail tracking is not compatible with some e-mail systems, however, so not receiving a receipt does not necessarily mean that a message did not arrive.

Multiple accounts. Full featured e-mail clients usually allow you to receive e-mail messages from multiple e-mail accounts. You can view, send, and reply to messages sent to any account from one application window, without changing software.

Synchronization. If you collect e-mail from various digital devices, you must understand how each system works so that messages don't slip between the cracks. When you collect mail, make sure you understand if it will be removed from the mail server. To avoid downloading mail to a mobile device that you'd rather have on your computer, find out if your e-mail service allows you to selectively download messages while leaving the rest on the server.

Encryption. Your e-mail client might allow you to encrypt e-mail messages for enhanced security. If your e-mail software does not provide this feature, you can use third-party encryption software, such as PGP (Pretty Good Privacy). Recipients of encrypted messages must use a key to decrypt the message content. You can provide the key in a separate e-mail.

Signatures. An **e-mail signature** is a block of text or graphics automatically added to the end of every e-mail message you send. You could, for example, set up a signature that includes your name, title, and telephone number.

Backup. E-mail messages are usually stored together as one large file in a proprietary format. That fact explains the difficulty of moving messages and address books from one e-mail client to another. For local e-mail systems, the file containing e-mail messages is often buried deep within the Windows folder structure, making it difficult to find for a manual backup. Happily, most e-mail clients include a backup or archive command. Using it regularly ensures that you'll not lose all your e-mail correspondence in case of a hard disk failure.

FAQ Is e-mail safe?

E-mail is patterned after paper-based letters sent through the ground-based postal service. The advantage of e-mail is that it arrives quickly and costs nothing. It also maintains a "paper trail" of messages and replies that can be useful in verifying decisions and approvals.

One of e-mail's main disadvantages is **spam**—unwanted electronic junk mail about medical products, low-cost loans, and software upgrades that often carries viruses and other malicious software. Today's proliferation of spam is generated by marketing firms that harvest e-mail addresses from mailing lists, membership applications, and casual Web browsing. Legislation to minimize spam has so far been ineffective.

To protect your computer and data from spam and other risks associated with e-mail, consider the following precautions:

- Never reply to spam when you receive it.

- Never open suspicious attachments or click links in dubious e-mail messages.

- If your e-mail provider offers a way to report spam, use it.

- If your e-mail client provides spam filters to block unwanted messages, put them to use. A **spam filter** automatically routes advertisements and other junk mail to the trash folder maintained by your e-mail client. Although spam filters can be very effective for blocking spam and other unwanted e-mail, they sometimes block messages you want. After activating spam filters, periodically examine the folder that holds your e-mail trash to make sure the filters are not overly aggressive.

- Spam filters usually include a set of predefined rules designed to filter out junk mail with subject lines such as "p()rn" and "d0n8 now!". If spam bypasses the predefined rules, you can construct additional rules to filter out even more spam.

- When spam gets out of hand, you might have to consider changing your e-mail account so that you have a different e-mail address.

- Use an e-mail provider that filters out spam at its server to block unwanted mail from reaching your Inbox.

- Make sure your antivirus software is configured to scan incoming mail and attachments for viruses and other malicious exploits.

- Provide your e-mail address only to people from whom you want to receive e-mail. Be wary of providing your e-mail address at Web sites, entering it on application forms, or posting it in public places such as online discussion groups.

- Be cautious when sending sensitive data, such as credit card numbers and Social Security numbers. This data is best sent over a secure connection or in an encrypted message. Sometimes a phone call is the best way to convey sensitive information as it is unlikely to be intercepted.

- Understand policies relating to message storage and access. Regard e-mail as a postcard, rather than a sealed letter. Like a postcard, your e-mail can be read during the course of system maintenance. It can be forwarded to others, and it can be intercepted in transit. Even after you've downloaded and deleted messages, they can remain stored on e-mail servers and on backups for months or years. If you don't want your words made public, be cautious about enclosing them in an e-mail message.

FAQ How does netiquette apply to e-mail?

Netiquette is online jargon for "Internet etiquette." It is a series of customs or guidelines for avoiding misunderstandings, maintaining civilized discourse, and carrying on effective communication in online discussions, instant messages, text messages, and e-mail exchanges. The most important rules of netiquette include:

- Make sure you consider the purpose of the correspondence and tailor your message accordingly. Business correspondence is more formal than casual messages to friends.

- Avoid using abbreviations, slang, smileys, and text message shorthand in business communications. **Smileys** are symbols that represent emotions. For example the ;-) smiley means "just joking." Smileys can help convey the intent behind your words, but are most appropriate in casual correspondence; ditto for text messaging shorthand like LOL (laughing out loud).

- Review messages before you send them. Check spelling and grammar. Use uppercase and lowercase letters. An e-mail message that's typed in all uppercase means that you're shouting.

- Be cautious when using sarcasm and humor. The words in your e-mail arrive without facial expressions or voice intonations, so a sarcastic comment can easily be misinterpreted.

- Be polite. Avoid wording that could sound inflammatory or confrontational. If you would not say it face-to-face, don't say it in e-mail.

- Try to respond promptly to messages and make your reply concise and accurate. Although e-mail messages tend to be longer than instant messages or text messages, there is no need to ramble on.

- Avoid replying to all recipients. Use the Reply All command only when there is a specific need for everyone listed in the To:, Cc:, and Bcc: boxes to receive the message.

- Don't send huge attachments. Try to limit the size of attachments to 100 KB or less for recipients with dial-up connections, and 1 MB or less for recipients with broadband connections. If necessary, use a compression utility, such as WinZip, to shrink the attachment.

- Put a meaningful title on the subject line of every message and explain all attachments. Attachments can harbor computer viruses. To determine whether an attachment is legitimate, your correspondents will want to know the file name of the attachment, what the attachment contains, and the name of the software you used to create it. You can provide this information in the body of your e-mail message.

- Be careful when embedding Web links in e-mail messages. Although it's handy to include direct links to Web pages, not all e-mail systems support this feature. Only use embedded Web links when you want to reference information on Web pages that will still exist when the message is received.

- Make sure you follow school and company guidelines on the use of e-mail. National, state, and local laws may also apply. Don't use e-mail or other electronic communications for illegal or unethical activities, such as cheating on exams.

- Legal documents that require a signature should be sent through traditional delivery methods rather than electronically.

FAQ How do I troubleshoot common e-mail problems?

E-mail is one of the most dependable network technologies. However, problems sometimes prevent messages from being sent, prevent them from being delivered, or make their content difficult to view once they are received. Sending problems can be caused by antivirus software or an ISP outage. Delivery failures often stem from invalid addresses, Internet outages, spam filters, and storage overloads. Even when mail reaches your Inbox, the message might be garbled or the attachment might be difficult to open.

Blocked by antivirus software. Most computer owners use antivirus software to scan incoming and outgoing e-mail messages. When antivirus scanning is active, e-mail messages are sent from your Outbox to the virus scanner before going to your e-mail server. If the antivirus software detects a possible virus, it displays a warning and prevents the message from progressing to the server. Read the warning carefully. The virus was most likely spotted in the attachment. You can carry out a manual scan of the attachment to ascertain whether a virus does exist. If the scan does not detect a virus, renaming or zipping the attachment file might get the attachment through the scan.

No connection. When you ship mail from a local Outbox to an e-mail server, your e-mail client typically displays a progress report. If your computer cannot establish a connection to your e-mail server, the progress report stops and eventually indicates the mail cannot be sent (Figure 20-16). If you receive such a message, check your network connection by trying to open your browser. Network connections go out of service periodically and sometimes you have to wait a few minutes for service to be re-established. If the outage continues, you should contact your Internet service provider.

Figure 20-16

Alert

Connection to server mail.nmu.edu timed out.

OK

Internet outages. After an e-mail message leaves your Outbox, it travels from your e-mail server to the recipient's e-mail server. Problems on the Internet backbone or with the recipient's e-mail service can prevent delivery. Internet outages are not common, but localized power outages and malicious exploits such as denial of service attacks can cause Internet traffic jams that delay or lose data. You will not get any notification if a message is delayed or lost. When you want to know if messages have reached their destinations, use return receipts if your e-mail client provides them.

Blocked for abuse. E-mail servers sometimes block entire domains if they are the suspected source of spam. When an e-mail message cannot be delivered by the recipient's server, you usually receive an e-mail message explaining possible reasons for non-delivery. Sometimes, if you send the message again, it goes through the second time. You can avoid retyping the message by using the Forward button to resend the message to the same recipient.

• How do I troubleshoot common e-mail problems? (continued)

Invalid address. If you type the wrong e-mail address, the recipient's e-mail server cannot deliver the mail and instead generates a non-delivery message. If you check the recipient's address and discover it is incorrect, use the Forward button and then type the correct address.

Disk full. When the device that stores your mail becomes full, you must take steps to delete unwanted files to regain space. Although it is a good idea to regularly delete unwanted e-mail messages, they take up a very small portion of your multi-gigabyte hard disk or USB flash drive. Look for other large files, such as graphics and music, that you can delete to quickly regain disk space.

Inbox overflow. Webmail services typically limit the amount of storage space allocated to an account. When you fill your allocated space, you must delete old messages or purchase additional storage space. Your Webmail provider might store overflow files in a special storage area. As soon as you delete old messages, the mail in this storage area can be delivered and you can read it.

Attachment won't open. To open an attachment, your computer must have software that works with the attachment's file type. If your computer does not recognize the file extension, it displays a message asking which software to use to open the file (Figure 20-17). In this situation, you might have to ask for more information about the attachment from the person who sent it.

Figure 20-17

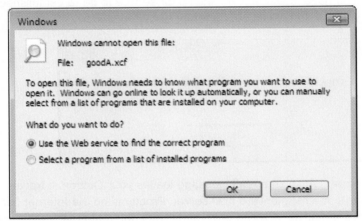

Garbled messages. Occasionally, e-mail and other transmissions across the Internet become garbled and the text appears as a series of random characters. This problem is typically caused by heavy traffic on the Internet or by errors on transmitting or receiving computers. The problem can also be caused if the sender uses a font or a language not installed on your computer. If you receive a garbled message, ask the sender to try to ship it to you again.

Lost formatting. Messages in HTML might lose their formatting when viewed using an e-mail client that has HTML disabled for security reasons. If you don't see expected bold, italics, and other formatting in a message, check the view options on your software's menu or toolbar.

QuickCheck A

1. Webmail is accessed using a(n) [＿＿＿＿＿＿＿] .

2. True or false? The To: field of an e-mail message can hold only one address—addresses for additional recipients must be placed in the Cc: or Bcc: boxes. [＿＿＿＿＿]

3. An e-mail [＿＿＿＿＿＿＿] is used to send word processing documents, spreadsheets, photos, and music clips along with an e-mail message.

4. [＿＿＿＿＿＿＿] is the term used to refer to electronic junk mail.

5. An e-mail [＿＿＿＿＿＿＿] consists of an original message and all of the replies and forwards that stem from it.

CheckIt!

QuickCheck B

Indicate the letter of the screen element that best matches the following:

1. A message with an attachment [＿＿＿]

2. The folder that holds a copy of all mail you've sent out [＿＿＿]

3. A high-priority message [＿＿＿]

4. An unread e-mail message [＿＿＿]

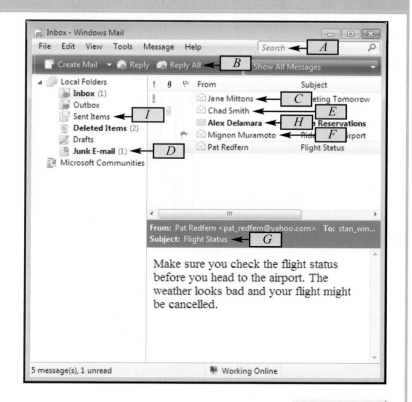

CheckIt!

CHAPTER 21

Browsing the Web

What's Inside and on the CD?

The Web is a modern rendition of an idea first developed in 1945 by an engineer named Vannevar Bush, who envisioned a microfilm-based machine called the "Memex" that linked associated information or ideas through "trails." The idea resurfaced in the mid-1960s when Harvard graduate Ted Nelson coined the term "hypertext" to describe a computer system that could store literary documents, link them according to logical relationships, and allow readers to comment on and annotate what they read. Tim Berners-Lee made this idea a reality in 1991 when he wrote the first software to locate and link documents over the Internet. In this chapter, you'll learn how the modern Web works to link information from all corners of the globe.

FAQ What is the Web?

The **Web** (short for "World Wide Web") is a collection of data that can be linked and accessed using HTTP. **HTTP** (Hypertext Transfer Protocol) is the communications protocol that sets the standard used by every computer that accesses Web-based information. The Web is not the same as the Internet. The Internet is a communications system; the Web is an interlinked collection of information that flows over that communications system.

A **Web page** is a specially coded document that can contain text, graphics, videos, animations, audio, and interactive elements. These pages are stored on Web servers all over the world. A **Web server** is a computer attached to the Internet that runs special Web server software and can send Web pages out to other computers over the Internet. A **Web site** consists of one or more Web pages located on a Web server.

Each Web page is assigned a **URL** (Uniform Resource Locator) that uniquely identifies its location on the Internet by referencing its server name, domain, and file name.

Figure 21-1

http://www.youcouldwin.com/currentcontest/rules.htm

| Web protocol | Server name | Domain | Folder name | File name |

To access a Web page, you can type its URL. You can also click an underlined word or phrase called a **hypertext link** (or simply a "link") to access related documents.

Web pages are created using **HTML** (Hypertext Markup Language), a set of specifications for creating documents that can be displayed as Web pages. Authors mark up documents by inserting special instructions, called **HTML tags**, that specify how the document should be displayed or printed. For example, a document might contain the HTML tag <b> to indicate a section of text that a browser should display in bold. The figure below shows the wide variety of elements that can be included in a Web page.

Figure 21-2

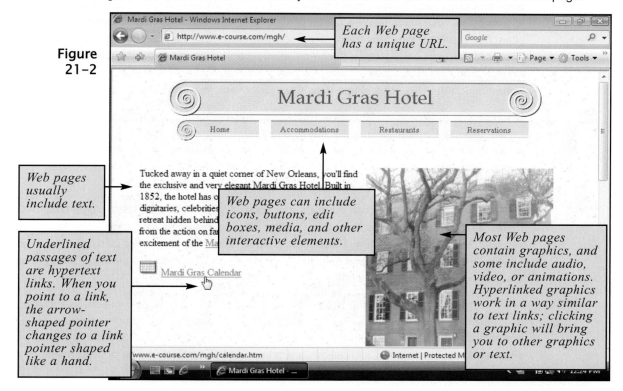

Each Web page has a unique URL.

Web pages usually include text.

Underlined passages of text are hypertext links. When you point to a link, the arrow-shaped pointer changes to a link pointer shaped like a hand.

Web pages can include icons, buttons, edit boxes, media, and other interactive elements.

Most Web pages contain graphics, and some include audio, video, or animations. Hyperlinked graphics work in a way similar to text links; clicking a graphic will bring you to other graphics or text.

FAQ What's on the Web?

The Web contains a variety of sites and understanding how they are classified can help you get to the right information quickly. These classifications can also help you select the right type of site for posting your own information; easy-to-use online tools are available for creating Web pages, Wikis, blogs, and podcasts. More complex Web design tools and programming languages can be used to produce commercial sites.

Commercial. When the Web opened for commercial use in 1998, businesses were quick to grasp the importance of creating a Web presence with informational or e-commerce sites. Informational sites explain a business's mission and provide access to technical support, product descriptions, and more. **E-commerce** is the practice of buying and selling merchandise and services online. URLs for commercial sites usually end in .com. Commercial sites also deliver online productivity applications, such as Google Docs, Yahoo! Mail, and mapping applications, such as Google Earth and MapQuest.

Academic and research sites. From private preschools to state universities, Web sites provide access to education-related information and services such as academic calendars, financial aid information, career services, tickets to sporting events, and course registration. Academic Web sites also provide **distance education**, which allows students to take classes from an off-campus location. URLs for academic sites usually end in .edu.

Organizational and governmental sites. Organizational sites with .org domains are usually managed by nonprofit organizations, such as churches and humanitarian groups. Sites operated by U.S. governmental agencies can be identified by URLs ending in .gov. URLs for government agencies in other countries typically use their country domains. For example, England's National Health Service Web site www.nhs.uk uses the United Kingdom .uk domain.

Search sites and portals. The Web is also home to search sites and portals. Search sites, such as Google and Yahoo!, make it possible to locate Web-based information by entering keywords and questions. A **Web portal** is a site that provides links to a collection of other sites. For example, the Canadian government site canada.gc.ca is a portal to commonly accessed government agencies such as Canada Council for the Arts, Canada Revenue Agency, and Canadian Coast Guard. Portals provide a single point of entry, so that by remembering the URL for a single Web site you can link to many other related sites.

Social networking sites. MySpace, Facebook, and Twitter are examples of popular social networking sites where participants can exchange information and photos, make business contacts and new friends, and keep in touch with family members and schoolmates. Many social networking sites are commercial sites with .com extensions and are supported by advertising revenues.

Public forums. Individuals can voice their opinions on personal Web sites, blogs, chat rooms, and RSS feeds as explained in Chapter 19. Podcasts and wikis offer additional vehicles for public commentary. **Podcasts** distribute audio content—your own radio show—to computers and mobile devices. A **wiki** such as Wikipedia is a series of Web pages that contributors can create, modify, and comment on.

Media sites. Two types of Web sites offer access to photos, music, and videos. File sharing sites, such as YouTube and Flickr, are designed so that contributors can post media files and share them publicly or with selected friends and family members. Commercial media sites, such as iTunes and CinemaNow, are primarily aimed at distributing photos, music, videos, and television programs to consumers for a fee.

FAQ Which browsers are most popular?

A **Web browser**—usually referred to simply as a "browser"—is a program that runs on your computer and helps you access Web pages. Browsers, such as Microsoft Internet Explorer, Mozilla Firefox, and Google Chrome, use HTTP to request Web pages and then interpret HTML tags to display the page on your computer screen.

Although many Web pages are stored as HTML documents, some are assembled from the data in databases or from XML (EXtensible Markup Language) documents with the help of additional components, such as scripts and style sheets. Using these components, most browsers can display database data and XML documents as well as HTML documents.

The browser you use depends on your computer platform and your personal preference. Regardless of the browser you use, it is a good idea to upgrade when a new version becomes available. Most upgrades are free. Therefore, you can get up-to-date browser functionality simply by spending a few minutes downloading and installing a new version.

Figure 21-3

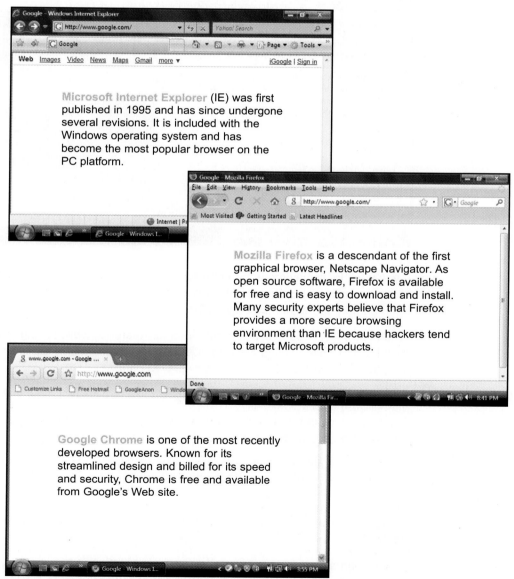

Microsoft Internet Explorer (IE) was first published in 1995 and has since undergone several revisions. It is included with the Windows operating system and has become the most popular browser on the PC platform.

Mozilla Firefox is a descendant of the first graphical browser, Netscape Navigator. As open source software, Firefox is available for free and is easy to download and install. Many security experts believe that Firefox provides a more secure browsing environment than IE because hackers tend to target Microsoft products.

Google Chrome is one of the most recently developed browsers. Known for its streamlined design and billed for its speed and security, Chrome is free and available from Google's Web site.

FAQ How do I start my browser?

No matter which browser you're using, you'll probably start it by clicking an icon on the Windows taskbar. To start Internet Explorer, click the 🅴 icon. The figure below identifies the main components of the Internet Explorer window.

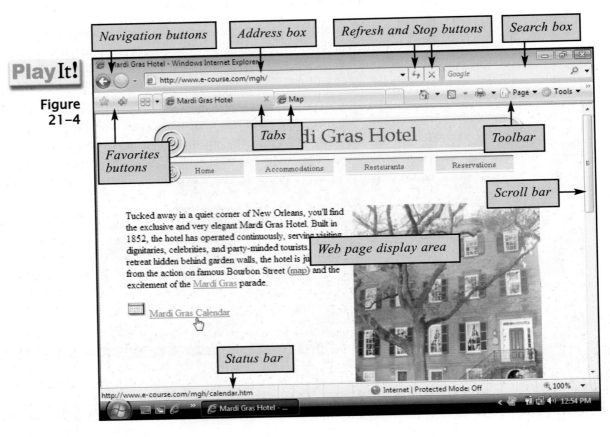

Figure 21-4

Play It!

- If you want to display more than one Web page at a time, you can open a second browser window by clicking the browser icon on the taskbar again. An alternative is to open another tab within the original browser window.

- When you want to keep a Web page open for reference while linking to another page, click the link while holding down the Ctrl key. IE creates a new tab in which to display the page. To close a tab, click the X displayed on it.

- Internet Explorer hides the menu bar. If you'd like to display it, hold down the Alt key.

- Enter keywords in the Search box to search the Web. Click the down arrow and select *Find on this page* to search just the displayed page.

- The Refresh button requests a fresh copy of a Web page in case you suspect the page did not load properly.

- Use the Stop button when a page takes too long to load. Server or communications errors sometimes delay Web pages. In such a case, use the Stop button, check the address, and try to access the page again.

- When using a dial-up connection, you can use the Control Panel's Connect to a Network option if your browser doesn't automatically connect to the Internet.

FAQ How do I use a URL to go to a Web site?

A URL serves as an address to uniquely identify a Web page. You'll see URLs on everything from billboard ads to soup cans and business cards. To enter a URL, first click the Address box on your browser window. Next, type the URL, then press the Enter key. Your browser sends a request for this URL to the Web server, which transmits the requested Web page back to your browser. Your browser then formats and displays the page on your computer screen.

Figure 21-5

* You must be very precise when entering a URL. Don't use any spaces—even before or after punctuation marks—and make sure that you exactly duplicate uppercase and lowercase letters.

* A complete URL usually starts with http:// as in http://www.ibm.com. However, you usually don't have to type the http:// part of the URL.

* The part of a URL that appears after the dot, such as .com, .edu, and .gov, indicates the top-level domain of the URL. Most commercial and e-commerce sites use the .com domain, but .biz is gaining popularity. Educational institutions use the .edu domain. The domain for U.S. government agencies is .gov. The U.S. military, the original sponsor of the Internet, uses the .mil domain. International Web sites might use .int, or an abbreviation indicating a specific country such as .ca for Canada or .fr for France.

FAQ How do I use links on a Web page?

A hypertext link is a connection, or path, between two Web pages. It contains the URL of a Web page, and so it can be used to "jump" from one Web page to another. Links are usually displayed on a Web page as underlined text or as a graphic. When positioned over a link, the arrow-shaped pointer turns into a 🖑 link pointer. When you click a link, the requested Web page is transmitted from the Web server and displayed on your computer.

Figure 21–6

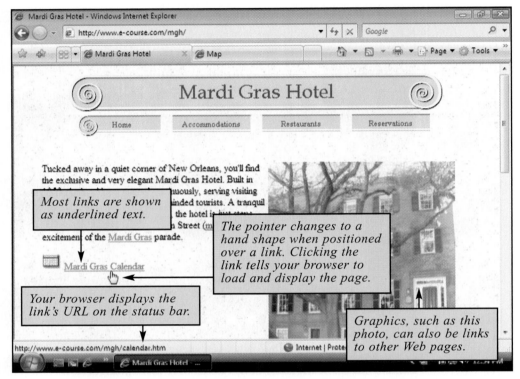

Most links are shown as underlined text.

The pointer changes to a hand shape when positioned over a link. Clicking the link tells your browser to load and display the page.

Your browser displays the link's URL on the status bar.

Graphics, such as this photo, can also be links to other Web pages.

- Text links typically change color after you click them. The color change makes it easy to see which links you have already clicked and viewed.

- To discover if a graphic is a link, move the pointer over the graphic. If the pointer changes to a hand shape, then the graphic is linked to another Web page or media element.

- If your browser is configured to display a status bar, when you move the pointer over a link, the link's URL is displayed in the status bar. For example, in the figure above, the hand is pointing to the Calendar link. On the status bar, you can see the URL for this link.

- By being aware of what's shown in the status bar, you can get an idea of a link's destination before you click it. This information can be important for your security. It might help you avoid fake Web sites designed to fool visitors into providing private information or downloading viruses.

- Most Web sites contain additional links that you can use to drill down to more and more specific material. In the figure above, the Calendar link might display a monthly calendar with days that you can click to see a list of events for a particular date.

FAQ How do the navigation buttons work?

Whereas hyperlinks help you jump to new Web pages, navigation buttons help you to jump back to pages that you've already viewed. Your browser maintains a list of Web pages that you view during the course of a session. A session starts when you open your browser and ends when you close it. Navigation buttons help you navigate through the Web pages you view during a session. If you'd like to return to pages you viewed during other sessions, use the Favorites or History lists as explained later in the chapter.

The Home button displays your **home page**—the page that appears when you first start your browser. Clicking this button at any time during a session returns you to your home page.

Figure 21–7

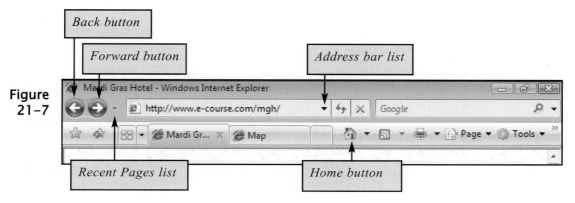

- When you first start your browser, the Back and Forward buttons are disabled or "grayed out." The Back button becomes enabled when you go to a new page. The Forward button becomes enabled after you use the Back button to go back to a previously viewed page.

- Contrary to what you might expect, the Forward button does not take you to new pages that you haven't yet viewed. Instead, the Forward button essentially counteracts the Back button. If you click the Back button to go back to a page, you can then click the Forward button to return to the page you viewed before you clicked the Back button.

- The Recent Pages list displays a list of Web sites visited during a session. Clicking the down-arrow button displays this list, allowing you to select a site and return to it.

- The Address bar list keeps track of URLs that you've entered in the Address bar. This feature is useful when you want to return to your Webmail site or any other site that you usually access by typing its URL.

- Although the page that appears when you first start your browser is called your "home page," that term is also applied to the main page of a Web site, such as the page you see when you connect to www.cnn.com or www.msn.com. To clarify the difference, most books use the term "your home page" for the page you set in your browser. References to a "site's home page" usually mean the main page of a Web site.

- To change your home page, first make sure your browser is displaying the page you'd like to designate as your home page. Click the down-arrow next to the Home button and select Add or Change Home Page.

FAQ How does the Favorites list work?

As you continue to use the Web, you'll visit some pages on a regular basis. For example, you might frequently visit www.weatherunderground.com to check your local weather. Or, you might periodically check consumer information at www.ftc.gov/bcp/consumer.shtm.

Rather than typing the URL every time you want to visit a particular Web page, you can add it to a **Favorites list** or create a **Bookmark**. Favorites and bookmarks work in a similar way; the terminology just varies from one browser to another. After you've added a Web page to your list of favorites, you can then just open the Favorites list and click the page you want to view.

PlayIt!

Figure
21–8

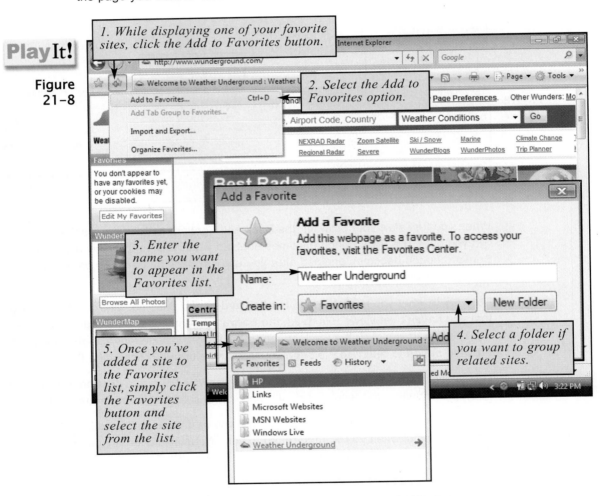

- If you have lots of favorites, grouping them into folders can make it easy to locate the Web page you want. You can drag a favorite into a folder even after you've added it.

- To delete a Web page or folder from the Favorites list, right-click the page name, then click Delete on the shortcut menu. Internet Explorer includes a number of predefined Favorite sites and folders. You can delete those that don't interest you.

- Favorites can be shared. Right-click any listing and select Copy. You can then paste the link into an e-mail message, add it to a document, or post it on a social networking site.

FAQ How does the History list work?

A **History list** displays the titles and/or URLs of individual Web pages you visited in the past. The list is maintained by your browser, so it typically includes every Web site and every Web page that you visit.

In some browsers, such as Firefox, the History list is treated separately from the Favorites list. Internet Explorer, however, provides access to the History list through the Favorites button.

Play It!

Figure 21-9

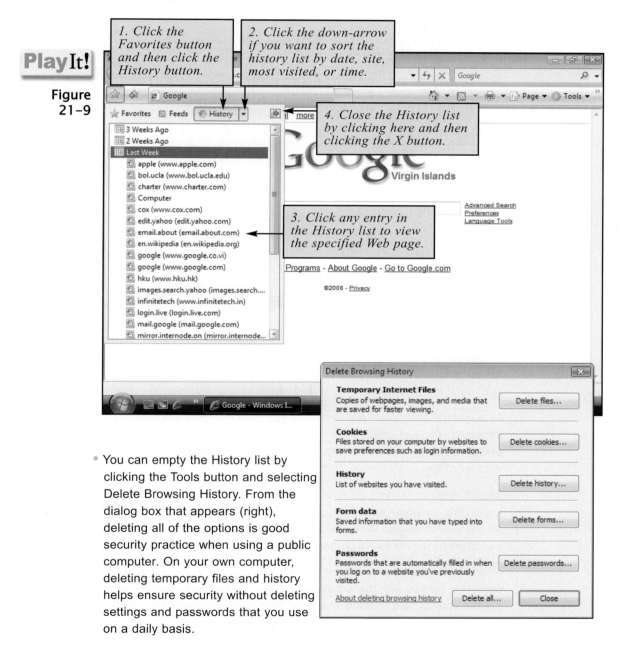

* You can empty the History list by clicking the Tools button and selecting Delete Browsing History. From the dialog box that appears (right), deleting all of the options is good security practice when using a public computer. On your own computer, deleting temporary files and history helps ensure security without deleting settings and passwords that you use on a daily basis.

* You can configure Internet Explorer to set the number of days it retains entries in the History list. Click Tools on the Internet Explorer menu bar, then click Internet Options. Click the General tab if necessary, then change the number in the *Days to keep pages in history* box.

FAQ How do I find information on the Web?

The most popular way to find information on the Web is by using a **search engine**, such as Google, Ask.com, Yahoo! Search, or Live Search. Depending on the search engine, you can look for information by entering keywords, filling out a form, or clicking a series of links to drill down through a list of topics and subtopics.

Play It!

Figure 21-10

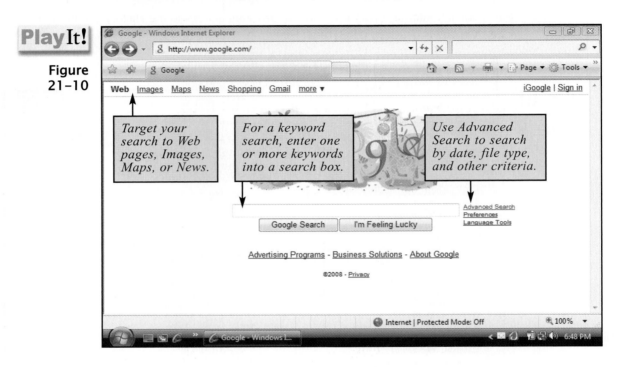

- When entering keywords, be as specific as possible. A keyword search for "Ford" produces thousands of links to pages about Ford automobiles, as well as pages about former president Gerald Ford and actor Harrison Ford. "Ford automobile" would result in a much more targeted search and return a more manageable number of results.

- As a general rule, the more keywords you use, the more targeted your search becomes. You can often refine your search by looking at the short descriptions presented by the search results and adding keywords from those results that seem most pertinent to your search.

- Search engines provide tools for advanced searches. These tools vary somewhat, depending on which search engine you're using, but are explained in detail somewhere on the search engine Web site. In general, advanced search tools help you formulate searches based on exact phrases, Boolean operators, dates, and file types.

- An exact-phrase search requires the search engine to find pages that include a particular phrase with the words occurring in a specified order. To specify an exact-phrase search, you typically surround the phrase with quotation marks.

- A Boolean search uses the operators (or symbols) AND(+), OR, and NOT(-) to specify how your keywords are to be combined. For example, if a search for "Model T automobile" turns up a lot of pages about car clubs that don't interest you, you can refine your search by entering: "Model T automobile" -club. Using the minus sign before the word "club" indicates you don't want to see links to any pages containing that word.

• How do I find information on the Web? (continued)

Generalized search engines such as Google, Ask.com, and Yahoo! Search are indispensable tools when it comes to searching the entire Web. There are also special purpose search engines, such as HotJobs, Westlaw, and WebMD. Even more specific searches can be carried out within a single site by using search-this-site technology.

**Figure
21–11**

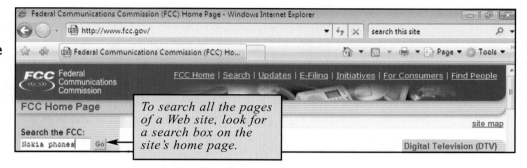

To search all the pages of a Web site, look for a search box on the site's home page.

You can also find information using Web-based indexes, lists of links, and links provided on the pages of wikis and other documents. Social networking tools are also handy; shared bookmarks, links from blogs, and references on Facebook pages can help you locate information. Even offline sources such as academic journals, television ads, magazines, and library databases can provide URLs for Web-based information.

The Web includes a staggering amount of information, but not all of it is necessarily reliable or accurate. You might need to access several sites to gather sufficient information for your purpose. Factors such as reliability, validity, and completeness contribute to the quality of information.

Reliability. A reliable source has a track record of good quality information.

Bias. Information can be biased, so examine the mission behind the academic, political, commercial, or media organization that sponsors the Web site.

Accessibility. Sites with reliable information tend to provide a way to communicate questions, comments, and corrections to the Web page author.

Professionalism. Be suspicious of sites that appear homemade, and sites that contain spelling and grammar errors.

Search ranking. Typically, the sites appearing at the top of a search engine list are the most popular and tend to be the most reliable.

Venue. Some Web venues, such as blogs, tend to present the views of the blog owner; social networking sites are notorious for their misleading information; wikis may accept contributions from participants without subject-matter expertise or qualifications.

Validity. Don't depend on a single site as the source for information; get verification by cross checking other Web sites and offline sources, such as academic journals and reference books.

Completeness. Quality information should address a topic without omitting important details.

FAQ Can I save Web pages, graphics, and text?

You can easily save a Web page on your computer's hard disk so that you can view it while you are offline. Use the Save As option on Internet Explorer's Page menu to initiate the save.

Most browsers give you the option of saving a Web page as an HTML file or as a plain text file. Internet Explorer also provides an option for saving a Web page as an MHT file, which is not a widespread standard. You should save the page as an HTML file if you want to share or modify it. The saved file includes all the HTML tags present in the original Web page document.

Alternatively, you can save the page as a plain text file without embedded HTML tags. A plain text file is easier to read if you open it with word processing software. It also works better than an HTML file if you want to later cut and paste text from the file into your own documents.

Figure 21–12

- Depending on your browser, the graphics might not be included with the saved page. If the graphics are not saved with the page, you can save the graphics individually as explained on the next page.

• **Can I save Web pages, graphics, and text? (continued)**

From time to time, you'll run across graphics or photos that you'd like to save for future reference. You don't have to save the entire page on which the graphic appears; you can save just the graphic, storing it in its own file on your computer's hard disk. Right-click the Web page graphic you want to save. A shortcut menu provides options for checking the graphic's file size and saving it.

Figure 21-13

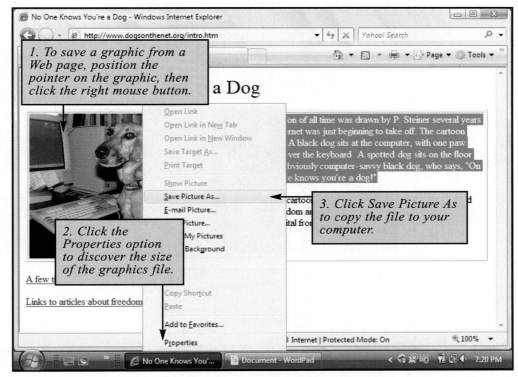

1. To save a graphic from a Web page, position the pointer on the graphic, then click the right mouse button.

2. Click the Properties option to discover the size of the graphics file.

3. Click Save Picture As to copy the file to your computer.

• Most photos and pictures on the Web are copyrighted. You can usually save them for personal use, but you should not use them in any commercial product or in your own Web pages unless you obtain permission from the copyright holder.

• The graphics you see on Web pages typically exist as either JPEG, GIF, or PNG files. If graphics files are fairly small in size, they travel quickly over the Internet and appear in your browser without much delay. You can use the Properties option on the shortcut menu to determine the size of a graphic.

• Once you've saved a file on your computer, you can access it while offline by using your browser or any graphics software that works with the type of file you've saved.

• You can also copy a graphic and paste it directly into your favorite graphics software. To do so, right-click the graphic and select the Copy option. Start your graphics software and use the Edit menu's Paste option. After pasting the graphic, make sure you save the file.

• Can I save Web pages, graphics, and text? (continued)

Suppose that you're searching the Web for information about a specific topic and taking notes for a research paper. It might be very useful to snip out a passage of text from a Web page and then paste it into the document that contains your notes. Later, when you compose the paper, you can incorporate the ideas from the passage or you can quote the passage in its entirety—including, of course, a reference citation to its source.

Figure 21-14

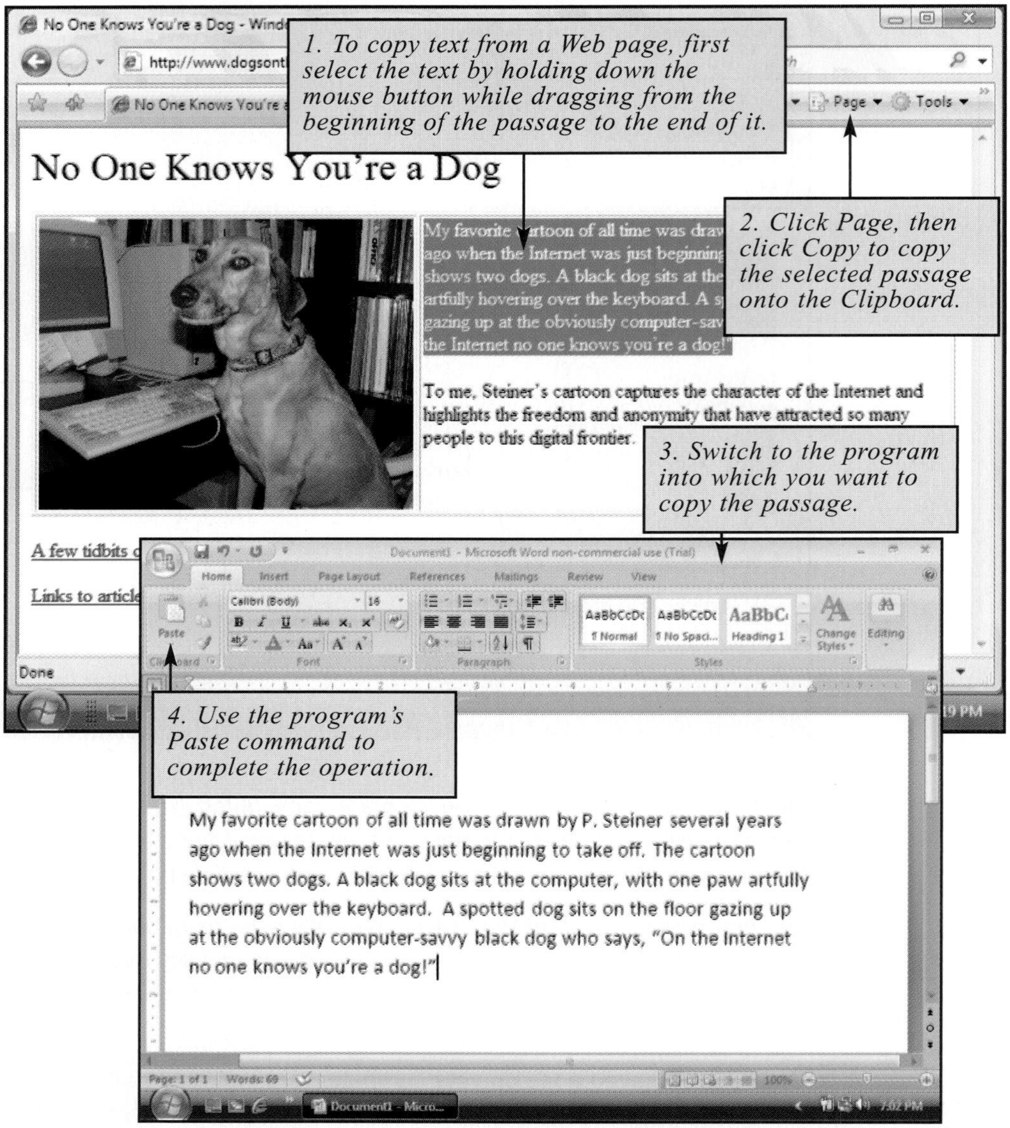

1. To copy text from a Web page, first select the text by holding down the mouse button while dragging from the beginning of the passage to the end of it.

2. Click Page, then click Copy to copy the selected passage onto the Clipboard.

3. Switch to the program into which you want to copy the passage.

4. Use the program's Paste command to complete the operation.

• Like material in printed books, content published on the Web is protected by copyrights. Make sure to provide a citation for any material you copy from the Web and then incorporate into your own work. Style guides such as *The Chicago Manual of Style* provide guidelines for formatting Web citations.

• After you copy a section of text from the Web, move the pointer up to your browser's Address box and select the URL. Copy the URL and paste it into the document that contains your notes. Using the URL as a reference, you'll be able to return to the original site whenever you need additional data to complete a citation.

FAQ How do I print a Web page?

Once you locate a Web page with relevant information, you might want to print it for future reference. For example, when you complete an online purchase, you might want to print your order confirmation. Most browsers make it easy to print a Web page using a toolbar button or menu option.

Figure 21-15

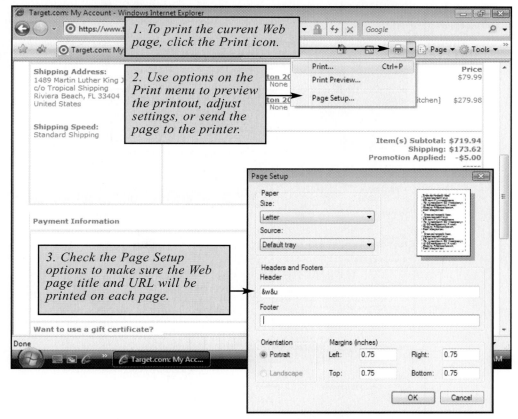

1. To print the current Web page, click the Print icon.

2. Use options on the Print menu to preview the printout, adjust settings, or send the page to the printer.

3. Check the Page Setup options to make sure the Web page title and URL will be printed on each page.

- Some Web pages include a link to a printer friendly version of the page, designed to print on standard size paper. This version is also designed to use color in such a way that a single page won't use all of your printer ink. Look for the "printer friendly" link before you start a printout.

- Many Web "pages" are very long—the equivalent of 10 to 20 printed pages. Some browsers divide long Web pages into a series of printable pages and let you select which of those pages you want to print. Other browsers do not have this capability. To print a part of a long Web page, you can use the copy and paste technique described in the previous FAQ.

- You might find it useful to include both the Web page's URL and title as a header on your printout. You'll need to make this setting before you begin the print process. Click your browser's File menu, then click Page Setup. If you're using Internet Explorer, make sure that the Header box contains &w&u. The code &w displays the Web page title; &u displays the URL.

FAQ How do I download and stream files from the Web?

Many Web sites offer a variety of music, software, photo, and data files you can download from a Web server to your own computer. The process for downloading and installing software was explained in Chapter 4. The process for downloading data files is similar.

Play It!

Figure 21-16

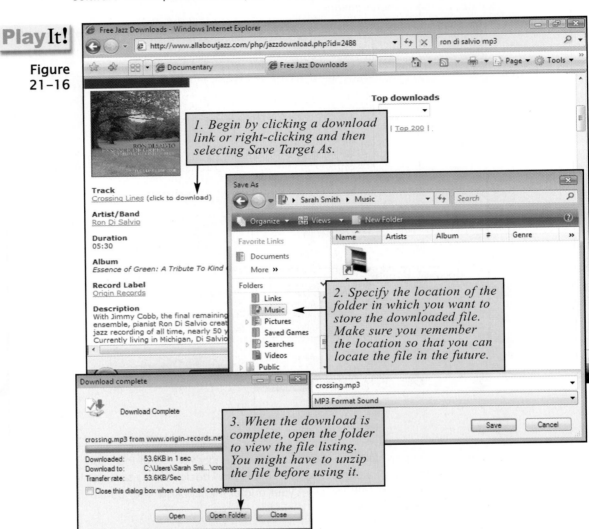

1. Begin by clicking a download link or right-clicking and then selecting Save Target As.

2. Specify the location of the folder in which you want to store the downloaded file. Make sure you remember the location so that you can locate the file in the future.

3. When the download is complete, open the folder to view the file listing. You might have to unzip the file before using it.

- When you download a data file such as an MP3 music file, a photo, or a document, you'll have to open the file with an appropriate application program or media player. In the case of an MP3 music file, you can open it using an MP3 player. Open a photo with Microsoft Paint or other graphics software. To view a document, open it with a word processing program such as Microsoft Word.

- Some downloadable files have been compressed or zipped to make the files smaller and decrease transfer time. If Windows does not automatically unzip these files, use a utility program, such as WinZip.

- Check the file size before you start the download process. Many Web sites provide file sizes and estimated download times. If the file is really huge, you might find out if you can get it delivered via surface mail on a CD-ROM.

• How do I download and stream files from the Web? (continued)

When you download a file and save it on your computer, you can access it whenever you like. You have to wait, however, for the file to download before you can open it. With large media files, such as full-length movies, that can be a disadvantage.

For media files, such as music and videos, streaming is an alternative to downloading. **Streaming** is a delivery method that plays music or displays video in real time as it arrives from the Web to your computer. Sites such as YouTube, Hulu, and Napster offer streaming music and video clips for sample tracks, trailers, TV shows, and video shorts.

While streaming takes place, parts of the media file might be temporarily stored on your computer, but the music or video is not stored in a format that you can use to replay the music or video when you are offline. This limitation helps to protect the media from unauthorized use and distribution.

Figure 21-17

In a streaming environment, selecting a media element opens a media player window.

You can use the player's controls to start, stop, and pause the playback. Additional controls let you adjust volume and the size of the player window.

• If your computer doesn't have the required plug-in for presenting the music or video stream, a link on the Web site will help you download and install it.

FAQ What should I do when I get an error message?

If a Web page does not exist or if the server cannot, for some reason, send the requested Web page, your browser eventually displays a "Page Cannot be Found" message, also referred to as a **404 error**. Assuming you haven't mistyped the URL, this error message usually means that the Web site has been updated and the page has been moved, renamed, or deleted.

To recover from the error, click the Back button to return to the previous page. You can then enter a different URL or try another link. Another strategy is to enter the URL for the site's home page and then try to navigate to a specific page from there. For example, suppose the link to www.starbucks.com/recipes/latte.html produces a 404 error because the latte.html file has moved to a different folder. Enter the URL www.starbucks.com and search the site for "latte" or follow links that have the potential to eventually lead to information about latte recipes.

Figure 21–18

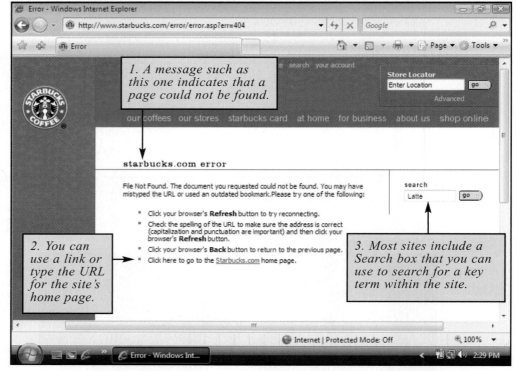

- Sometimes when you click a link, a message indicates that the page has moved to a new location. Usually, you are automatically redirected to the new site. If not, you are provided with a link to the new location of the page.

- If the text of a Web page appears garbled, you might not have the correct fonts installed, the Web site might be in a language your browser does not support, or the site might not have been tested with the browser you're using.

FAQ Why do browsers block pop-ups and ActiveX components?

Most browsers are equipped to block activities, such as pop-up ads and ActiveX components, that are annoying or could compromise your computer's security.

Pop-up ads are a pervasive type of online advertising that open new browser windows to promote cheap loans, software, Web sites, contests, and other products. A **pop-up blocker** prevents pop-up ads from appearing in your browser window.

Your browser might also be configured to block **ActiveX components**, which work in conjunction with Internet Explorer as plug-ins for playing media and running Web applications. Although the majority of ActiveX controls are legitimate, some harbor viruses, spyware, and other potentially damaging programs. Most browsers can be configured to check ActiveX components when they arrive as downloads.

The tools that block pop-ups and filter ActiveX components cannot always distinguish legitimate sites from harmful ones. Internet Explorer displays an Information Bar to alert you to pop-ups and ActiveX components.

Figure 21–19

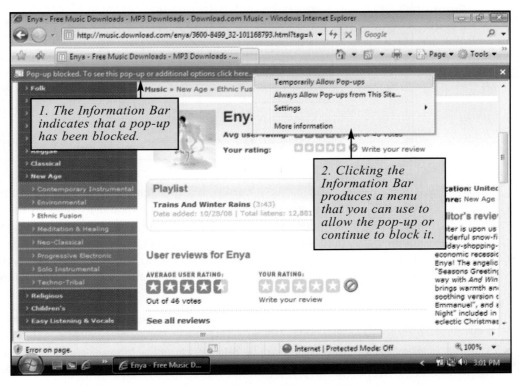

1. The Information Bar indicates that a pop-up has been blocked.

2. Clicking the Information Bar produces a menu that you can use to allow the pop-up or continue to block it.

- You can turn IE's pop-up blocker on and off by clicking the Tools button and then selecting Pop-up Blocker. From this menu, you can also adjust settings for how aggressively the pop-up blocker works and you can specify sites that have pop-ups you trust.

- Legitimate ActiveX components are signed and dated. You should be suspicious of any components that the Information Bar identifies as unsigned or expired.

- To adjust ActiveX settings, click the Tools button, select Internet Options, and then select the Security tab. The Custom button leads to a dialog box that you can use to change ActiveX settings.

FAQ Is the Web safe?

Among the millions of businesses and individuals that offer products, services, and information on the Web, some are unscrupulous and try to take advantage of unwary shoppers, chat group participants, and researchers. Internet-borne viruses and online credit card fraud are regularly featured on news reports. However, security tools and some common sense can make using the Web as safe, or safer than, shopping at your local mall or eating at a local restaurant.

Use a secure connection for sensitive data. Most commercial Web sites encrypt sensitive information sent to and from the site using SSL (Secure Sockets Layer) or TLS (Transport Layer Security) technology. URLs for secure Web connections begin with *https* instead of *http*. Before submitting credit card numbers, Social Security numbers, or other sensitive data, look for https in the URL and a padlock icon in the browser window.

Figure 21-20

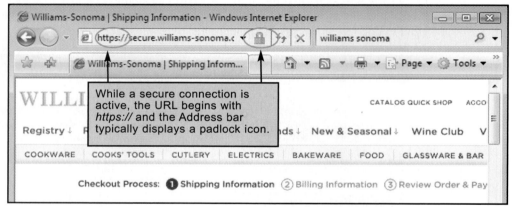

While a secure connection is active, the URL begins with *https://* and the Address bar typically displays a padlock icon.

Block third-party cookies. A **cookie** is a small chunk of data generated by a Web server and stored in a text file on your computer's hard disk. Cookies can be used to keep track of the pages you view at a site, the merchandise you select, and other profile information. You don't want to block cookies from legitimate sites because Web features such as shopping carts require them. You should, however, make sure your browser is configured to block third-party cookies that can be used to track the sites you've visited and to generate targeted ads.

Monitor temporary Internet files. A **browser cache** is a temporary local storage area for Web page elements. As you jump back to previously viewed pages, the text and graphics for those pages can be retrieved from the browser cache in your computer's memory or on the hard disk, rather than being downloaded again from a Web server. Web pages in the cache are a sort of record of your activities on the Web. Like cookies, a cache is relatively safe; but you might want to clear it if you use a public computer, if you're concerned that people with access to your computer might be curious about your Web activities, or if you're short on hard disk space.

Run antivirus software. Antivirus software modules contain several defensive tools that block Web-based exploits. Make sure your antivirus software is configured to run at all times and that it is up to date.

Keep your browser and operating system updated. Browsers and operating systems are updated frequently to patch security vulnerabilities. To maintain good security, apply these updates as soon as they are available.

QuickCheck A

1. A(n) [＿＿＿＿＿＿＿] , such as www.yahoo.com/automobiles or www.msu.edu/fac, uniquely defines a particular Web page.

2. When you start a browser, it automatically loads and displays a page from a Web site. This starting page is known as your [＿＿＿＿＿＿] page.

3. Assume that you type a URL in order to go to Web page A, then you click a link to go to Web page B. If you click the Back button, then click the Forward button, page [＿＿＿＿] will be displayed on your screen.

4. True or false? The History list shows only Web pages you visited during the current computing session. [＿＿＿＿]

5. A(n) [＿＿＿＿＿＿＿] is generated by a Web server and then stored on your computer to keep track of the pages you view at a site, the merchandise you select, and other profile information.

CheckIt!

QuickCheck B

Indicate the letter of the browser element that best relates the following:

1. Favorites [＿＿＿]

2. Home page [＿＿＿]

3. Tabs [＿＿＿]

4. URL [＿＿＿]

5. Pop-ups [＿＿＿]

CheckIt!

What's Inside and on the CD?

Computer technology offers opportunities for everyone. Individuals with physical challenges, for example, can use adaptive technologies, such as voice recognition and screen readers to access information, work, and communicate. Adaptive technologies spill over to other populations as well. For example, screen reader technology is also useful for children learning to read. Computers and the Internet can be harnessed to provide public services, such as public Internet centers where job seekers can participate in online training, develop their resumes, and contact potential employers.

Although there are some tasks not really suited to computerization—stand-up comedy and gardening come to mind—computers are essential tools for storing data, crunching numbers, and producing written work. The importance of computers and their widespread use raise issues about their safety, security, and ethical application.

In this chapter, you'll learn how computers affect society, your health, and the environment. You'll also find out about the potential risks computers pose to your privacy and security. As you read, you'll find many tips for protecting your privacy, avoiding scams, spotting hoaxes, and thwarting identity thieves.

FAQ How do computers benefit society?

Computers have become an important part of society, helping us with mundane tasks as well as contributing to the complex dynamics of business, politics, the economy, and personal relationships. Consider, for example, Figure 22-1, which summarizes the uses for computer tools mentioned in earlier chapters.

Figure 22-1

Collecting and organizing information	databases, search engines
Evaluating information and solving problems	spreadsheets, financial software
Communications	e-mail clients, Voice over IP, instant messaging, text messaging, blogs, Web sites, podcasts
Increasing productivity	word processing, presentation software
Collaborating with others	Web apps, FTP, groupware, Web conferencing
Creating communities	social networking sites, chat rooms, online bulletin boards, newsgroups
Facilitating learning and critical thinking	distance education, e-learning, Wikipedia
Promoting creativity	graphics software, video editing software, music software
Facilitating daily life	e-commerce; government Web portals; music, photo, and video sharing sites; music and video download sites; online job listings; online multi-player games
Assisting individuals with special needs	voice recognition, screen readers

Computers, the Web, and the Internet have done more than simply facilitate life-as-usual; they have transformed many aspects of the way we live.

Socializing. The social scene has evolved in some surprising directions. Online dating became popular when sites like Matchmaker.com and eHarmony opened. The club scene is now supplemented by online social networking and virtual reality sites such as Second Life, where digital people meet, interact, purchase real estate, start businesses, and earn cash that sometimes makes the jump to real life.

News. At one time, daily newspapers and televised news were the main sources of information about current events. Today, a wide ranging group of citizen journalists use blogs, vlogs, and podcasts to disseminate news and opinions. Citizen reporters and commentators present a diverse range of opinions and cover events that are often ignored by mainstream media.

Education. Today, many students take online classes instead of commuting to campus. Assisted by online tutorials and learning management systems (LMSs) such as Blackboard, Moodle, and Angel, access to education is much more convenient than in the past and that's especially useful for single parents and individuals with physical challenges.

• How do computers benefit society? (continued)

Business. The same technologies that make distance education possible enable workers to telecommute, attend Web conferences instead of traveling to meetings, collaborate using Web apps, and communicate using e-mail. Using tools like WebEx and GoToMeeting, what used to be commuting time can be spent more productively, travel costs are reduced, and fuel savings increase.

Manufacturing. Factories have changed, too. Hazardous jobs can now be handled by computer controlled robots and automated systems. In addition to increased worksite safety, these systems can also increase efficiency, and those efficiencies help to maintain reasonable product prices by offsetting increases in labor and material costs.

Banking. Our financial system, once based on paper currency and checks, has gone digital. Trips to the bank have been replaced by access to ATMs in malls and other handy locations. Electronic banking, income tax filing, and PayPal transactions happen from your computer keyboard. Point-of-sale systems connect to worldwide credit card processing systems that reduce paperwork and create an electronic "paper trail" of transactions.

Shopping. E-commerce is, perhaps, one of the most transformative technologies. Not only can shoppers purchase merchandise using their computers, but they can access stores far distant from their physical location and use shopping aggregators like PriceGrabber and NexTag to find the best deal. Businesses use similar online tools to shop suppliers for raw goods, parts, and services.

Travel. The travel industry is another example of fundamental change brought about by digital technologies. Instead of using travel agents, travelers now book their own flights, hotels, and rental cars. Online reviews and ratings posted by ordinary travelers at sites such as TripAdvisor provide information for selecting hotels, restaurants, and itineraries.

Although our focus is usually on personal computers because they are always close at hand, computers of all sizes contribute to the modern digital world.

Complex distributed computer reservation systems, such as Sabre, Amadeus, and Worldspan, track airline schedules and interconnect to online travel reservation sites such as Travelocity and Orbitz. Huge law enforcement databases help officers using portable computer units mounted in patrol cars to identify criminals. Premises security can be handled by a variety of devices such as simple motion detectors, electronic keys, and biometric devices that digitally scan fingerprints and retinal images. Large scale computer systems used to track and predict the weather also provide scientists with data pertaining to climate change. Communications networks provide the infrastructure for disaster-relief efforts and military operations.

Embedded computers play a role, too. Microcontrollers control household appliances, such as washing machines and microwave ovens. In automobiles, microcontrollers direct braking and fuel systems. Microcontrollers are also found in scientific and medical equipment such as personal blood pressure monitors, hearing aids, and glucose meters. Small RFID (Radio Frequency Identification) tags sewn into clothing communicate with inventory tracking systems.

Handheld digital devices also contribute to today's digital lifestyle. Handheld GPS receivers, GPS-enabled cell phones, and automobile navigation systems communicate with satellites to aid land and sea navigation. Portable media players such as the iPod keep us tuned in; smartphones keep us connected to each other and to the Internet.

FAQ How can I avoid computer-related health risks?

Computers and digital technologies offer uncountable benefits, but those benefits come with associated health, safety, security, and privacy risks.

Many people in today's information society spend long hours gazing at computer screens and typing on keyboards. Computers are an important part of the work environment—not only for people with traditional desk jobs, but also for telecommuters. A **telecommuter**, or "teleworker," uses a home-based computer and telecommunications equipment to perform work-related tasks. Today, telecommuters often work for call centers that provide technical support, take reservations for hotels, or process catalog orders.

Telecommuters and on-site employees who work with computers for most of the workday sometimes experience health problems related to computer use, such as eye strain caused by screen glare or small fonts. Computer users are also susceptible to musculoskeletal strain, such as back pain related to improper arrangement of desk, chair, and computer equipment. Long hours at the computer and prolonged typing sessions can also contribute to repetitive motion injuries, such as carpal tunnel syndrome.

To avoid computer-related health hazards, it is important to take frequent breaks to rest your eyes and move your muscles. You should also be aware of the ergonomics of your work areas. **Ergonomics** is the study of work and work environments. Results of ergonomics research have produced guidelines for making work environments safer and healthier.

Figure 22–2

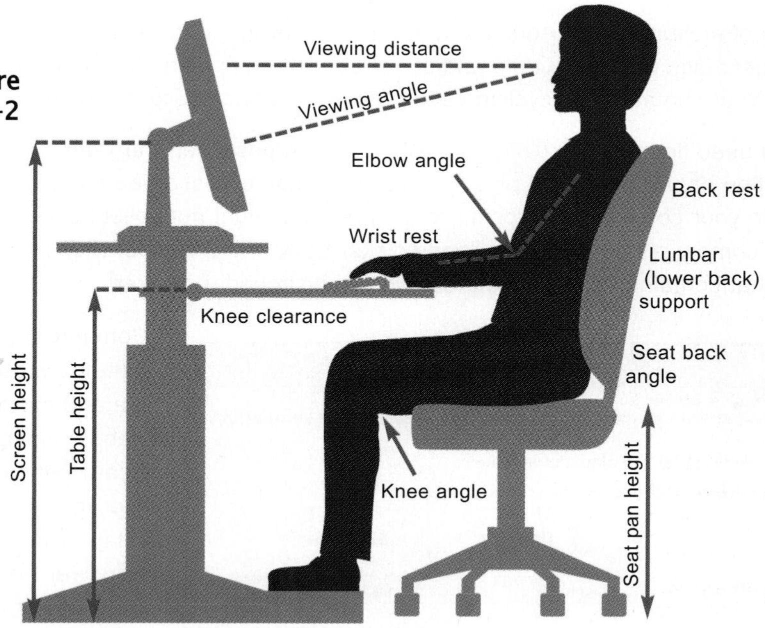

Viewing distance
Viewing angle
Elbow angle
Wrist rest
Back rest
Lumbar (lower back) support
Knee clearance
Seat back angle
Screen height
Table height
Knee angle
Seat pan height

For your computer work environment, adequate lighting and ventilation are important. A large screen can reduce eye strain. A wrist rest can reduce the risk of carpal tunnel syndrome.

Adjustable chairs and desks allow you to position equipment and maintain good posture. For example, Figure 22-2 illustrates how to set up your computer, desk, and chair to avoid potentially disabling musculoskeletal injuries.

In addition to taking steps to avoid health risks, computer owners should make sure their work areas are safe. Equipment should rest on a secure surface and have adequate air circulation. Cables should be stowed where they cannot become tangled in feet and arms, or cause a fire hazard. It is also important not to overload electrical circuits.

FAQ How do computers affect the environment?

Keeping up with technology means replacing your computer every few years. But what should you do with your old, outdated computer? Millions of computers are discarded every year. Billions of printer ink cartridges, floppy disks, CDs, and DVDs end up in landfills. Computers contain toxic materials, such as lead, phosphorus, and mercury, which can contaminate groundwater if not disposed of properly. Discarded disks and toner cartridges add materials to overburdened landfills. Computer owners can take some simple steps to have a positive effect on the environment:

- Recycle consumable products such as paper. If possible, use the back of discarded printouts for notes or bundle them off to your local recycling center.

- Use electronic documents whenever possible to reduce the use of paper.

- Refill or recycle printer ribbons, ink cartridges, and toner cartridges. Check your local office store for reinking and refill supplies. Also check your ink and toner packaging for disposal instructions. Many manufacturers provide mailing labels so that you can return these items for recycling.

- Donate your old computer, monitor, and printer to a charitable organization. By doing so, you not only keep equipment out of the waste stream for several more years, but you help others by providing opportunities to use empowering technologies. Just make sure you delete personal data from the hard disk.

- Dispose of malfunctioning equipment at a facility designed to handle electronic waste. Some manufacturers accept old and out-of-service equipment. Check their Web sites for details. Your community recycling center usually accepts electronic components, too.

- Recycle used floppy disks, CDs, and DVDs, when possible. The Web contains lots of information about great craft projects that make use of discarded storage media. Although your community curbside recycling team might not collect used media, several companies accept used floppy disks, CDs, and DVDs for a small recycling fee. Media that contains personal data should be destroyed, however.

Figure 22–3

- Computers use electricity, but they are becoming more and more efficient. Notebook computers typically consume less power than desktops. LCD display devices consume less power than CRTs. To reduce power consumption, you can configure your computer to enter standby mode when not in use. Depending on the settings you select, standby mode can turn off the monitor, power down the hard disk, or power down the entire computer (Figure 22-3).

FAQ How can I protect my data from loss and damage?

Data stored on a computer is susceptible to loss and damage from many sources. Equipment failures—especially a hard disk failure—can wipe out all your data. Fires, floods, and water leaks can damage computer components and storage media. Power failures can wipe out the data in open files. Electrical surges can damage chips on your computer's motherboard and drive controllers.

A thief can physically break into your home or office, steal your computer, and get access to all the data it contains. Given enough time, an intruder can download passwords, e-mail addresses, and private files—you might not even notice they've fallen into the wrong hands. To protect your data from loss and damage, you can take some simple steps.

Keep your computer secure. To prevent a thief from walking off with your desktop computer, lock it to your desk with a computer security lock that you can purchase at most computer stores. Lock your notebook computer in a drawer or cabinet when it is not in use, and don't leave it unattended in a library, airport, or café.

Establish password access to your computer. To prevent unauthorized access to your data by a nosy houseguest or roommate, use the password protection provided by your operating system. For Windows users, that means setting up a user account other than the system administrator.

Use a surge strip or UPS. For your desktop computer, consider using an uninterruptible power supply (UPS) to supply battery backup and surge protection. A surge strip is great for a notebook computer because it prevents electrical surges and spikes from damaging circuitry. The notebook's internal battery kicks into action in case of a power outage, so a UPS is typically not necessary.

Save your files frequently. As you work, don't let too much time elapse before you save open files. An unexpected power outage or someone tripping over your computer cord can wipe out hours of work. To provide even more protection for work in progress, check if your application software can be configured to autosave the file you're working on every 15 minutes or so.

Keep your computer's hard disk tuned up. Periodically defragmenting your computer's hard disk and checking it for errors can prevent data loss from bad sectors that cannot reliably hold data. When using Windows, you can access disk tuneup utilities by selecting the Computer option from the Start menu and right-clicking the icon for local disk C. From the menu that appears, select Properties, and then select the tools tab to display the window shown in Figure 22-4.

Figure 22-4

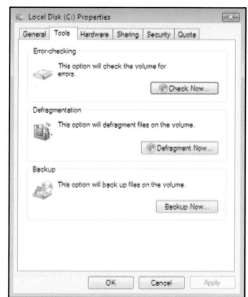

● How can I protect my data from loss and damage? (continued)

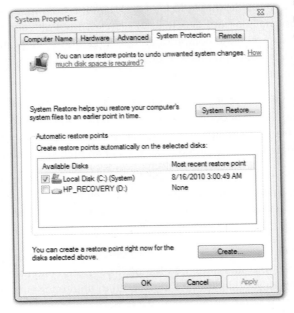

**Figure
22–5**

Pay attention to restore points. A **restore point** is a snapshot of your computer settings. Restore points are essentially backups of the Windows Registry. If a hard disk problem causes system instability, you might be able to roll back to a restore point when your computer was operational.

Restore points are set automatically when you install new software. You can manually set restore points, too. For example, you might want to set a restore point before setting up a network or installing new hardware. Restore point settings shown in Figure 22-5 can be set by accessing System Restore (Windows XP) or System Protection (Windows Vista).

Make regular backups. Develop a schedule for periodic backups and stick to it. The frequency of your backups depends on how much data you generate. The more files you create, the more frequently you should back up. Store your backups in a location away from your computer, so that they are not scooped up by the same thief who steals your computer, or damaged by the leaky hot water heater that destroys your computer system.

To access the Windows Vista Backup and Restore Center, enter Backup in the Start menu search box. In Windows XP, click All Programs, Accessories, and System Tools.

**Figure
22–6**

Backup Status and Configuration

Back Up Files

Restore Files

Automatic file backup is configured but turned off

Windows is not scanning your computer for new and updated files.

What file types are not included in the backup?

Backup status

ⓘ The last file backup was successful.

Backup location: HP_RECOVERY (D:)

Last successful backup: 3/2/2010 11:41 AM
Next backup: Disabled

To initiate a manual backup, click this option.

● Back up now
Scan for new or updated files and add them to your backup.

● Change backup settings
Adjust your current backup settings or start a new, full backup.

Automatic backup is currently off   🔘 Turn on

You can activate automatic backups by first adjusting settings to specify when and where the data is to be backed up, then clicking the Turn on button.

FAQ How can I protect my computer from intrusions?

Intruders don't even have to enter your premises to access your computer. Hackers use various technologies to gain unauthorized access to computers via networks. Often hackers transmit port probes that circulate over the Internet looking for unsecured computer systems. If a probe discovers that your computer is vulnerable, hackers can surreptitiously copy your data or use your computer as a base of operations for sending out viruses, spam, and other disruptive programs.

Hackers can also use packet sniffers to intercept data as it travels over the Internet. To thwart hackers and protect your computer from physical damage, consider the following tips.

Use encryption software. If you scramble your files, even a successful hacker or intruder will not find your data of much use. **Encryption software** scrambles your data by using a multi-digit key. A key is also necessary to decrypt the data into a useable format. Windows offers some specialized encryption capabilities. Check Windows Help to find out if these encryption capabilities are suitable for your needs. For more widespread use, consider third-party encryption options, such as PGP (Pretty Good Privacy) shareware.

Use a firewall when connected to a network. To prevent unauthorized access to your data by network hackers, activate personal firewall software, such as Windows Firewall. **Firewall software** is designed to analyze the flow of traffic entering your computer from a network. It makes sure that incoming information was actually requested and is not an unauthorized intrusion. It blocks activity from suspicious Internet addresses, and it reports intrusion attempts so that you know when hackers are trying to break into your computer.

To access Windows Firewall when using Windows Vista, type "firewall" in the Start menu's Search box. For Windows XP, open the Control Panel and select Windows Firewall.

Figure 22-7

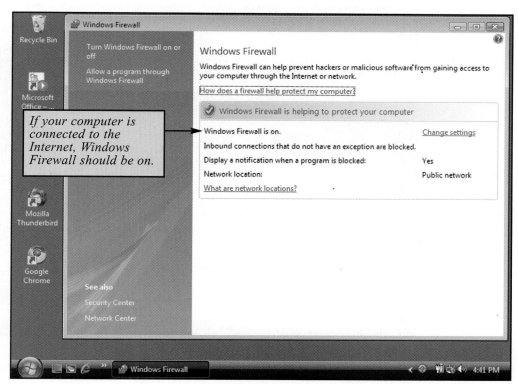

• How can I protect my computer from intrusions? (continued)

Use a router to filter out unauthorized network traffic. As an alternative to firewall software, you can set up a router to protect your computer from the prying eyes of hackers. The router is assigned a public Internet address and it passes legitimate messages to a private address assigned to your computer. A hacker who uses the public Internet address can only reach the router, which has no computing capabilities and stores no data. You connect the router between your computer and your cable or DSL modem. Make sure you change the default password for the router when you set it up.

Activate encryption on wireless networks. Airborne transmissions are easily captured by hackers or by innocent neighbors who just happen to be within the range of your wireless network. The data carried by Wi-Fi signals can be encrypted with WEP, WPA, or PSK.

The original wireless encryption was called WEP (Wired Equivalent Privacy) because it was designed to provide a level of confidentiality similar to that of a wired network. WEP is very easy to bypass. It does, however, protect a wireless network from casual hacks and inadvertent crosstalk from nearby networks.

WPA (Wi-Fi Protected Access) and its follow-up version, WPA2, offer stronger protection by making sure that packets have not been intercepted or tampered with in any way. PSK (pre-shared key), also referred to as "personal mode," is a type of WPA used on most home networks.

When setting up wireless encryption, you will create an encryption key, which works like a password. When a computer tries to join the network, the encryption key will be required. To activate encryption for your wireless network, open the router's configuration software as explained in Figure 22-8.

Figure 22-8

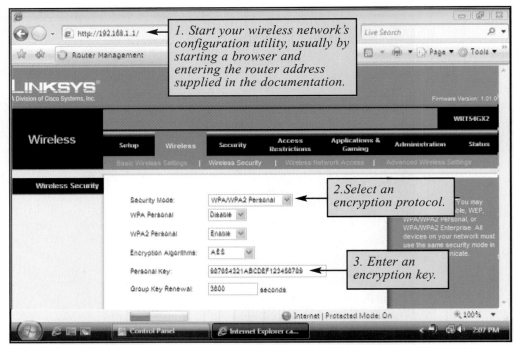

1. Start your wireless network's configuration utility, usually by starting a browser and entering the router address supplied in the documentation.

2. Select an encryption protocol.

3. Enter an encryption key.

FAQ How can I protect my computer from viruses?

The term **malicious code** refers to any program or set of program instructions designed to surreptitiously enter a computer and disrupt its normal operations. The most prevalent types of malicious code include viruses, worms, and Trojan horses.

A **computer virus** is a set of program instructions that can attach itself to a file, reproduce itself, and spread to other files. It can corrupt files, destroy data, display an irritating message, or otherwise disrupt computer operations. A common misconception is that viruses spread themselves from one computer to another. On the contrary, they can replicate themselves only on the host computer. Viruses are spread from one computer to another by human actions, such as sharing infected floppy disks, downloading infected software, and opening infected e-mail attachments.

A key characteristic of viruses is their ability to lurk in a computer for days or months, quietly replicating themselves. While this replication takes place, you might not be aware that your computer has contracted a virus; therefore, it is easy to inadvertently spread infected files to other people's computers. After several days or months go by, a trigger event, such as a specific date, can unleash a virus payload. Payloads can be as harmless as displaying an offensive message, or as devastating as erasing all the data on your computer's hard disk.

A **Trojan horse** is a computer program that seems to perform one function while actually doing something else. Technically, it is not the same as a virus because, unlike a virus, a Trojan horse is not designed to make copies of itself. Trojan horses are notorious for stealing passwords, but they can also delete files and cause other trouble. Some Trojan horses contain a virus or a worm, which can replicate and spread. Virus experts call this a **blended threat** because it combines more than one type of malicious code. In addition to Trojan-horse/virus combinations, worm/virus combinations are also becoming prevalent.

With the proliferation of network traffic and e-mail, worms have become a major concern in the computing community. Unlike a virus, which is designed to spread from file to file, a **worm** is designed to spread from computer to computer over local area networks and the Internet. Worms deliver payloads that vary from harmless messages to malicious file deletions. A **mass-mailing worm** makes use of information on an infected computer to mail itself to everyone listed in the e-mail address book. Other worms deliver denial of service attacks. A **denial of service attack** is designed to generate a lot of activity on a network by flooding it with useless traffic—enough traffic to overwhelm the network's processing capability and essentially bring all communications to a halt.

Most malicious code is stored in executable files, usually with .exe file name extensions. However, some infected files have .sys, .drv, .com, .bin, .vbs, .scr, or .ovl extensions. Malicious code in these types of executable files cannot infect your computer unless you open them, thereby executing the virus code they contain.

Malicious code can slip into your computer from a variety of sources. Be cautious of floppy disks, homemade CDs, and disreputable Web sites that offer pirated games and other supposedly fun stuff. They are a common source of viruses and Trojan horses.

E-mail attachments are another common source of malicious code. A seemingly innocent attachment could harbor a virus, worm, or Trojan horse. Typically, infected attachments look like executable files, usually with .exe file name extensions. These files infect your computer if you open them.

• **How can I protect my computer from viruses? (continued)**

A data file with a .doc or .xls extension can sometimes contain a **macro virus**. Legitimate macros are used to automate common word processing or spreadsheet tasks. An infected macro contains malicious code that is activated when its corresponding document or spreadsheet is opened. Today, most software that executes macros includes security features designed to protect your computer from macro viruses.

Antivirus software is a set of utility programs that looks for and eradicates viruses, Trojan horses, and worms. Typically, computer owners configure their antivirus software to run constantly in the background to check files and e-mail messages as they are downloaded.

Modern antivirus software attempts to locate viruses by watching for virus signatures. A **virus signature** is a section of code, such as a unique series of instructions, that can be used to identify a known virus, Trojan horse, or worm, much as a fingerprint is used to identify an individual.

The information that your antivirus software uses to identify and eradicate malicious code is stored in one or more files usually referred to as "virus definitions." New viruses and variations of old viruses are unleashed just about every day. To keep up with these newly identified pests, antivirus software publishers offer virus definition updates, which are usually available as Web downloads. Most antivirus software can be configured to automatically check for updates and download them when available. Figure 22-9 provides additional information about using antivirus software.

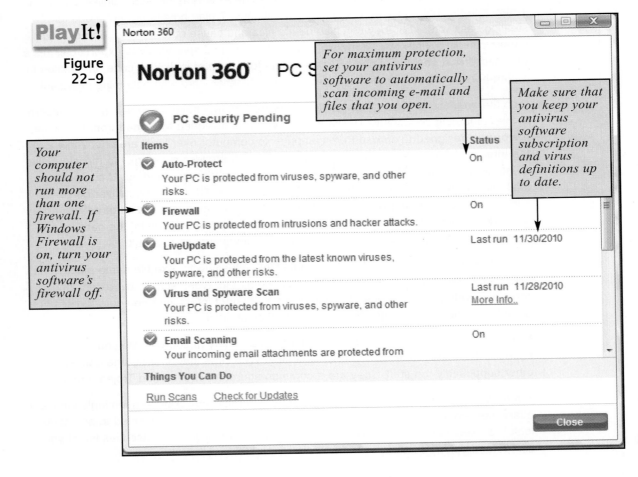

PlayIt!

Figure 22-9

Norton 360

Norton 360 PC S...

For maximum protection, set your antivirus software to automatically scan incoming e-mail and files that you open.

Make sure that you keep your antivirus software subscription and virus definitions up to date.

PC Security Pending

Items	Status
Auto-Protect Your PC is protected from viruses, spyware, and other risks.	On
Firewall Your PC is protected from intrusions and hacker attacks.	On
LiveUpdate Your PC is protected from the latest known viruses, spyware, and other risks.	Last run 11/30/2010
Virus and Spyware Scan Your PC is protected from viruses, spyware, and other risks.	Last run 11/28/2010 More Info..
Email Scanning Your incoming email attachments are protected from	On

Your computer should not run more than one firewall. If Windows Firewall is on, turn your antivirus software's firewall off.

Things You Can Do

Run Scans   Check for Updates

Close

● How can I protect my computer from viruses? (continued)

Avoiding viruses, Trojan horses, and worms is preferable to trying to eliminate these pesky programs after they have taken up residence in your computer. After they infiltrate your computer, they can be difficult to eradicate, even with antivirus software. The process of eradicating a virus—sometimes called "disinfecting"—might include deleting the virus code from files or deleting infected files. If your computer contracts a virus, check your antivirus software publisher's Web site for information on identifying the virus and eradicating it. To protect your computer against malicious code, you can take the following steps:

● Install antivirus software and keep it running full-time in the background so that it scans all files as they are opened and checks every e-mail message as it arrives. The scanning process requires a short amount of time, which creates a slight delay in downloading e-mail and opening files. The wait is worth it, however, when you can feel confident that the files you open are free from viruses.

● Before you download a file—especially a file containing software—make sure the file's source is reputable. Stay away from Web sites that offer pirated software. Do not open a downloaded file unless your antivirus software is active.

● Whenever you receive a disk, use your antivirus software to scan the files it contains before you copy them to your hard disk, run them, or open them.

● Never open an e-mail attachment unless you know whom it is from, you have an idea what it contains, and you were expecting to receive it.

● Watch for information about the latest virus threats. Many threats make headline news. You can also find out about threats at antivirus software publisher Web sites.

● Keep your antivirus software up to date by allowing it to automatically download updates when they become available.

Figure 22-10

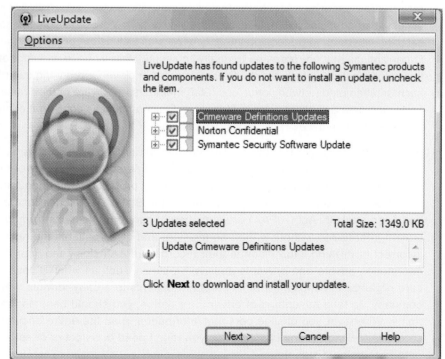

FAQ Can I depend on companies to respect my privacy?

Personal information can be defined as any data that is associated with you as an individual. For example, a database that includes names, addresses, and purchase records for an e-commerce merchant contains personal information. If Greta Hanson purchased merchandise from this company, the database can tell you what she bought. That information is personal because Greta might not want it known to the general public. In contrast, a database containing customer purchasing statistics without names and addresses would not hold personal information. There would be no way to discover what Greta has purchased from this database.

Personal information about your health, grades, charitable donations, and purchases is stored in a mind-boggling number of places. Your school records are stored by your grade school, high school, and college. Your doctor, health insurance company, employer, and hospital maintain your health care records. Government agencies store information related to your driver's license, passport, voting, income taxes, property taxes, and police contacts. Financial information is stored by your bank, credit card company, and credit bureaus. Your credit card company and a variety of merchants also hold information about the types of goods and services you purchase. If someone was able to access all of this information, it would be possible to compile a very accurate profile of your life—one that could be used for unscrupulous purposes.

Databases that contain personal information are typically protected by the policies and procedures of businesses that maintain the data. Many businesses that collect data online offer a **privacy policy** that describes how your personal data might be used, whether it might be sold or distributed, and how it might be protected from unauthorized access. Before supplying personal information online, check the privacy policy. Be aware, however, that the privacy policy is not necessarily a binding legal statement. If the company is sold or goes out of business, the privacy statement might no longer apply.

Maintaining privacy is a function of an organization's information security capabilities. **Information security** refers to the techniques used to protect information from unauthorized access, damage, disclosure, loss, modification, or use. Most organizations adopt proactive security measures to protect the integrity of data as well as the privacy of clients. Organizations that are prepared to deal with security threats have an information security policy for handling sensitive data. Procedures are in place for reporting security incidents, such as attempted network intrusions. Staff members are aware of their responsibilities in protecting data and client privacy. Users are assigned access rights that control the data they are allowed to view, add, modify, or delete.

Voluntary security and privacy measures have not proven to be sufficient, however, to protect privacy. Today, the use and distribution of personal data is governed by laws and rules designed to provide some degree of privacy protection and encourage the ethical use of personal data. For example, in the United States, the Health Insurance Portability and Accountability Act (HIPAA) prevents health care organizations from distributing patient information without written permission, and gives patients the right to amend incorrect or missing information in their records. HIPAA helps keep your medical information private and prevents abusive practices, such as when a cash-strapped health care organization sells a list of its pregnant patients to a baby-formula marketing company. To take advantage of privacy legislation, you should become familiar with your rights. Whenever you divulge personal information, read the entire document or screen carefully, looking for any check boxes you might need to select or deselect to keep your data from being distributed.

FAQ How can I protect my privacy online?

Privacy violations take place when your personal information is distributed or your online activities are tracked without your permission. Unscrupulous organizations can use your personal information to inundate you with ads and marketing offers, while criminals can use this data to stalk you or steal your identity. Despite legislation, a number of quasi-legal schemes exist for collecting your personal data. These schemes have flourished online. Currently, spyware is a major online privacy threat.

Spyware is any technology that surreptitiously gathers information. In the context of the Web and e-commerce, spyware secretly gathers information and relays it to advertisers or other interested parties. Web-based marketers use several spyware techniques, including ad-serving cookies and clear GIFs.

When you connect to a Web site, you expect it to store an innocuous cookie on your computer's hard disk. Some Web sites, however, feature banner ads supplied by third-party marketing firms. If you click the ad, this third party can create an **ad-serving cookie** and use it to track your activities at any site containing banner ads from that third party.

The marketing firms that distribute ad-serving cookies claim that this data is simply used to select and display ads that might interest you, but privacy advocates are worried that these cookies can be used to compile shopper profiles, which can be sold and used for unauthorized purposes. You can check the list of cookies on your computer to look for ad-serving cookies (Figure 22-11). They are typically generated by sites you have never visited and sometimes contain the word "ad" or "log."

Figure 22–11

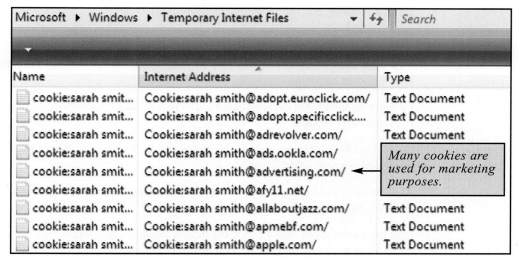

A **clear GIF** or "Web bug" is a 1x1 pixel graphic on a Web page. Clear GIFs can be used to set cookies to third-party Web sites. Unlike ad-serving cookies, you don't have to click a banner ad to receive a GIF-activated cookie. Simply viewing the page that contains a clear GIF sets the cookie. Cookies created with clear GIFs have the same uses and potential for misuse as ad-serving cookies.

Several software products are designed to block ad-serving cookies, clear GIFs, and other spyware—some even block banner and pop-up ads altogether. These products are becoming quite popular, despite their tendency to slightly slow down your browser's response time.

• How can I protect my privacy online? (continued)

You can violate your own privacy by unintentionally releasing information about yourself that can be exploited by aggressive marketing companies, hackers, and criminals. For example, to gain access to a **protected Web site**, you typically have to register for an account and password. The registration process includes filling out a form and perhaps answering several questions related to merchandise or service preferences. You must consider whether access to a protected Web site is worth the information you are required to divulge.

You might also inadvertently supply personal information in e-mail messages sent using a computer at school or at work. Legal rules and policies covering use of school and work computers vary, but typically you have more rights to data that you create on your own computer than to data created on school or work computers. For example, although most schools and businesses usually refrain from reading your e-mail messages, under certain circumstances it is legal to do so. Further, creative work that you generate on school or work computers could be regarded as the property of your school or employer. Read computer use policies at your school or workplace to learn your e-mail privacy rights and data ownership rights.

To protect your privacy, you should keep the following guidelines in mind:

* Do not reveal your e-mail address to any organization unless you want to receive correspondence from it.

* Be careful about posting your physical address and phone number in online public forums, bulletin boards, or your online resume.

* Be wary about sharing information about your family and friends.

* Use an alias when participating in chat rooms and do not divulge personal information to other chat room participants.

* Be wary of online surveys, especially those that ask for information about your job, finances, and income.

* When registering for an account or password to a protected Web site, supply a minimum amount of information.

* After using a public computer, make sure you sign out, log off, delete temporary Internet files, and shut down Windows.

* Regard e-mail more like a postcard than a sealed letter, especially if your e-mail account is supplied by your school or employer.

FAQ Are children safe online?

Web site filtering, the process of intentionally blocking access to certain sites, is controversial. It is practiced by concerned parents, litigation-averse librarians, and repressive governments. The Web contains all kinds of information, music, and images. Some of its less savory content includes pornography, information on bombs and poisons, extremist propaganda, and quack medicines. Balancing online freedom of speech with restrictions that ensure safety, security, and cultural ethics is becoming increasingly complex.

Parents are especially concerned with maintaining their children's privacy and safety online. Many sites are not suitable for children. Technology can mask the true identity of participants in chat rooms—even at sites sponsored by reputable child-centered organizations. Children have not yet developed the experience and judgment that sets up red flags when an offer is too good to be true. They are vulnerable to cajoling and threats. Parents should consider the following guidelines for keeping their children safe online.

Supervise as much as possible. Spend time with your children online. Let them show you their favorite sites and meet some of their chat buddies. Don't let your child remain online for long periods of time without supervision. Drop in and check the screen occasionally.

Keep the computer public. Your child should understand that the computer is public equipment and you or other family members might use it. Periodically, you might want to check for any potentially inappropriate activity by looking at your child's e-mail, the History list, and the list of sites stored in the Web cache.

Install filtering software. Several software publishers offer tools that filter out inappropriate Web sites. Programs such as Net Nanny and utilities such as Windows Parental Controls typically come pre-loaded with a long list of sites that are not child-friendly. They also offer tools for parents to adjust the list and monitor online activity.

Figure 22–12

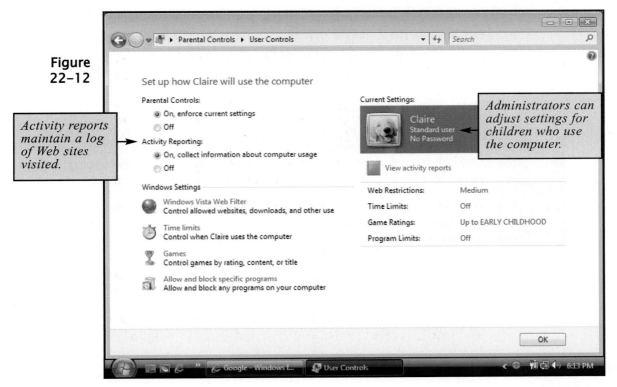

Activity reports maintain a log of Web sites visited.

Administrators can adjust settings for children who use the computer.

FAQ Can I prevent online identity theft?

Identity theft occurs when someone obtains your personal information and uses it without your permission to commit fraud or other crimes. A person whose identity has been stolen can spend months or years trying to restore a favorable reputation and credit record. In the meantime, an identity theft victim might be refused loans, jobs, and educational opportunities. Victims might even get arrested for crimes they didn't commit.

Identity thieves obtain personal information using a variety of high-tech and low-tech schemes. They rummage through your trash and mail looking for pay stubs and credit card receipts. They might ransack your home, steal your purse, or pilfer your wallet to obtain credit cards and your driver's license. Identity thieves posing as restaurant and store employees sometimes use a special information storage device to "skim" your credit card number as it is processed. High-tech thieves can hack into your personal computer, or the computer databases of your employer, bank, or credit card company.

Thwarting identity thieves requires vigilant supervision of your identity data, such as Social Security number, credit card numbers, driver's license, passport, pay stubs, credit card receipts, and medical records. Consider these tips.

Don't divulge personal information. Before you divulge any personal information on the phone, through the mail, or over the Internet, confirm that you're dealing with a legitimate representative of a reputable organization. Double-check by calling customer service using the number on your account statement or in the telephone book.

Shred your trash. Use a shredder or tear up your charge receipts, pay stubs, copies of credit applications, insurance forms, physician statements, cancelled checks, and bank statements. Cut up expired charge cards.

Guard your mail. Deposit sensitive outgoing mail in a post office collection box instead of an unsecured mailbox. For incoming mail, use a post office box or a mail slot, rather than trusting mail to a mailbox on your porch or curb.

Protect your identification documents. Keep your Social Security card and passport in a secure place. Keep a list of credit cards that you carry, along with the customer service number to call if a card is lost or stolen. Keep your driver's license in a clear window of your wallet, so that you don't have to hand it to clerks.

Divulge your Social Security number only when absolutely necessary. Your employer and bank have a legitimate need for your Social Security number to report wages and taxes. Other businesses might request your Social Security number for credit checks when you apply for a loan. Before you supply your Social Security number in any other situation, find out why it is needed, how it will be used, and how it will be secured.

Keep track of computer data. Before you dispose of an old computer, use file shredder software to delete any personal information stored on it. **File shredder software** overwrites the entire hard disk with random 1s and 0s to make data unrecoverable.

Keep passwords secret. Do not share your e-mail account, network password, protected Web site account, or credit card numbers with friends or coworkers.

Keep informed. Check www.ftc.gov/consumer for additional information on protecting your identity, and to learn what to do if you think your identity has been stolen.

FAQ How can I avoid scams and hoaxes?

Scam artists fooled unsuspecting victims long before computers were invented. Today, scammers take advantage of the Internet to reach across borders and access millions of potential victims. The most pervasive scams include phishing exploits, fake Web sites, and fraudulent e-mail messages.

Phishing is the use of fraudulent Web sites and e-mail links to trick people into revealing sensitive, personal, and financial information. A typical phishing scam begins with a faked (or "spoofed") e-mail message that seems to be an official notice from a trusted source, such as a credit card company, online payment service, software vendor, or bank. Under the guise of updating your password, reactivating your credit card, or confirming your address, the e-mail message offers a handy link to a supposedly legitimate site. However, the link leads to a fake site; and if you enter your password, credit card number, bank account number, or Social Security number, you're handing it over to a hacker.

Fake sites often look similar to real sites. They include corporate logos and they may even offer you a secure connection, padlock icon and all, when you enter sensitive information. Identifying these sites is not easy. Most browsers include built-in antiphishing features that compare URLs you might visit with a list of known phishing sites. Unfortunately, phishing sites spring up faster than the list can be updated, so don't depend on your browser as your only defense against phishing attacks.

Digital certificates offer another layer of protection. A **digital certificate** is issued by a certificate authority that essentially vouches for the certificate holder's identity. The certificate contains the holder's name, a serial number, an expiration date, and an encryption key. Digital certificates can be attached to e-mail messages, documents, and software, but they are useful antiphishing tools when attached to Web sites. If a site has a digital certificate, clicking it should display the certificate holder's name and other details.

Figure 22-13

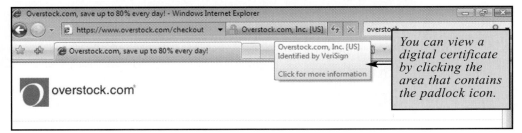

You can view a digital certificate by clicking the area that contains the padlock icon.

Digital certificates can also protect you from getting bamboozled by a fraudulent Web site masquerading as a well-known merchant. Sometimes these sites have URLs that are easy-to-mistype versions of the real sites; EdieBauer.com instead of EddieBauer.com, for example. Unfortunately, some legitimate sites do not subscribe to a digital certificate service, so that is not a security feature you can rely on to evaluate every Web site you visit.

Your best protection from phishing attacks is caution. First, pay careful attention to make sure you correctly type URLs. Before doing business with an unknown company, give its toll free number a call, check the Better Business Bureau online, and look for site reviews using Google. Never click links in e-mail messages that request passwords, sensitive personal data, or financial information. If you think the message is legitimate, close the e-mail message, open your browser, type in the legitimate Web site address for the business, and use links at the site to check if your account needs any maintenance.

• How can I avoid scams and hoaxes? (continued)

Phishing is only one type of scam carried by e-mail. E-mail messages are also used to distribute malicious software, advance-fee frauds, and hoaxes. For example, you might receive e-mail that appears to be from Microsoft. It warns of a new security hole in Windows and offers to install a patch directly to your computer when you click the www.microsoft.com/patch link—included right in the body of the e-mail message for your convenience. If you hover the pointer over this link and look at the status bar, you might discover that the link actually connects to www.microsoft.ru/patch. Checking the link and realizing it leads to a fake site can protect you from downloading malicious software.

You might also receive e-mail from various foreign businessmen and political widows who are looking for a reliable person to help them transfer large sums of money to safe U.S. or European banks. You are offered a substantial handling fee for your assistance. This multi-layered scheme, called advance-fee fraud, begins with a request for your bank account number and then escalates to pleas for money to initiate the transaction. Advance-fee fraud grosses hundreds of millions of dollars every year, and some victims have been lured abroad to complete the transaction, then kidnapped or killed. Never respond to an unsolicited request that seeks personal information or involves a transfer of funds.

Plenty of e-mail messages about nonexistent viruses circulate on the Internet. A typical virus hoax warns of a devastating new virus, describes some outlandish procedure for eradicating it, and encourages you to notify all your friends (Figure 22-14). The e-mail itself might contain a virus. Or, a virus might lurk in the file you are instructed to download for eradicating the non-existent virus. If you send panicked e-mails to all your friends, you invariably end up with egg on your face. Before you take any action based on an e-mail virus notification, check one of the many antivirus sites, such as www.symantec.com, www.f-secure.com, mcafee.com, or hoaxbusters.org.

Figure 22–14

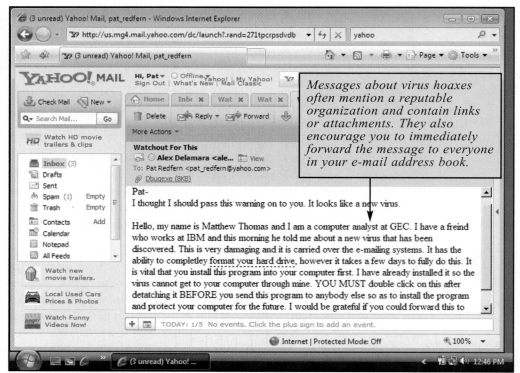

Messages about virus hoaxes often mention a reputable organization and contain links or attachments. They also encourage you to immediately forward the message to everyone in your e-mail address book.

FAQ What should I know about intellectual property online?

Intellectual property refers to intangibles, such as ideas, music, art, photos, logos, movies, and programs, that are the result of creativity and intellectual effort. Although intellectual property can be fixed in tangible media—CDs, DVDs, film, and sheet music—the underlying "property" is not necessarily tied to a particular media. It is the content that is important, rather than a particular format of the content.

People who create intellectual property deserve to benefit from their ideas. Therefore, many laws and regulations have been established to govern the use and distribution of intellectual property online as well as offline. Trademarks, patents, and copyrights are important legal protections for intellectual property.

Trademarks typically protect corporate logos and product names. They are important tools for businesses that want to maintain corporate reputations and prevent shoddy imitations from being sold by unscrupulous vendors.

Patents usually protect inventions from being used without permission from the inventor. In the digital world, encryption algorithms and file formats have been patented. The MP3 file format, so popular for digital music, is patented by a company that regulates its use and demands fees from software publishers that include MP3 algorithms in their software.

In the United States, the Digital Millennium Copyright Act of 1998 updated many key aspects of intellectual property law to meet the challenges of new digital realities, such as the ease with which music, software, and photos can be copied and distributed over the Internet.

Copyrights typically protect works such as software, photos, movies, and music. Many copyrighted works include a copyright notice, such as "Copyright 2010 eCourse Inc." This notice is not required by law, however, so works without a copyright notice can still be protected by copyright law.

Copyright law makes it illegal to copy and distribute protected works without the permission of the author or the author's representative. People who circumvent copyright law and illegally copy, distribute, or modify protected works are sometimes called "pirates."

Figure 22-15

Several organizations are dedicated to eradicating piracy. In the music industry, the Recording Industry Association of America (RIAA) is attempting to stop rampant MP3 music sharing on the Internet. The Software Information Industry Association (SIIA) is trying to stop illegal software distribution (Figure 22-15).

The material published on Web sites, in blogs, and in other online forums is protected by copyright. When you publish your own material online, it is automatically covered by copyright. You have a responsibility, however, to make sure your information is factual, relevant, and reliable. Clearly label your opinions, and treat opposing views with respect. You should try to avoid bullying in any online forum or communications. It is also important to respect people's privacy, especially at social networking sites where photos and gossip are commonly exchanged.

● **What should I know about intellectual property online? (continued)**

Copyright law does not prohibit all copying. You can make copies for your own use and you can make copies under **fair use** regulations, which allow you to copy small excerpts of copyrighted works for use in educational materials and critical reviews. Fair use allows you to insert fragments of literary works in research papers without first gaining permission from their authors. You should, however, always cite the source of such material. To determine whether you can use material under the fair use regulations, make sure it fits the following criteria:

● You are using the material for educational purposes or for critical review.

● The work has been previously published in some manner, such as in print or on the Web.

● You are not using a substantial part of the entire work.

● Your use does not provide a level of functionality that replaces the work so consumers would not need to purchase it.

It is easy, of course, to cut and paste large sections of someone else's material into your own reports and essays. Failure to cite your source or pretending the material is your own is plagiarism. Not only is plagiarism unethical, it is unlawful. In educational environments, plagiarism is considered especially egregious. Penalties, typically set forth in the student code of conduct, can be severe.

Make sure that you use source material accurately and do not modify statements attributed to your sources. Libel is defined as false and malicious statements published for the purpose of damaging the reputation of a living person. Charges of libel can arise from misquoted statements. Always cross-check material you attribute to named sources—especially if the material is controversial.

When your intended use of copyrighted material is not covered by fair use, you should obtain the author's permission. If you want to use a photo or music clip on your Web site, for example, contact the copyright holder. You can often do so via e-mail. You should also be aware that many clip art collections and other products billed as "copyright free" actually contain copyrighted material. If you read the small print, you might discover that you can use the material without permission only for personal, non-commercial use.

Laws do not seem to be sufficient deterrents to piracy. **Copy protection** refers to any physical method used to prevent works from being copied. Copy protected software CDs are designed to be used for installation purposes a limited number of times. They might also include technology that makes copies of the CD unusable. Music CDs and movie DVDs can also be copy protected, so that even with two writable CD or DVD drives, the disks produced do not work.

Copy protection methods can be hacked and circumvented. They have an additional disadvantage—copy protected media occasionally does not work on valid devices. If you've watched a movie DVD that paused for a moment and then did not continue, you might assume that the DVD is damaged. However, it might also be the case that the DVD checked its copy protection, decided it was not a legitimate copy, and therefore did not continue. Intellectual property is big business. You can expect further developments in copyright law, anti-piracy campaigns, and copy protection.

FAQ How can I keep informed about technology related issues?

Whether you're buying a computer, working in a computer career, investing for retirement, or just casually browsing the Internet, it pays to keep informed about current technology. As you might expect, numerous sources provide access to such information.

Computer publications. Popular computer magazines include *Computer Power User (CPU)*, *Computer Shopper*, *Wired*, and *PC World*. Two of the most prominent online sources for computer news are CNET News and Computerworld.

Mailing lists and RSS feeds. Subscribing to a mailing list or RSS feed from Ars Technica or InfoWorld can bring computer news and commentary right to your desktop.

Figure 22-16

Professional organizations. If you have a professional interest in computers, you should consider joining a professional organization such as the Association for Computing Machinery. Membership typically provides access to professional libraries, online or print journals, computer conferences, job listings, and special interest groups.

Corporate sites. Computer company Web sites often contain valuable information about corporations, products, and employment. Investors can find plenty of financial data in corporate reports. When you have a problem with a product, the first place to look for solutions is the manufacturer's customer support Web page or knowledge base.

Consumer reviews. If you're interested in purchasing computer equipment, check out consumer sites, such as epinions.com, consumerreports.org, and consumersearch.com. Also check computer-related blogs. These sites carry hundreds of reviews and ratings for computers, printers, and other peripheral devices.

School and work policies. Make sure you're aware of computer-use policies at your school or workplace. These policies typically specify what kinds of personal activities are allowed on school-owned or business-owned computers. They also should indicate the level of privacy you can expect with respect to e-mail and electronic communications over school or business networks.

• **How do I keep informed about computer-related issues?** (continued)

Figure 22-17

Laws and regulations. Computer use is governed by many laws and regulations. The most significant U.S. laws pertaining to computers are described briefly in Figure 22-17.

United States Copyright Act (1976) extends copyright protection beyond print media to "original works of authorship fixed in any tangible medium of expression, now known or later developed, from which they can be perceived, reproduced, or otherwise communicated, either directly or with the aid of a machine or device."

Fair Use Doctrine, a part of the U.S. Copyright Act, generally allows copying if it is for educational or personal use, if only a portion of the original work is copied, and if it does not have a substantial effect on the market for the original work.

Sony Corp. v. Universal City Studios (1984) sets a precedent that companies are not liable for user infringements, such as using VCRs to make unauthorized copies of videotapes, so long as the technology has valid, non-infringing uses, such as copying personal home videos. In recent cases, the defense for peer-to-peer file sharing networks was based on this decision.

Computer Fraud and Abuse Act (1986 amended in 1994, 1996, 2001, and USA PATRIOT Act) makes it a criminal offense to knowingly access a computer without authorization; transmit a program, information, code, or command that causes damage; or distribute passwords that would enable unauthorized access.

Electronic Communications Privacy Act (1986) extends telephone wiretap laws by restricting government agents and unauthorized third parties from tapping into data transmissions without a search warrant. The law does not apply to data, such as e-mail, transmitted on employer-owned equipment.

Health Insurance Portability and Accountability Act (1996) requires health care providers to take reasonable procedural and technical safeguards to insure the confidentiality of individually identifiable health information.

Digital Millennium Copyright Act (1998) makes it illegal to circumvent copy-protection technologies, such as those used to prevent unauthorized copying of software CDs, music CDs, and movie DVDs. In addition, it is illegal to distribute any type of cracking software technology that would be used by others to circumvent copy protection. Protects ISPs against copyright infringement by subscribers if the ISP takes prompt action to block the infringement as soon as it discovers illegal activity.

Communications Decency Act (1996) protects ISPs from liability for defamatory statements made by customers. Prohibits material deemed offensive by local community standards from being transmitted to minors. The latter section was overturned in 2002.

Children's Online Privacy Protection Act (1998) attempted to protect children from Internet pornography. Overturned in 1999.

Gramm-Leach-Bliley Act (1999) requires financial institutions to protect the confidentiality and security of customers' personal information.

Children's Internet Protection Act (2000) requires schools and libraries that receive federal funds to implement filtering software that protects adults and minors from obscenity and pornography.

USA PATRIOT Act (2001) enhances the authority of law enforcement agents to preempt potential terrorist acts by various means, such as monitoring electronic communications without first obtaining a search warrant in situations where there is imminent danger. Offers safe harbor to ISPs that voluntarily disclose potentially threatening activities of users. Increases maximum penalties for hackers.

Homeland Security Act (2002) establishes a Department of Homeland Security with an agency to monitor threats to the communications infrastructure, including the Internet, and exempts from the Privacy Act any information about infrastructure vulnerabilities to terrorism submitted by individuals or non-federal agencies.

Sarbanes-Oxley Act (2002) establishes financial reporting regulations to prevent corporate fraud. Requires full disclosure in accounting systems and protects corporate whistleblowers.

CAN-SPAM Act (2003) establishes national standards for sending commercial e-mail by requiring senders to use a valid subject line, include the sender's legitimate physical address, and provide an opt-out mechanism.

Green v. America Online (2003) interprets sections of the Communications Decency Act to mean that ISPs are not responsible for malicious software transmitted over their services by hackers.

MGM v. Grokster (2005) refines the precedent set in the 1984 Sony Corp. v. Universal Studios case. Companies that actively encourage infringement, as seemed to be true of peer-to-peer file-sharing networks such as Grokster, can be held accountable for user infringement.

QuickCheck A

1. [_____] guidelines help you position your computer, desk, and chair to avoid potentially disabling musculoskeletal injuries.

2. To prevent unauthorized access to your data by hackers, install and activate [_____] software that can analyze and control the flow of traffic entering your computer.

3. A mass-mailing [_____] can make use of information on an infected computer to mail itself to everyone listed in the e-mail address book.

4. Web-based marketers use several [_____] technologies, including ad-serving cookies and clear GIFs.

5. [_____] use regulations allow you to legally copy small excerpts of copyrighted works for use in educational materials and critical reviews.

CheckIt!

QuickCheck B

Based on the screen displayed at right, answer T if the statement is true, F if the statement is false.

1. Antivirus software is installed. [____]

2. Your computer has been given a digital certificate. [____]

3. You don't have to worry about fake e-commerce sites. [____]

4. Virus signatures will not be automatically updated. [____]

5. This computer will not be secure unless connected to a router. [____]

PC Security Pending	
Items	**Status**
Auto-Protect	On
Your PC is protected from viruses, spyware, and other risks.	
Firewall	On
Your PC is protected from intrusions and hacker attacks.	
LiveUpdate	Off
Your PC is protected from the latest known viruses, spyware, and other risks.	
Email Scanning	Off
Your incoming email attachments are protected	

CheckIt!

Projects

Introduction to Projects

The projects in this section are designed to help you review and develop skills you learned by reading the chapter material and working with Play It! activities. Projects serve as a valuable intermediate step between the *Practical Literacy* learning environment and working on your own. Even if you are not required to complete the projects for a class, you'll find that trying some of the projects can enhance your ability to use Windows, Microsoft Office, e-mail, and the Web.

Required software. Although not required for interacting with the Play It! activities in Chapters 1–22, Windows and Microsoft Office 2007 must be installed on the computer you use to complete the projects in this section. For projects in Chapter 20, you need an e-mail account. For projects in Chapter 21, you need access to the Internet and a browser, such as Internet Explorer.

To discover if Microsoft Office 2007 software has been installed on your computer, click the Start button, click All Programs, and then look for Microsoft Office on the programs list. Click Microsoft Office to display the shortcut menu. Microsoft Word 2007, Microsoft Excel 2007, Microsoft Access 2007, and Microsoft PowerPoint 2007 should be on the menu. The instructions and sample screens for *Practical Literacy* pertain to the applications in Office 2007.

Project Help. If you don't remember how to complete a task for a project, refer to Chapters 1–22. They are designed to provide quick reference to the skills you've learned. Keep the *Practical Literacy* book handy as you work on the projects and when working on your own.

Project Files. For many of the projects, you'll start by copying project files from the CD supplied with this book. You can copy a project file from the CD using the Copy It! button on the first page of a project. As another option, you can use the Start menu's Computer button, Windows Explorer, or the My Computer icon to copy the files directly from the CD to a removable storage device—such as a USB flash drive or floppy disk— or to your computer's hard disk. We suggest keeping all of the project files together in one location. We will refer to this location as your Project Folder.

How to Submit Assignments. At the completion of each project, you will have created a file that demonstrates your ability to apply your skills. To submit a completed project to your instructor, use one of the methods indicated by the instructions at the end of the project. Most projects can be printed, turned in on a USB flash drive or floppy disk, or sent as an e-mail attachment. Your instructor might have a preference for one of these methods. You'll find additional information about printing, saving, and e-mailing projects on the next three pages.

Submitting an Assignment as a Printout or on a Removable Storage Device

You can print or save your project files in one of two ways. For project files created in Microsoft Office, you can use the Microsoft Office button, as shown in the figure below.

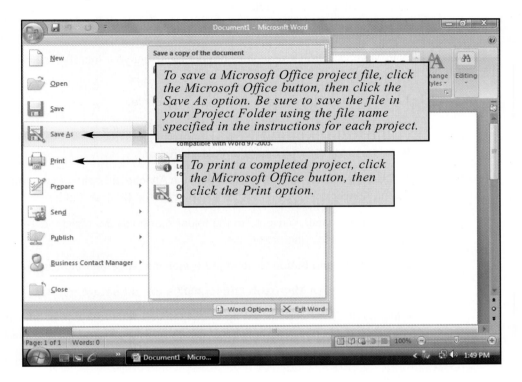

- To print a project file:

1. Make sure that a printer is attached to your computer and that it is turned on.

2. In Microsoft Office, click the Microsoft Office button, then click Print. When using other software, click the File menu, and then click Print.

3. If the printout doesn't already include your name, student ID number, class section number, date, and project name, be sure to write this information on the printout.

- To save your file on a removable storage device, such as a USB flash drive or floppy disk:

1. In Microsoft Office, click the Microsoft Office button, then select the Save As option. When using other software, click the File menu, then select Save as.

2. When the Save As dialog box appears, navigate to the removable storage device.

3. In the *File name* box, enter the name specified by the project instructions.

4. Click the Save button to complete the process.

5. Before submitting a USB flash drive or floppy disk to your instructor, make sure that it is labeled with your name, student ID number, class section number, date, and project name.

Submitting an Assignment as an E-mail Attachment

You can typically use either Method 1 or Method 2, as explained below, to submit most projects. Access projects, however, require Method 1. America Online (AOL) users must use Method 1 for all projects.

• Method 1—Add Attachments Manually

With Method 1, you'll send your project file using your local e-mail client or Webmail account.

1. Make sure that you have saved the project file.

2. Start your e-mail software and start a new message.

3. Address the new message to your instructor.

4. Click the Attachment button or select the Attachment option from a menu. If you don't see an Attachment option, look for a File option on the Insert menu.

5. When prompted, navigate to the folder that holds the attachment—usually your Project Folder—and select the project file.

6. Click the Send button to send the e-mail message and attachment.

• Method 2—Use Microsoft Office 2007's Send Feature

If Microsoft Office 2007 is set up in conjunction with your e-mail software, you can send your project file directly from Word, Excel, or PowerPoint by using the following steps:

1. After saving your project, keep your application (Paint, Word, Excel, or PowerPoint) window open.

2. Click the Microsoft Office button.

3. Select the Send option, then select the E-mail option. Enter your instructor's e-mail address in the To: box, enter the body of the e-mail and then send it.

• Getting an E-mail Account

If you don't have an e-mail account, refer to Project EM-1 to set up a Gmail account. When you use a Webmail account, complete your project offline. Then, connect to your Webmail account, create a new message addressed to your instructor, and then attach your project file to the message before sending it.

If you prefer to use local e-mail, you'll need to set up an account with an ISP or some other provider, such as your school. To set up a local e-mail account, you might need to obtain the following information from your ISP:

- The Internet access phone number (dial-up service only)

- Your e-mail address (such as hfinn5678@verizon.net)

- Your e-mail password (such as huck2finn)

- The incoming mail server type (usually POP3)

- Your incoming mail server's name (often the part of your e-mail address that comes after the @ symbol, i.e., aol.com)

- Your outgoing SMTP mail server's name (such as mailhost.att.net)

- The primary and secondary domain name server (DNS) numbers (such as 204.127.129.1)

Microsoft Office 2007 Configuration

Microsoft Office 2007 provides many ways for you to configure and modify the way its applications look and operate. While this adaptability can be a positive feature, it can potentially cause confusion if your version of Microsoft Office 2007 is not configured to look or work the same way as the version used for the examples in *Practical Literacy*. Here's how to configure your software to match the settings that were used for the figures and animations in Chapters 1–22.

- **To configure Microsoft Word, Excel, and PowerPoint:**

1. Click the Microsoft Office button. Click either the Word Options, Excel Options, or PowerPoint options button. On the Popular tab, make sure *Show Mini Toolbar on selection* and *Enable Live Preview* are selected.

- **To configure Microsoft Access:**

1. The entire ribbon should be visible. If it is not, double-click one of the tabs at the top of the application window.

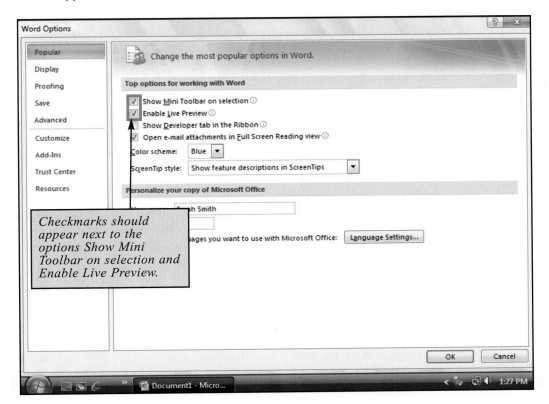

Checkmarks should appear next to the options Show Mini Toolbar on selection and Enable Live Preview.

Project WI-1: Exploring the Windows Vista Desktop

In this project, you will apply what you have learned about elements on the Windows Vista desktop.

Requirements: This project requires Microsoft Windows Vista and Paint.

Project file: No project file is required for this project.

1. You can personalize your Windows Vista desktop by changing the default desktop items to your preferred choices. Open the Start menu by clicking the Start button. Select the Control Panel and click *Appearance and Personalization*.

2. Suppose you want to change your desktop background. Under Personalization, select *Change desktop background*. For this project, choose one of the Windows Wallpapers. If the Picture Location box does not contain Windows Wallpapers, click the down-arrow button of the box and select it.

3. Under Light Auras, click img26. You should see the name of the picture when you rest your pointer on it. When you've selected the image, click the OK button. Close the Desktop Background screen by clicking the ☒ Close button in the upper-right corner of the screen. Your desktop should now display the orange and yellow backdrop of img26.

4. You can also customize the desktop Sidebar. If your desktop does not have a Sidebar, click the Start button and type sidebar in the Search box. Click Windows Sidebar. The Sidebar should appear on the right side of your screen.

5. Click the + button at the top of the Sidebar to display the list of available gadgets. Write down three gadgets that you think would be useful to have on the Sidebar. To find out more about each gadget, click *Show details* at the bottom left of the Add gadgets box.

6. Suppose you want a notepad on your Sidebar. Double-click Notes. The Notes gadget should appear above any other gadgets on the Sidebar. Some of the other gadgets might no longer be visible if there is not enough room on the Sidebar, but they should still be running. Close the Add gadgets box by clicking the ☒ Close button in the upper-right corner of the box. Use the Notes gadget to give yourself a reminder. Click the notepad, type Submit Project WI-1, and then press Enter.

7. For this project and some future projects, you will be required to take snapshots of your screen (also called "screen shots"). To learn how to take screen shots, open the Start menu and select Help and Support. A rectangular window appears and displays Help and Support options. Type screen capture in the Search box at the top of the window and press Enter. Click *Take a screen capture (print screen)* from the list of results. Read the information about how to take a screen capture, but don't capture anything yet. Click the ▬ Minimize button in the upper-right corner of the Windows Help and Support window. The window is reduced to a button on the taskbar.

8. Now, to take the screen shot, press the PrtSc or Print Screen key, located somewhere at the top of your keyboard. On some computers, you might have to hold down a key marked Fn as you press the PrtSc key.

• **Exploring the Windows Vista Desktop (continued)**

9. The screen shot is temporarily held in your computer's memory. To view it, you can use the Paint program or Microsoft Word. In this example, we will use Paint. Open Paint by clicking the Start button and typing paint in the Search box. Click Edit on the Paint menu bar, then select Paste on the menu. The snapshot of your screen should now be displayed. Except for the desktop icons and some Sidebar gadgets, your screen shot should be very similar to the example below.

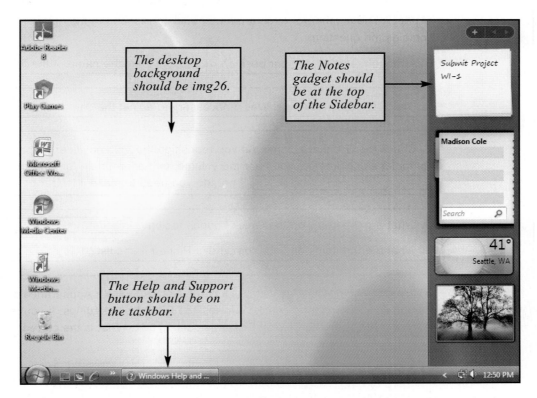

10. You can print your screen shot by clicking File on the Paint menu bar, then selecting Print from the menu. Click the Print button in the Print dialog box. Click the ▬ Minimize button of the Paint window.

11. You can view a three-dimensional representation of the windows for all the programs you've been running by clicking the *Switch between windows* icon on the Quick Launch toolbar. After you do so, click the Help and Support window to display it at its full size. Take a few minutes to browse more Help topics. When you're done, click the ⊠ Close button to close Help and Support.

12. You can click a program's taskbar button to view the program window; but when you right-click the button, a list of options appears. Right-click the Paint taskbar button. Select the Close option to close the program. When asked if you want to save your changes, click the Don't Save button.

13. Submit your screen shot to your instructor. Include your name, student ID number, class section number, date, and PrjWI-1.

Project WI-2: Checking Your Windows Settings

In this project, you will apply what you have learned about Windows to view and adjust system settings.

Requirements: This project requires Microsoft Windows.

Project file: No project file is required for this project.

As you complete each step, write your answers to the questions in the book or on a sheet of paper. The number for each answer should correspond to the number of the step that contains the question.

1. Arrange the icons on your desktop by type. What is the name of the first icon?

2. Check the date and time. Was it necessary to adjust the date or time?

3. Check the Speaker volume. As you reposition the Volume slider bar, a beep from your computer's speaker lets you hear the volume. Is it appropriate for your work setting? If not, do you need to make it louder or softer?

4. What are the items on the Quick Launch toolbar?

5. What are the items on your computer's Pinned Items list?

6. If you're using Windows Vista, select the Control Panel's Appearance and Personalization option to check your desktop and screen settings. If you're using Windows XP, open the Display Properties dialog box. What is the current theme?

7. What is the background wallpaper?

8. Does your computer have a screen saver activated? If so, what is its name and what is the wait period?

9. What is the screen resolution?

10. If you would like to save any settings you changed, click the OK button. Otherwise, click the Cancel button to return to the Control Panel.

11. Use the Control Panel to explore the options in the Ease of Access Center (Vista) or Accessibility Options (XP). List five options that Windows offers to improve accessibility for individuals with physical disabilities.

12. Use the Control Panel to access the Windows Security Center. Indicate your computer's security status for firewall protection, automatic updates, and malware (virus) protection.

• Checking Your Windows Settings (continued)

13. Open the Control Panel's Mouse tool. Do you need to adjust the mouse sensitivity so that it is comfortable for you? [_____] Close the Mouse Properties dialog box, and save the new settings.

14. Open the Control Panel's Printers tool in Windows Vista or *Printers and Other Hardware* tool in Windows XP. How many printers can your computer access? [_____] How many of the printers are accessed over a network? [_____]

15. Which version of Windows and service packs are installed on your computer?
[_____]

16. Hold down the Ctrl and Alt keys while you press the Delete key. If you're using Windows Vista, select Start Task Manager. If you're using Windows XP, the Task Manager should appear automatically. Click the Applications tab. Make a list of the programs that are running on your computer. For each program, indicate its status. If an application is "hung up" and not responding, you can use the End Task button to close the application. Otherwise, close the Task Manager.

17. Submit your answer sheet to your instructor. If your instructor prefers to receive your assignment via e-mail, use Method 1 or Method 2, as described on page 348. Type your instructor's e-mail address in the To: box. Click the Subject: box, then type Project WI-2, your student ID number, and your class section number. Transfer your answers from your answer sheet to the body of the e-mail message. Click the Send button or perform any additional steps required by your e-mail software to send an e-mail message.

Project WI-3: Organizing the Windows Desktop

In this project, you will apply what you have learned about application windows to start several programs and arrange your desktop.

Requirements: This project requires Microsoft Windows, Notepad, Paint, and Microsoft Word.

Project file: No project file is required for this project.

1. If you are using a lab computer that does not allow students to create desktop icons, proceed to Step 9. Otherwise, add a new desktop icon using the Text Document option. Enter To-Do.txt as the file name.

2. Use the new To-Do icon to open the file. This action launches the Notepad program. An empty document window should appear with the flashing insertion point positioned at the top-left corner of the blank work area. The file name To-Do should be in the Notepad window's title bar.

3. Enter a list of five To-Do items. As you enter the list, you can use the Backspace key to correct typing errors. After typing each item on the list, press the Enter key to go to the next line.

4. Close the file by closing the Notepad program. You will be asked if you want to save the changes to your file. Click the Save button in Windows Vista or the Yes button in Windows XP.

5. Rename the desktop icon To-Do List.txt.

6. Create a new folder icon on the desktop called Troubleshooting Documents. Right click the folder and examine its properties. Use the Customize tab to select a different folder icon.

7. Create a shortcut on the desktop. Enter www.wikipedia.com as the location and Wikipedia as the name. Test the shortcut to make sure it starts your browser and connects to the Wikipedia Web site. Close the browser.

8. Delete the Troubleshooting Documents desktop icon.

9. Click the Start button, point to Recent Items in Windows Vista or My Recent Documents in Windows XP, and then wait for a list of files to appear. Open any document that was created with Microsoft Word. Make sure that the newly opened window is maximized.

10. Start the Paint program, which is located in the Accessories group of the All Programs list on the Start menu. Make sure that the Paint window is maximized.

11. Switch to the Word window and close it.

12. Use the Start menu to open Microsoft Word. An empty document window should appear with the insertion point positioned at the top-left corner of the window. The file name Document1 should be in the title bar.

13. Type the title WI-3 Project and press the Enter key. Type your name and press the Enter key. Type today's date and press the Enter key twice.

14. Make sure that the Document1 window is maximized.

15. Right-click a blank area of the taskbar and select *Show Windows Side by Side* in Windows Vista or *Tile Windows Vertically* in Windows XP.

16. Adjust the size and position of the two windows so that the To-Do List and Wikipedia desktop icons, if you created them, are also visible. To adjust window size, position the pointer at the edge of the window until a two-sided arrow appears. Hold down the mouse button while you drag the borders of the window to the size you want it to be.

● Organizing the Windows Desktop (continued)

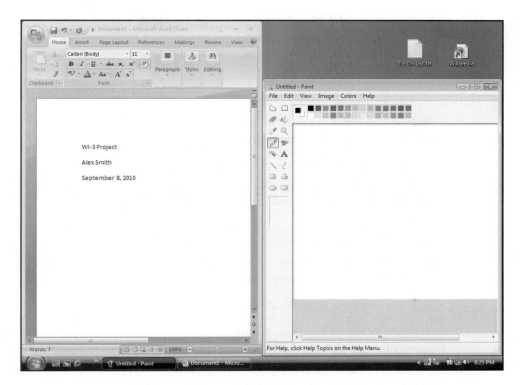

17. Compare your screen to the one above. Your screen should show the Paint window, the Document1 window, the Wikipedia icon, and the To-Do List icon.

18. Press the Print Screen key on your keyboard. Maximize the Document1 window. To paste the screen shot into Word, right-click anywhere in the Document1 window, then select Paste from the shortcut menu. The screen shot of your desktop should appear in the Word window.

19. Close the Document1 window. You will be asked if you want to save the changes to your document. Answer Yes to open the Save As dialog box. The Address bar in Vista or the *Save in* box in XP should point to the Documents or My Documents folder.

20. In the File name box, enter PrjWI-3-XXXXX-9999, where XXXXX is your student ID number and 9999 is your class section number. Click the Save button to complete the process.

21. Close the Paint window. Delete the To-Do List desktop icon.

22. Use one of the following options to submit your project on a USB flash drive or floppy disk, as a printout, or as an e-mail attachment, according to your instructor's directions:

● To submit the file from the Documents or My Documents folder where it is currently stored, copy the file to the Project Folder on a USB flash drive or floppy disk. Include your name, student ID number, class section number, date, and PrjWI-3 when you submit the file.

● To print the project, click the Microsoft Office button in Windows Vista or the File menu in Windows XP. Click Print, then click the OK button. Write your name, student ID number, class section number, date, and PrjWI-3 on the printout.

● To e-mail the file, use Method 1 or Method 2, as described on page 348. Type your instructor's e-mail address in the To: box. Click the Subject: box and type PrjWI-3, your student ID number, and your class section number. Click the Send button or perform any additional steps required by your e-mail software to send an e-mail message.

Project WI-4: Organizing Directories and Folders

In this project, you will apply what you have learned about Windows file management to organize your personal files.

Requirements: This project requires Microsoft Windows and Microsoft Word.

Project file: No project file is required for this project.

Note: If you are using a lab or work computer, make sure that you have permission to modify files and folders in the Documents or My Documents folder.

You can write your answers to the questions on a sheet of paper with your name and the title WI-4 Answers. The number for each answer should correspond to the number of the step that contains the question. For example, your first answers will be for Step 1.

1. Use the Start menu's Search box in Windows Vista or Search Companion and wildcards in Windows XP to search your entire hard disk for DOC files that contain the word sample in the file name. What did you enter for search specifications? [　　　　　　] How many files were found? [　　　　　　]

2. If you used the Search Companion, close it.

3. Open Windows Explorer. If drive C is expanded, click the black triangle or minus symbol to hide its folders. List the storage devices attached to your computer and take note of the icons that represent them. Indicate if your computer is connected to any remote storage devices. Hint: Look carefully at the icons.

4. Expand drive C and open the Documents or My Documents folder. Look at the status bar. How many objects are stored in this folder? [　　　　　　] How many subfolders does the My Documents folder contain? [　　　　　　]

5. Open one of the Documents or My Documents subfolders. Arrange the files by type. How many files of each type are stored in the subfolder? [　　　　　　]

6. Arrange the files by size. What are the name and size of the largest file? [　　　　　　] What are the name and size of the smallest file? [　　　　　]

7. Arrange the files by date. What are the name and date of the most recent file? [　　　　　　] What are the name and date of the oldest file? [　　　　　　]

8. Use the Start menu to open Microsoft Word. An empty document window should appear with the cursor positioned at the top-left corner of the window. The file name Document1 should be at the top of the screen.

9. Type the title WI-4 Project. Press the Enter key.

10. Type your name. Press the Enter key.

11. Type the date. Press the Enter key twice.

12. Minimize the Word window.

13. On your answer sheet, create a sketch of the folder hierarchy for the Documents or My Documents folder. Create a second sketch that shows a more efficient directory structure. Provide examples of the files you would move into each of these directories.

• Organizing Directories and Folders (continued)

14. Carry out your plan from the previous step. Create and delete folders as necessary, then move files into them.

15. Press the Print Screen or PrtSc key on your keyboard to take a screen shot of the new directory structure.

16. Restore the Word window.

17. Right-click anywhere in the Word window, and then select Paste. The screen shot of the new directory should appear in the Word window.

18. Switch to the Documents or My Documents window. Review the name of each file in the various folders you have created. Which of these files would benefit from a new name? [   ] What would those names be?

19. Use the Views button on the Windows Explorer toolbar to experiment with various Views, such as Tiles, Icons, List, and Details. Which view do you prefer?
[   ]

20. Right-click one of the DOC or DOCX files and display its properties. Is the file read-only or hidden? [   ] If you change the status of the file to read-only, what does this mean? [   ]

21. Close the Documents or My Documents window.

22. Close the Word window. When asked if you want to save the changes to your document, answer Yes to open the Save As dialog box. The Address bar in Vista or *Save in* box in XP should point to the Documents or My Documents folder.

23. In the File name box, enter Project WI-4 XXXXX 9999, where XXXXX is your student ID number and 9999 is your class section number. Click the Save button to complete the process.

24. Stop the Word program by closing the Word window.

25. Submit your sketch and the Word document that contains your screen shot and your answers.

Project WI-5: Compressing Files

In this project, you will learn how to compress files using the Windows compression utility or WinZip.

Requirements: This project requires Microsoft Windows Vista or XP and Paint.

Project file: PrjWI-5.zip.

1. Copy the file PrjWI-5.zip to your Project Folder using the Copy It! Button on this page in the BookOnCD.

2. The file PrjWI-5.zip contains four graphics that were zipped using a compression utility called WinZip. Open Windows Explorer to display the list of files in your Project Folder. Double-click the PrjWI-5 file. A window should appear with a list of the files contained in PrjWI-5. Your application window might look slightly different, but you should see the four files shown in the figure below.

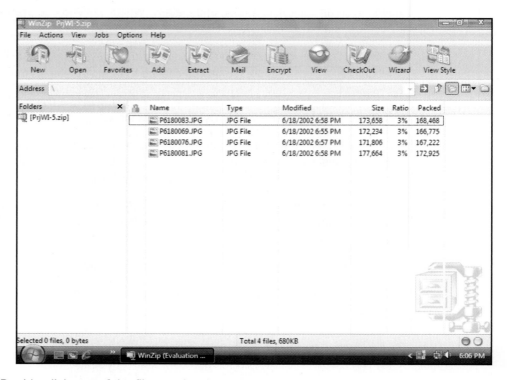

3. Double-click one of the files to view it.

4. Close the application window after you view the file.

5. Suppose you want to create two graphics and compress them into one object that you can ship as an e-mail attachment. First, create your graphics. Use the Start menu to open the Paint program, which is located in the Accessories group of the All Programs list. Create two simple graphics. Use the text tool to include your name on the graphics, and then store them in the My Pictures or Pictures folder as Picture1.jpg and Picture2.jpg. Close Paint.

• Compressing Files (continued)

6. Use the Start Menu to open the Pictures or My Pictures folder. Make sure the two graphics that you created are located in this folder.

7. The next step is to create a "container" to hold the files when you compress them. Depending on your Windows configuration, you will create either a compressed folder or a zipped file to hold these graphics. (Instructions for zipped files are in parentheses.) In Windows XP, click File on the Windows Explorer menu bar, select the New option, and then click Compressed (zipped) folder (or click WinZip File). In Windows Vista, right-click Picture1.jpg, select Send To from the shortcut menu, then click Compressed (zipped) Folder.

8. Enter FYI for the folder (file) name.

9. Now you can place copies of your graphics into FYI. In Windows XP, hold the Ctrl key down while you click each of the files you want to compress. Drag the selected files to the FYI folder (file). In Windows Vista, simply drag Picture2 to the FYI folder.

10. If a WinZip dialog box appears, click the Add button to add the files to FYI. That's it! Your files are compressed.

11. To check that FYI contains your files, open the compressed folder (zipped file) by double-clicking it. It should contain your graphics.

12. Send your compressed folder or zipped file to your instructor as an attachment in an e-mail by using Method 1 on page 348. Type your instructor's e-mail address in the To: box. Click the Subject: box, then type PrjWI-5, your student ID number, and your class section number. Click the Send button or perform any additional steps required by your e-mail software to send an e-mail message.

Project AP-1: Working with Windows Applications

In this project, you'll apply what you've learned about application windows to start several programs and arrange your desktop.

Requirements: This project requires Microsoft Windows, WordPad, and Paint.

Project file: No project file is required for this project.

1. Start the WordPad program, which is located in the Accessories group of the All Programs list on the Start menu.

2. Make sure that the WordPad window is maximized.

3. Start the Paint program, which is located in the Accessories group of the All Programs list on the Start menu.

4. Make sure that the Paint window is maximized.

5. Switch to the WordPad window.

6. Switch back to the Paint window.

7. Restore the Paint window.

8. Adjust the size and position of the Paint window so that your screen looks similar to the one on the next page.

• Working with Windows Applications (continued)

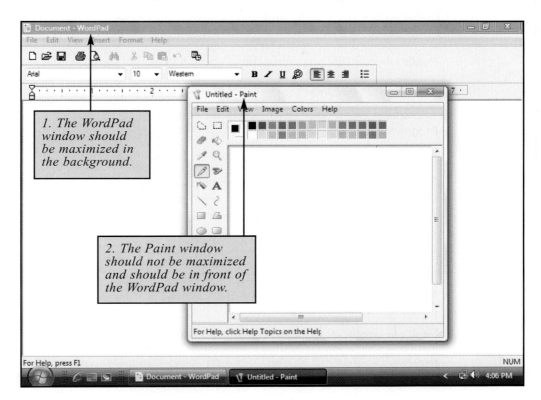

1. *The WordPad window should be maximized in the background.*

2. *The Paint window should not be maximized and should be in front of the WordPad window.*

9. Press the PrtSc or Print Screen key on your keyboard.

10. Maximize the Paint window. Click Edit on the Paint menu bar, then click Paste. If you are given the option of enlarging the bitmap, click the Yes button.

11. Save the graphic in your Project Folder as PrjAP-1-XXXXX-9999, where XXXXX is your student ID number and 9999 is your class section number.

12. Use one of the following options to submit your project on a USB flash drive or floppy disk, as a printout, or as an e-mail attachment, according to your instructor's directions:

• To submit the project from your Project Folder where it is currently stored, stop the Paint program by closing its window. Copy the file to a USB flash drive or floppy disk. Include your name, student ID number, class section number, date, and PrjAP-1 when you submit the file.

• To print the project, click File on the Paint menu bar, then click Print. Click the OK button. Write your name, student ID number, class section number, date, and PrjAP-1 on the printout.

• To e-mail the file, use Method 1 as described on page 348. Type your instructor's e-mail address in the To: box. Click the Subject: box, then type PrjAP-1, your student ID number, and your class section number. Click the Send button or perform any additional steps required by your e-mail software to send an e-mail message.

Project AP-2: Working with Files

In this project, you'll apply what you've learned about Windows applications to create, save, and open a file.

Requirements: This project requires Microsoft Windows and WordPad.

Project file: No project file is required for this project.

1. Start the WordPad program, which is located in the Accessories group of the All Programs list on the Start menu.

2. Make sure that the WordPad window is maximized.

3. Click anywhere in the blank section of the document window and type the following short memo. Type your own name on the FROM: line and type today's date on the DATE: line. (Hint: Press the Enter key at the end of each line.)

MEMO
TO: Professor Greer
FROM: [Your name]
DATE: [Today's date]
SUBJECT: This week's lesson
I will not be able to attend my music lesson this week.

4. Save the document in your Project Folder as PrjAP-2.txt.

5. Stop the WordPad application by closing its window.

6. Start WordPad again. Open the file PrjAP-2.txt from your Project Folder.

7. Type the word IMPORTANT so that the first line of the document reads IMPORTANT MEMO. Your document should now look like the one shown on the next page.

• Working with Files (continued)

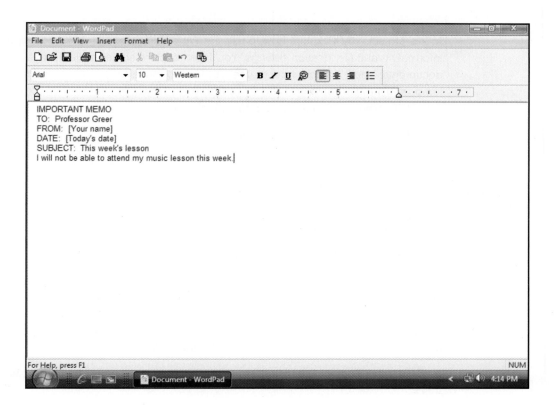

8. Save the new version of your document under a different name on your Project Folder. Use PrjAP-2-XXXXX-9999 as the new name, where XXXXX is your student number and 9999 is your class section number.

9. Use one of the following options to submit your project on a USB flash drive or floppy disk, as a printout, or as an e-mail attachment, according to your instructor's directions:

• To submit the memo from your Project Folder where it is currently stored, stop the WordPad program by closing its window. Copy the file to a USB flash drive or floppy disk. Include your name, student ID number, class section number, date, and PrjAP-2 when you submit the file.

• To print the project, click File on the WordPad menu bar, then click Print. Click the Print button. Write your name, student ID number, class section number, date, and PrjAP-2 on the printout.

• To e-mail the memo file, use Method 1 as described on page 348. Type your instructor's e-mail address in the To: box. Click the Subject: box and type PrjAP-2, your student ID number, and your class section number. Click the Send button or perform any additional steps required by your e-mail software to send an e-mail message.

Project AP-3: Configuration and Navigation Basics

In this project, you'll explore how to use the Word Options dialog box to configure user information and file location settings. You'll also explore some efficient ways to move around documents. You'll find out how to use Ctrl-End to move to the end of a document in one jump. You'll experiment with the Page Up, Page Down, Home, and End keys, then use the Go To command to jump to a specified page.

Requirements: This project requires Microsoft Word.

Project file: PrjAP-3.docx

1. Copy the file PrjAP-3.docx to your Project Folder using the Copy It! button on this page in the BookOnCD.

2. Start Microsoft Word.

3. Open the file PrjAP-3.docx from your Project Folder.

4. Click the Microsoft Office button, and then click the Word Options button. When the Word Options dialog box appears, click the Save tab on the left and notice the storage device set to hold your documents. Click the Browse button to view the dialog box that allows you to change these locations. Unless you want to change these locations now, click the Cancel button to return to the Word Options dialog box.

5. Select the Popular tab. Enter your name in the User name text box if it is not already there.

6. Click the OK button to save your User Information.

7. Click the View tab, then click Print Layout.

8. Press Ctrl-End to move to the end of the document.

9. Press Ctrl-Enter to insert a page break.

10. Click anywhere in the blank section near the top of the new page and type the following:
BREAKOUT SESSION EVALUATION

Please provide comments on the effectiveness of each breakout session. Do not sign your evaluation.

11. Use the scroll bar to scroll to the beginning of the document.

12. Press the Page Down key a few times and notice how this key changes the position of the insertion point. Press the Page Up key to return to the top of the document.

13. Click in the middle of any full line of text in the document. Press the Home key and notice how this key changes the position of the insertion point. Press the End key to see what it does.

14. On the Home tab, click the down-arrow button next to Find in the Editing group, then click Go To. Type 5, click Go To, and then click Close.

15. Add the following line to the end of the memo.
Drop it off on the table at the conference room door before you leave.

The last page of your document should now look like the one shown on the next page.

• Configuration and Navigation Basics (continued)

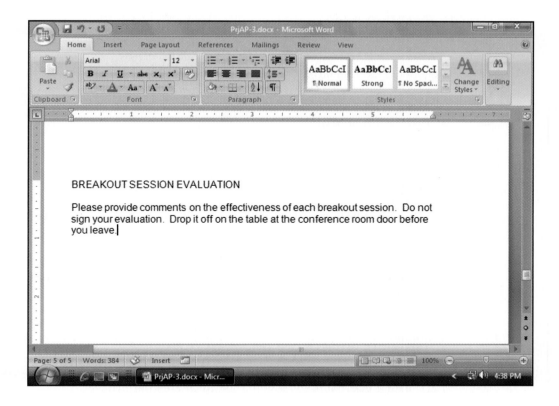

16. Save the new version of your document under a different name in your Project Folder. Use PrjAP-3-XXXXX-9999 as the new name, where XXXXX is your student number and 9999 is your class section number.

17. Use one of the following options to submit your project on a USB flash drive or floppy disk, as a printout, or as an e-mail attachment, according to your instructor's directions:

• To submit the memo from your Project Folder where it is currently stored, stop the Word program by closing its window. Copy the file to a USB flash drive or floppy disk. Include your name, student ID number, class section number, date, and PrjAP-3 when you submit the file.

• To print the project, click the Microsoft Office button, then click Print. Click the OK button. Write your name, student ID number, class section number, date, and PrjAP-3 on the printout.

• To e-mail the memo file, use Method 1 or Method 2, as described on page 348. Type your instructor's e-mail address in the To: box. Click the Subject: box and type PrjAP-3, your student ID number, and your class section number. Click the Send button or perform any additional steps required by your e-mail software to send an e-mail message.

Project WD-1: Creating a Word Document

In this project, you'll apply what you've learned about Microsoft Word to create a document, modify it, and insert a hyperlink.

Requirements: This project requires Microsoft Word.

Project file: No project file is required for this project.

1. Start Microsoft Word.

2. Create a new document containing the text below, placing a blank line between each paragraph.

Dear Marjorie,

Hi! I was happy to receive your letter and learn that all is going well with you, Bob, and the kids. I really miss you all!

Your new job at the bookstore sounds great! How do you manage to keep your mind on work where there are so many fascinating books and magazines just begging to be read?

You mentioned that your first big assignment is to create a display appropriate for the month of February, but without featuring Valentine's Day or Presidents' Day. Did you know that I keep a database of offbeat events, like International Tuba Day and National Accordion Awareness Month? Let me know if you're interested and I'll create a query and send you a list of interesting events.

Sorry for the shortness of this note, but I have to run off to class. I promise to write more soon.

Good luck with the new job!

3. Compare the text that you typed with the text shown above and correct any typing mistakes that you might have made.

4. Use the Delete key to delete the phrase create a query and from the last sentence of the third paragraph. The Delete key deletes text without copying it to the clipboard.

5. Copy the phrase for the month of February from the paragraph that starts with the words You mentioned. Paste the copied phrase before the period at the end of the sentence that ends with send you a list of interesting events.

6. Select the sentence I really miss you all! in the first paragraph. Drag and drop the sentence after the sentence Good luck with the new job! at the end of the document.

7. Delete the fourth paragraph of the document, which starts with the words Sorry for the shortness.

8. Use the Undo button to restore the deleted paragraph.

9. While holding down the mouse button, drag the pointer over the phrase "International Tuba Day" to select it.

10. Right-click the selected phrase and select Hyperlink from the shortcut menu. Make sure the *Text to display* box contains "International Tuba Day."

11. In the Address box, enter www.tubaday.com and then click the OK button.

• **Creating a Word Document (continued)**

12. You've created a hyperlink in your document. To test it, hold down the Ctrl key and click the link. Once you've connected to the International Tuba day site, you can close your browser and complete the remaining steps in the project.

13. Compare your letter with the document below. Don't worry if the sentences in your document break in different places at the right margin.

Dear Marjorie,

Hi! I was happy to receive your letter and learn that all is going well with you, Bob, and the kids.

Your new job at the bookstore sounds great! How do you manage to keep your mind on work where there are so many fascinating books and magazines just begging to be read?

You mentioned that your first big assignment is to create a display appropriate for the month of February, but without featuring Valentine's Day or Presidents' Day. Did you know that I keep a database of offbeat events, like International Tuba Day and National Accordion Awareness Month? Let me know if you're interested and I'll send you a list of interesting events for the month of February.

Sorry for the shortness of this note, but I have to run off to class. I promise to write more soon.

Good luck with the new job! I really miss you all!

---

14. Add your name as the last line of the letter.

15. Save your document in your Project Folder as PrjWD-1-XXXXX-9999, where XXXXX is your student ID number and 9999 is your class section number.

16. Use one of the following options to submit your project on a USB flash drive or floppy disk, as a printout, or as an e-mail attachment, according to your instructor's directions:

• To submit the file from your Project Folder where it is currently stored, stop the Word program by closing its window. Copy the file to a USB flash drive or floppy disk. Include your name, student ID number, class section number, date, and PrjWD-1 when you submit the file.

• To print the project, click the Microsoft Office button, then click Print. Click the OK button. Write your name, student ID number, class section number, date, and PrjWD-1 on the printout.

• To e-mail the file, use Method 1 or Method 2, as described on page 348. Type your instructor's e-mail address into the To: box. Click the Subject: box and type PrjWD-1, your student ID number, and your class section number. Click the Send button or perform any additional steps required by your e-mail software to send an e-mail message.

Project WD-2: Using the Mail Merge Wizard

In this project, you'll use the Microsoft Word's Mail Merge Wizard to create an address list and perform a mail merge.

Requirements: This project requires Microsoft Word.

Project file: No project file is required for this project.

1. Start Microsoft Word.

2. Click the Mailings tab. Click Start Mail Merge in the Start Mail Merge group, then click Step by Step Mail Merge Wizard.

3. In the Mail Merge task pane, select *Letters* as the type of document, then click *Next: Starting document*.

4. In the Mail Merge task pane, select *Start from a template*, then click the *Select template* option. Select the Urban Letter template from the Letters tab, then click OK. Click *Next: Select recipients*.

5. In the Mail Merge task pane, select the *Type a new list* option, then click the *Create* option. Enter the following information in the New Address List dialog box.

First Name	Last Name	Address 1	City	State
Jim	Gallagos	1420 Elm Pass	Springfield	IL
Ed	Zimmerman	1562 River Way	Springfield	IL
Alice	Wegin	523 West Ave	Oak Grove	IL

Use the New Entry button to insert new rows. Click the OK button to close the New Address List dialog box.

6. Save the list as Address List.mdb in your Project Folder. Click the OK button to close the Mail Merge Recipients dialog box. Click the *Next: Write your letter* option.

7. In the upper-right corner of the letter, delete the name placeholder and then replace the sender company address placeholder with the following return address:

Perfect Pizza
1320 W. Oak Grove Rd.
Springfield, IL

8. Delete the placeholders for the recipient's address and name. Click the *Address block* option from the Mail Merge task pane and then click the OK button to close the Insert Address Block dialog box.

9. Select today's date for the date placeholder.

10. Delete the placeholder for the salutation. Click the *Greeting line* option from the Mail Merge task pane, select any salutation, then click the OK button.

11. Replace the placeholder for the letter's text with:

I'm pleased to announce that Perfect Pizza has opened a new branch in your neighborhood! Stop by anytime this week for a free slice of pizza!

12. Delete the placeholder for the name at the bottom of the page. Replace the placeholder for the closing with:

Sincerely,

Paul DiCella

• Using the Mail Merge Wizard (continued)

13. From the Mail Merge task pane, click *Next: Preview your letter*s. Use the Forward and Back buttons on the Mail Merge task pane to view the merged letters.

14. From the Mail Merge task pane, click *Next: Complete the merge*. On the task pane, click *Edit individual letters*. Click All, then click the OK button. The mail merge is complete. Scroll down the document. You should have three individually addressed letters.

15. Compare the first letter to the document shown below. Don't worry if the date is different.

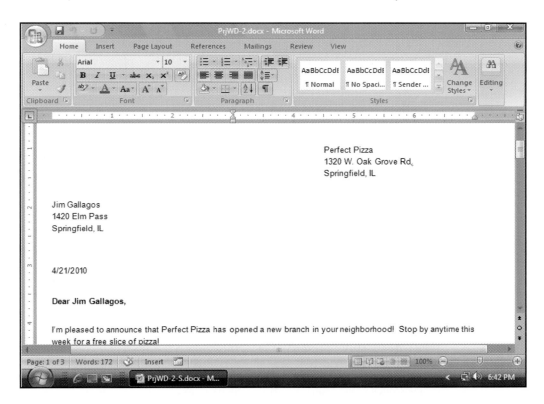

16. Save your document in your Project Folder using the file name PrjWD-2-XXXXX-9999, where XXXXX is your student ID number and 9999 is your class section number.

17. Use one of the following options to submit your project on a USB flash drive or floppy disk, as a printout, or as an e-mail attachment, according to your instructor's directions:

• To submit the file from your Project Folder where it is currently stored, stop the Word program by closing its window. Copy the file to a USB flash drive or floppy disk. Include your name, student ID number, class section number, date, and PrjWD-2 when you submit the file.

• To print the project, click the Microsoft Office button, then click Print. Click the OK button. Write your name, student ID number, class section number, date, and PrjWD-2 on the printouts.

• To e-mail the file, use Method 1 or Method 2, as described on page 348. Type your instructor's e-mail address in the To: box. Click the Subject: box and type PrjWD-2, your student ID number, and your class section number. Click the Send button or perform any additional steps required by your e-mail software to send an e-mail message.

Project WD-3: Cut, Copy, and Paste

In this project, you'll apply what you've learned about Microsoft Word to copy and paste text, and automatically insert special symbols such as the date and time.

Requirements: This project requires Microsoft Word and Microsoft Excel.

Project file: PrjWD-3.xlsx

CopyIt!

1. Copy the file PrjWD-3.xlsx to your Project Folder using the Copy It! button on this page in the BookOnCD.

2. Start Microsoft Word.

3. Create a new document containing the text below, placing a blank line between each paragraph.

MEMO

To: All staff

Date:

Congratulations to Maria, winner of our quarterly sales bonus! Maria has sold over 1,000 SuperWidgets this year!

Sales totals are as follows:

4. Press the Enter key.

5. Start Microsoft Excel.

6. Click the Microsoft Office button, then click Open to open the file PrjWD-3.xlsx from your Project Folder.

7. Highlight cells A1 through D9. To do this, first click cell A1 where it says "Monthly Sales Totals by Salesperson." Next, hold down the Shift key and click cell D9 that contains $1,004.26.

8. Copy the cells using the Copy button in the Clipboard group on the Home tab. As an alternative, you can use the Ctrl-C key combination.

9. Switch back to Microsoft Word.

10. Make sure the insertion point is positioned below the last line of the document.

11. Use the Paste button in the Clipboard group on the Home tab (or press Ctrl-V) to paste the spreadsheet data into the document.

12. Switch back to Microsoft Excel. Copy the Congratulations clip art from the spreadsheet. Switch to Microsoft Word and paste the clip art into the document. Use the Text Wrapping options on the Picture Tools contextual tab to size and position the clip art just to the right of the memo heading lines containing: MEMO, To, and Date.

13. If the Paste operation was successful, switch back to Microsoft Excel and close it.

14. In your Microsoft Word document, position the insertion point after the word "Date" on the third line of the memo. If necessary, press the Spacebar to create a space after the colon.

• Cut, Copy, and Paste (continued)

15. Click the Insert tab, then click Date & Time in the Text group. Choose the third option to insert the date in the format *March 16, 2010*. Click the OK button to insert the date and time.

16. Position the insertion point at the end of the word SuperWidgets.

17. On the Insert tab, click Symbols in the Symbols group, then click More Symbols. Select the trademark symbol. Click Insert, then click Close.

18. Your memo should look similar to the one below.

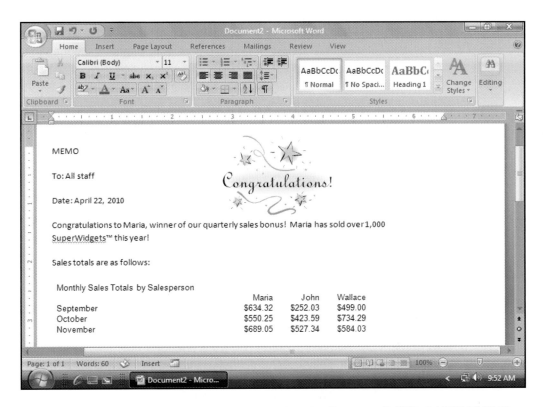

19. Save your memo in your Project Folder using the file name PrjWD-3-XXXXX-9999, where XXXXX is your student ID number and 9999 is your class section number. Use one of the following options to submit your project:

- To submit the file from your Project Folder where it is currently stored, stop the Word program by closing its window. Copy the file to a USB flash drive or floppy disk. Include your name, student ID number, class section number, date, and PrjWD-3 when you submit the file.

- To print the project, click the Microsoft Office button, then click Print. Click the OK button. Write your name, student ID number, class section number, date, and PrjWD-3 on the printouts.

- To e-mail the file, use Method 1 or Method 2, as described on page 348. Type your instructor's e-mail address in the To: box. Click the Subject: box and type PrjWD-3, your student ID number, and your class section number. Click the Send button or perform any additional steps required by your e-mail software to send an e-mail message.

Project WD-4: Troubleshooting Printing Problems

Sometimes documents fail to print. In this project, you'll experiment with various techniques to troubleshoot common printing problems.

Requirements: This project requires Microsoft Word.

Project file: No files are needed for this project.

1. Start Microsoft Word.

2. Create a new document containing the title below. As you go along, you can add to the document your answers for questions posed in Steps 4–6.

Exploring Printing Problems

3. Before printing, it is important to make sure your printer is plugged in, turned on, and online. Draw a diagram of the printer currently connected to your computer and label the power switch, power light, online light, and control panel. Also, look for the brand name and model of the printer and write it down.

4. One of the most common causes of printing problems is selecting the wrong printer. Use the Microsoft Office button to select Print. When the Print dialog box appears, write the name of the printer displayed in the Name box in your Exploring Printing Problems document. Is it the same as the printer you worked with in Step 3? If not, select the correct printer using the down-arrow button on the Name box.

5. Microsoft Windows provides help for troubleshooting printing problems. Open Windows Help and Support by clicking the Start button, then clicking Help and Support. Enter printer problems in the Search box and press the Enter key. If you are using Windows Vista, select *Troubleshoot printer problems* to view a list of possible problems. If you are using Windows XP, first select *Fixing a printing problem*, and then select *Use the Printing Troubleshooter*. Choose three problems from the list displayed and look at the suggested solutions. Summarize what you learn in your Exploring Printing Problems document.

6. Printers are ultimately controlled by the Windows operating system. Use the Start menu to access the Control Panel. If you are using Windows Vista, use the Printer option under Hardware and Sound to view a list of printers. If you are using Windows XP, use the Printers and Other Hardware option. Add the names of these printers to your Exploring Printing Problems document. Indicate which printer is the default. Check the print queue for the default printer. If it contains documents, list them and their status.

7. You can print a test page to make sure the printer is working properly. Right-click your printer, and then select Properties. From the General tab, select Print Test Page. The test page might look similar to the figure on the next page.

• Troubleshooting Printing Problems (continued)

Windows
Printer Test Page

Congratulations!

If you can read this information, you have correctly installed your SnagIt 8 Printer on D7SQJZB1.

The information below describes your printer driver and port settings.

```
Submitted Time: 10:03:59 AM 4/22/2010
Computer name:   D7SQJZB1
Printer name:    SnagIt 8
Printer model:   SnagIt 8 Printer
Color support:   Yes
Port name(s):    C:\ProgramData\TechSmith\SnagIt 8\PrinterPortFile
Data format:     RAW
Share name:
Location:
Comment:
Driver name:     UNIDRV.DLL
Data file:       SNAGITP8.GPD
Config file:     UNIDRVUI.DLL
Help file:       UNIDRV.HLP
Driver version:  6.00
Environment:     Windows NT x86

Additional files used by this driver:
  C:\Windows\system32\spool\DRIVERS\W32X86\3\SNAGITD8.DLL          (8.2.1.215)
  C:\Windows\system32\spool\DRIVERS\W32X86\3\STDNAMES.GPD
  C:\Windows\system32\spool\DRIVERS\W32X86\3\UNIRES.DLL   (6.0.6000.16386
(vista_rtm.061101-2205))
  C:\Windows\system32\spool\DRIVERS\W32X86\3\SNAGITP8.INI

This is the end of the printer test page.
```

8. Save your Exploring Printing Problems document in your Project Folder using the file name PrjWD-4-XXXXX-9999, where XXXXX is your student ID number and 9999 is your class section number.

9. Print your Exploring Printing Problems document and submit it along with your printer sketch and the test printout. Write your name, student ID number, class section number, date, and PrjWD-4 on all the submitted papers.

Project WD-5: **Formatting a Document**

In this project, you'll apply what you've learned about Microsoft Word to format an existing document.

Requirements: This project requires Microsoft Word.

Project file: PrjWD-5.docx

1. Copy the file PrjWD-5.docx to your Project Folder using the Copy It! button on this page in the BookOnCD.

2. Start Microsoft Word.

3. Open the file PrjWD-5.docx from your Project Folder.

4. Apply the bold text attribute to the line Memorandum - Novel-Tea & Coffee, Inc.

5. Apply italics to the phrase air-tight in the sentence that begins Please don't forget.

6. Apply bold and underlining to the phrase number one in the last sentence.

7. Select the Memorandum line, then change its font to Book Antiqua, size 18.

8. Center the Memorandum line.

9. Select the word Memorandum. Use the Change Case button in the Font Group on the Home tab to select UPPERCASE.

10. Select the list of items starting with Bean quality, then format the list as a bulleted list.

11. Indent the first line of the main paragraphs by .4". The three paragraphs that you'll indent begin Just a reminder, Please don't forget, and Thanks for helping.

12. Change the line spacing to 1.5 lines for the paragraphs that begin Just a reminder, Please don't forget, and Thanks for helping.

13. Remove the underlining from the phrase number one in the last sentence.

14. Justify the paragraphs that begin Just a reminder, Please don't forget, and Thanks for helping so that both the left and right margins are straight.

15. For justified paragraphs, hyphenation can reduce some of the extra spacing added between words. On the Page Layout tab, click Hyphenation in the Page Setup group, then click Hyphenation Options. Place a checkmark in the box *Automatically hyphenate document*. Uncheck the box *Hyphenate words in CAPS*.

16. Change the number in the Hyphenation zone box to .35" to increase the space allowed between the end of a line and the right margin. This setting produces fewer hyphens in a document, but allows the right margin to become somewhat ragged.

17. Enter the number 1 for the *Limit consecutive hyphens to* box. Professional publishers prefer not to have more than one consecutive line ending with hyphens.

18. Click the OK button to close the Hyphenation dialog box, then compare your document with the document in the figure on the next page.

• **Formatting a Document (continued)**

MEMORANDUM - Novel-Tea & Coffee, Inc.

To: Tea n' Coffee Shop Managers
From: Food and Beverage Director, Novel-Tea & Coffee
RE: Reminder – Fundamentals of Coffee-making

Just a reminder to all Tea n' Coffee Shop managers that it takes more than our fine beans to make a quality cup of coffee. Sometimes our employees are so busy frothing cream or sprinkling cinnamon that they can forget the five key factors to creating the best possible cup of coffee. Listed below are the five fundamentals of superb coffee creation:

- Bean quality
- Water purity
- Elapsed time from roasting beans to perking
- Cleanliness of equipment
- Elapsed time from grinding beans to perking

Please don't forget to store all beans in clean, glass, *air-tight* containers to retain the freshness and aroma of the coffee beans. Beans from your weekly shipment that you don't anticipate using within the week must be kept in the refrigerator or freezer. This retains flavor by preventing chemical reactions in the beans.

Thanks for helping to make Tea n' Coffee Shops **number one** in the tri-state area.

---

19. Save your document in your Project Folder using the file name PrjWD-5-XXXXX-9999, where XXXXX is your student ID number and 9999 is your class section number.

20. Use one of the following options to submit your project on a USB flash drive or floppy disk, as a printout, or as an e-mail attachment, according to your instructor's directions:

- To submit the file from your Project Folder where it is currently stored, stop the Word program by closing its window. Copy the file to a USB flash drive or floppy disk. Include your name, student ID number, class section number, date, and PrjWD-5 when you submit the file.

- To print the project, click the Microsoft Office button, then click Print. Click the OK button. Write your name, student ID number, class section number, date, and PrjWD-5 on the printout.

- To e-mail the file, use Method 1 or Method 2, as described on page 348. Type your instructor's e-mail address in the To: box. Click the Subject: box and type PrjWD-5, your student ID number, and your class section number. Click the Send button or perform any additional steps required by your e-mail software to send an e-mail message.

Project WD-6: Using Tabs and Paragraph Alignment

In this project, you'll focus on font formats and tab settings.

Requirements: This project requires Microsoft Word.

Project file: PrjWD-6.docx

1. Copy the file PrjWD-6.docx to your Project Folder using the Copy It! button on this page in the BookOnCD.

2. Start Microsoft Word.

3. Open the file PrjWD-6.docx from your Project Folder.

4. Select the document title How Much Lead Is in Your Cup?, then use the Font dialog box to change the title font to size 26, dark blue, bold italic with a shadow effect.

5. Select the list of items starting with Perked coffee 90-150 mg and ending with Tea 30-70 mg. Use the Tabs dialog box to set a left tab at the 1" position. Set another left tab at the 3" position, with a dotted leader. Close the Tab dialog box.

6. Position the insertion point to the left of Perked coffee, then press the Tab key to move it to the first tab position. Place the insertion point to the left of 90-150 mg, then press the Tab key to move it to the second tab position and display the dotted leader. Use a similar process with the remaining two list items.

7. Position the insertion point at the end of the line that ends with 30-70 mg, then press the Enter key to create a new line. Add this fourth list item, with appropriate tabs: Colas 30-45 mg.

8. Click the ¶ Show/Hide button in the Paragraph group on the Home tab to display non-printing characters. Notice that the locations in which you pressed the Tab key are indicated by arrows. The locations where you pressed the Enter key are indicated by the ¶ symbol.

9. Position the insertion point to the left of any ¶ symbol in the document. Press the Delete key to delete it. By removing this line break symbol, you joined two lines together.

10. To reestablish the original line break, click the Undo button on the Quick Access toolbar near the Microsoft Office button.

11. At the top of the document, replace Juan T. Sposito with your name.

12. Compare your completed document with the document in the figure on the next page.

● Using Tabs and Paragraph Alignment (continued)

Novel-Tea News
Reporter: [Student name here]

How Much Lead is in Your Cup?

Caffeine is a product found in many popular beverages. Yet most people are trying to curb their daily caffeine intake. After all, the effects of excessive caffeine have recently received a lot of press coverage.

As employees of Novel-Tea & Coffee, you will often get caffeine-related questions from customers. The following list of common drinks paired with their caffeine content may help you answer many of those questions.

Perked coffee .... 90-150 mg
Instant coffee .... 60-80 mg
Tea .... 30-70 mg
Colas..................................... 30-45 mg

Most customers also associate caffeine with chocolate. A typical chocolate bar contains 30 mg of caffeine. Yes, a cup of perked coffee does have three to five times the caffeine of a chocolate bar, but doesn't a chocolate bar have a few more calories than a cup of perked coffee?

So hopefully this information will help you answer commonly asked questions about caffeine and help us better serve our customers.

---

13. Save your document in your Project Folder using the file name Project WD-6 XXXXX 9999, where XXXXX is your student ID number and 9999 is your class section number.

14. Use one of the following options to submit your project on a USB flash drive or floppy disk, as a printout, or as an e-mail attachment, according to your instructor's directions:

● To submit the file on the Project Folder where it is currently stored, stop the Word program by closing its window. Copy the file to a USB flash drive or floppy disk. Include your name, student ID number, class section number, date, and Project WD-6 when you submit the file.

● To print the project, click File on the Word menu bar, then click Print. Click the OK button. Write your name, student ID number, class section number, date, and Project WD-6 on the printout.

● To e-mail the file, use Method 1 or Method 2, as described on page 348. Type your instructor's e-mail address in the To: box. Click the Subject: box and type Project WD-6, your student ID number, and your class section number. Click the Send button or perform any additional steps required by your e-mail software to send an e-mail message.

Project WD-7: Finalizing a Document

In this project, you'll apply what you've learned about Microsoft Word to check a document for errors, correct mistakes, set margins, use styles, display document statistics, add headers, and add footers. You'll also add footnotes, endnotes, and citations, plus find out how to assemble citations into a bibliography.

Requirements: This project requires Microsoft Word.

Project file: PrjWD-7.docx

1. Copy the file PrjWD-7.docx to your Project Folder using the Copy It! button on this page in the BookOnCD.

2. Start Microsoft Word.

3. Open the file PrjWD-7.docx from your Project Folder.

4. Use the Margins button on the Page Layout tab to set the right and left margins of the document to 1.25".

5. Use the right-click method to check the spelling of any words with a wavy red underline. If the spell checker catches any proper names that you'd like to add to your custom dictionary, right-click and choose Add to Dictionary.

6. Use the right-click method to correct the grammar of any phrases with wavy green underlines.

7. Use the thesaurus to select a more appropriate word to replace serious in the first sentence of the third paragraph.

8. Add a header to the document that includes your name and your student ID number on one line; add your class section number and PrjWD-7 on a second line.

9. Add a left-justified footer that shows the word Page followed by the page number.

10. Apply the Heading 1 style to the first line in the document.

11. Click the Office button and then click the Word Options button. Select the Proofing option and make sure that the boxes for checking grammar and showing readability statistics are checked. Return to the document and perform a spelling check to view readability statistics.

12. Use the Find button on the Home tab to locate the word "BAR." Select the Reference tab and then add an endnote "Browning Automatic Rifle."

13. Position the insertion point at the end of the paragraph on the first page that ends "...shot as spies." Use the Insert Citation button to add a citation to the book, *Insights into History* by Jefferson MacGruder, published in 2008 by Random House (New York).

14. Go to the end of the document and right-click the endnote. Select Convert to Footnote to move it to the bottom of the page on which it is referenced.

15. Go to the end of the document once again. Cursor down to a blank line and then Click the Bibliography button on the References tab. Select the Works Cited option. Make sure that that the Works Cited section of your document looks like the sample on the next page.

• Finalizing a Document (continued)

In the big picture of World War II, Art and Ron were part of a desperate effort to repulse a last-ditch German attack that began on December 16. Many historians (Jones, 1998) now note that the Axis was on the brink of collapse and further struggle simply prolonged the course of the war and needlessly increased the number of casualties on both sides of the struggle.

Works Cited

Jones, G. (1998). *World War II Reconstructed.* Boston: Little Brown.

MacGruder, J. (2009). *Insights into History.* New York: Random House.

---

16. Save your document in a Project Folder using the file name PrjWD-7-XXXXX-9999, where XXXXX is your student ID number and 9999 is your class section number.

17. Click the Office button and select the Send option. To find out if you can fax this document, select the Internet Fax option. If your computer is not configured for faxing, click the OK button to read about fax services. You do not have to sign up with a fax service for this project, so close your browser and proceed to the next step.

18. Click the Office button again, but this time select Publish. Notice the Blog option that would let you post this document directly to your blog. To use this option, however, you would have to sign up for a blog and then configure Word with the name and location of your blog. It is not necessary to post this document to a blog for this project.

19. Review your document. Make sure it contains citations in parentheses for MacGruder on page 1 and Jones on page 3, a footnote at the bottom of page 1, and a Works Cited section at the end of the document.

20. Use one of the following options to submit your project on a USB flash drive or floppy disk, as a printout, or as an e-mail attachment, according to your instructor's directions:

- To submit the file from your Project Folder where it is currently stored, stop the Word program by closing its window. Copy the file to a USB flash drive or floppy disk. Include your name, student ID number, class section number, date, and PrjWD-7 when you submit the file.

- To print the project, click the Microsoft Office button, then click Print. Click the OK button. Write your name, student ID number, class section number, date, and PrjWD-7 on the printout.

- To e-mail the file, use Method 1 or Method 2, as described on page 348. Type your instructor's e-mail address in the To: box. Click the Subject: box and type PrjWD-7, your student ID number, and your class section number. Click the Send button or perform any additional steps required by your e-mail software to send an e-mail message.

Project WD-8: Creating a Table

In this project, you'll apply what you've learned about Microsoft Word to create a table in a document.

Requirements: This project requires Microsoft Word.

Project file: PrjWD-8.docx

1. Copy the file PrjWD-8.docx to your Project Folder using the Copy It! button on this page in the BookOnCD.

2. Start Microsoft Word.

3. Open the file PrjWD-8.docx from your Project Folder.

4. Insert a table before the paragraph that starts Because of the special nature. The table should consist of four columns and seven rows and have a fixed column width.

5. Enter the following four labels into the first row of the table:

COFFEE (16 oz.)　　TOTAL CALORIES　　CALORIES　　FROM FAT

6. Select the leftmost column. Resize it by using the Table Tools Layout contextual tab. Change Width in the Cell Size group to 2.5 inches. Center the label using the Align Top Center button in the Alignment group.

7. You can combine two cells into one cell. Select the cells containing the labels CALORIES and FROM FAT. Click Merge Cells in the Merge Group. Fix the label so that it fits on one line.

8. With the merged cell still selected, create a new cell next to the merged cell by clicking Split Cells in the Merge Group. Select 2 for number of columns and 1 for number of rows.

9. Enter the label FAT (grams) in the new cell.

10. Your labels should look similar to the example below. Enter the following data into the cells of the table, under the appropriate labels:

COFFEE (16 oz.)	TOTAL CALORIES	CALORIES FROM FAT	FAT (grams)
Black Coffee	0	0	0
Cafe Latte (non-fat milk)	126	0	0
Cafe Latte (whole milk)	204	99	11
Cappuccino (non-fat milk)	75	0	0
Cappuccino (whole milk)	120	54	6
Cafe Mocha (non-fat milk)	174	18	2

11. Insert one more row into the table and enter the following data:

Cafe Mocha (whole milk)	234	90	10

12. You can split a table if you need to. Select the cell in the first column, fifth row, and click Split Table in the Merge group. Click the Undo button in the Quick Access toolbar to go back to your original table.

13. Using the Table Tools Layout contextual tab, delete the row containing Black Coffee.

• Creating a Table (continued)

14. Click Sort in the Data Group of the Table Tools Layout contextual tab to sort the data in ascending order, first by TOTAL CALORIES, then by COFFEE. Select the number type for TOTAL CALORIES and the text type for COFFEE.

15. Click the Table Tools Design contextual tab. Highlight all the labels, click Shading in the Table Styles group, and select the Light Blue standard color.

16. With all the labels still highlighted, click Borders in the Table Styles group and select No Borders. Click the Undo button in the Quick Access toolbar to restore the borders.

17. To automatically format the table, use the Table Styles group on the Table Tools Design contextual tab. Select the Medium List 2 - Accent 2 format.

18. If needed, insert a blank line so that the table is separated from the paragraphs above and below it.

19. At the top of the document, replace the reporter's name with your own name.

20. Compare your document to the figure below.

Novel-Tea News
Reporter: [Student Name]

How Much Fat Is in Your Cup?

As employees of Novel-Tea & Coffee, you may be asked about the calories and the fat content of some of our standard and specialty drinks. The following list of standard drinks with their caloric and fat contents may help you answer those questions.

COFFEE (16 oz.)	TOTAL CALORIES	CALORIES FROM FAT	FAT (grams)
Cappuccino (non-fat milk)	75	0	0
Cappuccino (whole milk)	120	54	6
Café Latte (non-fat milk)	126	0	0
Café Mocha (non-fat milk)	174	18	2
Café Latte (whole milk)	204	99	11
Café Mocha (whole milk)	234	90	10

Because of the special nature of our monthly spotlight drinks, they are likely to be higher in both calories and fat content than any of the above drinks. We'll try to get you the data on a spotlight drink when we announce the drink.

If a customer is troubled by the calories or fat content of a particular drink, suggest a drink that's similar, but with fewer calories or less fat. For example, suggest a cappuccino instead of a café latte, or recommend using non-fat milk instead of whole milk. Hopefully this information will help you answer commonly asked questions and help us better serve our customers.

---

21. Save your document in your Project Folder using the file name PrjWD-8-XXXXX-9999, where XXXXX is your student ID number and 9999 is your class section number. Submit your project on a USB flash drive or floppy disk, as a printout, or as an e-mail attachment, according to your instructor's directions.

Project WD-9: Using SmartArt Graphics

In this project, you'll use the SmartArt Graphics options to customize a document.

Requirements: This project requires Microsoft Word.

Project file: PrjWD-9.docx

CopyIt!

1. Copy the file PrjWD-9.docx to your Project Folder using the Copy It! button on this page in the BookOnCD.

2. Start Microsoft Word.

3. Open the file PrjWD-9.docx from your Project Folder.

4. Position the insertion point in the text box that contains the text *SmartArt*, then delete the text.

5. With the insertion point still in the text box, click the Insert tab, then click the SmartArt button in the Illustrations group.

6. From the List tab, select the Basic Block List option, then click the OK button.

7. Insert the following items in the text boxes:

   Sledding
   Skating
   Sled Dog Racing
   Ice Sculptures

8. Delete the extra text box by selecting it, then pressing the Delete key on your keyboard.

9. From the Layouts group on the SmartArt Tools Design contextual tab, select the Vertical Box List layout.

10. From the SmartArt Styles group on the SmartArt Tools Design contextual tab, select the Subtle Effect Style.

11. Compare your document to the one on the next page.

• Using SmartArt Graphics (continued)

12. Save your document in your Project Folder using the file name PrjWD-9-XXXXX-9999, where XXXXX is your student ID number and 9999 is your class section number. Use one of the following options to submit your project on a USB flash drive or floppy disk, as a printout, or as an e-mail attachment, according to your instructor's directions:

• To submit the document from your Project Folder where it is currently stored, stop the Word program by closing its window. Copy the file to a USB flash drive or floppy disk. Include your name, student ID number, class section number, date, and PrjWD-9 when you submit the file.

• To print the project, click the Microsoft Office button, then click Print. Click the OK button. Write your name, student ID number, class section number, date, and PrjWD-9 on the printout.

• To e-mail the file, use Method 1 or Method 2, as described on page 348. Type your instructor's e-mail address in the To: box. Click the Subject: box and type PrjWD-9, your student ID number, and your class section number. Click the Send button or perform any additional steps required by your e-mail software to send an e-mail message.

Project EX-1: Creating a Worksheet

In this project, you'll apply what you've learned to create a worksheet using Microsoft Excel.

Requirements: This project requires Microsoft Excel.

Project file: No file is required for this project.

1. Start Microsoft Excel.

2. Use the Microsoft Office button to open the Excel Options dialog box. Use the Popular and Save tabs to make sure the user name and default file locations are correct. Click the OK button to save these settings if you have permission to modify them. Otherwise, click the Cancel button.

3. Enter the labels and values shown below:

	A	B	C	D	E	F
1	Phone Charges Per Roommate for February					
2	Basic Monthly Service Rate		20.44			
3	Long Distance Charges for Each Roommate:					
4			Jamesson	Coleman	Depindeau	Struthers
5			5.65	0.25	1.35	3.75
6			0.45	0.65	2.15	0.88
7			1.68	0.56	3.78	1.23
8				4.15	5.77	0.95
9				1.25		0.88
10				3.67		1.95
11						3.88
12	Total Long Distance					
13	Share of Basic Rate					
14	Total					

4. In cell C12, use the AutoSum button to calculate the sum of the cells in column C. Use a similar procedure to calculate the long distance call totals for Coleman, Depindeau, and Struthers in cells D12, E12, and F12.

5. In cell C13, create a formula to calculate Jamesson's share of the $20.44 basic monthly service rate by dividing the contents of cell D2 by 4. Create a similar formula for each roommate in cells D13, E13, and F13.

6. In cell C14, create a formula to calculate Jamesson's share of the total phone bill by adding the contents of cell C12 to the contents of cell C13. Create a similar formula for each roommate in cells D14, E14, and F14.

7. Change the contents of Cell A1 to Feb Phone.

8. Use the Undo button to change the label in cell A1 back to the original wording.

9. Compare your worksheet to the one shown in the figure on the next page.

• Creating a Worksheet (continued)

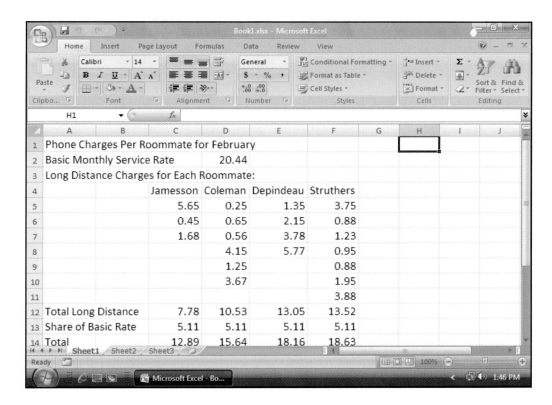

The worksheet (columns A–J) shows:

	A	B	C	D	E	F
1	Phone Charges Per Roommate for February					
2	Basic Monthly Service Rate		20.44			
3	Long Distance Charges for Each Roommate:					
4			Jamesson	Coleman	Depindeau	Struthers
5			5.65	0.25	1.35	3.75
6			0.45	0.65	2.15	0.88
7			1.68	0.56	3.78	1.23
8				4.15	5.77	0.95
9				1.25		0.88
10				3.67		1.95
11						3.88
12	Total Long Distance		7.78	10.53	13.05	13.52
13	Share of Basic Rate		5.11	5.11	5.11	5.11
14	Total		12.89	15.64	18.16	18.63

10. Save your worksheet in your Project Folder using the file name Project EX-1-XXXXX-9999, where XXXXX is your student ID number and 9999 is your class section number.

11. Use one of the following options to submit your project on a USB flash drive or floppy disk, as a printout, or as an e-mail attachment, according to your instructor's directions:

• To submit the file from your Project Folder where it is currently stored, stop the Excel program by closing its window. Copy the file to a USB flash drive or floppy disk. Include your name, student ID number, class section number, date, and PrjEX-1 when you submit the file.

• To print the project, click the Microsoft Office button, then click Print. Click the OK button. Write your name, student ID number, class section number, date, and PrjEX-1 on the printout.

• To e-mail the file, use Method 1 or Method 2, as described on page 348. Type your instructor's e-mail address in the To: box. Click the Subject: box and type PrjEX-1, your student ID number, and your class section number. Click the Send button or perform any additional steps required by your e-mail software to send an e-mail message.

Project EX-2: Using Functions

In this project, you'll apply what you've learned about AutoSum plus the MAX, MIN, AVERAGE, and IF functions to complete a Microsoft Excel worksheet.

Requirements: This project requires Microsoft Excel.

Project file: PrjEX-2.xlsx

1. Copy the file PrjEX-2.xlsx to your Project Folder using the Copy It! button on this page in the BookOnCD.

2. Start Microsoft Excel.

3. Open the file PrjEX-2.xlsx from your Project Folder.

4. Use the AutoSum button to display the total number of flights in cells B11 and C11.

5. In cell B12, use the MIN function to display the lowest number of Mango Air flights from the list that begins in cell B4 and ends in cell B10. Enter a similar function in cell C12 for Econo Air flights.

6. In cell B13, use the MAX function to display the highest number of Mango Air flights from the list that begins in cell B4 and ends in cell B10. Enter a similar function in cell C13 for Econo Air flights.

7. In cell B14, use a function to display the average number of Mango Air flights from the list that begins in cell B4 and ends in cell B10. Enter a similar function in cell C14 for Econo Air flights.

8. In cell D3, enter the label Most Flights and adjust the column width so the label fits in a single cell.

9. In cell D4, use the Logical button in the Function Library group on the Formulas tab to create an IF function that compares the number of flights for Mango Air and Econo Air. The IF function should display Econo Air in cell D4 if that airline has the most flights for Costa Rica. It should display Mango Air in cell D4 if that airline has the most flights. (Hint: Place quotation marks around "Econo Air" and "Mango Air" when you create the function, and remember that the Insert Function dialog box provides help and examples.)

10. Use the Fill option in the Editing group on the Home tab to copy the IF function from cell D4 down to cells D5 through D10.

11. In cell B16, use the Count function to display the number of destination countries for Mango Air flights from the list that begins in cell B4 and ends in cell B10. Enter a similar function in cell C16 for Econo Air flights.

12. Enter your name in cell E1.

13. Compare your worksheet to the one shown in the figure on the next page, but don't save it yet. You have one change to make in Step 14.

● Using Functions (continued)

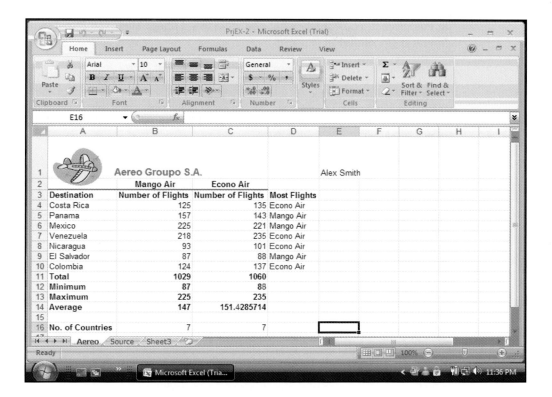

14. Change the number in cell C9 to 85.

15. Save your worksheet in your Project Folder using the file name PrjEX-2-XXXXX-9999, where XXXXX is your student ID number and 9999 is your class section number.

16. Use one of the following options to submit your project on a USB flash drive or floppy disk, as a printout, or as an e-mail attachment, according to your instructor's directions:

● To submit the file from your Project Folder where it is currently stored, stop the Excel program by closing its window. Copy the file to a USB flash drive or floppy disk. Include your name, student ID number, class section number, date, and PrjEX-2 when you submit the file.

● To print the project, click the Microsoft Office button, then click Print. Click the OK button. Write your name, student ID number, class section number, date, and PrjEX-2 on the printout.

● To e-mail the file, use Method 1 or Method 2, as described on page 348. Type your instructor's e-mail address in the To: box. Click the Subject: box and type PrjEX-2, your student ID number, and your class section number. Click the Send button or perform any additional steps required by your e-mail software to send an e-mail message.

Project EX-3: Formatting a Worksheet

In this project, you'll apply what you've learned about Microsoft Excel to complete and format a worksheet.

Requirements: This project requires Microsoft Excel.

Project file: PrjEX-3.xlsx

1. Copy the file PrjEX-3.xlsx to your Project Folder using the Copy It! button on this page in the BookOnCD.

2. Start Microsoft Excel.

3. Open the file PrjEX-3.xlsx from your Project Folder.

4. Click the  empty block between the "A" and "1" labels in the upper-left corner of the worksheet to select the entire worksheet.

5. Change the font size of the entire worksheet to 12 point.

6. Copy the formula from cell C6 to cells D6 and E6.

7. Copy the formula from cell C15 to cells D15 and E15.

8. Copy the formula from cell F4 to cells F5 through F6, and cells F9 through F15.

9. Insert a new, empty row before row 15.

10. Change the color of the text in cell A1 to dark blue.

11. Change the font in cell A1 to Times New Roman, size 14, bold.

12. Merge the contents of cells A1 through F1 so that the title is centered across those columns.

13. In cell A2, enter today's date.

14. Use the Dialog Box Launcher in the Number group to open the Format Cells dialog box. Select a date format that displays dates in the format *Wednesday, March 14, 2010*.

15. Merge the contents of cells A2 through F2 so that the date is centered.

16. Format cells A3 through F3 as bold text. Format cells A8 and A16 as bold text.

17. Format the numbers in cells C4 through E16 as currency.

18. Format the numbers in cells F4 through F16 as percentages (no decimal places).

19. Right-align the labels in cells C3 through F3.

20. Add both inside and outline borders to two cell ranges: B4 through F5 and B9 through F13.

21. Adjust the width of all columns so that all labels and values fit within the cells.

22. Now, explore what happens when you align some of the worksheet labels at a 90° angle. Select cells C3 through F3. Click the Orientation button in the Alignment group, then click Angle Counterclockwise.

• Formatting a Worksheet (continued)

23. Aligning column headings at a 90° angle is useful for worksheets that have many narrow columns. On this worksheet, however, the labels looked better at the normal angle, so use the Undo button in the Quick Access toolbar to undo the 90° angle.

24. Compare your worksheet to the one shown below.

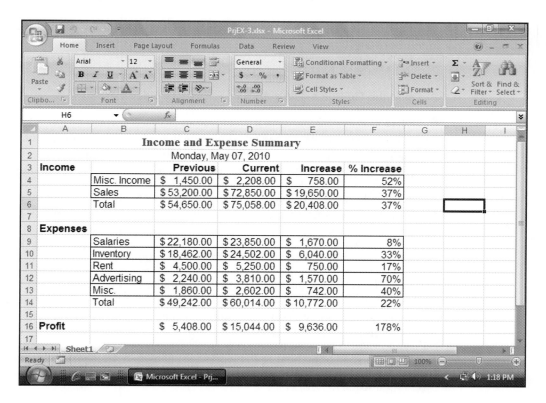

25. Save your worksheet in your Project Folder using the file name PrjEX-3-XXXXX-9999, where XXXXX is your student ID number and 9999 is your class section number.

26. Use one of the following options to submit your project on a USB flash drive or floppy disk, as a printout, or as an e-mail attachment, according to your instructor's directions:

• To submit the file from your Project Folder where it is currently stored, stop the Excel program by closing its window. Copy the file to a USB flash drive or floppy disk. Include your name, student ID number, class section number, date, and PrjEX-3 when you submit the file.

• To print the project, click the Microsoft Office button, then click Print. Click the OK button. Write your name, student ID number, class section number, date, and PrjEX-3 on the printout.

• To e-mail the file, use Method 1 or Method 2, as described on page 348. Type your instructor's e-mail address in the To: box. Click the Subject: box and type PrjEX-3, your student ID number, and your class section number. Click the Send button or perform any additional steps required by your e-mail software to send an e-mail message.

Project EX-4: Using Absolute and Relative References

In this project, you'll apply what you've learned about absolute and relative references to complete a sales commission worksheet.

Requirements: This project requires Microsoft Excel.

Project file: PrjEX-4.xlsx

CopyIt!

1. Copy the file PrjEX-4.xlsx to your Project Folder using the Copy It! button on this page in the BookOnCD.

2. Start Microsoft Excel.

3. Open the file PrjEX-4.xlsx from your Project Folder.

4. Notice that cell B2 contains a sales commission rate. Each salesperson receives a commission equal to his or her total sales multiplied by the commission rate. The commission rate changes periodically. The worksheet is set up so that if the sales manager changes the rate in cell B2, all the sales commissions will be recalculated.

5. Create a formula in cell B10 to calculate the sales commission for column B by multiplying the Total Sales in cell B9 by the Commission Rate in cell B2. (Hint: You must use an absolute reference for the Commission Rate in the formula.)

6. Copy the formula from cell B10 to cells C10 through E10.

7. Check the results of the copied formulas to make sure that they show the correct results. If cells C10 through E10 contain zeros, you did not use the correct absolute reference for the formula that you entered in Step 5. If necessary, modify the formula in B10, then recopy it to cells C10 through E10.

8. Compare your worksheet to the worksheet shown in the figure on the next page, but don't save it until you complete Steps 9 and 10.

• **Using Absolute and Relative References (continued)**

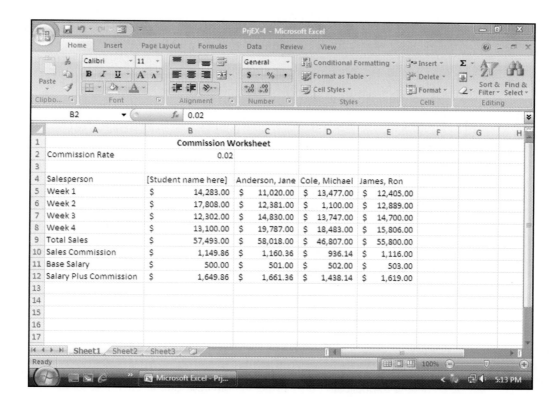

9. Change the contents of cell B2 to 0.03.

10. Enter your name in cell B4.

11. Save your worksheet in your Project Folder using the file name PrjEX-4-XXXXX-9999, where XXXXX is your student ID number and 9999 is your class section number.

12. Use one of the following options to submit your project on a USB flash drive or floppy disk, as a printout, or as an e-mail attachment, according to your instructor's directions:

• To submit the file from your Project Folder where it is currently stored, stop the Excel program by closing its window. Copy the file to a USB flash drive or floppy disk. Include your name, student ID number, class section number, date, and PrjEX-4 when you submit the file.

• To print the project, click the Microsoft Office button, then click Print. Click the OK button. Write your name, student ID number, class section number, date, and PrjEX-4 on the printout.

• To e-mail the file, use Method 1 or Method 2, as described on page 348. Type your instructor's e-mail address in the To: box. Click the Subject: box and type PrjEX-4, your student ID number, and your class section number. Click the Send button or perform any additional steps required by your e-mail software to send an e-mail message.

Project EX-5: Finalizing a Worksheet

In this project, you'll apply what you've learned about Microsoft Excel to complete a worksheet, freeze its titles, and finalize it for printing.

Requirements: This project requires Microsoft Excel.

Project file: PrjEX-5.xlsx

CopyIt!

1. Copy the file PrjEX-5.xlsx to your Project Folder using the Copy It! button on this page in the BookOnCD.

2. Start Microsoft Excel and open the file PrjEX-5.xlsx from your Project Folder.

3. Notice that when you scroll the worksheet, the title and column headings are no longer visible. To freeze the titles at the top of the screen, click cell A3. You've clicked this cell because you want the titles above row 3 to remain fixed in place when you scroll.

4. Click the View tab, click Freeze Panes in the Window group, then select Freeze Panes. Now scroll the worksheet and make sure that rows 1 and 2 remain in view.

5. Scroll down the worksheet and notice that data for the miniature gargoyles is not complete. Select cell B43 and use the Fill option and then the Series option to consecutively number the products. For example, The Miniature Dragon Gargoyle should have a product number of 359 and the Miniature War Horse should be 381.

6. All of the miniatures are the same size, weight, price, and shipping cost. Use the Fill command to duplicate the information from cells C43 through F43 for all miniature gargoyles.

7. Select cell B2. Use the Wrap Text button in the Alignment group to wrap the text.

8. Adjust the width of column B so that Product Number fits on two lines.

9. Right-justify the data in columns B through F, then center the titles for those columns.

10. Sort the data in cells A3 through F68 in A to Z order by Description.

11. Check the spelling of the worksheet and correct misspellings as needed.

12. Unfreeze the panes so that you can scroll the entire worksheet.

13. Add a right-justified header to the worksheet that includes your name, your student ID number, your class section number, today's date, and Prj EX-5.

14. Add a centered footer to the worksheet that includes the word Page followed by the page number. Hint: If you can't see header and footer elements such as Page Number, select the Design tab.

15. Switch back into Normal view and check the Print Preview to see how this worksheet is set up to print. Does it print all the miniature gargoyles? What's printed on the second page?

16. Close the Print Preview and look at the current print area, A1:I43. Part of the sheet is not included. Clear the print area so the entire sheet will be printed.

17. Use the options on the Page Layout tab to adjust the Width and Height settings to print the worksheet on a single piece of paper. Print your worksheet.

• Finalizing a Worksheet (continued)

18. The text on the single-page printout is quite small and let's suppose that you don't want to print the Discount Schedule. On the Page Layout tab, change the width and height to Automatic, and the scale to 100%.

19. Select cells A1 through F68 and designate this range as the print area, so that the Discount Schedule is not printed.

20. Use the Print Titles button to designate cells A1 through F2 as the title to print on every page.

21. Using Sheet Options, designate that you want to print gridlines and headings so that you can see the row numbers and column letters on the printout.

22. Set a page break at row 33. Hint: Select cell G33 before you click the Breaks button.

23. Look at a print preview of your worksheet. It should look similar to the two pages below.

Sara Smith
ID 345672342
Section 1020
January 20, 2010
Prj EX-5

	A	B	C	D	E	F
1	Gothic Gargoyle Collection					
2	Description	Product Number	Size	Weight	Price	Shipping
33	Medium Lion Gargoyle	889	3"Wx3"H	1.5	$29.95	$4.95
34	Medium Mounted Knight	891	3"Wx3"H	1.5	$29.95	$4.95
35	Medium Ring-Bearer	892	3"Wx3"H	1.5	$29.95	$4.95
36	Medium Treasure Chest Gargoyle	880	3"Wx3"H	1.5	$29.95	$4.95
37	Medium Troll	893	3"Wx3"H	1.5	$29.95	$4.95
38	Medium War Horse	900	3"Wx3"H	1.5	$29.95	$4.95
39	Medium Warrior with Axe	899	3"Wx3"H	1.5	$29.95	$4.95

Sara Smith
ID 345672342
Section 1020
January 20, 2010
Prj EX-5

	A	B	C	D	E	F
1	Gothic Gargoyle Collection					
2	Description	Product Number	Size	Weight	Price	Shipping
3	Ancient Burden Gargoyle	872	4"Wx2"H	16	$32.95	$5.95
4	Dwarf Dragon Gargoyle	561	3"Wx5"H	4	$12.95	$5.95
5	Dwarf Dragon Gargoyle	731	3"Wx7"H	5	$19.95	$5.95
6	Dwarf Florentine Gargoyle	810	2"Wx4"H	9	$14.95	$5.95
7	Dwarf Gnawing Gargoyle	994	3"Wx7"H	8	$10.95	$5.95
8	Dwarf Gothic Gruff	741	3"Wx7"H	7	$19.95	$5.95

24. Save your worksheet in your Project Folder using the file name PrjEX-5-XXXXX-9999, where XXXXX is your student ID number and 9999 is your class section number.

25. Submit your project on a USB flash drive or floppy disk, as a printout, or as an e-mail attachment, according to your instructor's directions.

Project EX-6: Creating Charts

In this project, you'll apply what you've learned about Microsoft Excel to create a column chart and a pie chart for an e-commerce worksheet.

Requirements: This project requires Microsoft Excel.

Project file: PrjEX-6.xlsx

1. Copy the file PrjEX-6.xlsx to your Project Folder using the Copy It! button on this page in the BookOnCD.

2. Start Microsoft Excel.

3. Open the file PrjEX-6.xlsx from your Project Folder.

4. Select the data in cells B3 through C6. Use the Insert tab to create a 3D pie chart. Add the chart title, Which Activities Lead?, above the chart. Use the Data Labels button to show percentages on the pie slices. Place the chart on a new sheet and name the sheet Comparison Chart.

5. Change the style of the chart to *Style 12* in the Chart Styles group on the Design contextual tab.

6. Change the chart background color to *Subtle Effect, Accent 2* in the Shape Styles group on the Format contextual tab.

7. Select the data in cells H4 through H9. Use the Insert tab to create a Clustered Column chart. Click the Select Data button in the Data group on the Design contextual tab. Click the Edit button for the Horizontal (Category) Axis Labels, then select cells G4 through G9, click the OK button to close the Axis Labels dialog box, then click the OK button to close the Select Data Source dialog box. Add the chart title, U.S. Projections, above the chart. Add a vertical Y-axis title, $ Billions. Remove the legend from the chart. Place the chart on a new sheet and name the sheet Growth Chart.

8. Change the chart type to *Line with markers* in the Type group on the Design contextual tab. Click the OK button to apply the chart type.

9. Examine the charts to ensure that the spreadsheet data is accurately represented. One easy verification technique is to identify a data trend and see if the trend is shown both in the data and on the chart. A trend in this data is the trend for projected growth to increase from one year to the next. Verify that the line chart corresponds to this trend by making sure the line moves up as it moves to the right.

Use care when identifying trends; make sure the conclusions you draw are accurate. Be aware of what can and can't be concluded from data. For example, although this data shows that 52% of e-commerce business activity is from business to consumer, it would be incorrect to assume that 52% of monetary transactions on a given day are from consumers to businesses.

10. Copy both charts to the E-Commerce tab.

11. Size and position the pie chart so that the top-left corner of the chart is in cell A10 and the bottom-right corner is in cell E23.

● Creating Charts (continued)

12. Size and position the line chart so that the top-left corner of the chart is in cell G11 and the bottom-right corner is in cell L23.

13. Click a blank cell in the worksheet, then open the Print Preview. Use Page Setup options to change the page orientation to Landscape and fit the worksheet on one page. The worksheet preview should look like the one shown in the figure below.

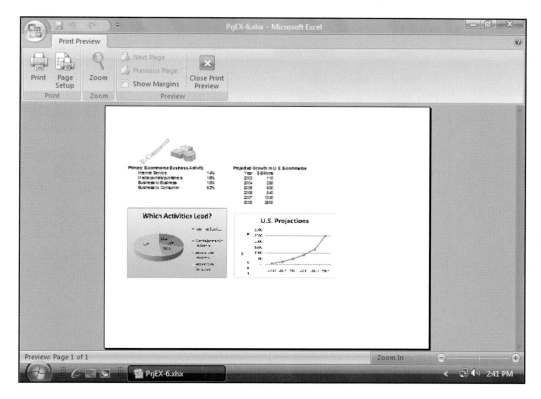

14. Save your worksheet in your Project Folder using the file name PrjEX-6-XXXXX-9999, where XXXXX is your student ID number and 9999 is your class section number.

15. Use one of the following options to submit your project on a USB flash drive or floppy disk, as a printout, or as an e-mail attachment, according to your instructor's directions:

● To submit the file from your Project Folder where it is currently stored, stop the Excel program by closing its window. Copy the file to a USB flash drive or floppy disk. Include your name, student ID number, class section number, date, and PrjEX-6 when you submit the file.

● To print the project, click the Microsoft Office button, then click Print. Click the OK button. Include your name, student ID number, class section number, date, and PrjEX-6 on the printout.

● To e-mail the file, use Method 1 or Method 2, as described on page 348. Type your instructor's e-mail address in the To: box. Click the Subject: box and type PrjEX-6, your student ID number, and your class section number. Click the Send button or perform any additional steps required by your e-mail software to send an e-mail message.

Project EX-7: Interpreting Worksheets and Charts

In this project, you'll practice identifying simple trends and drawing conclusions based on tabular information and charts. You'll also try your hand at sorting, ranking, and filtering data.

Requirements: This project requires Microsoft Excel.

Project file: PrjEX-7.xlsx

1. Copy the file PrjEX-7.xlsx to your Project Folder using the Copy It! button on this page in the BookOnCD.

2. Start Microsoft Excel and open the file PrjEX-7.xlsx from your Project Folder.

3. The worksheet contains raw data from the National Climatic Data Center. It is a 100-year record (1909–2008) of mean temperatures in the U.S. for the month of January. Examine the data. What would you guess is the average temperature for this 100-year period? Can you tell if temperatures seem to be increasing or decreasing? [   ]

4. To make it easier to analyze the data, highlight cells A3:B102 and use the Data tab's Sort button to arrange the temperatures in order from smallest to largest. The lowest temperature should be 22.57 in 1979. If your results are different, undo the sort and try it again, making sure to highlight both columns A and B.

5. Which year had the highest mean temperature and what was it ? [   ]

6. Do all of the highest temperatures appear to have occurred in the last 50 years? [   ]

7. Suppose you'd like to answer the question "In which years was the average temperature greater than 34 degrees?" Select Cells A2 and B2, which contain the Year and Temperature labels. Click the Data tab, and then click the Filter button. Click the down-arrow in column B, select Number Filters, and then click Greater Than. Enter 34 and then click the OK button. How many years had temperatures above 34 degrees? [   ]

8. Clear the filter by clicking the Filter button again.

9. Now, sort columns A and B by year from smallest to largest.

10. In cell E3, calculate the average temperature. Do temperatures before 1920 appear to be above or below average? [   ]

11. To identify trends in the temperatures, enter formulas in column E to compute the average January temperatures for each of the ten-year intervals listed in the Decade column. Which decade appears to have the highest average January temperatures? [   ]

12. Excel can automatically rank the decades so that you can easily see which decade was the warmest, which was the second warmest, and so on. Click cell F6 and enter the formula =RANK(E6, $E$6:$E$15). That formula should produce the number 8 to indicate that 1910-1919 was the 8th warmest decade. Copy the formula down through row 15. Which decade is ranked #9? [   ]

13. Create a pie chart of the data in cells E6 through E15. Does that chart make sense? Change the chart type and look at the data formatted as a column chart, a scatter chart, and a line chart. Which chart best shows the temperature trends over time, and which one best lets you compare temperatures from one decade to the next? [   ]

• Interpreting Worksheets and Charts (continued)

14. Select the clustered column chart type once again. Click the Select Data button on the Design tab. Click the Edit button for the Horizontal (Category) Axis Labels, then select cells D6 through D15 to display the decades on the horizontal axis. Click the OK button to close the Axis Labels dialog box, and then click the OK button to close the Select Data Source dialog box.

15. Use the Layout tab to add the chart title, Average Temperatures Per Decade, above the chart. Add a vertical Y-axis title, Degrees Fahrenheit. Remove the "Series 1" legend from the chart. Format the horizontal axis so the temperatures are displayed without decimal places. Compare your chart to the example below.

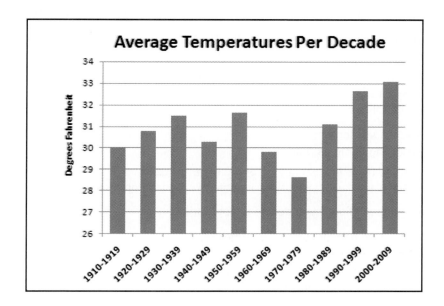

16. Move the chart on a new sheet tab and name the sheet Chart by Decade.

17. Examine the chart to ensure that the spreadsheet data is accurately represented. One easy verification technique is to identify a data trend and see if the trend is shown both in the data and on the chart. A trend in this data is the trend for the lowest temperatures in the 60s and 70s, and the highest in the last 20 years. Verify that the column chart corresponds to this trend.

18. You can add a trendline to your chart using the Trendline button on the Layout tab. Select Linear Trendline. According to this trendline, how would you characterize the temperature differences now compared to a hundred years ago? [_____]

19. To forecast trends based on your chart, select Trendline Options in the Format Trendline dialog box. Under Forecast, enter 2 in the Forward box. Based on this trendline what would you expect as the average temperature for the decade 2020-2029? [_____]

20. Add your name to cell G1 on the first worksheet. Save your project using the file name PrjEX-7-XXXXX-9999, where XXXXX is your student ID number and 9999 is your class section number. Submit your project on a USB flash drive or floppy disk, as a printout, or as an e-mail attachment, according to your instructor's directions.

Project PP-1: Creating a Presentation

In this project, you'll apply what you've learned to create a "tongue-in-cheek" PowerPoint presentation about e-commerce business trends.

Requirements: This project requires Microsoft PowerPoint.

Project file: No file is required for this project.

1. Start Microsoft PowerPoint.

2. Create a new presentation using any theme. The example on the next page shows the Trek theme.

3. Add a title slide, then enter Money Machine as the title. Enter your name as the subtitle.

4. Add a Title and Content slide. Enter The Web Economy as the slide title. Enter the following items as bullets:

> Growth is more important than profit.
> Scalability is crucial–we must be able to grow faster than the competition.
> It's OK to lose money–as long as we keep growing.

5. Add a Two Content slide. Enter We don't need profits because: as the slide title. Add the following items as bullets:

> Even if we lose money on every item, we can make it up in volume.
> What we can't make up in volume, we'll make up by selling banner ads.

Add whatever clip art you decide is appropriate.

6. Add a Title and Content slide. Enter Here's the Plan! as the slide title. Add the following items as bullets:

> Quickly expand to credit card sales!
> Expand into major international markets!

7. Experiment with changing the slide background by clicking Background Styles in the Background group on the Design tab. Select Format Background. Click the down-arrow button for Color and change the background color to *Light Turquoise, Background 2*. Close the Format Background dialog box.

8. Use the Undo button on the Quick Access toolbar to display the original background.

9. Compare your slides to those shown in the figure on the next page.

● Creating a Presentation (continued)

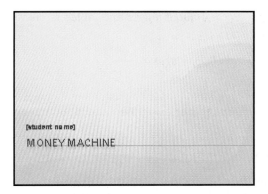

THE WEB ECONOMY

※ Growth is more important than profit.
※ Scalability is crucial – we must be able to grow faster than the competition.
※ It's OK to lose money – as long as we keep growing.

WE DON'T NEED PROFITS BECAUSE:

※ Even if we lose money on every item, we can make it up in volume.
※ What we can't make up in volume, we'll make up by selling banner ads.

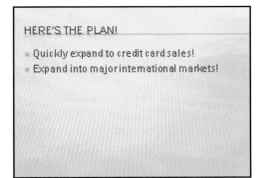

HERE'S THE PLAN!

※ Quickly expand to credit card sales!
※ Expand into major international markets!

10. Save your presentation using the file name PrjPP-1-XXXXX-9999, where XXXXX is your student ID number and 9999 is your class section number.

11. Use one of the following options to submit your project on a USB flash drive or floppy disk, as a printout, or as an e-mail attachment, according to your instructor's directions:

● To submit the file from your Project Folder where it is currently stored, stop the PowerPoint program by closing its window. Copy the file to a USB flash drive or floppy disk. Include your name, student ID number, class section number, date, and PrjPP-1 when you submit the file.

● To print the project, click the Microsoft Office button, then click Print. In the Print dialog box, look for the *Print what* section and use its pull-down list to select Handouts. Make sure that the *Handouts* section specifies 6 slides per page in Horizontal order. Also, make sure that the *Scale to fit paper* check box contains a checkmark. Click the OK button. Write your name, student ID number, class section number, date, and PrjPP-1 on the printout.

● To e-mail the file, use Method 1 or Method 2, as described on page 348. Type your instructor's e-mail address in the To: box. Click the Subject: box and type PrjPP-1, your student ID number, and your class section number. Click the Send button or perform any additional steps required by your e-mail software to send an e-mail message.

Project PP-2: Creating Slides with Charts and Tables

In this project, you'll apply what you've learned about charts and tables to create PowerPoint slides for a fitness center.

Requirements: This project requires Microsoft PowerPoint.

Project file: PrjPP-2.pptx

CopyIt!

1. Copy the file PrjPP-2.pptx to your Project Folder using the Copy It! button on this page in the BookOnCD.

2. Start Microsoft PowerPoint.

3. Open the file PrjPP-2.pptx from your Project Folder.

4. Add a Title and Content slide. Enter Target Heart Rates as the slide title. Add a table consisting of three columns and four rows, then enter the following data into the table:

Age	Minimum Rate	Maximum Rate
20	120	170
30	114	162
40	108	163

5. Select the slide you just made in the pane that contains the Slides and Outline tabs. Right-click the slide and select Duplicate Slide in the shortcut menu. Select the duplicate slide and change the slide title to Caloric Expenditures by Body Weight. Delete the table and create a column chart that shows the following data:

	125 Lbs.	175 Lbs.
Jogging	7.3	10.4
Swimming	6.9	9.8

Make sure you have the weight categories as the labels for the X-axis.

6. Compare your slides to those shown in the figure on the next page.

• Creating Slides with Charts and Tables (continued)

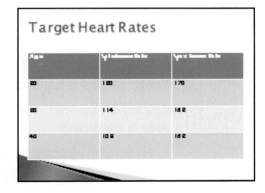

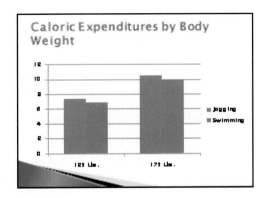

7. Save your presentation in your Project Folder using the file name PrjPP-2-XXXXX-9999, where XXXXX is your student ID number and 9999 is your class section number.

8. Use one of the following options to submit your project on a USB flash drive or floppy disk, as a printout, or as an e-mail attachment, according to your instructor's directions:

• To submit the file from your Project Folder where it is currently stored, stop the PowerPoint program by closing its window. Copy the file to a USB flash drive or floppy disk. Include your name, student ID number, class section number, date, and PrjPP-2 when you submit the file.

• To print the project, click the Microsoft Office button, then click Print. In the Print dialog box, look for the *Print what* section and use its pull-down list to select Handouts. Make sure that the *Handouts* section specifies 6 slides per page in Horizontal order. Also, make sure that the *Scale to fit paper* check box contains a checkmark. Click the OK button. Write your name, student ID number, class section number, date, and PrjPP-2 on the printout.

• To e-mail the file, use Method 1 or Method 2, as described on page 348. Type your instructor's e-mail address in the To: box. Click the Subject: box and type PrjPP-2, your student ID number, and your class section number. Click the Send button or perform any additional steps required by your e-mail software to send an e-mail message.

Project PP-3: Using Animations, Transitions, and Sounds

In this project, you'll apply what you've learned to add animations, transitions, and sounds to a PowerPoint presentation.

Requirements: This project requires Microsoft PowerPoint.

Project file: PrjPP-3.pptx

CopyIt!

1. Copy the file PrjPP-3.pptx to your Project Folder using the Copy It! button on this page in the BookOnCD.

2. Start Microsoft PowerPoint.

3. Open the file PrjPP-3.pptx from your Project Folder.

4. On the first slide, change the subtitle text *The time is right!* to Book Antiqua, size 44, bold, and italic.

5. Add the Uncover Down transition to the second slide.

6. Add the Fade Through Black transition to the third slide.

7. Add the Fly In animation (coming from the left) to the bulleted list on the third slide in the presentation. Add the Drum Roll transition sound effect to the animation.

8. View the presentation to see how the transition and animation effects work.

9. Switch to Slide Sorter View. You should see transition and animation icons under slides 2 and 3, as shown on the next page. Note: Don't worry about spelling errors. You will have an opportunity to fix them in the next project.

• Using Animations, Transitions, and Sounds (continued)

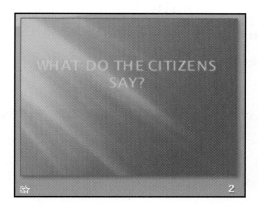

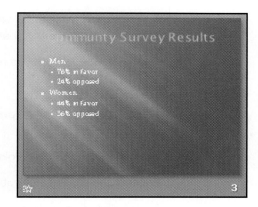

10. Save your presentation in your Project Folder using the file name PrjPP-3-XXXXX-9999, where XXXXX is your student ID number and 9999 is your class section number.

11. Use one of the following options to submit your project on a USB flash drive or floppy disk, as a printout, or as an e-mail attachment, according to your instructor's directions:

• To submit the file from your Project Folder where it is currently stored, stop the PowerPoint program by closing its window. Copy the file to a USB flash drive or floppy disk. Include your name, student ID number, class section number, date, and PrjPP-3 when you submit the file.

• To print the project, click the Microsoft Office button, then click Print. On the Print dialog box, look for the *Print what* section and use its pull-down list to select Handouts. Make sure that the *Handouts* section specifies 6 slides per page in Horizontal order. Also, make sure that the *Scale to fit paper* check box contains a checkmark. Click the OK button. Write your name, student ID number, class section number, date, and PrjPP-3 on the printout.

• To e-mail the file, use Method 1 or Method 2, as described on page 348. Type your instructor's e-mail address in the To: box. Click the Subject: box and type PrjPP-3, your student ID number, and your class section number. Click the Send button or perform any additional steps required by your e-mail software to send an e-mail message.

Project PP-4: Finalizing a Presentation

In this project, you'll apply what you've learned as you finalize a version of the Microsoft PowerPoint presentation that you worked with in Project PP-3.

Requirements: This project requires Microsoft PowerPoint.

Project file: PrjPP-4.pptx

1. Copy the file PrjPP-4.pptx to your Project Folder using the Copy It! button on this page in the BookOnCD.

2. Start Microsoft PowerPoint.

3. Open the file PrjPP-4.pptx from your Project Folder.

4. Use Slide Sorter View to move the Questions & Answers? slide to the end of the presentation.

5. Move the Best Site slide so that it comes immediately after the Potential Sites slide.

6. In Normal view, add the following speaker note to the first slide in the presentation: Introduce team members Jill Smith, David Byrne, and Tom Woods.

7. Add the following speaker note to the last slide in the presentation: Let's get a general idea of your reaction to the proposed golf course... raise your hand if you would like the project to proceed.

8. Delete the We need to proceed as quickly as possible! slide.

9. Check the spelling of all slides and make any necessary corrections.

10. Select the View tab and then click the Slide Master button. Select the first (and largest) master slide. Select "Click to edit Master title style." Go back to the Home tab and select a bright yellow color for the title text.

11. Look through the list of master slides and make sure that all the titles are bright yellow.

12. Switch back to Normal view and double-check the color of all the titles. If you need to make adjustments to the title colors, go back to Slide Master view.

13. In Slide Sorter View, compare your presentation to the one shown on the next page.

• Finalizing a Presentation (continued)

11. Save your presentation in your Project Folder using the file name PrjPP-4-XXXXX-9999, where XXXXX is your student ID number and 9999 is your class section number.

12. Use one of the following options to submit your project on a USB flash drive or floppy disk, as a printout, or as an e-mail attachment, according to your instructor's directions:

• To submit the file from your Project Folder where it is currently stored, stop the PowerPoint program by closing its window. Copy the file to a USB flash drive or floppy disk. Include your name, student ID number, class section number, date, and PrjPP-4 when you submit the file.

• To print the project, click the Microsoft Office button, then click Print. On the Print dialog box, look for the *Print what* section and use its pull-down list to select Handouts. Make sure that the *Handouts* section specifies 6 slides per page in Horizontal order. Also, make sure that the *Scale to fit paper* check box contains a checkmark. Click the OK button. Write your name, student ID number, class section number, date, and PrjPP-4 on the printout.

• To e-mail the file, use Method 1 or Method 2, as described on page 348. Type your instructor's e-mail address in the To: box. Click the Subject: box and type PrjPP-4, your student ID number, and your class section number. Click the Send button or perform any additional steps required by your e-mail software to send an e-mail message.

Project PP-5: Creating an Organization Chart

In this project, you'll explore the graphics capabilities of PowerPoint to create a presentation that includes an organization chart.

Requirements: This project requires Microsoft PowerPoint.

Project file: No file is required for this project.

1. Start Microsoft PowerPoint.

2. Create a new blank presentation. Select the first slide and change the layout to *Title and Content*.

3. Add the title Company Hierarchy.

4. Select the Insert SmartArt Graphic content icon. Select the Organization Chart option from the Hierarchy category.

5. Delete all boxes except the top tier by selecting the box, then clicking the Delete key. Add the title President to the top of the organization chart. Click the down-arrow button on the Add Shape button in the Create Graphic group on the SmartArt Tools Design contextual tab to create a second tier with three boxes containing the following text: VP Marketing, VP Research, and VP Operations.

6. Click any blank area of the President box. If you click the text and see an insertion bar, try again until the box itself is selected, not the text inside the box. Click the down-arrow button on the Add Shape button in the Create Graphic group to create an Assistant for the President.

7. Add the text Administrative Assistant to the new box.

8. Add four subordinates to the VP Marketing box. Type Marketing Rep in each subordinate box.

9. Select the VP Marketing box, select Layout in the Create Graphic group, and then select Left Hanging.

10. Remove one Marketing Rep box by selecting it, then clicking the Delete key.

11. Compare your slide to the one shown in the figure on the next page.

• **Creating an Organization Chart (continued)**

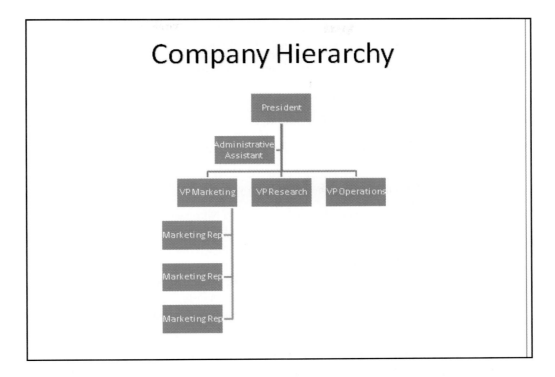

12. Add your name as a second line in the President box. To add text, click the text in the box. Use the End key to jump to the end of the line, and then press the Enter key. When the insertion point is on a new line, type the additional text.

13. Use the SmartArt Styles group to change the style for the organization chart to Subtle Effect.

14. Save your presentation in your Project Folder using the file name PrjPP-5-XXXXX-9999, where XXXXX is your student ID number and 9999 is your class section number.

15. Use one of the following options to submit your project on a USB flash drive or floppy disk, as a printout, or as an e-mail attachment, according to your instructor's directions:

• To submit the file from your Project Folder where it is currently stored, stop the PowerPoint program by closing its window. Copy the file to a USB flash drive or floppy disk. Include your name, student ID number, class section number, date, and PrjPP-5 when you submit the file.

• To print the project, click the Microsoft Office button, then click Print. On the Print dialog box, look for the *Print what* section and use its pull-down list to select Handouts. Make sure that the *Handouts* section specifies 6 slides per page in Horizontal order. Also, make sure that the *Scale to fit paper* check box contains a checkmark. Click the OK button. Write your name, student ID number, class section number, date, and PrjPP-5 on the printout.

• To e-mail the file, use Method 1 or Method 2, as described on page 348. Type your instructor's e-mail address in the To: box. Click the Subject: box and type PrjPP-5, your student ID number, and your class section number. Click the Send button or perform any additional steps required by your e-mail software to send an e-mail message.

Project PP-6: Working with Slide Graphics

In this project, you'll explore how to use Microsoft PowerPoint to add simple graphical elements to slides and change existing slide graphics.

Requirements: This project requires Microsoft PowerPoint.

Project file: PrjPP-6.pptx

CopyIt!

1. Copy the file PrjPP-6.pptx to your Project Folder using the Copy It! Button on this page in the BookOnCD.

2. Start Microsoft PowerPoint.

3. Open the file PrjPP-6.pptx from your Project Folder.

4. Display the first slide, which is titled Nitrogen Cycling. Select the chart by clicking the area just above the legend that contains Ammonia, Nitrite, and Nitrate. Now that the chart is selected, you can change various formats, such as the background color. Right-click any blank background area of the chart, then select Format Chart Area. When the Format Chart Area dialog box appears, select Solid fill. Click the down-arrow button for Color, and then select Dark Red under Standard Colors. Click the Close button to close the Format Chart Area dialog box and apply the new color.

5. Suppose you want to change the color of the Ammonia line to light blue. Click anywhere inside the legend that contains Ammonia, Nitrite, and Nitrate. Now that the legend is selected, click Ammonia, then right-click it. Select Format Data Series from the shortcut menu. When the Format Data Series dialog box appears, select Line Color in the left pane, then select Solid line. Click the down-arrow button for Color, then select Light Blue under standard colors. Click the Close button to close the Format Data Series dialog box and apply the new color.

6. Switch to the slide titled Losses in Fish Hatch. Suppose you decide that a different chart type would be more appropriate for displaying the information. To change the chart type, double-click the chart to select it. Click Change Chart Type in the Type Group on the Design tab. When the Change Chart Type dialog box appears, select Pie in the left pane, then select *Pie in 3-D* as the chart sub-type. Click the OK button to apply the new chart type. Click Style 2 in the Chart Styles group on the Design tab of the Chart Tools contextual tab.

7. Suppose you want to position the pie chart toward the center of the slide, with the legend to the right of it. Click the blank area to the left of the chart. When the chart box appears, hold down the left mouse button and drag the box toward the center of the slide. (Hint: Make sure your pointer is in the box, but not on the chart, when you drag the box.)

8. Now, suppose you want to duplicate this chart to another slide. Make sure the chart is selected. Click Copy in the Clipboard group on the Home tab. Switch to the slide titled Causes of Mortality and click Paste in the Clipboard group on the Home tab to paste the chart and legend on the slide. Position and size the chart on the right side of the slide so it visually balances the bullets.

• Working with Slide Graphics (continued)

9. You can use elements in the Drawing group on the Home tab to draw your own graphics that tie slide elements together. Switch to the slide titled Biological Cycling. You can follow the next set of steps to make the slide look like the one below:

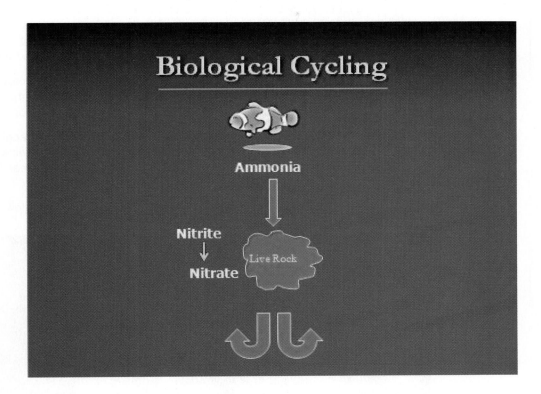

10. You can draw a line under the slide title by clicking the Line icon in the Drawing group. Position the pointer under the first letter of the title. While holding down the left mouse button, draw the line across the bottom of the title. Release the mouse button.

11. To draw the arrow that points down from Ammonia, click the Down Arrow icon in the Drawing group. Drag the pointer in the area under Ammonia. Resize and reposition the arrow as necessary.

12. Now, to add the thin arrow between Nitrite and Nitrate, click the Arrow icon in the Drawing group. Position the cursor below the word Nitrite. While holding down the left mouse button, draw an arrow to the word Nitrate, and then release the mouse button. Position the arrow so it is centered between the two text items.

13. Suppose you want to change the format of the thin arrow. Double-click the arrow, then click Shape Outline in the Shape Styles group of the Format tab. Select Yellow under Standard Colors. You can also change the line thickness using the Shape Outline option. Select Weight in the shortcut menu, and then select the 3 point option.

14. Suppose you want to duplicate a drawn object. Click the U-Turn arrow and click Copy in the Clipboard group on the Home tab. Now click Paste in the Clipboard group to paste the duplicate U-Turn arrow on the slide. To flip the arrow, click the left square (sizing handle) on the side of the arrow and hold your mouse pointer down to drag it to the right without changing the size of the arrow. Position the flipped arrow so it is right beside the original arrow, as illustrated above.

• **Working with Slide Graphics** (continued)

15. To add text to the slide, click the Insert tab and click Text Box in the Text group. Position the pointer just above the two U-Turn arrows. Drag a box shape and then type Live Rock.

16. Now, suppose you want to draw a freeform object. Click Shapes in the Illustrations group on the Insert tab. Under Lines, click the Freeform icon. Next, position the pointer just above your new text box; and while holding the left mouse button, draw a freeform object shaped somewhat like a cloud large enough to cover the new text box.

17. Notice that the new object is covering the text box. To change the order of your objects so that the text box is on top and the freeform object moves to the back, double-click the freeform object, then click *Send to Back* in the Arrange group of the Format tab.

18. Suppose you want to change the style of your freeform object. To apply a shadow effect, make sure your freeform object is selected, then click Shape Effects in the Shape Styles group of the Format tab. Select Shadow, then click *Inside Diagonal Top Left* in the Inner options list.

19. The set of slides in the PrjPP-6 presentation should look like the following:

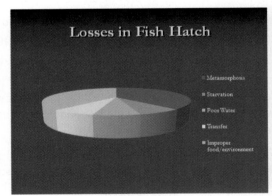

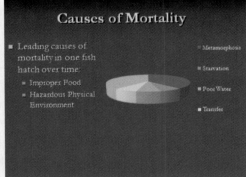

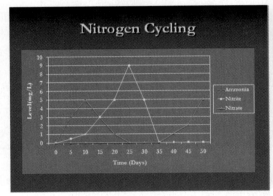

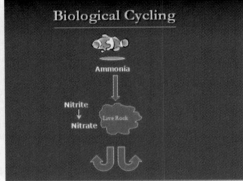

• Working with Slide Graphics (continued)

20. Now, create a new presentation using any design template you like. The presentation should contain one title slide and one blank slide. Enter Biological Cycling as the title for slide 1. Save the presentation in your Project Folder with the file name Executive Summary.

21. Next, duplicate the objects from slide 2 of the PrjPP-6 presentation to slide 2 of the Executive Summary presentation. To do so, switch to the PrjPP-6 presentation and display slide 2. Position the cursor at the top-right corner, hold down the left mouse button, and drag the box to the bottom-left corner. When you release the mouse button, all the objects should be selected. If not, repeat this step again. Click Copy in the Clipboard group of the Home tab. Switch to slide 2 of the Executive Summary presentation and click Paste in the Clipboard group to paste the objects on the blank slide.

22. Save the revised version of the Executive Summary presentation.

23. Save the PrjPP-6 presentation in your Project Folder using the file name PrjPP-6A-XXXXX-9999, where XXXXX is your student ID number and 9999 is your class section number. Save the Executive Summary presentation as PrjPP-6B-XXXXX-9999.

24. Use one of the following options to submit your project files on a USB flash drive or floppy disk, as printouts, or as e-mail attachments, according to your instructor's directions:

• To submit the files from your Project Folder where they are currently stored, stop the PowerPoint program by closing its window. Copy the files to a USB flash drive or floppy disk. Include your name, student ID number, class section number, date, and the project names when you submit the files.

• To print the two project files, click the Microsoft Office button, then click Print. On the Print dialog box, look for the *Print what* section and use its pull-down list to select Handouts. Make sure that the *Handouts* section specifies 6 slides per page in Horizontal order. Also, make sure that the *Scale to fit paper* check box contains a checkmark. Click the OK button. Write your name, student ID number, class section number, date, and PrjPP-6A and PrjPP-6B, respectively, on the printouts.

• To e-mail the two project files, use Method 1 or Method 2, as described on page 348, attaching both files to one e-mail message. Type your instructor's e-mail address in the To: box. Click the Subject: box and type PrjPP-6A and PrjPP-6B, your student ID number, and your class section number. Click the Send button or perform any additional steps required by your e-mail software to send an e-mail message.

Project PP-7: Working with Slide Text

In this project, you'll explore how to zoom in or zoom out to view a slide, and how to use the PowerPoint Options dialog box to configure user information and file location settings. You'll also explore how to copy, cut, and paste clip art and text; and you'll experiment with text formatting, and Undo and Redo options.

Requirements: This project requires Microsoft PowerPoint.

Project file: PrjPP-7.pptx

1. Copy the file PrjPP-7.pptx to your Project Folder using the Copy It! Button on this page in the BookOnCD.

2. Start Microsoft PowerPoint and open the file PrjPP-7.pptx from your Project Folder.

3. To explore what happens when you adjust the magnification level, click the View tab, then click Zoom in the Zoom group. When the Zoom dialog box appears, select 100%, then click OK. Notice that the slide is too big to fit in the window. Now, zoom to 50%. For the most practical magnification level, select the Fit option in the Zoom dialog box or click *Fit to Window* in the Zoom group on the View tab.

4. To explore how to configure a presentation's author information, click the Microsoft Office button, then click PowerPoint Options. When the PowerPoint Options dialog box appears, enter your name and initials in the boxes provided.

5. To adjust the Save options, click Save in the left pane. Typically, PowerPoint is configured to save presentations in the Documents or My Documents folder. If you want to change this setting, use the *Default file location* box to do so now.

6. To apply your new settings and close the PowerPoint Options dialog box, click the OK button.

7. Add a new slide at the end of the presentation. Select the *Title and Content* layout. Enter Top Three Sponsors as the slide title. Add the following items as three bullets:

Titleist

PepsiCo

PGA

8. Select the bullets and change them to a numbered list using the Numbering button in the Paragraph group on the Home tab.

9. Make sure all the bullets are selected, and then click Line Spacing in the Paragraph group on the Home tab. Select *Line Spacing Options*. When the Paragraph dialog box appears, change the line spacing from Single to Double, then click the OK button.

10. Switch to the slide titled *We need to proceed as quickly as possible*. Duplicate the clip art from this slide to the slide titled *Top Three Sponsors*. Adjust the position of the graphic so that it looks visually pleasing.

11. Switch back to the slide titled *We need to proceed as quickly as possible*. Suppose you would rather have this clip art image on the slide titled *What do the citizens say?* Select the clip art, copy it to the Clipboard, and paste it on the slide. Adjust the position of the graphic so that it looks visually pleasing.

• Working with Slide Text (continued)

12. Select the quoted text from the *What do the citizens say?* slide. To apply a shadow effect to the text, click the Text Shadow button in the Font group.

13. To explore the best alignment for the quoted text, click the Align Text Left button in the Paragraph group. Next, click the Align Text Right button. Finally, click the Center button.

14. Use the Undo button on the Quick Access toolbar to change back to right alignment. Use the Redo button to return the alignment to centered.

15. Make sure the rectangular quote text box is selected by clicking on the border of the text box. Move the entire text box to the *Top Three Sponsors* slide. You might need to reposition the text box just below the bullets.

16. Suppose you want to use the contents of this slide for another presentation. To select the entire contents of the slide, position the cursor at the top-right corner, hold down the left mouse button, and drag the box to the bottom-left corner. When you release the mouse button, all the objects should be selected. Click the Copy button in the Clipboard group on the Home tab. Now, create a new, blank PowerPoint presentation and select the blank layout for the first slide. Paste the contents of the golf slide into the new presentation. Your slide should look similar to the one shown in the figure below.

Top Three Sponsors

1. Titleist

2. PepsiCo

3. PGA

"We can depend on our current corporate sponsors to assist us with our plans for a new course, and it is likely that we can find additional sponsors once construction begins."

17. Switch to the *Advantages of a New Golf Course* slide in the original presentation. Use Cut in the Clipboard group on the Home tab to delete this slide from the presentation. Switch to your new presentation and paste the slide there. Your new presentation should now contain two slides.

18. Save the original presentation in your Project Folder using the file name Prj-PP-7A-XXXXX-9999, where XXXXX is your student ID number and 9999 is your class section number. Save the new presentation in your Project Folder as PrjPP-7B-XXXXX-9999.

19. Submit both presentations for this project on a USB flash drive or floppy disk, as printouts, or as e-mail attachments, according to your instructor's directions.

Project PP-8: Final Presentation Details

In this project, you'll explore how to add footers to slides and how to change slide setup.

Requirements: This project requires Microsoft PowerPoint.

Project file: PrjPP-8.pptx

1. Copy the file PrjPP-8.pptx to your Project Folder using the Copy It! Button on this page in the BookOnCD.

2. Start Microsoft PowerPoint and open the file PrjPP-8.pptx from your Project Folder.

3. Suppose you would like all the slides to display the date slides were created, slide numbers, and your name. Select any slide, then select Header & Footer in the Text group of the Insert tab. When the Header and Footer dialog box appears, click the Slide tab.

4. To add the date the slides were created, click the Date and time check box. Make sure the Fixed option is selected and then type today's date in the box.

5. To add sequential numbers to every slide, place a checkmark in the Slide number box. To add your name to a footer, place a checkmark in the Footer box and type your name in the box. Place a checkmark in the *Don't show on title slide* box. This step prevents the footer from appearing on the title page. Click the Apply to All button to add the footer to all the slides and close the Header and Footer dialog box. Look through the slides to make sure your footer appears on every slide except the title slide.

6. Suppose that you want to display the current date on the title slide each time the presentation is given. Select the title slide, then click Header and Footer in the Text group. When the Header and Footer dialog box appears, click the Slide tab. Place a checkmark in the *Date and time* option box, and then click *Update automatically*. To change the date format, click the down-arrow button on the date box and select the second option (e.g., Monday, April 19, 2010).

7. Remove the checkmarks from the three check boxes at the bottom of the dialog box. You do not want this slide numbered, nor do you want your name on it. To apply this footer to just the title slide and close the Header and Footer dialog box, click the Apply button. Today's date now appears in the lower-left corner of the title slide.

• Final Presentation Details (continued)

8. Now, suppose you want to print the presentation on 8 1/2 inch by 11 inch paper and you would like to stretch each slide to fit the entire page. Click Page Setup in the Page Setup group on the Design tab. When the Page Setup dialog box appears, click the down-arrow button for the *Slides sized for* box and select Letter Paper (8.5x11 in). Change the orientation of the slides to Portrait and then click the OK button. Your title slide should look similar to the one shown in the figure below.

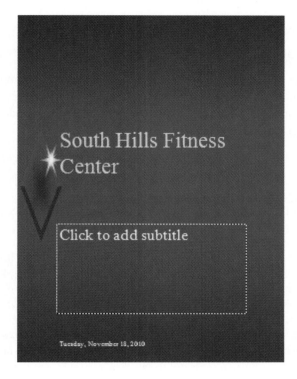

9. Save your presentation in your Project Folder using the file name PrjPP-8-XXXXX-9999, where XXXXX is your student ID number and 9999 is your class section number.

10. Use one of the following options to submit your project on a USB flash drive or floppy disk, as a printout, or as an e-mail attachment, according to your instructor's directions:

- To submit the file from your Project Folder where it is currently stored, stop the PowerPoint program by closing its window. Copy the file to a USB flash drive or floppy disk. Include your name, student ID number, class section number, date, and PrjPP-8 when you submit the file.

- To print the project, click the Microsoft Office button, then click Print. On the Print dialog box, look for the *Print what* section and use its pull-down list to select Handouts. Make sure that the *Handouts* section specifies 6 slides per page in Horizontal order. Also, make sure that the *Scale to fit paper* check box contains a checkmark. Click the OK button. Write your name, student ID number, class section number, date, and PrjPP-8 on the printout.

- To e-mail the file, use Method 1 or Method 2, as described on page 348. Type your instructor's e-mail address in the To: box. Click the Subject: box and type PrjPP-8, your student ID number, and your class section number. Click the Send button or perform any additional steps required by your e-mail software to send an e-mail message.

Project AC-1: Creating a Database Table

In this project, you'll apply what you've learned about Microsoft Access to create a database, create a table, and enter data into the table. You'll also explore data formats and validation rules.

Requirements: This project requires Microsoft Access.

Project file: No project file is required for this project.

1. Start Microsoft Access.

2. Create a new blank database in your Project Folder. Name the database PrjAC-1.accdb.

3. Use the Table Template option to create a table. Select the Contacts sample table. Include the following fields in the table: ID, Company, LastName, FirstName, Job Title, Business Phone, Fax Number, Address, City, State/Province, ZIP/PostalCode, and Country/Region. Name the table Contacts.

4. In Design View, add a field at the end of the field list called ContactDate, with a data type of Date/Time.

5. Select ContactDate, and change the format of the field to General Date. To do this step, use the Format option on the General tab in the Field Properties box near the bottom of the window.

6. Create a validation rule to restrict the dates entered in the ContactDate field to later than 1/1/2009. Select ContactDate, and type >=#1/1/2009# in the Validation Rule found on the General tab under Field Properties. In the Validation Text box enter Please enter a date later than 1/1/2009.

7. Select ZIP/PostalCode, and change the field size to 5 using the Field Size option on the General tab under Field Properties. Note that changing format options, such as field size, might result in changes to data in your database. For example, for records that include ZIP/PostalCodes longer than five characters, changing the field size to 5 would result in some fields being truncated. Save the changes to the table, then switch to Datasheet View.

8. Move the ContactDate column heading and drag it so that it is positioned just to the right of the FirstName column.

9. Delete the Company column.

10. Add the following record to the database. Leave fields, such as Fax Number, blank if you don't have the data. If you can't see the full text for a field, drag the dividing line between field headers to resize the column.

Last Name	First Name	Contact Date	Business Phone	Address	City	State/ Province	ZIP/ Postal Code	Country/ Region
Brown	Luke	5/9/2010	(812) 928-3828	4702 Lakewood Lane	Stone's Throw	GA	83928	USA

11. What happens to the ZIPCode when you enter the following record?

Last Name	First Name	Contact Date	Business Phone	Address	City	State/ Province	ZIP/ Postal Code	Country/ Region
Cho	Alison	9/30/2010	(702) 737-2781	337 Center Street	Stockton	KY	83748-7707	USA

• Creating a Database Table (continued)

12. What happens when you try to add the data for the following record?

Last Name	First Name	Contact Date	Business Phone	Address	City	State/ Province	ZIP/ Postal Code	Country/ Region
McGuire	Joe	10/10/2002	(303) 383-7478	1147 Old Mill Road	Hanover	OH	57373	USA

Enter today's date instead of 10/10/2002, and then complete the record.

13. Check the data you entered and correct any typing mistakes. Your table should look similar to the one in the figure below.

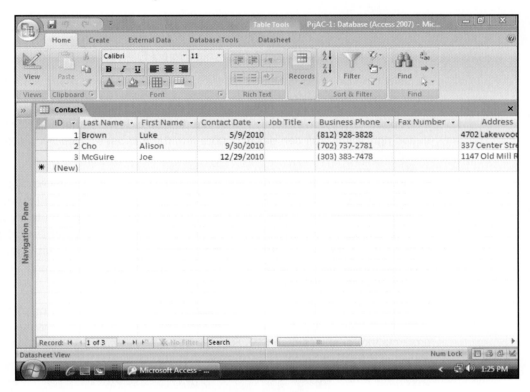

14. Use one of the following options to submit your project on a USB flash drive or floppy disk, as a printout, or as an e-mail attachment, according to your instructor's directions:

• To submit the file from your Project Folder where it is currently stored, stop the Access program by closing its window. Copy the file to a USB flash drive or floppy disk. Include your name, student ID number, class section number, date, and PrjAC-1 when you submit the file.

• To print the file, make sure that the Contacts table is open. Click the Microsoft Office button, click Print, then click OK. Write your name, student ID number, class section number, date, and PrjAC-1 on the first page of the printout.

• To e-mail the file, exit Access and start your usual e-mail program. Type your instructor's e-mail address in the To: box. Type PrjAC-1, your student ID number, and your class section number in the Subject: box. Attach the file PrjAC-1.accdb from your Project Folder to the e-mail. Click the Send button or perform any additional steps required by your e-mail software to send an e-mail message.

Project AC-2: Creating Queries

In this project, you'll apply what you've learned about Microsoft Access to find specific records and create queries for finding specific information in a database.

Requirements: This project requires Microsoft Access.

Project file: PrjAC-2.accdb

CopyIt!

1. Copy the file PrjAC-2.accdb to your Project Folder using the Copy It! button on this page in the BookOnCD.

2. Start Microsoft Access.

3. Open the file PrjAC-2.accdb from your Project Folder.

4. Select the Contacts table and delete it. When asked if you really want to delete this table, click the Yes button.

5. Suppose you hadn't intended to delete this table. If you remember to click the Undo button right away, you can easily restore it to the database. Click the Undo button on the Quick Access toolbar.

6. Open the Products table and find the first Description that matches "Signal Kit." To complete this step, click the Home tab and then click Find in the Find group to open the Find and Replace dialog box. This dialog box allows you to type the text you want to find and select options such as which table to search and how to match the criteria. Enter Signal Kit in the *Find What* box. Set the *Look In* box to Products. Set *Match* to Whole Field. Set *Search* to All. Click the Find Next button to initiate the search. When the record has been located, click the Cancel button.

7. Use the Query Wizard to create a query that includes all fields from the Products table. Name the query Products Under $10. Add query criteria to limit the query results to products that cost less than $10. Run the query and compare your results to those shown in the figure below:

Products Under $10			✕
ID ▾	Product Number ▾	Description ▾	Price ▾
1	72838	8 oz Coffee Mug	$3.45
2	82892	12 oz Coffee Mug	$4.15
3	18372	Cup Holder	$2.85
5	83827	Auto Trash Bag	$7.95
7	23702	Lock De-icer	$2.89
8	37027	Windshield Scraper	$3.25
* (New)	0		$0.00

8. Save and close the updated query.

• Creating Queries (continued)

9. Use the Query Wizard to create a query that includes only the State/Province and EmailName fields from the Contacts table. Name the query Ohio E-mail Addresses. Add query criteria to limit the query results to records of people located in the state of Ohio (OH). Uncheck the Show check box for the State/Province field so that data from that field is not displayed in the query results. Run the query and compare your results to those shown in the figure below.

10. Save and close the updated query.

11. Delete the query named E-mail Address List by clicking its title and then pressing the Delete key on your keyboard.

12. Use one of the following options to submit your project on a USB flash drive or floppy disk, as a printout, or as an e-mail attachment, according to your instructor's directions:

• To submit the file from your Project Folder where it is currently stored, stop the Access program by closing its window. Copy the file to a USB flash drive or floppy disk. Include your name, student ID number, class section number, date, and PrjAC-2 when you submit the file.

• To print the project, make sure that the *Products Under $10* query is open, then click the Microsoft Office button, click Print, then click OK. Close the *Products Under $10* query, then open the *Ohio E-mail Addresses* query. Click the Microsoft Office button, click Print, then click OK. Staple the pages together, then write your name, student ID number, class section number, date, and PrjAC-2 on the first page.

• To e-mail the file, exit Access and start your usual e-mail program. Type your instructor's e-mail address in the To: box. Type PrjAC-2, your student ID number, and your class section number in the Subject: box. Attach the file PrjAC-2.accdb from your Project Folder to the e-mail. Click the Send button or perform any additional steps required by your e-mail software to send an e-mail message.

Project AC-3: Creating Forms

In this project, you'll apply what you've learned about Microsoft Access to create forms that would allow a data entry person to easily update the Products and Contacts tables.

Requirements: This project requires Microsoft Access.

Project file: PrjAC-3.accdb

1. Copy the file PrjAC-3.accdb to your Project Folder using the Copy It! button on this page in the BookOnCD.

2. Start Microsoft Access.

3. Open the file PrjAC-3.accdb from your Project Folder.

4. Use the Form Wizard to create a form containing all the fields from the Products table. Specify the Columnar layout and the Foundry style. Enter Product Inventory as the form title.

5. Compare your form to the one shown below:

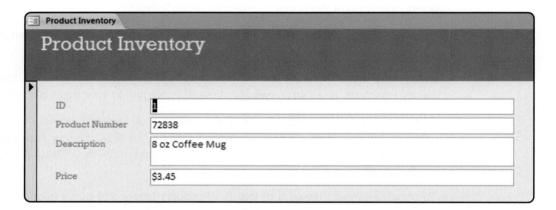

6. Use the Product Inventory form to add a new record for product number 54431, which is Fix-a-Flat priced at $1.89.

7. Close the Product Inventory form.

8. Use the Form Wizard to create a form containing the following fields from the Contacts table: LastName, FirstName, and EmailName. Use the Justified layout and the Paper style. Enter E-Mail List as the form title.

9. Compare your form to the one shown below.

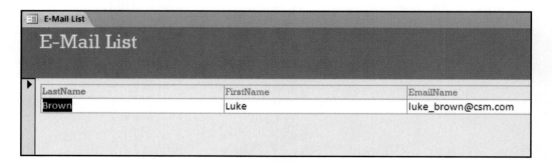

• Creating Forms (continued)

10. Suppose you would like the date and time on a header for each form. Switch to Layout View. Select *Date and Time* in the Controls group on the Format tab. In the Date and Time dialog box, check the format you prefer, then click the OK button. The form should now have the date and time in its upper-right corner.

11. Switch to Design View and edit the title so that it says "E-Mail Address List" instead of "E-Mail List." Resize the text box so that the title is displayed on one line.

12. Forms are usually displayed on the screen for data entry and editing. You can print one or more forms. For example, you might print and mail a form to a client so that he or she can verify the data it contains. To print the form you are viewing, click the Microsoft Office button, then click Print. Click the OK button.

13. When working with small forms, such as the E-Mail List, you might want to print all the forms on a single page. To do so, make sure the Print dialog box is set to print All.

14. Use a form to add the e-mail address for a friend or relative.

15. Close the E-Mail List form.

16. Sometimes forms become obsolete and should be deleted. Delete the form called Client Addresses. To do so, highlight the form name and then press the Delete key on your keyboard. When asked if you want to permanently delete the form, click the Yes button.

17. Use one of the following options to submit your project on a USB flash drive or floppy disk, as a printout, or as an e-mail attachment, according to your instructor's directions:

- To submit the file from your Project Folder where it is currently stored, stop the Access program by closing its window. Copy the file to a USB flash drive or floppy disk. Include your name, student ID number, class section number, date, and PrjAC-3 when you submit the file.

- To print the data as it appears in the form, make sure that the Product Inventory form is open. Click the Microsoft Office button, click Print, then click OK. Close the Product Inventory form and open the E-Mail List form. Click the Microsoft Office button, click Print, then click OK. Staple the pages together, then write your name, student ID number, class section number, date, and PrjAC-3 on the first page.

- To e-mail the file, exit Access and start your usual e-mail program. Type your instructor's e-mail address in the To: box. Type PrjAC-3, your student ID number, and your class section number in the Subject: box. Attach the file PrjAC-3.accdb from your Project Folder to the e-mail. Click the Send button or perform any additional steps required by your e-mail software to send an e-mail message.

Project AC-4: Creating Reports

In this project, you'll apply what you've learned about Microsoft Access to generate printed reports.

Requirements: This project requires Microsoft Access.

Project file: PrjAC-4.accdb

1. Copy the file PrjAC-4.accdb to your Project Folder using the Copy It! button on this page in the BookOnCD.

2. Start Microsoft Access.

3. Open the file PrjAC-4.accdb from your Project Folder.

4. Use the Report Wizard to create a report containing only the LastName, FirstName, and EmailName fields from the Contacts table. Do not add any grouping levels. Sort the records by last name in ascending order. Use the Tabular layout and the Foundry style for the report. Enter Contact E-Mail Addresses for the report title.

5. Compare your report to the one shown in the figure below, then close the report.

	Contact E-Mail Addresses

Contact E-Mail Addresses

LastName	FirstName	EmailName
Brown	Kim	brown_kim@mindspring.com
Brown	Luke	luke_brown@csm.com
Cho	Alison	acho@centnet.net
Glenn	Candace	
Lowe	Sharon	slowe@aol.com
Maki	John	john_maki@aol.com
McGuire	Joe	jmc@cnet.net
Nakamura	Yukiko	ynaka@cnet.net
Smith	Heidi	heidis@aol.com

● **Creating Reports (continued)**

6. Use the Report Wizard to create a report containing all fields *except the ID field* in the Query: Products Under $10. Group by department. Sort the records by Description in ascending order. Use the Stepped layout and Module style for the report. Enter Products Under $10 by Department for the report title.

7. Compare your report to the one shown in the figure below, then close the report.

Products Under $10 by Department			✕

Products Under $10 by Department

Department	Description	Product Number	Price
Automotive			
	Auto Trash Bag	83827	$7.95
	Cup Holder	18372	$2.85
	Fix-a-Flat	54431	$1.89
	Lock De-icer	23702	$2.89
	Windshield Scraper	37027	$3.25
Floral			
	Herb Garden	77543	$3.49
Housewares			
	12 oz Coffee Mug	82892	$4.15
	8 oz Coffee Mug	72838	$3.45
	Plastic Hangers/12	78662	$3.99
	Rock Key Safe	986443	$5.99
	Votive Candles	887611	$0.99

8. Use one of the following options to submit your project on a USB flash drive or floppy disk, as a printout, or as an e-mail attachment, according to your instructor's directions:

● To submit the file from your Project Folder where it is currently stored, stop the Access program by closing its window. Copy the file to a USB flash drive or floppy disk. Include your name, student ID number, class section number, date, and PrjAC-4 when you submit the file.

● To print the project, open the *Contact E-Mail Addresses* report, click the Microsoft Office button, click Print, then click OK. Open the *Products Under $10 by Department* report, click the Microsoft Office button, click Print, then click OK. Staple the pages together, then write your name, student ID number, class section number, date, and PrjAC-4 on the first page.

● To e-mail the file, exit Access and start your usual e-mail program. Type your instructor's e-mail address in the To: box. Type PrjAC-4, your student ID number, and your class section number in the Subject: box. Attach the file PrjAC-4.accdb from your Project Folder to the e-mail. Click the Send button or perform any additional steps required by your e-mail software to send an e-mail message.

Project AC-5: Indexing and Filtering

In this project, you'll explore how indexes can be used to make databases more efficient. You'll also find out how to use filters to create a quick "query by example."

Indexes are used to find and sort records quickly. A primary key is an example of an index. It is a good idea to create an index on any field commonly used as a sort or search field. Indexes can also be used to restrict fields to unique values. For example, a customer number field must contain only unique customer numbers because no two customers can share a customer number. A "No Duplicate" index restricts values entered into the field to only unique values.

Requirements: This project requires Microsoft Access.

Project file: PrjAC-5.accdb

1. Copy the file PrjAC-5.accdb to your Project Folder using the Copy It! button on this page in the BookOnCD.

2. Start Microsoft Access.

3. Open the file PrjAC-5.accdb from your Project Folder.

4. Create an index by opening the Contacts table in Design View. Select the State/Province field and select *Yes (Duplicates OK)* from the Indexed option on the General tab under Field Properties.

5. Select the ID field and use the General tab to verify that the index for this field does not allow duplicates. Close Design View and save the changes you just made. Now that you have indexes for the State/Province field and ID field, sorts and searches on these fields will require less time—especially in databases that contain thousands of records. You can't tell the difference with a short database that fits on a removable storage device, but keep this important database design technique in mind for your own large databases.

6. Now explore the way filters help you quickly sift through a table to find records. Open the Contacts table. Click the down-arrow button on the column header in the State/Province field. Remove the checkmarks from all of the selections except OH, then click the OK button.

7. Compare your screen to the one shown on the next page, then cancel the filter by clicking the Toggle Filter button in the Sort & Filter group on the Home tab.

• Indexing and Filtering (continued)

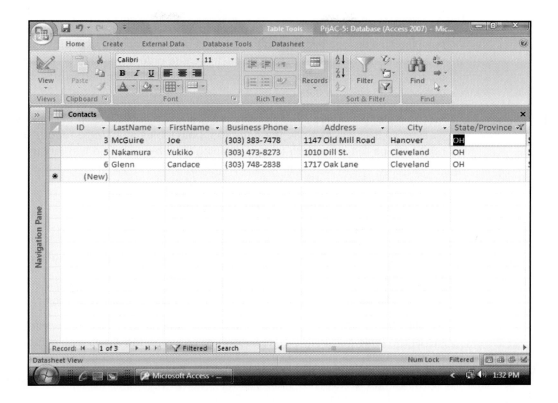

8. Use one of the following options to submit your project on a USB flash drive or floppy disk, as a printout, or as an e-mail attachment, according to your instructor's directions:

• To submit the file from your Project Folder where it is currently stored, stop the Access program by closing its window. Copy the file to a USB flash drive or floppy disk. Include your name, student ID number, class section number, date, and PrjAC-5 when you submit the file.

• To print the project, open the Contacts table, set the filter, click the Microsoft Office button, click Print, then click OK. Write your name, student ID number, class section number, date, and PrjAC-5 on the printout.

• To e-mail the file, exit Access and start your usual e-mail program. Type your instructor's e-mail address in the To: box. Type PrjAC-5, your student ID number, and your class section number in the Subject: box. Attach the file PrjAC-5.accdb from your Project Folder to the e-mail. Click the Send button or perform any additional steps required by your e-mail software to send an e-mail message.

Project AC-6: Creating Relationships

In this project, you'll learn how to create and use one-to-many relationships. A one-to-many relationship links one record in a table to one or more records in another table. Examples of one-to-many relationships include customers to orders (one customer can place many orders), authors to titles (one author can write multiple books), and students to classes (several students can take one class).

To complete this project, you'll create a one-to-many relationship between students and classes so that you can use the data from both tables in a single report. One-to-many relationships require a third table containing links between the two tables in the relationship. The project database provides you with three tables, so that you will create the relationships and generate a report based on the linked data.

Requirements: This project requires Microsoft Access.

Project file: PrjAC-6.accdb

1. Copy the file PrjAC-6.accdb to your Project Folder using the Copy It! button on this page in the BookOnCD.

2. Start Microsoft Access. Open the file PrjAC-6.accdb from your Project Folder.

3. Click the Database Tools tab, then click Relationships in the Show/Hide group. Click the Show Table button in the Relationships group on the Relationship Tools Design contextual tab.

4. Hold down the Ctrl key while you click Classes, click Students, then click Rosters. Click the Add button, then click the Close button to close the Show Table dialog box. The Relationships window now contains three field lists—one for each of the tables. Drag the borders of the field lists so that you can see their entire contents.

5. Drag the field list title bars so that Rosters is between Classes and Students.

6. Note that the Classes table and the Rosters table both include a ClassID field. To create a relationship between these tables, drag ClassID from the Classes table and drop it on ClassID in the Rosters table.

7. When the Edit Relationships window appears, make sure it says *One-to-Many* at the bottom, and then click the Create button. If the window says *One-to-One*, click the Cancel button, then repeat Step 6, making sure to drop on the word ClassID.

8. Next, create a one-to-many relationship between the Rosters table and the Students table using the StudentID field.

9. Close the Relationships window and save the changes.

10. With the relationships created, you can generate a class roster report. Click the Create tab, then click Report Wizard in the Reports group.

11. Choose all the fields from the Classes table by first choosing *Table: Classes* from the Tables/Queries list, then clicking the >> button to move all the fields to the Selected Fields list.

12. Choose *Table: Students* from the Tables/Queries list, select LastName, and click > . Also add the FirstName field. Click the Next button to continue.

13. Verify that the next dialog box indicates that you'll view your data by Classes, and click the Next button.

● Creating Relationships (continued)

14. Do not choose any grouping levels, and click the Next button.

15. Sort records by student last names in ascending order by choosing LastName. Click Next.

16. Choose to lay out your report using the *Outline* layout. Click Next.

17. Choose the Foundry style, and click Next.

18. Type Class Roster as the report title. Verify that *Preview the Report* is selected, and click the Finish button.

19. Compare your results to those shown below.

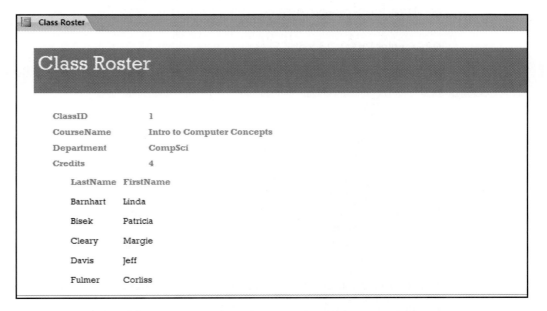

20. Use one of the following options to submit your project on a USB flash drive or floppy disk, as a printout, or as an e-mail attachment, according to your instructor's directions:

● To submit the file from your Project Folder where it is currently stored, stop the Access program by closing its window. Copy the file to a USB flash drive or floppy disk. Include your name, student ID number, class section number, date, and PrjAC-6 when you submit the file.

● To print the relationships, open the relationships window. Click the Relationship Report button in the Tools group on the Relationship Tools Design contextual tab. Click the Print button in the Print group on the Print Preview tab, then click OK. Close the Print Preview. Save and close the relationships report using the default report name. Write your name, student ID number, class section number, date, and PrjAC-6 on the printouts.

● To e-mail the file, exit Access and start your usual e-mail program. Type your instructor's e-mail address in the To: box. Type PrjAC-6, your student ID number, and your class section number in the Subject: box. Attach the file PrjAC-6.accdb from your Project Folder to the e-mail. Click the Send button or perform any additional steps required by your e-mail software to send an e-mail message.

Project AC-7: Setting Up Referential Integrity

In this project, you'll explore how to use relationships to maintain referential integrity between tables, and how to create queries that use relationships.

Referential integrity can be used to ensure that data entered in tables is correct in the context of the database. Let's suppose you are working with two tables from a school database. One table contains a list of classes. The other table contains prerequisites. The school uses two tables for this data because the database designer did not want to waste disk space to store empty fields for classes that have no prerequisites.

Assume that a class can have no more than one prerequisite. You can activate referential integrity to make sure that prerequisites cannot be added for a course that does not exist. You can also use it to avoid entering more than one prerequisite for a class.

Requirements: This project requires Microsoft Access.

Project file: PrjAC-7.accdb

1. Copy the file PrjAC-7.accdb to your Project Folder using the Copy It! button on this page in the BookOnCD.

2. Start Microsoft Access.

3. Open the file PrjAC-7.accdb from your Project Folder.

4. Click the Database Tools tab, then click Relationships in the Show/Hide group. Click the Show Table button in the Relationships group on the Relationship Tools Design contextual tab. Hold down the Shift key while you click Classes, and then click Prerequisites. Click the Add button, then click the Close button. The Relationships window now contains two field lists—one for the Classes table and one for the Prerequisites table. Drag the borders of the field lists so that you can see their entire contents.

5. Note that both tables include a ClassID field. To create a relationship between these tables, drag ClassID from the Classes table to the Prerequisites table.

6. When the Edit Relationships window appears, make sure the box for *Enforce Referential Integrity* contains a checkmark.

7. Click the Create button to create a one-to-one relationship between Classes and Prerequisites.

8. The line that connects the two tables indicates the one-to-one relationship you just created. Close the Relationships window and save the changes.

9. Take a look at the Prerequisites table by double-clicking the table name. The ClassID field lists classes by number. If you want to find the name of a class, you can simply click the + sign next to it. What is the name of class 4? If you click the + sign, you'll see that it is Applied Math. Click the minus sign to hide the class name. The PrerequisiteName field lists the title of the prerequisite course. For example, the prerequisite for course 4 is Math Basics.

10. Now, what happens when you try to enter a prerequisite of English 101 for a class (numbered 11) that does not exist? Add a new record with the following values: *Class ID:* 11, *Prerequisite Name:* English 101. Press the Tab key to move to the next record. A warning message appears because no classes exist with a Class ID of 11. Therefore, no prerequisites for that class can be added. Click the OK button to close the warning message.

● Setting Up Referential Integrity (continued)

11. Now, try to change the Class ID to 6. Press the Tab key twice to move to the next record. Another warning message appears because you can see from the record above that class 6 already has a prerequisite of English 101.

12. Click the OK button and enter the following data:

ClassID: 1 PrerequisiteName: Math Basics

13. Create a query using the Query Wizard that includes all the fields from the Classes table and the PrerequisiteName field from the Prerequisites table. Save the query with the name Classes and Prerequisites.

14. Run the query and compare your results to those shown below.

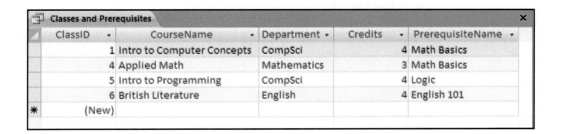

ClassID ▾	CourseName ▾	Department ▾	Credits ▾	PrerequisiteName ▾
1	Intro to Computer Concepts	CompSci	4	Math Basics
4	Applied Math	Mathematics	3	Math Basics
5	Intro to Programming	CompSci	4	Logic
6	British Literature	English	4	English 101
* (New)				

15. Use one of the following options to submit your project on a USB flash drive or floppy disk, as a printout, or as an e-mail attachment, according to your instructor's directions:

● To submit the file from your Project Folder where it is currently stored, stop the Access program by closing its window. Copy the file to a USB flash drive or floppy disk. Include your name, student ID number, class section number, date, and PrjAC-7 when you submit the file.

● To print the project, make sure that the Classes and Prerequisites query is open, click the Microsoft Office button, click Print, then click OK. Write your name, student ID number, class section number, date, and PrjAC-7 on the first page.

● To e-mail the file, exit Access and start your usual e-mail program. Type your instructor's e-mail address in the To: box. Type PrjAC-7, your student ID number, and your class section number in the Subject: box. Attach the file PrjAC-7.accdb from your Project Folder to the e-mail. Click the Send button or perform any additional steps required by your e-mail software to send an e-mail message.

Project AC-8: Managing Tables and Relationships

In this project, you'll explore basic database management techniques, such as viewing tables in different ways and deleting old or obsolete items from the database.

Requirements: This project requires Microsoft Access.

Project file: PrjAC-8.accdb

1. Copy the file PrjAC-8.accdb to your Project Folder using the Copy It! button on this page in the BookOnCD.

2. Start Microsoft Access and open the file PrjAC-8.accdb from your Project Folder.

3. Open the Student Names table and the Students table. Click Switch Windows in the Window group on the Home tab. Select Tile Horizontally to arrange both tables as shown below so that they do not overlap.

4. Does data in one of these tables simply duplicate data in the other table? The Student Names table seems to include only students from Alabama. To more easily see if the same students are in the Students table, sort the Students table in ascending order by state.

5. Examine the data in the two tables. The records in the Student Names table also appear to be in the Students table. Are their student numbers the same? Students in the Student Names table are sorted in descending order by Student ID. To match this order, sort the Students table in descending order by Student ID.

• **Managing Tables and Relationships (continued)**

6. It is still a bit difficult to compare the data. You can apply a filter to show only the students in Alabama in the Students table. In the Students table, right-click any state field that contains "AL." Click Selection in the Sort&Filter group on the Home tab. Select Equals "AL." Now Access displays only students who live in Alabama, sorted by Student ID. Compare the two tables. The data in the Student Names table is already stored in the Students table.

7. Remove the filter on the Students table by clicking Filter in the Sort&Filter group. Select *Clear filter from State*.

8. Close both tables. Click No if you are asked if you want to save the changes.

9. Assume you've seen enough to convince yourself that the Student Names table is not needed. You can delete the table, but first you should check if the table is related to any other tables. Click Relationships in the Show/Hide group on the Database Tools tab. Notice the relationship between Student Names and Students and Classes. Right-click the relationship and select Delete. Click the Yes button when prompted to delete the relationship. Close the Relationships window.

10. Click the down-arrow button for Tables and select Queries. The Student Name query is based on data from the table you want to eliminate. To delete the query, right-click the Student Name query, and select Delete. Click the Yes button to complete the deletion.

11. Now that you have deleted the relationships and queries associated with the Student Names table, you can delete the table itself. Navigate back to the Tables list. Right-click Student Names, and choose Delete. Click Yes to delete.

12. Use one of the following options to submit your project on a USB flash drive or floppy disk, as a printout, or as an e-mail attachment, according to your instructor's directions:

• To submit the file from your Project Folder where it is currently stored, stop the Access program by closing its window. Copy the file to a USB flash drive or floppy disk. Include your name, student ID number, class section number, date, and PrjAC-8 when you submit the file.

• To print the project, make sure that the Relationships window is open, click the Microsoft Office button, click Print, then click OK. Write your name, student ID number, class section number, date, and PrjAC-8 on the first page.

• To e-mail the file, exit Access and start your usual e-mail program. Type your instructor's e-mail address in the To: box. Type PrjAC-8, your student ID number, and your class section number in the Subject: box. Attach the file PrjAC-8.accdb from your Project Folder to the e-mail. Click the Send button or perform any additional steps required by your e-mail software to send an e-mail message.

Project AC-9: Grouped Reports

In this project, you'll explore how to use Microsoft Access to create reports containing "control breaks" that group, summarize, and total data.

Requirements: This project requires Microsoft Access.

Project file: PrjAC-9.accdb

1. Copy the file PrjAC-9.accdb to your Project Folder using the Copy It! button. Start Microsoft Access and open the file PrjAC-9.accdb from your Project Folder.

2. Open the table called Mutual Fund. Notice that it contains a list of funds, such as American Value, that are managed by various companies, such as Dean Witter. The funds are categorized as GR, MP, SC, etc. Each record includes the fund's value, and its value over the past year and past five years.

3. Print this table by clicking the Microsoft Office button, selecting Print, and then clicking the OK button in the Print Dialog box.

4. Next, highlight just the Dean Witter records. To print just these records, open the Print dialog box and click Selected Record(s) before you click the OK button. Printing the raw data contained in a table does not provide much flexibility for formatting and organizing report data, so it is rarely done. The Reporting features provided by Access offer much more flexibility.

5. Use the Report Wizard to create a report for the Mutual Fund. Include the fields Company, Fund Name, and Net Asset Value. Group by Company. These groups are sometimes referred to as "break points." Sort the records by Fund Name in ascending order. To include a subtotal for each company, click the Summary Options button and click the Sum box. Make sure that the *Detail and Summary* option is selected, so that the report includes the records in each group, not just a summary for each group. Click the OK button to close the Summary Options dialog box. Use the Stepped layout and Concourse style for the report. Enter Company Net Asset Value for the report title.

6. Compare your report to the one shown in the figure below.

Company Net Asset Value

Company	Fund Name	Net Asset Value
Dean Witter		
	Pacific Growth	19.28
	Natural Resources	13.64
	Intermediate Income	9.59
	High Yield	6.66
	European Growth	16.62
	Dividend Growth	44.57
	Development Growth	22.70
	Convertible	13.01
	Capital Growth	14.47
	American Value	27.01
Summary for 'Company' = Dean Witter (10 detail records)		
Sum		187.55

• Grouped Reports (continued)

7. Print only the first page of the report. To do so, open the Print dialog box, click the Pages option in the Print Range section, and then type 1 in the From box. Click the OK button to start printing. Click the Close button to close the report preview.

8. When you no longer need to generate a particular report, you can delete its template. To delete the *Fund Objective by Category* report, click its name and click the Delete key on your keyboard. When asked if you want to permanently delete this report, click the Yes button.

9. Now, suppose you want to create a report that contains the average, minimum, and maximum 1-year and 5-year totals for each fund management company. Use the Report Wizard to create a report for the Mutual Fund table containing all fields except Category and Net Asset Value. Group by Company. Click the Summary Options button and then select the boxes for Avg, Min, and Max for 1 Year and 5 Years. Select the Summary Only option under Show. Click the OK button. Use the Stepped layout and Concourse style for the report. Enter Company 1 Year and 5 Year Summary for the report title. Click the Finish button.

10. Notice that the report does not include individual funds, such as American Value. These details are not displayed because you selected Summary Only. Therefore, the column heading "Fund Name" is not needed. Click the Close Print Preview button to switch to Design View. Delete Fund Name from the page header. To do so, click Fund Name in the Page Header area, then press the Delete key on your keyboard. Reposition the field boxes so that they are directly under the correct headers. Switch back to Print Preview by clicking the View button in the Views group of the Design tab, then selecting Print Preview.

11. Now, suppose that your boss wants you to change the setup of the report so that it fits on a single page in landscape orientation. Click Landscape in the Page Layout group on the Print Preview contextual tab. To explore changing the page size, click Size in the Page Layout group. Make sure that Letter is selected to print on standard 8.5" x 11" paper. Now, click Margins in the Page Layout group and change the top and bottom margins to .75" and the left and right margins to .35". Compare your report to the one shown in the figure below, and then print it.

Company 1 Year and 5 Year Summary

Company	One Year	Five Years
Dean Witter		
Summary for 'Company' = Dean Witter (10 detail records)		
Avg	14.7	12.4
Min	3.1	5.0
Max	28.9	18.7
Dreyfus		
Summary for 'Company' = Dreyfus (10 detail records)		
Avg	17.1	12.1
Min	-2.6	5.5
Max	25.7	15.3
Evergreen		
Summary for 'Company' = Evergreen (10 detail records)		

12. Submit the four printed reports you produced by following the steps of this project.

Project AC-10: Exporting Information

In this project, you'll practice exporting Access data to a spreadsheet, to a Word document, and into comma-delimited format.

Requirements: This project requires Microsoft Access, Microsoft Excel, Microsoft Word, and WordPad.

Project file: PrjAC-10.accdb

1. Copy the file PrjAC-10.accdb to your Project Folder using the Copy It! button on this page in the BookOnCD.

2. Start Microsoft Access and open the file PrjAC-10.accdb from your Project Folder.

3. Open the Products table. Switch to Design View and add a field named Quantity with a data type of number.

4. Switch back to Datasheet View and save your table design changes when prompted. Enter a number in the Quantity field for all records in the table.

5. Now, suppose you want to compute a product's total price, based on the quantity you had entered. You might also want to group the products by department and compute the total price per department, so you can better analyze the data. You can export the data to an Excel spreadsheet to do all the computations. To do so, open the Products table, click the External Data tab, then click Excel in the Export group.

6. In the *Export - Excel Spreadsheet* dialog box, name the file PrjAC-10A.xlsx and save it in your Project Folder. Select the export options *Export data with formatting and layout* and *Open the destination file after the export operation is complete*, then click the OK button.

7. Now you can edit the exported data in your Excel spreadsheet. First, delete the ID field in column A. Add a field called Total Price in column F and use the PRODUCT function to compute the total price per product. Your spreadsheet should look similar to the example below.

	A	B	C	D	E	F
1	**Department**	**Product Number**	**Description**	**Price**	**Quantity**	**Total Price**
2	Housewares	72838	8 oz Coffee Mug	$3.45	100	345
3	Housewares	82892	12 oz Coffee Mug	$4.15	100	415
4	Automotive	18372	Cup Holder	$2.85	100	285
5	Automotive	28383	Dash Compass	$11.80	50	590
6	Automotive	83827	Auto Trash Bag	$7.95	75	596.25
7	Automotive	42702	Signal Kit	$14.00	50	700
8	Automotive	23702	Lock De-icer	$2.89	75	216.75
9	Automotive	37027	Windshield Scraper	$3.25	125	406.25
10	Automotive	40070	Car Brush	$10.25	60	615
11	Automotive	51102	AutoVac	$19.95	30	598.5
12	Automotive	54431	Fix-a-Flat	$1.89	25	47.25
13	Housewares	785422	Hot-Air Popper	$16.95	20	339
14	Housewares	78662	Plastic Hangers/12	$3.99	30	119.7
15	Housewares	99877867	Wood Hangers/12	$24.99	35	874.65
16	Housewares	887611	Votive Candles	$0.99	45	44.55
17	Floral	77543	Herb Garden	$3.49	30	104.7

Products

Ready   100%

• Exporting Information (continued)

8. Close the Excel program, go back to Microsoft Access, and close the Export dialog box using the Close button.

9. Use the Report Wizard to create a report containing only the LastName, FirstName, BusinessPhone, City, and State/Province from the Contacts table. Group by State/Province. Sort the records by LastName in ascending order. Use the Stepped layout and None for the report style. Enter Phone Contacts for the report title. Click the Finish button.

10. You can export reports to Word documents where you can add explanatory text. You can also export tables, queries, and forms to Word. All data is exported to Word in Rich Text Format (rtf). To export the Phone Contacts report, open it in Report View, click the External tab, then click Word in the Export group.

11. In the *Export - RTF File* dialog box, name the file PrjAC-10B.rtf and save it in your Project Folder. Select the export option *Open the destination file after the export operation is complete*, then click the OK button. Your Word document should look very similar to the Phone Contacts report.

12. Close the Word program, go back to Microsoft Access, and close the Export dialog box using the Close button.

13. You can also export Access data as comma-delimited files for processing by programs such as Notepad and Excel. Open the Contacts table, click the External Data tab, then click Text File in the Export group.

14. In the *Export - Text File* dialog box, name the file PrjAC-10C.txt and save it in your Project Folder. Click the OK button. Select Delimited for the export format, examine the sample format, and click the Next button. Make sure the delimiter that separates your fields is a comma, then click the Next button. When once again prompted for the file name for your exported data, use PrjAC-10C.txt and save it in your Project Folder. Click the Close button to close the Export dialog box.

15. Open the txt file to view it. The Notepad program should start automatically.

16. Use one of the following options to submit the three project files on a USB flash drive or floppy disk, as printouts, or as e-mail attachments, according to your instructor's directions:

- To submit the files from your Project Folder where they are currently stored, close any open application windows. Copy the files to a USB flash drive or floppy disk. Include your name, student ID number, class section number, date, and PrjAC-10 when you submit the files.

- To print each project file, double-click the file to open it. The correct application program should start. In Excel or Word, click the Microsoft Office button, click Print, then click OK. In Notepad, click the File menu, then select Print. Staple the pages together, then write your name, student ID number, class section number, date, and PrjAC-10 on the first page.

- To e-mail the file, exit Access and start your usual e-mail program. Type your instructor's e-mail address in the To: box. Type PrjAC-10, your student ID number, and your class section number in the Subject: box. Attach the three project files from your Project Folder to the e-mail. Click the Send button or perform any additional steps required by your e-mail software to send an e-mail message.

Project EM-1: Exploring Webmail

In this project, you will learn how to open, use, and manage a Webmail account. Signing up for Gmail also provides access to Google Docs, an SaaS (software as a service) online application.

Requirements: This project requires Microsoft Windows and a browser, such as Internet Explorer.

1. Start your browser.

2. In this exercise, you will work with Google Gmail. If Google is displayed as your home page, click Gmail in the upper-left corner of the Google page. Otherwise, click your browser's address bar, type mail.google.com, and press the Enter key.

3. If you already have a Gmail account, sign in and proceed to Step 9. If not, click *Sign up for Gmail* on the lower-right side of the page. Enter your first name, last name, and desired login name in the online form.

4. Click *check availability!* to make sure no one else has chosen the same login name. If the name is unavailable, a list of available names similar to the one you've selected is displayed. Click a login name from the list if your original login name is unavailable.

5. Before typing a password, click *Password strength* on the right of the *Choose a password* box for tips on selecting secure passwords. Enter a password and change it if the password strength is not labeled Strong. Now retype the password in the *Re-enter password* box.

6. Type a secondary e-mail address if you have one. You can skip the Location box if you want the location to default to United States, or you can click the down-arrow button to display a list.

7. In the Word Verification box, type the characters exactly as you see them. Scroll up to the top of the form to review all your information and make changes if necessary. Read the Google Terms of Service at the bottom of the page, and then click the *I accept* button. On the *Introduction to Gmail* screen, click the *I'm ready - show me my account* link in the upper-right corner.

8. You should be back to the Gmail home page. Sign in to Gmail with your new username and password.

9. You should now be viewing the contents of your mailbox. Compare your screen to the example on the next page.

• Exploring Webmail (continued)

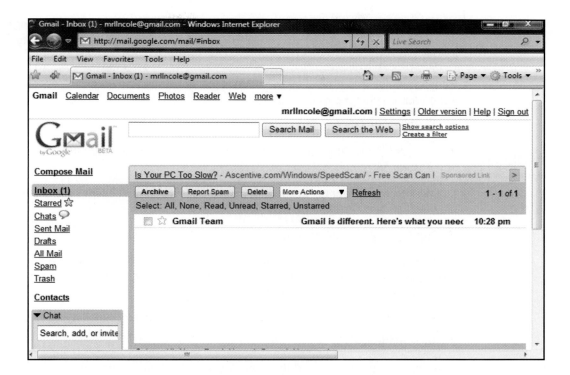

10. Take a screen shot and paste it into a Word document. Name the file PrjEM-1.docx.

11. To view your account settings, click the Settings link in the upper-right corner of the screen. Click each tab and study the various features associated with your account. Write down on paper five features that you think might be most useful for you.

12. Click Compose Mail on the left side of the screen, and then enter your instructor's e-mail address in the To: box.

13. Type Project EM-1 in the Subject: box. Insert the file PrjEM-1.docx as an attachment.

14. In the body of the message, type the five Gmail features you had written down on paper, then send the message.

15. Sign out of Gmail and then close your browser.

16. The e-mail message you sent to your instructor is the only material you need to submit for this project.

Project EM-2: E-mail Basics

In this project, you will practice sending, receiving, formatting, and forwarding e-mail messages. You will also explore how to designate a message as high priority, and how to add attachments.

Requirements: This project requires Microsoft Windows and an e-mail account. You also need your instructor's e-mail address.

Project file: PrjEM-2.txt

1. Copy the file PrjEM-2.txt to your Project Folder using the Copy It! button on this page in the BookOnCD.

2. Log into your Webmail account or open your local e-mail client software, such as Microsoft Outlook or Outlook Express.

3. Create a new message to jack_hill@infoweblinks.com.

4. Enter Join our club in the subject line. Use your own words to write a short message inviting Jack to join an investment club where members discuss the stock market and exchange information about retirement planning.

5. At the end of the message, type your name as a closing.

6. Send the message.

7. Wait a minute or two, and then check your mail. You should have a message from Jack Hill. If the message does not seem to arrive, try refreshing your screen or try switching to a different mail folder and then switch back to your Inbox.

8. Open the message and read it.

9. If you are using Outlook or Thunderbird, add Jack's address to your address book by right-clicking the From box and selecting the Add button from the shortcut menu. If you are using other e-mail software, use Help to find out how to add Jack's address.

10. Click the link or button for forwarding mail. Enter your instructor's e-mail address, but don't forward the message just yet.

11. Add the file PrjEM-2.txt as an attachment.

12. Add the following text to your message: It looks like Jack is going to pass on our offer to join, but I sent him some links to the sites we like.

13. Start a new paragraph and add a sentence to tell your instructor what e-mail software (Outlook, Thunderbird, Gmail, Hotmail, etc.) you used for this assignment. Italicize the software name.

14. Search for "importance" or "priority" using your e-mail software's Help option to find out if you can designate a message as high importance or priority. If you can do so, designate the reply to Jack Hill as high priority. If your e-mail system does not offer prioritization, add [HIGH PRIORITY] to the subject line.

• E-mail Basics (continued)

15. Your message should look similar to the one below. The exact appearance of your screen depends on the e-mail client you are using. Send the message.

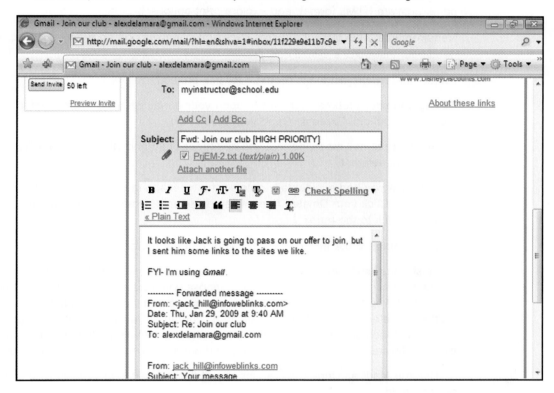

16. Periodically, it is a good idea to empty the contents of your junk, spam, and trash folders. Select your Trash folder and make sure that it contains no mail that you want to keep. If you are using local e-mail client software, you can probably right-click the folder and select Delete from a shortcut menu. If you are using Webmail, look for a Delete link.

17. Select your Inbox and initiate a search for all messages that contain "Join" in the subject line. Most local e-mail clients provide a search box for this purpose. Gmail provides a search box with an adjoing Search Mail button.

18. Find out if your e-mail client allows you to sort messages by sender, subject, or date. If possible, sort your mail according to sender and identify who has sent you the most e-mail.

19. Use the Help provided by your e-mail client to find out how to archive or back up your mail folders and address book. Print out a copy of the instructions and keep them handy so you can periodically back up your e-mail data.

20. Close any e-mail messages that are open.

21. Close your e-mail software.

22. The e-mail message you sent to your instructor is the only material you need to submit for this project.

Project EM-3: Customizing Your E-mail Environment

In this project, you will delete and undelete messages, mark messages as read and unread, organize your mail folders, work with your address book, activate the preview pane, activate HTML format, and explore print options.

Requirements: This project requires Microsoft Windows and an e-mail account. You also need your instructor's e-mail address.

Project file: No project file is required for this project.

1. Log into your Webmail account or open your e-mail client software, such as Microsoft Outlook or Outlook Express. Open your Inbox.

2. Select an e-mail message that you no longer need and click the Delete key on your keyboard to delete it.

3. Suppose you had accidentally deleted the message in Step 2, and you'd like it back in your Inbox. Click your Deleted Items folder to open it. Drag the message that you deleted in Step 2 back to the Inbox.

4. Switch back to the Inbox and make sure that the message is listed.

5. Most e-mail software is configured to display unread mail in bold font. After you read a message, it is displayed in normal font. Suppose you read a message, but don't have time to respond. You can mark a message as unread, so that it appears in bold as a reminder to read it at a later time. To mark a message as unread in Outlook or Outlook Express, right-click it, and then select *Mark as Unread* from the shortcut menu. If you're using other e-mail software, refer to its Help menu to find out how to designate a message as unread.

6. Use the Mark as Unread option for one of the messages in your Inbox that you have already read.

7. You can also mark messages as read if you don't need to read them, but don't want to delete them either. Mark the message from Step 5 as read by right-clicking it and selecting Mark as Read (in Outlook and Outlook Express). If you're using other e-mail software, use its Help menu to find out how to designate a message as read.

8. Open your address book. Create a group mailing address or distribution list consisting of five e-mail addresses from your address book. Name the list "Good Friends" and save it.

9. Open the "Good Friends" address list. Delete an address from the list, and save the list. Close the address book.

10. Check if your e-mail software provides toolbar options by clicking View and looking for a Toolbar menu item. Display all the toolbars by selecting each of the listed toolbars. Most people simply want the Standard toolbar displayed. If you would prefer not to display and use the other toolbars, uncheck their names from the toolbar list.

11. Experiment with making a new folder. In Outlook or Outlook Express, click File, point to Folder, and click New Folder. Name the folder School E-mail and click the OK button. The folder is not displayed until you add it as a mail shortcut. To do so, click File, point to New, and select Outlook Bar Shortcut. Select School E-mail and then click the OK button. You can now use this folder and shortcut to keep your Inbox more organized. If you would rather not use this shortcut, you can delete it by right-clicking it and selecting Remove from Outlook Toolbar.

12. Experiment with saving an e-mail message as a file called Mail Message in your Project Folder. Click a message to select it, then click Save As. Use the Save As dialog box to indicate the file location and name.

• Customizing Your E-mail Environment (continued)

13. Click View and look for an option to show previews, such as AutoPreview or Preview Pane. When the preview pane is activated, you can see the first few lines of a message, while also viewing the Inbox. Previews are handy, but they might allow e-mail viruses to automatically run when they reach your Inbox. Click View and turn off message previews.

14. HTML formatted mail allows you to use some formatting, such as colored text, bold, underlines, and italics. You can also insert graphics into HTML messages, as shown below. Most e-mail software allows you to activate and deactivate HTML format using the Tools or Options menu or tab. HTML mail is more likely to harbor viruses than plain text messages, so some experts recommend deactivating HTML format.

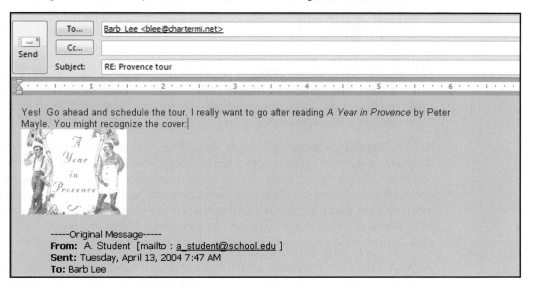

15. Find out if your e-mail is set for HTML format. In Outlook, click the Options tab and check if HTML is highlighted. In Outlook Express, click Tools on the menu bar, click Options, then select the Mail Format tab. The current setting is displayed in the *Compose in this message format* box. If HTML format is activated, you might consider changing the format to plain text. Unfortunately, in Outlook this setting only applies to your outgoing mail. It does not convert incoming mail to plain text format, which would be necessary to avoid viruses that arrive in HTML scripts.

16. Typically, your e-mail software displays data about e-mail messages in columns, such as From, Subject, Received, and Size. Some e-mail software allows you to customize these columns. Use your e-mail Help menu to find out how to display additional fields or remove fields from your Inbox. (Hint: Right-click one of the Inbox column headers, and see if there's an option to customize the view.) Adjust the columns to display the information that is most important to you.

17. Open an e-mail message, highlight only the text in the message area, and select Print in Outlook Express. In Outlook, click the Microsoft Office button, then click Print. Look at the Print dialog box. Most e-mail software includes options to print the entire message or only the selected portion. You might also be able to adjust other print options, such as the number of copies to print. Experiment with the Print settings to create three different printouts of the open e-mail message.

18. On each printout, indicate the print options you used. Make sure that you add your name, student ID number, date, class section number, and PrjEM-3 to each printout. Submit the printouts to your instructor.

Project WW-1: Exploring Your Internet Connection

In this project, you will learn to test your Internet connection using the Ping and Traceroute tools, view Internet connection speeds worldwide, locate your IP address, and test your computer's ports using the ShieldsUP!! utility.

Requirements for this project: This assignment requires Microsoft Windows, Paint, and a browser, such as Internet Explorer or Firefox.

Project file: No project file is required for this project.

1. To check your Internet connection speed, you can "ping" an Internet address, such as www.yahoo.com. To do so in Windows Vista, enter command prompt in the Start menu's Search box. In Windows XP, click Run in the Start menu, then enter command prompt in the Open box. A window displaying a command line prompt should appear.

2. Type ping www.yahoo.com and then press the Enter key. The Ping utility is not sensitive to uppercase or lowercase letters. If you make a typing error, you can use the Backspace key to correct your mistake as long as you have not pressed the Enter key. If you press the Enter key before you make the correction, you will most likely receive an error message. Simply re-enter ping www.yahoo.com.

3. The Ping utility automatically pings www.yahoo.com four times, and then reports the minimum, maximum, and average times for data to make a round trip between your computer and the Yahoo! Web site. Note that average times above 200 ms are not fast enough for online gaming. Ping sometimes displays "request timed out" messages, which mean that the Web site you specified is down or is not accepting pings for security reasons. Take a screen shot of the Ping report using the Print Screen key and Paint. Print the screen shot, then circle the minimum, maximum, and average times. Close the Paint window.

4. You can run the Traceroute utility to gather more information about your Internet connection. At the next command prompt, type tracert www.yahoo.com and press the Enter key. Compare your results to the example below.

```
Tracing route to www.yahoo-ht3.akadns.net [69.147.114.210]
over a maximum of 30 hops:

  1   30 ms    2 ms    2 ms  c-24-271-294-232.ma.comcast.net [24.271.294.232]
  2    9 ms                       B.1
  3    *                     ur01.ma.comcast.net [68.87.156.201]
  4   11 ms                  ur01        68.87.144.125]
  5   23 ms                  ur01        68.87.144.121]
  6   15 ms   10 ms   11 ms  te-7-1-ar02.ma.comcast.net [68.87.145.53]
  7   10 ms   24 ms   11 ms  po-11-ar01.ma.comcast.net [68.87.146.37]
  8   29 ms   13 ms   15 ms  po-10-ar01.ma.comcast.net [68.87.146.22]
  9   23 ms   15 ms   16 ms  po-11-ar01.ma.comcast.net [68.87.146.26]
 10   18 ms   25 ms   17 ms  68.86.90.69
 11   20 ms   18 ms   20 ms  te-9-2.car1.NewYork1.Level3.net [4.71.172.117]
 12   25                     ae-31-53.ebr1.NewYork1.Level3.net [4.68.97.94]
 13                          ae-3.ebr1.Washington1.Level3.net [4.69.132.89]
 14   24                     ae-11-51.Washington1.Level3.net [4.68.121.18]
 15   29 ms   25 ms   25 ms  4.79.228.2
 16   25 ms   25 ms   32 ms  ge-3-1-0-p140.re1.yahoo.com [216.115.108.5]
 17   36 ms   25 ms   31 ms  ge-1-42.bas-a2.re3.yahoo.com [66.196.112.203]
 18   24 ms   24 ms   26 ms  f1.www.vip.re3.yahoo.com [69.147.114.210]

Trace complete.
```

An asterisk indicates that a router along the route did not respond to the ping.

Your IP address

Hop number

• Exploring Your Internet Connection (continued)

5. Take a screen shot of the Ping report using the Print Screen key and Paint. Print the screen shot, then close the Paint window. Type *exit* at the next command prompt to close the Command Prompt window.

6. Analyze the Traceroute results. Circle your IP address in the screen shot, which is on the first line. Circle the total number of hops. For each hop, Traceroute pings three times to test the speed of data travel. An asterisk in the report indicates that one of the routers along the data's route did not respond. Three asterisks indicate that a ping timed out, revealing a potential problem. Circle any asterisks in your report.

7. If you want to compare your Internet connection speed to the rest of the country, you can look at the Internet Traffic Report. Start your browser. In the Address bar, type www.internettrafficreport.com and press the Enter key. Take a screen shot of the report using the Print Screen key and Paint. Print the screen shot, then close the Paint window. How much slower or faster is your average response time compared to that of the rest of the country? Write this result on the printout.

8. You can run the *ShieldsUP!!* utility to check your computer for any open ports, which can attract unauthorized access. Go to www.grc.com. Click the *ShieldsUP!!* logo.

9. Scroll through the list of software offerings, look for the Hot Spots heading, and then click *ShieldsUP!!*. In the middle of the page, *ShieldsUP!!* displays your IP address. Above the IP address, click the Proceed button.

10. Under *ShieldsUP!!* Services, click Common Ports. A TruStealth Analysis should be displayed. Scroll down to the bottom of the page and click the Text Summary button. Take a screen shot of your summary, then print it. Close the Paint window. If you are running the test on your computer, you might consider following the instructions to beef up security.

11. Submit the following items to your instructor and include your name, student ID number, class section number, date, and PrjWW-1:

• A screen capture of the Ping report for www.yahoo.com, along with the minimum, maximum, and average times encircled

• A screen capture of the Traceroute report for www.yahoo.com, with your IP address, the total number of hops, and potential problems encircled

• A screen capture of the Internet Traffic Report, plus a comparison of your average response time to that of the rest of your country

• A screen capture of the scan summary displayed by the ShieldsUP!! utility

Project WW-2: Basic Browsing

This project will help you to apply basic navigation skills needed to successfully surf the Internet, find information, and submit an HTML form.

Requirements for this project: This assignment requires Microsoft Windows and a browser such as Firefox or Internet Explorer.

Project file: No project file is required for this project.

1. Start your browser and have a pencil ready to jot down answers to questions posed in the steps. What is the URL for your home page? [   ]

2. If your browser opens to a site other than Google, type www.google.com in the address bar and press the Enter key to connect to the Google search engine.

3. Enter Mardi Gras History in the Search box.

4. Use the links to answer the question: When and where was the first "American" Mardi Gras? [   ]
Don't rely on a single Web site for information. Make sure you cross-check the information for accuracy at several sites.

5. Use the Address bar to access the site http://www.e-course.com/mgh/. What does the title bar show as the title of this site? [   ]

6. Once at the site, click the Mardi Gras link. Add this page to your Favorites or Bookmarks. How many sites are listed in your Favorites/Bookmarks list? [   ]

7. Open the Favorites list and experiment with organizing it by creating a new Folder called Travel. Move the Mardi Gras link to this folder.

8. Use the Back button to return to the original Mardi Gras Hotel page, then select the Accommodations link. Which of the hotel's suites would you reserve if you were going to stay there? [   ]

9. Use the Back button to return to the main hotel page, then select the Reservations link. What does the title bar show as the title of this page? [   ]

10. Connect to the site www.ross-simons.com. Click the Stop button. Did the entire page load? [   ]

11. Can you access the site www.mardigras.com from your History list? Explain why or why not. [   ]

• Basic Browsing (continued)

12. Go back to the Reservations page on the Mardi Gras Hotel site. Fill in the newsletter form. Click the Submit button to submit the form. (Note: For your privacy, the information you supply is not actually transmitted to the Web site.)

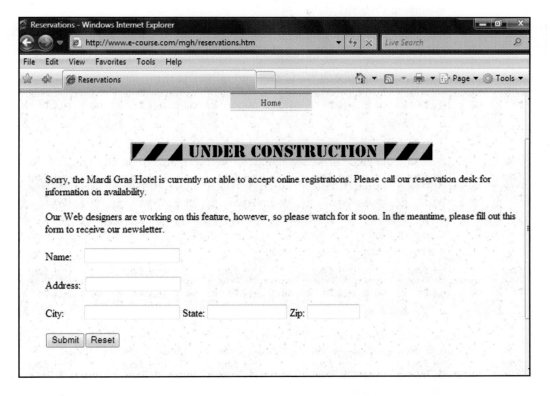

13. Go back to the Mardi Gras Hotel home page.

14. Use the File menu (Firefox) or the down-arrow on the Print button (Internet Explorer) to access the Page Setup dialog box. Change the paper orientation to landscape. Notice that if your printer handles various paper sizes, you can adjust that setting on this dialog box. Change the top and bottom margins to 1". Change the left and right margins to 2". Click the OK button to save these settings.

15. Use the File menu (Firefox) or the down-arrow on the Print button (Internet Explorer) to display a Print Preview.

16. Make sure that the information fits on two pages, then print it.

17. Submit your printout and the answers to questions according to your instructor's guidelines.

Project WW-3: Exploring the Web

In this project, you will learn to identify the elements in a browser's user interface, use a search engine and formulate searches, analyze a Web site's home page, navigate to various Web pages using text and graphics links, and research topics using the Wikipedia Web site.

Requirements for this project: This assignment requires Microsoft Windows and a browser, such as Internet Explorer or Firefox.

Project file: No project file is required for this project.

1. Start your browser. Your home page should appear. Using the Print Screen key and the Paint program, take a screen shot of your home page and print it. Close the Paint window. On your screen shot, circle the URL of your home page.

2. Study the browser's user interface. Rest your pointer on all icons in the interface to display their tooltips. On your screen shot, label five icons with their corresponding functions.

3. Suppose you have to research Renaissance art. If Google is not displayed as your home page, click your browser's address bar, type www.google.com, and press the Enter key. In Google's Search box, type Renaissance art and click the Google Search button. Write down the number of hits from this search.

4. In Step 3, Google returned all occurrences of the words "Renaissance" *and* "art." To search for an exact phrase, enclose the phrase in quotes. Put quotes around *Renaissance art*, click the Google Search button, and then write down the number of hits.

5. Suppose you want to focus on Renaissance art in Italy. Type Italy after "Renaissance art" and click the Google Search button. Write down the number of hits.

6. You can use Google's Advanced Search feature to help formulate your search. Suppose you want to exclude architecture from your research and you don't know how. Click the Advanced Search link to the right of the Search box. On the Advanced Search page, Google has automatically filled in the first two boxes with your original search criteria. Note that in the box beside *with the exact phrase*, Renaissance art does not have to be in quotes.

7. Position your pointer in the box beside *without the words.* Type architecture, then press the Enter key. Write down the number of hits. For future reference, note that Advanced Search used the minus sign (without a space after) to exclude *architecture* from the search.

8. Formulate a search that will return at least one hit but not more than ten. You can use the Advanced Search feature to help you further refine your search. When you have met the requirements for your search, take a screen shot of the Google results page and print it. Close the Paint window.

9. In the browser's address bar, type www.weather.com and press the Enter key. Study The Weather Channel's home page. Click various text and graphics links. Check your local weather. You can use the Web site's Home tab or your browser's Back button to go back to the site's home page. Write down five things you like and five things you don't like about the home page.

• Exploring the Web (continued)

10. Wikipedia is a free encyclopedia that is open to public editing. To find out more about it, go to en.wikipedia.org/wiki/Main_page. Familiarize yourself with the Web site by clicking several links.

11. Now go back to the main page and use your browser's scroll bar to scroll to the middle of the page. Wikipedia's Search box is located on the left-hand side. Enter Palm trees and click Go.

12. Use your browser's Find command to search the Wikipedia article for "date." In Internet Explorer, click the down-arrow next to the magnifying glass to access the Find command. Use the Match whole word only option and count the number of references to "date palms."

13. Suppose that you are having a problem printing a PDF file when using Adobe Reader software. Go to the Adobe site www.adobe.com and use the Support link to find a solution to this problem. List one of the offered solutions.

14. Click a blank browser tab to open a new browser workspace. Can you create a Google search to find the same information that you found in #12? You can make sure you reached the same page by switching back and forth between tabs. Indicate the Google search terms and links you used to find information on the PDF problem. Close the browser tab.

15. Submit the following items to your instructor and include your name, student ID number, class section number, date, and PrjWW-3:

• A document containing the following:

    a. The number of hits resulting from the searches for *Renaissance art*, *"Renaissance art," Italy* and *"Renaissance art," Italy* and *"Renaissance art"* excluding architecture

    b. Five things you like and five things you don't like about The Weather Channel's home page

    c. The number of references to "date palms" you found in the Wikipedia Palm Trees article.

    d. The solution you found to the problem of being unable to print a PDF file, and the links you followed to find that solution.

• A screen capture of your home page with the home page URL circled and five browser interface icons labeled

• A screen capture of the Google page after you've entered a search that returns at least one hit but not more than ten hits

Project WW-4: Customizing Your Browser

In this project, you will explore various ways to configure your browser, change the display of Web pages, check security and privacy levels, and use Help.

Requirements for this project: This assignment requires Microsoft Windows, Microsoft Word, and Internet Explorer.

Project file: No project file is required for this project.

1. Start your browser. Also start your word processing software and use it to record answers to the questions presented. Number each answer using the same number as in the corresponding step. For example, your first answer will be for Step 5.

2. Connect to the site www.cnn.com.

3. Usually, clicking a link opens a new Web page in the same browser window. You can, however, continue to look at the current page and display the new page in a different window. To do so, hold down the Shift key as you click any link on the CNN page.

4. When you are done viewing the information in the new window, click the Close button in the upper-right corner of the window.

5. With a very slow dial-up connection, you might find it advantageous to turn off graphics, which require much more transmission time than text. Use the Help menu to search for "graphics" and follow the links to find instructions on how to turn off Web page graphics. Follow the instructions and then connect to www.ebay.com. What does your browser use to indicate missing graphics? [_____]

6. Restore the previous configuration so that your browser shows graphics again. Click View and then click Refresh to reload the eBay page with graphics visible.

7. Close the browser Help window, if it has remained open.

8. Use your browser's View menu to list the toolbars shown in your browser window. If the Links toolbar is checked, remove the checkmark so that the Links toolbar is no longer displayed. Also use the View menu to make sure the Status bar is displayed.

9. Use the Tools menu to display the Internet Options dialog box. This dialog box contains most of the settings you can configure for your browser.

10. Make sure the General tab is displayed. In the Web chapter, you learned that some people believe it is important to delete the list of cached Web files—especially when using public computers. Deleting this data can also regain some hard disk space. If you want to empty the History folder, click the Clear History button.

• Customizing Your Browser (continued)

11. Click the Security tab. What is your browser's security level? ☐

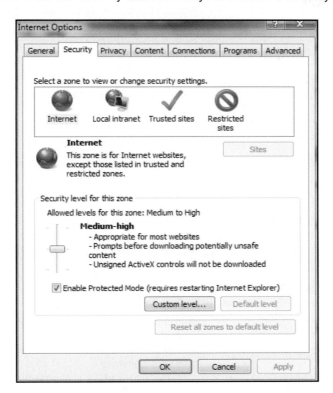

12. Click the Privacy tab. What is your browser's privacy level? ☐
How are cookies handled at this level of privacy? ☐

13. If you want to block all cookies, what security level would you select? ☐

14. Click the Advanced tab. Look through the list of settings and select two that you would like to change. Which settings would you like to change and why?
☐

15. Save the document in which you've written your answers in your Project Folder using the file name PrjWW-4-XXXXX-9999, where XXXXX is your student ID number and 9999 is your class section number. Use one of the following options to submit your project:

• To submit the answer document from the Project Folder where it is currently stored, stop the Word program by closing its window. Copy the file to a USB flash drive or floppy disk. Include your name, student ID number, class section number, date, and PrjWW-4 when you submit the file.

• To print the answer document, click the Microsoft Office button, then click Print. Click the OK button. Write your name, student ID number, class section number, date, and PrjWW-4 on the printout.

• To e-mail the answer document, use Method 1 or Method 2, as described on page 348. Type your instructor's e-mail address in the To: box. Click the Subject: box and type PrjWW-4, your student ID number, and your class section number. Click the Send button or perform any additional steps required by your e-mail software to send an e-mail message.